The Alternative Modernity of the Bicycle in British and French Literature, 1880–1920

Edinburgh Critical Studies in Victorian Culture

Recent books in the series:
Rereading Orphanhood: Texts, Inheritance, Kin
Diane Warren and Laura Peters

Plotting the News in the Victorian Novel
Jessica R. Valdez

Reading Ideas in Victorian Literature: Literary Content as Artistic Experience
Patrick Fessenbecker

Home and Identity in Nineteenth-Century Literary London
Lisa C. Robertson

Writing the Sphinx: Literature, Culture and Egyptology
Eleanor Dobson

Oscar Wilde and the Radical Politics of the Fin de Siècle
Deaglán Ó Donghaile

The Sculptural Body in Victorian Literature: Encrypted Sexualities
Patricia Pulham

New Media and the Rise of the Popular Woman Writer, 1832–1860
Alexis Easley

Elizabeth Robins Pennell: Critical Essays
Dave Buchanan and Kimberly Morse-Jones

Reading Bodies in Victorian Fiction: Associationism, Empathy and Literary Authority
Peter Katz

The Alternative Modernity of the Bicycle in British and French Literature, 1880–1920
Una Brogan

For a complete list of titles published visit the Edinburgh Critical Studies in Victorian Culture web page at www.edinburghuniversitypress.com/series/ECVC

Also Available:
Victoriographies – A Journal of Nineteenth-Century Writing, 1790–1914, edited by Diane Piccitto and Patricia Pulham
ISSN: 2044-2416
www.eupjournals.com/vic

The Alternative Modernity of the Bicycle in British and French Literature, 1880–1920

Una Brogan

EDINBURGH
University Press

Edinburgh University Press is one of the leading university presses in the UK. We publish academic books and journals in our selected subject areas across the humanities and social sciences, combining cutting-edge scholarship with high editorial and production values to produce academic works of lasting importance. For more information visit our website: edinburghuniversitypress.com

© Una Brogan, 2022, 2024

Edinburgh University Press Ltd
The Tun – Holyrood Road
12(2f) Jackson's Entry
Edinburgh EH8 8PJ

First published in hardback by Edinburgh University Press 2022

Typeset in 11/13 Adobe Sabon by
IDSUK (DataConnection) Ltd,
Croydon, CR0 4YY

A CIP record for this book is available from the British Library

ISBN 978 1 4744 8860 0 (hardback)
ISBN 978 1 4744 8861 7 (paperback)
ISBN 978 1 4744 8862 4 (webready PDF)
ISBN 978 1 4744 8863 1 (epub)

The right of Una Brogan to be identified as the author of this work has been asserted in accordance with the Copyright, Designs and Patents Act 1988, and the Copyright and Related Rights Regulations 2003 (SI No. 2498).

Contents

List of Illustrations	vi
Series Editors' Preface	vii
Acknowledgements	ix
Introduction	1
1. Text and Transport	19
2. Liberation on Two Wheels: Class, Gender and the Bicycle in Literature	69
3. The Body and the Machine: The Sensory Discoveries of the Cyclist	140
4. Moving Forward: Space, Time and the Bicycle	204
Conclusion	249
Bibliography	253
Index	272

Illustrations

I.1 Anonymous, 'The American Velocipede' and 'Velocipede Race in Paris–Sunday Afternoon', *Harper's Weekly*, New York, 19 December 1868, 812. Public domain. 3

I.2 An 1880 'Ordinary' bicycle or high-wheeler and J. K. Starley's 1885 'Safety Bicycle', from *Lexikon der gesamten Technik*, ed. Otto Lueger (Berlin: Deutsche Verlags-Anstalt, 1904). Public domain. 4

1.1 R.T.M., 'How to Mount a Bicycle: A Drama in Four Acts', *The Jarvey*, 12 January 1889 (Dublin: Mecredy and Kyle). By permission of National Library of Ireland. 46

1.2 Anonymous, cover of Edmond Redmond, *Lyra Cyclus: Or, The Bards and the Bicycle* (Rochester, NY: Bacon, 1897). Public domain. 55

2.1 Frederick Pegram, 'A Contrast', *Punch, or the London Charivari*, 4 May 1895, 207. By permission of TopFoto. 74

2.2 Georges Massias, advertising poster for Cycles Gladiator, c. 1895. Public domain. 124

3.1 Edward Tennyson Reed, 'A Warning to Enthusiasts', *Punch, or the London Charivari*, 6 July 1889, 5. By permission of TopFoto. 149

3.2 Anonymous, 'Division of Labour', *Punch, or the London Charivari*, 24 January 1896, 6. By permission of TopFoto. 154

3.3 Anonymous, 'A Spill', from W. J. Coppen, *Romances of the Wheel* (Coventry: Iliffe and Son, 1880), frontispiece. Public domain. 163

Series Editor's Preface

'Victorian' is a term, at once indicative of a strongly determined concept and an often notoriously vague notion, emptied of all meaningful content by the many journalistic misconceptions that persist about the inhabitants and cultures of the British Isles and Victoria's Empire in the nineteenth century. As such, it has become a by-word for the assumption of various, often contradictory habits of thought, belief, behaviour and perceptions. Victorian studies and studies in nineteenth-century literature and culture have, from their institutional inception, questioned narrowness of presumption, pushed at the limits of the nominal definition, and have sought to question the very grounds on which the unreflective perception of the so-called Victorian has been built; and so they continue to do. Victorian and nineteenth-century studies of literature and culture maintain a breadth and diversity of interest, of focus and inquiry, in an interrogative and intellectually open-minded and challenging manner, which are equal to the exploration and inquisitiveness of its subjects. Many of the questions asked by scholars and researchers of the innumerable productions of nineteenth-century society actively put into suspension the clichés and stereotypes of 'Victorianism', whether the approach has been sustained by historical, scientific, philosophical, empirical, ideological or theoretical concerns; indeed, it would be incorrect to assume that each of these approaches to the idea of the Victorian has been, or has remained, in the main exclusive, sealed off from the interests and engagements of other approaches. A vital interdisciplinarity has been pursued and embraced, for the most part, even as there has been contest and debate amongst Victorianists, pursued with as much fervour as the affirmative exploration between different disciplines and differing epistemologies put to work in the service of reading the nineteenth century.

Edinburgh Critical Studies in Victorian Culture aims to take up both the debates and the inventive approaches and departures from convention that studies in the nineteenth century have witnessed for the last half century at least. Aiming to maintain a 'Victorian' (in the most positive sense of that motif) spirit of inquiry, the series' purpose is to continue and augment the cross-fertilisation of interdisciplinary approaches, and to offer, in addition, a number of timely and untimely revisions of Victorian literature, culture, history and identity. At the same time, the series will ask questions concerning what has been missed or improperly received, misread, or not read at all, in order to present a multi-faceted and heterogeneous kaleidoscope of representations. Drawing on the most provocative, thoughtful and original research, the series will seek to prod at the notion of the 'Victorian', and in so doing, principally through theoretically and epistemologically sophisticated close readings of the historicity of literature and culture in the nineteenth century, to offer the reader provocative insights into a world that is at once overly familiar, and irreducibly different, other and strange. Working from original sources, primary documents and recent interdisciplinary theoretical models, Edinburgh Critical Studies in Victorian Culture seeks not simply to push at the boundaries of research in the nineteenth century, but also to inaugurate the persistent erasure and provisional, strategic redrawing of those borders.

Julian Wolfreys

Acknowledgements

I am grateful to the many professors who stimulated my interest in history and literature, especially Kate Astbury at the University of Warwick, and Christina Howells, Marianne Ailes, Michel Abecassis and Jane Garnett at the University of Oxford. Thank you to my supervisor at Paris 7-Diderot, Sara Thornton, whose enthusiasm provided the necessary spark to my PhD project and helped carry it to fruition. My thanks go also to all my colleagues who welcomed me warmly into the English department and LARCA research group at Université Paris 7-Diderot while showing sustained interest in my research. I am grateful to the undergraduate students I taught for their input, energy and ideas. LARCA's financial support allowed me to attend conferences and make research trips to the British Library and the National Cycle Archives in Warwick. A special thanks to the staff at the Bibliothèque des Grands Moulins, whose efforts in searching out books via interlibrary loan saved me many research trips. Thank you also to the editors at Edinburgh University Press for helping me transform my thesis into a book.

I was lucky enough to come across several academic communities working on bicycles in the course of this research. I am grateful to Jeremy Withers and Daniel P. Shea, the editors of the collection *Culture on Two Wheels*, for bringing together an academic community working on the cultural and literary significance of cycling. I am indebted to Glen Norcliffe both for his insightful research on bicycles and for inviting me to work with a team of researchers on a forthcoming *Companion to Cycling*. Thanks to Dave Buchanan for sharing his insight and enthusiasm about literary cycle pilgrims. I am grateful to the organisers and participants of the International Cycle History Conference for welcoming me into a wide community of bicycle scholars. Thank you also to Will Noonan from Université de Bourgogne for our enlightening exchanges on bicycles and humour.

I wish to thank the bicycle community in Paris, whose belief in a better world and dedication to put it into practice inspired me to begin this research. To all *vélorutionnaires* and bike workshop members and volunteers, *vive la vélorution*! My heartfelt thanks to all my friends and family for their support, ideas and eagerness to provide editorial assistance, as well as for coming to Paris for my *soutenance de thèse*.

Thanks finally to Paul for always being there and to Cara for providing plenty of opportunities for distraction.

Note on Translations

Unless otherwise stated, all translations from French to English are my own.

Introduction

The bicycle is a technology that extends and transforms the range of human experience. Voted the greatest invention since 1800 by BBC listeners in 2005,[1] over the past two centuries cycling has played a key role in human mobility and society at large. The empowering experience of people-powered locomotion points an alternative route to progress, one that remains rooted in an awareness of the past, the environment, the body and humanity while moving steadily into the future. This study aims to reinstate the turn-of-the-century bicycle as a crucial element in the wide-ranging project of modernity, to which it contributed by helping to introduce such concepts as rapid individual mobility, an intimate connection to both the body and the machine, and a subjective, embodied relationship to space and time. By interrogating the very definition of modernity – often automatically associated with fossil-fuelled technologies, commodification and acceleration – early twentieth-century cyclists formulated an alternative, human-centred vision of progress. At the same time, this research seeks to (re)define the bicycle itself, by uncovering the utopian meanings attributed to it at the point of its introduction. The alternative paradigm of human-propelled mobility that the bicycle established at its inception continues to offer a road map for more environmentally and socially responsible societies in the present day. Far from pointing to a regression to a previous state, it offers a responsible, convivial and just means of moving forward, one that moves counter to the individualistic, profit-driven thrust of many contemporary societies.

Given the fact that the basic technology of the wheel had been understood for millennia, it might come as a surprise to learn that it took until the nineteenth century for humans to design an object that allowed them to balance and move on two aligned wheels. Indeed, the object seemed such an obvious companion to human locomotion once invented that some nineteenth-century writers imagined a more ancient history for the technology. Cycling historians over the past thirty years have helped to correct many inaccuracies concerning the origin of the bicycle, disproving as fraudulent a Leonardo da Vinci sketch that was claimed to have featured in his *Codex Atlanticus* in 1493, and the claim that Comte de Sivrac developed a bicycle prototype (the *célérifère*) in 1791. A general consensus now exists in the academic community that the first two-wheeled, human-powered vehicle was invented by Baron Karl von Drais in Mannheim in 1817.[2] A version of his wooden draisine, also called a 'running machine' or 'dandy horse', was subsequently manufactured in London by Denis Johnson in 1818, when it enjoyed a brief moment of popularity among wealthy young men, before the two-wheeler was largely forgotten for over forty years.

Various three- and four-wheeled machines were tested throughout the nineteenth century without great success, and it was not until the early 1860s that the first commercial pedal-powered machine – the velocipede – made its appearance in the Paris workshop of the blacksmith Pierre Michaux.[3] The outbreak of the Franco-Prussian war has been held responsible for stopping the 1860s velocipede craze in its tracks, but the machine would be adapted and improved in numerous ways across Europe and the USA over the following twenty years. The most influential model to come out of this period of innovation (and the first to be termed a 'bicycle') was the Coventry manufacturer James Starley's steel-framed, wire-spoked 'Ariel' high-wheel bicycle in 1871. Starley's subsequent invention of the tangentially spoked wheel and the search for greater power from increasing wheel size resulted in the Ordinary bicycle, also known as the high-wheeler or penny farthing. Alongside these models made for sporting, daring riders, various manufacturers produced single or tandem tricycles, which were popular with women, couples and older people in the 1880s. Various attempts to build a less perilous machine while maintaining the advantage of high gearing resulted in John Kemp Starley's chain-driven, low-wheeled 'Rover' safety bicycle of 1885. The final touch was the replacement of solid rubber tyres with pneumatic ones, patented in 1888 by John Dunlop. This last design differs little from the bicycles ridden today.

Two-wheeled, human-powered transportation was thus conceived at the outset of the industrial revolution, spent several decades in hibernation, and only reached its perfected, lasting form in the closing decades of the nineteenth century. The Irish champion cyclist, newspaper editor and writer R. J. Mecredy adopted Darwinian terms

Figure I.1 Anonymous, 'The American Velocipede' and 'Velocipede Race in Paris–Sunday Afternoon', *Harper's Weekly*, New York, 19 December 1868, 812. Public domain.

Fig. 2. Bicycle (Hochrad) von 1880.   Fig. 3. Rover (Niederrad) von 1886.

Figure I.2 An 1880 'Ordinary' bicycle or high-wheeler and J. K. Starley's 1885 'Safety Bicycle', from *Lexikon der gesamten Technik*, ed. Otto Lueger (Berlin: Deutsche Verlags-Anstalt, 1904). Public domain.

to boast in 1890 that 'it would be difficult to find any more beautiful example of evolution, and the survival of the fittest, than the development of the modern cycle from the rude hobby-horse of 1818'.[4] As well as participating in contemporary scientific discourses such as the theory of evolution, the bicycle's invention was a deeply cosmopolitan one, with innovators in Germany, France, the UK and the USA variously collaborating on, improving and commercialising the machine.

This brief overview of bicycle history allows us to define the term 'bicycle' as a human-powered vehicle consisting of a rigid frame, a drive chain propelled by the rider's feet, two aligned wheels and a steering mechanism. My engagement with early texts on cycling reveals that the human-powered dimension – and the absence of any external energy sources that necessarily rely on some form of exploitation, pollution, commodification or obsolescence – is central to the philosophy and meaning of cycling. It is my opinion that we are at risk of obscuring this fundamental characteristic of the bicycle amid the current electric bike craze, with industry seeking to sell these marketable novelties by brushing over the crucial differences between human-powered and battery-assisted technology.

This book focuses on literature written at the end of the highwheel period and during the era of the first popularity of the safety bicycle, c. 1880–1920, when Europe and the USA witnessed an explosion in the manufacture, purchase and use of the two-wheeler. The first bicycle boom reached its peak in the last years of the nineteenth century. In 1890, twenty-seven factories in the UK produced around 40,000 bicycles; six years later, 250 factories were producing some 1.2 million machines annually.[5] Although the dandy horse, velocipede and Ordinary bicycle each enjoyed their moment in the limelight, the difficulty and expense of acquiring and riding these machines meant that their use was largely limited to daring, aristocratic young men. However, in the safety bicycle era, mass production techniques meant that cycling grew steadily as a pursuit among diverse social groups. Even if the price of new machines was prohibitive right up to the First World War,[6] the rapid development of the technology meant that cheaper, second-hand machines appeared on the market, making cycling accessible to the working and middle classes. According to the social construction of technology (SCOT) model developed by Wiebe Bijker et al.,[7] technologies do not arise as a result of a specific need; rather, artefacts first appear in society and their meanings are subsequently negotiated by relevant social groups. This takes place during a period of 'interpretive flexibility', which is followed by 'closure' and finally 'stabilisation', when the cultural meaning of the artefact becomes fixed.[8] The SCOT theory is of particular interest to the present study since Bijker et al. argue that in the case of the safety bicycle, this tripartite process leading to stabilisation occurred from 1879 to 1898.[9] This was the era in which a social and cultural space was carved out for and by the bicycle.

The period of the bicycle boom is a particularly compelling moment in history as it allows us to examine the first contact of society at large with a revolutionary new technology. As Tom Gunning notes:

> To imagine an old technology as something that was once new means [...] to try to recapture a quality it has lost. It means examining a technology or device at the point of introduction, before it has become part of a nearly invisible everyday life of habit and routine. But it also must mean examining this move from dazzling appearance to nearly transparent utility, from the spectacular and astonishing to the convenient and unremarkable. This transformation needs to be interrogated for the cultural myths of modernity it assumes and creates.[10]

Literature gives us a privileged means of reimagining the now familiar technology of the bicycle when it was new, and tracing the contours of the 'myths of modernity' that it engendered. Gunning concentrates on society's encounter with the cinema, while others have focused on the impact of the railway or a range of turn-of-the-century inventions such as the typewriter, telephone or automobile. Like these other major technologies, at the moment of its introduction the bicycle offered a vision of the future that soon became outdated in the rapid forward march of technological development. This book seeks to establish contact with the bicycle's particular vision of progress by analysing works of literature that incorporated the technology when it was still dazzlingly new.

Bruno Latour, like Gunning, argues that it is by re-engaging with the newness of the technologies of modernity that we can draw beneficial insight from them. He argues:

> We can keep the Enlightenment but discard modernity, if we are able to write the objects of science and technology back into the Constitution [. . .] The origin of these objects must no longer be hidden, but closely followed, from the heady events that gave birth to them, up until the gradual cooling that transforms them into essences of nature or society.[11]

Modernity, for Latour, is a force that threatens to overpower the benefits of culture and nature; yet he recognises that the technologies that modernity engendered can have a positive impact on society, depending on the uses to which they are put. It is by engaging with the stories and origins of these technologies that we can come to understand the social changes that they wrought and the possible new interpretations or applications they could have in the present day. This study delves into literature to recast the imaginary of the bicycle, now that it has 'cooled', in Latour's terms, into a fixed representation. Texts allow us to encounter the technology when it was fresh, and observe the roles it came to play in society and culture.

The geographical criteria selected for this investigation reflect the fact that the invention of the bicycle in the second half of the nineteenth century may be considered a cross-Channel initiative, with the UK and France vying to improve the existing technology during the era of the velocipede, Ordinary and safety bicycles. These were both cultures in which cycling was enthusiastically and widely adopted and written about, yet they are just one part of a global picture. Recent criticism has rightly drawn attention to the Eurocentrism of studies of bicycle history and literature, a bias that occults the major cultural impact that the bicycle has had across the world during the past century and a half.[12] Even when focusing on the British and French context, it is important to remain aware of the bicycle's complex imbrication in a wider colonial network, notably its reliance on the provision of rubber from central Africa.[13] While conscious of my focus on a much-discussed European colonial centre, I attempt to come to an understanding of the literary and cultural dimension of the bicycle in this context in order to better apprehend the technology's relation to humanity at large. Rather than offering a rapid bird's-eye view of the global picture, I closely follow the bicycle's route through the literature of two countries whose languages and cultures are familiar to me, and whose relationship to the technology in question is rich and varied.[14]

The fascinating relationship between books and bicycles has already drawn critical attention. Several anthologies of cycling literature have been published in the USA, the UK and France, and a number of websites and blogs are dedicated to this subject.[15] While this book aims to actively engage with and contribute to this growing field, it by no means seeks to provide an exhaustive list of literary appearances of the bicycle. Rather, a select group of texts allows us to focus on a specific period in order to come into contact with contemporary points of view on a novel technology at the moment of its introduction. As such, I aim to reach a better understanding of the overarching significance of the bicycle in turn-of-the-century texts than can be offered by cycling bibliographies or anthologies, which lack sufficient analysis and contextualisation. Cycling literature anthologies have nonetheless helped to draw attention to overlooked portraits of cyclists by well-known authors such as H. G. Wells (1866–1946), Jerome K. Jerome (1859–1927), Maurice Leblanc (1864–1941) and Alfred Jarry (1873–1957). Taking the extracts included in several anthologies as a starting point, I also sought out lesser-known texts and authors.[16] Any fictional text in which bicycles played a significant narrative or symbolic role was taken into consideration, including obscure works no longer in print,[17] before a final selection of the works of some twenty authors was made.

A wealth of written material is available in both English and French, but for reasons of space and coherence the decision was made to anchor my corpus in English literature, making comparisons with a smaller selection of relevant primary texts in French. In choosing texts, I privilege accounts of utilitarian or recreational cycling, rather than sport, as my focus is on how the experience of cycling transformed the fabric of people's everyday lives.[18] While I include some accounts of racing (in Jarry's *The Supermale* [*Le Surmâle*], for instance), and do not downplay the major cultural impact of cycle racing in this period, this study concentrates on cycling as a transformative, individual locomotive experience rather than as a spectator sport. Minor or lowbrow authors were willingly included alongside canonical ones. Novels and short stories form the bulk of the corpus, but some non-fiction travel writing and guides are included because of the important insights they provide on the experience of the cyclist. The large number of texts taken into consideration reflects that fact that few texts are analysed in their entirety. With some exceptions, I mainly conduct close readings of isolated scenes in novels and stories whose overall plot does not necessarily centre on the bicycle, but which nonetheless make compelling use of the object. The myriad cycling magazines, newspapers, advertisements, posters, guides and manuals published in this period provide a valuable source of contextual information on the social and cultural impact of the bicycle.

I adhere to a systemic approach to the study of the bicycle, like that favoured by Frédéric Héran, who argues that 'the history of the bicycle is principally the history of its relationship to other modes of transport'.[19] It is important to recall that nineteenth-century societies became increasingly mobile, multiplying the forms of transport they used rather than adopting a single one. Trains, for example, did not negate the need for horse- and human-powered transport, but rather stimulated these modes.[20] Furthermore, cycling made its appearance at a time of dizzying technological innovation in the communications sector, where inventions such as the gramophone, the typewriter and cinema led to what Friedrich Kittler termed 'the media revolution of 1880', which transformed our relationship to the spoken and written word.[21] The 'iron horse' – as the bicycle was named – was consistently understood and portrayed in relation to other transportation and communication technologies, which multiplied throughout the century. As such, throughout this book I foreground the connections between the bicycle and these other technologies.

Foremost among these technologies, in terms of its role in shaping modernity, was the railway. This book follows in the footsteps of the cultural historian Wolfgang Schivelbusch, who studied the creation of the industrial subject through the experience of railway travel in his seminal book *The Railway Journey* (1979). Schivelbusch contends that society's encounter with trains rapidly made previous modes of behaviour redundant and necessitated the formulation of new forms of social interaction and perception. In the case of the train, this meant, for example, the birth of a train reading culture (alongside a taboo on conversation in carriages, in contrast to the traditionally convivial stagecoach journey) and the development of a specific form of perception which favoured a 'panoramic view' of landscapes, framed by the train window and seen as an object to be contemplated as visual spectacle.[22] Further work on the cultural significance of railways has focused on the connections between train travel and the silent cinema, and the manifold cultural and literary transformations that accompanied the spread of railways.[23]

The role of the horse in fiction has also been explored in several articles and anthologies,[24] while Carsten Meiner's monograph *Le carrosse littéraire et l'invention du hasard* (2008) provides a compelling overview of the literary functions of carriages, from the seventeenth to the twentieth centuries.[25] Meiner argues that the carriage's role in literature is much more than a purely utilitarian or representational one; rather, these vehicles serve specific ends, having symbolic and narrative functions in the text. 'Carriage scenes' became a convention or topos in literature, functioning to inscribe the sensation of random chance or contingency that would come to define the modern era.

A number of studies have also explored the relationship between walking and literature in the Romantic period, when 'pedestrianism' became a favoured sport and pastime, shedding the taboo status it had previously held for the well-to-do. As a number of critical works convincingly show, the experience of travelling on foot impacted on the subject matter, form and rhythms of Romantic literature.[26] In the twentieth century, motor cars and aeroplanes have been considered from a literary angle by several critics.[27] The literary and cultural impact of communications technologies such as the postal system and the telegraph have also been explored.[28] These studies have provided precious methodological and thematic backgrounds for my examination of the question of the interaction between literature and technology.

In recent decades, cultural critics have become increasingly interested in the role of technology, movement, speed and individual mobility in the construction of modernity. As Stephen Kern argues:

> From around 1880 to the outbreak of WW1 a series of sweeping changes in technology and culture created distinctive new modes of thinking about and experiencing time and space. Technological innovations, including the telephone, wireless telegraph, x-ray, cinema, bicycle, automobile, and airplane, established the material foundation for this reorientation; independent cultural developments such as the stream of consciousness novel, psychoanalysis, Cubism and the theory of relativity shaped consciousness directly.[29]

Kern's compelling study demonstrates how a renewed relationship to time and space was inaugurated at the turn of the century in response to the new capabilities provided by technologies such as the bicycle. Kern is exceptional in including a brief consideration of the bicycle, as in most cultural studies of modernity – even those that specifically address the significant role of transportation technologies – the bicycle's role is sidelined. Marc Desportes, for instance, offers a transversal analysis in *Paysages en mouvement* (2005), in which he studies the ways in which transportation technologies from the eighteenth century onwards offered altered means of perception and interaction.[30] Despite the fact that he engages with the period around 1900 – when taxation figures for France indicate some three and a half million bicycles compared to just three thousand automobiles[31] – Desportes occults two-wheeled transportation in his study, leapfrogging from the train to the car to the aeroplane. Critics tend to consider the bicycle's ingenious industrial harnessing of human energy as an inconsequential blip between the train and the motor car age. Other transport technologies are widely considered to have made a momentous impact on shaping mentalities, introducing fresh modes of perception and forging new cultural and social formations, while the bicycle's role is all too frequently overlooked.

Nonetheless, this area of study is growing increasingly vibrant, perhaps thanks to the upsurge in cycling in European and North American societies in recent years. Lately a number of monographs on the bicycle's cultural significance have appeared. Glen Norcliffe offers a compelling portrait of the bicycle's participation in the momentous changes occurring in the late nineteenth century in *Ride to Modernity: The Bicycle in Canada, 1869–1900* (2001) and provides a global cultural perspective on bicycles in his volume *Critical Geographies of Cycling* (2015).[32] Another critic to whom my research is indebted is Zack Furness, whose *One Less Car: Bicycling and the Politics of Automobility* (2010) contains an excellent first chapter on the sociocultural impact of cycling in the 1890s. Further studies on the bicycle's impact on society and culture that have actively enriched my research include works by Ivan Illich, Catherine Bertho-Lavenir, Gordon Wilson et al., Paul Rosen et al., Wiebe Bijker et al. and Christopher Thompson.[33] In the wake of these studies, this book engages with the bicycle as a means of transport that has made and continues to make a lasting impact on society and culture. What sets my approach apart from these cultural, historical, sociological and scientific studies is that I place literary texts at the core of my research. This particular area of study is as yet poorly furnished, yet it is beginning to attract critical attention. Testament to this is the edited collection *Culture on Two Wheels* (2016), edited by Jeremy Withers and Dan Shea, which provides a rich selection of essays on the bicycle in literature and film.[34]

This research has also been influenced by a specific branch of cultural and literary studies that addresses the crucial role of the machine, and objects more broadly, in human societies. Critics such as Leo Marx, Herbert Sussman, Friedrich Kittler, Mark Seltzer, Sara Danius, Nicholas Daly, Christine MacLeod, Andrew Thacker and Alex Goody have all sought to integrate an understanding of the machine's role into cultural and literary criticism.[35] Connected to this area of study is the appreciation of objects as historical actors. Gilles Deleuze and Félix Guattari's concept of assemblages, the actor-network theory of Bruno Latour, Bill Brown and Arjun Appadurai's research into how things have shaped the modern subject and Jane Bennett's work on vital materialism have all influenced my approach to the study of a particular cultural artefact.[36] This book explores both how literature produced the object of the bicycle and how the bicycle in turn helped shape new modes of consciousness and literary production. Bicycles are particularly compelling objects for thing theory; indeed, the critics Ian Hodder and Jane Bennett were both inspired to illustrate the challenging concept of an assemblage by using the example of a cyclist riding a bicycle along a rough road.[37] The bicycle is an inanimate object forged of industrial steel, colonial rubber and mass-produced, precisely manufactured components, yet it becomes animate once ridden, when the line between rider and machine is suddenly blurred. Propelled solely by human energy, the agency of the bicycle and its complex relationship to the human body are remarkable. This was something that fascinated its first riders, many of whom wrote about the bicycle as an extension of the human body, but also as an object that seemed capable of gaining an uncanny measure of autonomy.

The first chapter deals with the bicycle's tangible interaction with fiction, text and publishing, drawing attention to the connections established between texts and cycling from the outset. This is exemplified in a group of cycling travel 'pilgrims' including F. W. Bockett,[38] Joseph Pennell (1857–1926), Elizabeth Robins Pennell (1855–1936) and Edward Thomas (1878–1917). A parallel reading of two cycling novellas by H. G. Wells and Maurice Leblanc allows us to engage with the narrative role of the bicycle at close range. The vehicle's interaction with various genres, styles and formats is examined, with a focus on its role in adventure, detective and comic fiction. I then turn my attention to the publishing context to argue that the emergence of the cheaply produced pocket classic was symptomatic of a democratisation of knowledge that accompanied major changes in people's everyday mobility at the turn of the century.

Chapter 2 focuses on the bicycle's revolutionary role in class and gender relations. Close readings of three of Wells's social novels allow us to appreciate the evolving symbolism and narrative function of a vehicle that seemed capable of eroding strict Victorian class and moral structures. In Wells's novels, the bicycle emerges as a means of negotiating, subverting or corrupting the complex and often baffling English class system. Secondly, I examine the bicycle's relationship to the changing status of women in society, asking whether the bicycle really was the 'freedom machine' recent criticism has seen fit to call it.[39] By exploring texts from a range of British, Irish and French authors such as Grant Allen (1848–99), Mary E. Kennard (1850–1936), Matthias Mc Donnell Bodkin (1850–1933) and Émile Zola (1840–1902), I seek to complicate the picture of the bicycle's role in women's emancipation by shedding light on the machine's ambivalent role in a society that remained decidedly patriarchal. A study of the role of bicycles in *A la recherche du temps perdu* (*In Search of Lost Time*) by Marcel Proust (1871–1922) closes this chapter, where I highlight the object's crucial role as a feminist and queer symbol in literature. The bicycle emerges from these texts as a subversive technology that allows its users to transgress and blur gender and social boundaries.

The third chapter examines the new aesthetic and sensory experiences of the cyclist. Returning to some of the above authors and integrating others such as J. W. Allen (1865–1944), J. H. Rosny (1856–1940), Alfred Jarry and Dorothy Richardson (1873–1957), I analyse the ways in which the bicycle offered direct contact with speed and mechanism alongside a rich sensory experience. Cyclists enjoyed a hybrid of mechanical and corporeal sensations which provided rich ground for literary experimentation. The close relationship between rider and machine allowed a questioning of the man/machine dichotomy, moving away from the alienation of the industrial era in order to achieve a more empowering and meaningful interaction with technology.

The final chapter builds on the phenomenological findings of Chapter 3 in order to examine the cyclist's specific engagement with time and space. Combining theory and literature, I present the bicycle as both a modernising influence and a counter-cultural technology. In performing a human-centred interaction with time and space, the cyclist proposed an alternative path at a critical juncture. The spatial theories of French critics including Henri Lefebvre, Michel de

Certeau and Paul Virilio are mobilised to analyse spatial representations in texts by Ford Madox Ford (1873–1939), G. K. Chesterton (1874–1936) and Aldous Huxley (1894–1963), among others. I examine the cyclist's nostalgic, backward-looking gaze, inherited in part from the *flâneur*. The bicycle allowed these and other authors to propose an interactive geography based on individual exploration and criss-crossing of urban and rural environments, while reviving spaces racked by industrialisation, the railways and the emerging motor car. Reading spaces from a turn-of-the-century cyclist's perspective creates a vision of civilised, humane transport capable of enriching communities and retaining a vital link to the past.

I join with present-day writers such as Didier Tronchet in proposing a reflection on the bicycle as part of what he calls 'a long process of ideological reconquest, against the tidal wave of automobile imagery'.[40] Through an exploration of the early cultural impact of this technology, I hope to challenge the entrenched cultural dominance of motorised transport and point to the possibility, the desirability and indeed the necessity of a human-powered impetus for the twenty-first century.

Notes

1. 'Bicycle Chosen as Best Invention', BBC News, 5 May 2005, available at <http://news.bbc.co.uk/2/hi/technology/4513929.stm> (accessed 18 September 2020).
2. A number of well-documented histories of the bicycle are available, as well as the acts of the International Cycling History Conference (*Cycle History*), which has annually brought together experts on the subject since 1990. See Frederick Alderson, *Bicycling: A History* (New York: Praeger, 1972); Andrew Ritchie, *King of the Road: An Illustrated History of Cycling* (London: Wildwood House, 1975); James McGurn, *On Your Bicycle: An Illustrated History of Cycling* (New York: Facts on File, 1987); Pryor Dodge and David V. Herlihy, *The Bicycle* (Paris: Flammarion, 1996); David V. Herlihy, *Bicycle: The History* (New Haven, CT: Yale University Press, 2004); Frédéric Héran, *Le retour de la bicyclette: une histoire des déplacements urbains en Europe, de 1817 à 2050* (Paris: La Découverte, 2014); Paul Smethurst, *The Bicycle: Towards a Global History* (Basingstoke: Palgrave Macmillan, 2015).
3. Some historians maintain that this was the work of Michaux's apprentice Pierre Lallement, who began producing velocipedes in the US soon after emigrating there in 1865. See Keizō Kobayashi, 'The Inventor of the Lallement Pattern: Michaux, Olivier, or Lallement Himself?', *Cycle History* 1 (1990), 100–9; David V. Herlihy, 'Who Invented the

Bicycle – Lallement in 1863 or Michaux in 1861?', *Cycle History* 4 (1993), 11–26.
4. R. J. Mecredy, *The Art and Pastime of Cycling* (Dublin: Mecredy and Kyle, 1890), 40.
5. McGurn, *On Your Bicycle*, 98.
6. Herlihy, *Bicycle*, 7.
7. Wiebe E. Bijker, Thomas Parke Hughes and T. J. Pinch (eds), *The Social Construction of Technological Systems: New Directions in the Sociology and History of Technology* (Cambridge, MA: MIT Press, 1987). For critiques of the SCOT model, see Nick Clayton, 'SCOT: Does It Answer?', *Technology and Culture* 43, no. 2 (2002), 351–60; Glen Norcliffe, 'G-COT', *Science, Technology, & Human Values* 34, no. 4 (2009), 449–75.
8. Wiebe E. Bijker, *Of Bicycles, Bakelites, and Bulbs: Toward a Theory of Sociotechnical Change* (Cambridge, MA: MIT Press, 1995), 20.
9. Ibid., 39.
10. Tom Gunning, 'Re-Newing Old Technologies: Astonishment, Second Nature, and the Uncanny in Technology from the Previous Turn of the Century', in *Rethinking Media Change: The Aesthetics of Transition*, ed. David Thorburn and Henry Jenkins (Cambridge, MA: MIT Press, 2003), 39.
11. Bruno Latour, *Nous n'avons jamais été modernes* [1991] (Paris: La Découverte, 1997), 185.
12. Critics who have addressed this imbalance include Alon Raab, 'Wheels of Fire: Writers on Bicycles', *World Literature Today* 86, no. 5 (2012), 22–31; Smethurst, *The Bicycle*; Glen B. Norcliffe, *Critical Geographies of Cycling: History, Political Economy and Culture* (Burlington, VT: Ashgate, 2015).
13. See William Woodruff, *The Rise of the British Rubber Industry During the Nineteenth Century* (Liverpool: Liverpool University Press, 1958), 39.
14. The only PhD thesis I am aware of on the subject of bicycles in literature, by Josh Guevara, seems to me to cast the net too wide. Guevara explores many interesting avenues, yet his temporal and geographical ranges are extremely broad; he includes a wide variety of excerpts from global fiction across the twentieth century, paying little heed to the context in which they were written. See J. Josh Guevara, '"The Mechanisms. Light and Miraculous": The Convivial Bicycle in Literature and Film', PhD dissertation, University of California Santa Cruz, 2012. Some noteworthy Master's dissertations have been written on the subject, including Andrew Shrimpton, 'The Cultural Significance of Cycling c. 1870–1900', University of York, 1991; Nanci J. Adler, 'The Bicycle in Western Literature: Transformations on Two Wheels', Rollins College, 2012.
15. See Seamus McGonagle, *The Bicycle in Life, Love, War, and Literature* (South Brunswick: Pelham Books, 1969); Roderick Watson and Martin

Gray, *The Penguin Book of the Bicycle* (London: Penguin, 1978); James E. Starrs and Kevin Schaeffer, *The Literary Cyclist* (New York: Breakaway Books, 1997); Edward Nye, *A bicyclette: anthologie* (Paris: Sortilèges, 2000); Hélène Giraud, *Le goût du vélo* (Paris: Mercure de France, 2011); Keizō Kobayashi, *Pour une bibliographie du cyclisme: répertoire des livres en langue française édités entre 1818 et 1983: la bicyclette sous tous ses aspects* (Paris: Fédération française de cyclotourisme, 1984); Edward Williams, *The Pocket Bibliography of Cycling Books* (Wolverhampton: Edward Williams, 1993); Jeanne MacKenzie, *Cycling* (Oxford: Oxford University Press, 1981); Pierre Thiesset and Quentin Thomasset (eds), *Les bienfaits de la vélocipédie: anthologie* (Vierzon: le Pas de côté, 2013). The first two include somewhat outdated if interesting reflections on the bicycle's literary significance; the third, fourth and fifth are literary anthologies, the sixth and seventh bibliographies and the latter two provide extracts from the press and other sources in the late nineteenth and early twentieth centuries in the UK and France respectively. A number of online articles and blogs focus on the relationship between cycling and literature, such as Jasper Gates, 'Vélivre: Reading and Riding', *The Dusty Musette*, 25 November 2011, available at <http://dustymusette.blogspot.fr/2011/11/velivre-reading-and-riding.html> (accessed 15 January 2020); Katlin Hawkins and Eliza Robertson, 'Books on Two Wheels: The Cycling Reading List', *World Literature Today*, available at <http://www.worldliteraturetoday.org/books-two-wheels-cycling-reading-list#.VQl7HmZJ_m0> (accessed 18 March 2020); Micah Mattix, 'Literary Cycles', *Wall Street Journal*, 26 June 2013, available at <http://online.wsj.com/news/articles/SB10001424127887323683504578567760447206752> (accessed 16 October 2014); Philippe Orgebin, Hervé Le Cahain and Jean-Yves Mounier, *Biblio-Cycles*, available at <http://biblio-cyclesdephilippeorgebin.hautetfort.com> (accessed 18 March 2020); Jim Peirpert, 'Literary Musings', *Jim's Bike Blog*, 29 August 2012, available at <https://jimsbikeblog.wordpress.com/category/literary-musings/> (accessed 23 February 2020).
16. In some cases, reading the other novels of an author noted for one cycling novel allowed me to come into contact with overlooked literary treatments of the bicycle. This was notably the case for H. G. Wells; while he is widely recognised for his 1896 cycling novella *The Wheels of Chance*, criticism has generally neglected his compelling narrative and symbolic use of bicycles in a number of later novels, including *Kipps* (1905), *The War in the Air* (1908) and *The History of Mr Polly* (1910).
17. Examples of works in my corpus that are no longer in print include Jehan de La Pédale, *Contes modernes. Pédalons!* (Paris: Véloce-Sport, 1892); W. S. Beekman and Allan Eric, *Cycle Gleanings: Or, Wheels and Wheeling for Business and Pleasure, and the Study of Nature* (Boston: Skinner, Bartlett, 1894); Mary E. Kennard, *A Guide Book*

for Lady Cyclists (London: F. V. White, 1896); Mary E. Kennard, *The Golf Lunatic and his Cycling Wife* (London: Hutchinson, 1902); J. W. Allen, *Wheel Magic; Or, Revolutions of an Impressionist* (London: J. Lane, 1909).
18. I follow Andrew Ritchie's differentiation between three distinct categories of cycling: utilitarian, recreational and sporting. See Andrew Ritchie, *Quest for Speed: A History of Early Bicycle Racing 1868–1903* (Santa Clarita, CA: A. Ritchie, 2011), 18.
19. Héran, *Le retour de la bicyclette*, 16.
20. Matthew Beaumont and Michael J. Freeman, *The Railway and Modernity: Time, Space, and the Machine Ensemble* (Oxford: Peter Lang, 2007), 147.
21. Friedrich A. Kittler, *Gramophone, Film, Typewriter*, trans. Geoffrey Winthrop-Young and Michael Wutz (Stanford, CA: Stanford University Press, 1999), 16.
22. Wolfgang Schivelbusch, *The Railway Journey: The Industrialization of Time and Space in the 19th century* [1979], trans. Anslem Hollo (Berkeley, CA: University of California Press, 1986).
23. Lynne Kirby, *Parallel Tracks: The Railroad and Silent Cinema* (Durham, NC: Duke University Press, 1997); Beaumont and Freeman, *The Railway and Modernity*; see also John Lucas, 'Discovering England: The View from the Train', *Literature & History* 6, no. 2 (1997), 37–55; Jonathan H. Grossman, *Charles Dickens's Networks: Public Transport and the Novel* (Oxford: Oxford University Press, 2012).
24. See, for instance, Anne Grimshaw, *The Horse, a Bibliography of British Books, 1851–1976* (London/Phoenix, AZ: Library Association/Oryx Press, 1982); Gail Cunningham, 'Seizing the Reins: Women, Girls and Horses', in *Image and Power: Women in Fiction in the Twentieth Century*, ed. Sarah Sceats and Gail Cunningham (London: Longman, 1996), 65–77; Jennifer Mason, 'Animal Bodies: Corporeality, Class, and Subject Formation in *The Wide, Wide World*', *Nineteenth-Century Literature* 54, no. 4 (2000), 503–33; Helen Lenskyj, *Out on the Field: Gender, Sport, and Sexualities* (Toronto: Women's Press, 2003).
25. Carsten Henrik Meiner, *Le carrosse littéraire et l'invention du hasard* (Paris: PUF, 2008).
26. Jeffrey Cane Robinson, *The Walk: Notes on a Romantic Image* (Norman, OK: University of Oklahoma Press, 1989); Anne D. Wallace, *Walking, Literature, and English Culture: The Origins and Uses of Peripatetic in the Nineteenth Century* (Oxford: Clarendon Press, 1994); Robin Jarvis, *Romantic Writing and Pedestrian Travel* (Basingstoke: Macmillan, 1997); Rebecca Solnit, *Wanderlust: A History of Walking* (New York: Viking, 2000); Merlin Coverley, *The Art of Wandering: The Writer as Walker* (Harpenden: Oldcastle Books, 2012).
27. See, for instance, Robert Wohl, *A Passion for Wings: Aviation and the Western Imagination, 1908–1918* (New Haven, CT: Yale University

Press, 1994); Peter Thorold, *The Motoring Age: The Automobile and Britain 1896–1939* (London: Profile Books, 2003); Peter Wenzel and Sven Strasen (eds), *Discourses of Mobility, Mobility of Discourse: The Conceptualization of Trains, Cars and Planes in 19th- and 20th-Century Poetry* (Trier: WVT, 2010).

28. Bernhard Siegert, *Relays: Literature as an Epoch of the Postal System* (Stanford, CA: Stanford University Press, 1999); Richard Menke, *Telegraphic Realism: Victorian Fiction and Other Information Systems* (Stanford, CA: Stanford University Press, 2008).
29. Stephen Kern, *The Culture of Time and Space 1880–1918* (Cambridge, MA: Harvard University Press, 1983), 1.
30. Marc Desportes, *Paysages en mouvement: transports et perception de l'espace, XVIIIe–XXe siècle* (Paris: Gallimard, 2005), 8.
31. Eugen Weber, *France, Fin de Siècle* (Cambridge, MA: Belknap Press of Harvard University Press, 1986), 200. The population of France at the time was some 41 million. The tax on bicycles was introduced in 1893 and only abandoned in 1958.
32. Glen Norcliffe, *The Ride to Modernity: The Bicycle in Canada, 1869–1900* (Toronto: University of Toronto Press, 2001); Norcliffe, *Critical Geographies of Cycling*.
33. Ivan Illich, *Energy and Equity* (New York: Harper and Row, 1974); Bijker, *Of Bicycles, Bakelites, and Bulbs*; Catherine Bertho-Lavenir, *La Roue et le Stylo: comment nous sommes devenus touristes* (Paris: Editions Odile Jacob, 1999); David Gordon Wilson, Jim Papadopoulos and Frank Rowland Whitt, *Bicycling Science* (Cambridge, MA: MIT Press, 2004); Christopher S. Thompson, *The Tour de France: A Cultural History* (Berkeley, CA: University of California Press, 2006); Paul Rosen, Peter Cox and David Horton (eds), *Cycling and Society* (Aldershot: Ashgate, 2007).
34. Jeremy Withers and Daniel P. Shea (eds), *Culture on Two Wheels: The Bicycle in Literature and Film* (Lincoln, NE: University of Nebraska Press, 2016).
35. Leo Marx, *The Machine in the Garden: Technology and the Pastoral Ideal in America* (New York: Oxford University Press, 1964); Herbert L. Sussman, *Victorians and the Machine: The Literary Response to Technology* (Cambridge, MA: Harvard University Press, 1968); Friedrich A. Kittler, *Discourse Networks 1800/1900* (Stanford, CA: Stanford University Press, 1990); Mark Seltzer, *Bodies and Machines* (New York: Routledge, 1992); Sara Danius, *The Senses of Modernism: Technology, Perception, and Aesthetics* (Ithaca, NY: Cornell University Press, 2002); Andrew Thacker, *Moving through Modernity: Space and Geography in Modernism* (Manchester: Manchester University Press, 2003); Nicholas Daly, *Literature, Technology, and Modernity, 1860–2000* (Cambridge: Cambridge University Press, 2004); Christine MacLeod, *Heroes of*

Invention: Technology, Liberalism and British Identity, 1750–1914 (Cambridge: Cambridge University Press, 2007); Alex Goody, *Technology, Literature and Culture* (Cambridge: Polity, 2011).

36. Gilles Deleuze and Félix Guattari, *Capitalisme et schizophrénie: l'anti-Oedipe* (Paris: Les Éditions de minuit, 1980); Bruno Latour, *Aramis ou L'amour des techniques* (Paris: La Découverte, 1992); Bill Brown (ed.), *Things* (Chicago: University of Chicago Press, 2004); Jane Bennett, *Vibrant Matter: A Political Ecology of Things* (Durham, NC: Duke University Press, 2010). See also Arjun Appadurai (ed.), *The Social Life of Things: Commodities in Cultural Perspective* (Cambridge: Cambridge University Press, 1986).
37. Bennett, *Vibrant Matter*, 38; Ian Hodder, *Entangled: An Archaeology of the Relationships Between Humans and Things* (Malden, MA: Wiley-Blackwell, 2012), 110.
38. No biographical information is known about F. W. Bockett, the author of *Some Literary Landmarks for Pilgrims on Wheels* (London: J. M. Dent, 1901).
39. See, for instance, Sue Macy, *Wheels of Change: How Women Rode the Bicycle to Freedom* (Washington DC: National Geographic Society, 2011); Lena Wanggren, 'The Freedom Machine: The New Woman and the Bicycle', in *Transport in British Fiction: Technologies of Movement, 1840–1940*, ed. Adrienne E. Gavin and Andrew Humphries (London: Palgrave, 2015), 123–35.
40. Didier Tronchet, *Petit traité de vélosophie: réinventer la ville à vélo* (Paris: Plon, 2014), 13.

Chapter 1

Text and Transport

An intuitive interaction between writing and mobility has long existed; as far back as Homer's *Odyssey*, the rhythms of movement over land and sea have been linked to the inspiration required to begin writing and to the structure, style and literary qualities needed to produce text.[1] Cyclists and authors at the turn of the twentieth century used a new means of transport to explore fresh terrestrial and narrative possibilities. From acting as a device for bringing characters into contact to using the rhythms of cycling to structure a story, authors explored a rich literary terrain on two wheels. The cyclist made an appearance in late Victorian literature as a symbol of progressiveness, liberation and modernity, and quickly became interwoven with genres including adventure stories and comic writing. The bicycle also helped shape original literary forms in this period, which witnessed, for instance, the appearance of the New Woman novel, detective stories and new forms of travel writing. Moreover, cycling had a material relationship to print; the spread of this means of transport impacted on the production and consumption of literature, contributing to the significant changes occurring in the format of books and the manner in which they were read at the turn of the century. The visceral experience of this contemporary form of mobility had a palpable impact on the minds of writers and readers alike.

Romantic Walkers and Cycle Travel Literature

> Cycling [. . .] has brought nature and man together in a way that not even the arts of poetry and painting have hitherto succeeded in doing.
> F. W. Bockett[2]

Turn-of-the-century cyclists inherited and extended aesthetic, literary and social conceptions of movement and mobility that had begun to be formulated in the Romantic period, when walking was tightly bound up with the process of literary creation. Several Romantic poets were keen walkers, writing during a period described by some – even at the time – as an 'age of Pedestrianism'.[3] Wordsworth, Coleridge, Hazlitt and de Quincey each acknowledged the influence of walking on their writing, and Victorian critics readily recognised the importance of Pedestrianism to the Romantic movement. Leslie Stephen, for instance, claimed in his essay 'In Praise of Walking' (1901) that 'the literary movement at the end of the eighteenth century was [. . .] due in great part, if not mainly, to the renewed practice of walking'.[4] This close association between a human-powered means of locomotion and a literary movement is compelling for this study as it can shed light on the ways in which cycling, in its turn, came to shape the way both readers and writers interacted with text.

Since the late 1980s there has been an upsurge of critical interest in the place of pedestrian travel in Romantic literature. A number of monographs explore the manifold links between Romantic authors' passion for walking and the literature they produced.[5] Robin Jarvis notes that 'the creativity of Romantic verbal art is repeatedly referred to the conditions, qualities and rhythms of a body in motion, a travelling self making excited passage over the land, or through the streets, discovering locomotive and representational freedoms that were unavailable to previous generations'.[6] This representation of the body in motion in both rural and urban environments vividly prefigures the cyclist, who would inherit the freedom and bodily connection of the walker, while moving at greater speed. Anne D. Wallace's research reveals how the walk was a 'crucial metaphorical or narrative structure in Wordsworth's poetry' that laid the foundations for a peripatetic approach to literature.[7] These critics draw attention to the privileged relationship between walking and the processes of literary creation. This form of locomotion affords an intimate connection with nature and fellow humans. The mobile subject adopts a steadily evolving gaze that encourages what Eric Leed terms a 'progressional ordering of reality'.[8] In addition, walking allows for digressions and detours, and its pace may calm a troubled mind while provoking the rhythms of poetry. As we shall see, all of these concepts were handed down in greater or lesser degrees to late Victorian cyclists and were reflected in the texts they read and produced.

The Romantic era is not readily associated with the bicycle, yet it should be recalled that the first two-wheeled, human-powered vehicle was invented as early as 1817. From the outset, the machines were conceptualised as a technological improvement on the body's innate capacity for walking. Consisting of two wheels joined by a wooden bar, the draisine was known as a *Laufmaschine* in Germany and a 'swift walker' in Britain, since the rider's feet simply pushed off the ground to give impetus to the vehicle. Even once pedals were introduced in the 1860s, the etymological and conceptual link with the foot was conserved in the name Michaux gave to his new machine, *vélocipède* (from the Latin 'fast foot'). Although it would take until the end of the century for the bicycle to make a lasting impact on transport habits, it is significant that, from the first, the new vehicle was conceptualised as a 'walking machine' that could extend and optimise the body's innate means of locomotion. This precocious and revealing association between two-wheeled and pedestrian modes of locomotion would persist into the twentieth century, leading the French cycling advocate Louis Baudry de Saunier to claim in 1925 that 'we can see no fundamental difference between walking and cycling [. . .] The cyclist is a walker on wheels.'[9]

Despite its marginality at this time, the draisine's brief boom in popularity (along with the rise of ice-skating)[10] in the pre-train era should not be forgotten. When John Keats encountered young men on draisines in 1819, he termed the machine 'the nothing of the day', and he was right to predict that the fashion would be short-lived.[11] However, its cultural impact in the early nineteenth century was significant. Brian Rejack has examined 'the broader cultural narrative into which the draisine fell, albeit briefly', examining contemporary sources to point to the powerful symbolic potential of the object in Regency Britain.[12] Rejack argues that with the swift walker, 'the dandy trespasses on the grounds of country leisure, and in doing so figuratively trespasses on what constitutes public British identity'.[13] The two-wheeler's brief but significant appearance at this moment in the early nineteenth century reinforces its link to walking – an activity that was being established as a subversive and literary pursuit at the time – while simultaneously inscribing it in cultural discourses that would echo throughout the century.

Walkers in the Romantic period defined themselves in opposition to contemporary negative views of pedestrian travel (notably its association with poverty and crime) and sought to establish walking as at once a respectable and a literary pursuit.[14] Similarly, turn-of-the-century touring cyclists were a marginal group who struggled to forge an identity for themselves in the face of preconceptions and criticism, often by means of the written word. This is evident in Elizabeth Robins Pennell's *Our Sentimental Journey Through France and Italy* (1893) – illustrated by her husband Joseph[15] – which is littered with instances of locals ridiculing the couple's machine or cycling dress, or their being turned away from hotels and restaurants due to their means of locomotion.[16] In the midst of the polemic that raged around cycling from the mid-1880s, a strong pro-cycling discourse was developed in medical journals, newspapers, travel accounts and literature. Authors actively participated in this contemporary debate, and like their Romantic forefathers, they enlisted the written word in defence of their human-powered pastime.

While there is a vast body of travel writing by cyclists in this period, the Pennells, a London-based American couple, were part of a specific group of authors who looked to eighteenth-century and Romantic authors and their world by cycling to places connected with them, or by writing in a style that emulated them. These writers consciously chose bicycle journeys as a means to engage with past works of literature while producing new texts in response to the experiences cycling afforded them. Works such as F. W. Bockett's *Some Literary Landmarks for Pilgrims on Wheels* (1901) and Edward Thomas's *In Pursuit of Spring* (1914) recount journeys in which cycling 'pilgrims' seek out the birth and burial places of well-loved authors and poets, or retrace their journeys. Pennell rides a tandem tricycle along with her husband in order to retrace Laurence Sterne's famous journey through France and Italy, while Bockett goes on day trips to sites associated with a range of well-loved authors in the south of England. Thomas's journey 'on or with a bicycle' in the spring of 1913 brings him to Coleridge's home in the Quantocks.[17] Although these texts were written well after the Romantic period, each owes a major debt to the literary movement that occurred a hundred years previously, and to the pedestrian mode that was closely associated with it. In the case of Pennell, a legacy from eighteenth-century sentimental literature is also foregrounded in her overt emulation of Sterne. Not only are these authors inheritors of the concept of the slow-paced, subjective exploration of landscapes, they use their modern machines to seek out new and privileged connections with literature, the past and their environment. Each of these authors explores anew the vital connection between human-powered locomotion and literature, pointing to the ways in which cycling, like walking, can revive and shape spaces and texts.

These bookish cyclists all seek to draw closer to the texts and authors they admire by journeying to places associated with them, resurrecting both the person of the author and their fictional creations in the process. Temporal boundaries are crossed in both directions: Pennell and Bockett respectively invite Laurence Sterne and Thomas

Carlyle into the present by painting the anachronistic image of these admired authors riding bicycles. Pennell expresses the firm conviction that Sterne would have preferred her chosen vehicle, addressing him directly in the preface when she argues 'in these degenerate days, you, Sir, we are sure, would prefer it to a railway carriage, as little suited to your purposes as to those of Mr Ruskin'.[18] Pennell defends cycling against detractors such as Ruskin, arguing that 'the oft-regretted delights of travelling in days of coach and post-chaise, destroyed on the coming of the railroad, [are] once more to be had by means of tricycle or bicycle'.[19] It is Pennell's opinion that the speed and disconnection of the train necessarily result in a journey devoid of sentimental, aesthetic or artistic qualities. These cyclists opt for a human-powered mode of transport in order to discover meaning in their journey as well as the inspiration to write. The bicycle, thanks to its moderate speed, its openness to its surroundings and its affordability, permits the traveller to rediscover 'the delights of travelling' as experienced in the eighteenth century, when even coaches and post-chaises rarely surpassed the average walking speed of 4 miles per hour.[20] Pennell seeks to emulate sentimental literature which readily makes room for digression, a trope that had long been associated with travel on foot or by coach. Pennell ostensibly seeks to follow the tradition of travel writing established by Sterne in providing an account of her subjective experience of the journey, rather than penning a fact-based, Baedeker-style travel guide, which would have been more in keeping with late Victorian taste. Just as sentimental novels and travel writing may be seen as a reaction to the rationalism and empiricism of the eighteenth century, these writers position themselves against the qualitative, positivist outlook that had come to characterise the late Victorian age.

Bockett also makes the imaginative leap of placing an admired past author on a bicycle, going so far as to imagine that cycling would have improved Carlyle's writing style:

> Imagination fails one in the attempt to conceive what Carlyle might have been had he practised vaulting into the saddle over a pair of sound pneumatics [. . .] The adjuncts of cycling would have taken some of the objectionable philosophic starch out of Thomas.[21]

The fact that these texts present the unusual image of a deceased author on a bicycle reflects the literary potential of the vehicle as well as its power to transgress temporal boundaries. As Dave Buchanan highlights, Pennell's and Bockett's images 'illustrate how cycling in the late Victorian period was seen by some as having imaginative overtones connecting writers of the past with riders, writers, and readers of the present'.[22] The bicycle is not just a tool for the writer, but also for the reader, establishing a relationship with the past that allows a privileged connection to works of literature and the worlds that produced them. While inviting dead authors into the present, cycle pilgrims sought to journey into the past. Bockett, on departing from Shelley's home, remarks 'as I [. . .] mounted my cycle I felt that I should read "Alastor" that night with fresh interest, with a keener eye for its beauties, with a sense of possession such as I had never felt before'.[23] Cycling to the place where the famous poem was written provides Bockett with a sense of connection with the author that enhances his pleasure in reading the work.

Indeed, it is not only the texts that these cyclists seek to come into closer contact with, but the very person of the dead author. When Bockett cycles to Tennyson's home – which was still a private house – he makes an attempt 'to obtain almost the identical view seen from the poet's own windows' by standing on high ground nearby.[24] As such, he both summons the author into his imagination and attempts to stand in his shoes, experiencing the sensations he experienced. Pennell brings Sterne back to life by addressing her preface to him, expressing her sincere wish that he enjoy this homage to his famous journey. She includes an account of a recent visit to Sterne's grave, visited by 'many, who have come to breathe a sigh or drop a tear for poor Yorick' (the largely autobiographical hero of Sterne's *A Sentimental Journey*).[25] The familiarity Pennell establishes with Sterne in the preface acts as a pretext for liberal borrowings from his work throughout her account. She explains that 'as you will recognise your own words without our pointing them out, we have not even put them into quotation marks, an omission which you of all men can best appreciate'.[26] Pennell thus openly appropriates Sterne's journey and text as a structure and guide for her own, something that was commonplace in the eighteenth century, but disparaged in the Victorian age, when concepts of copyright and intellectual property came to the fore. Pennell displays irreverence towards these contemporary attitudes to literary creation, daring to enter into an open dialogue with and reappropriation of Sterne's classic text. These cyclists willingly blurred the lines between past and present, fiction and reality, living and dead, in an attempt to resurrect authors and journey with them to the places that shaped a well-loved text.

A further Romantic connection established by this group of cycle-travel writers was their revival of the eighteenth-century picturesque aesthetic, founded on the combination of beautiful landscapes and traces of the past, such as ruined buildings, road dwellers or wild spaces.[27] Buchanan argues that these authors were part of a broader practice of literary tourism, promoting a nostalgic and picturesque approach to landscape and literature that drew on pictorial models.[28] Pennell expresses an idealised view of road dwellers, as conveyed in a scene where Elizabeth congenially approaches a group of people she encounters in France and introduces herself, saying: 'I was a Gipsy come from over the seas, with news of their brothers in America. "But we're not Gipsies," said they, "we live in Boulogne, and we're busy."'[29] This amusing encounter is complemented by idyllic descriptions of the gypsies' traditional way of life, while several of Joseph's illustrations take them as their subject. Of course, the gap between the lifestyle of these middle-class cyclists and that of the people they encounter on the road is much greater than the former might be willing to admit.[30]

Elements of a picturesque outlook may also be traced in Edward Thomas's *In Pursuit of Spring*, in which the narrator describes an encampment of gypsies in the following terms:

> If they were not there, in fact, they would have to be invented. They are at home there. See them at nightfall, with their caravans drawn up facing the wind, and the men by the half-door at the back smoking, while the hobbled horses are grazing and the children playing near. The children play across the road, motor cars or no motor cars, laughing at whoever amuses them.[31]

These road dwellers appear to Thomas as a natural part of the landscape, and his imperative 'see' summons the image vividly to the reader's mind, resurrecting an idealised scene frequently represented in eighteenth-century paintings. The children's irreverent playfulness in spite of the presence of motor cars symbolises the backward-looking nature of Thomas's perspective; these gypsies enshrine a pre-industrial lifestyle that refuses to align itself with the symbols of technological progress and modernity. Cyclists such as Thomas associated the bicycle with this imaginary, refusing the tenets of a society based on ever-accelerating progress.

As Buchanan observes, attention to and depiction of wild elements in the landscape was another key element in both the picturesque and the Romantic aesthetic.[32] At the close of a century of intensive industrialisation, the need to maintain or re-establish contact with nature seemed both vital and urgent. Thomas explicitly invokes the dual motivation for his journey to the Quantocks, which he hopes will allow him to connect simultaneously with the change of season and with Coleridge's poetry. He explains that

> I had a wish of a mildly imperative nature that Spring would be arriving among the Quantocks at the same time as myself, that 'the one red leaf the last of its clan,' that danced on March 7, 1798, would have danced itself into the grave: that since my journey was to be in 'a month before the month of May,' Spring would come fast, not slowly, up that way.[33]

The rich intertextuality of this passage, which liberally quotes from Coleridge's poem 'Christabel', hints at the intimate connection the cyclist hopes to establish with the poet and his texts by travelling to the landscapes that inspired them, in the same season in which they were written. Like the Romantic poets he admires, natural rhythms are crucial for Thomas; in his *Pursuit of Spring* he attempts to embody the change of season, closely observing the transforming landscape as he journeys, and using it as a basis for his powerful nature writing.

The industrial artefacts that were part of the early twentieth-century landscape are carefully woven into Thomas's narrative, as we saw in the peripheral description of motor cars in the portrait of the gypsy encampment. Yet generally, symbols of modernity such as cars and advertising hoardings are perceived as oppressive, unwelcome elements in the cyclist's environment. Thomas rejoices in witnessing nature overcome man-made developments, remarking that: 'it was a pleasure to see on a wayside plot, where elms mingled with telegraph posts, a board advertising building sites, but leaning awry, mouldy, and almost illegible'.[34] Like Bockett, Thomas deplores urban sprawl, seeking a transcendental connection with the wild by voyaging beyond the city's limits.[35] He condemns the drive to build over any leftover land, arguing that 'if any waste be left under the new order, it will be used for conspicuously depositing rubbish. Little or no wildness of form or arrangement can survive, and with no wildness a landscape cannot be beautiful.'[36] Bockett similarly rejoices in the connection with nature that cycling affords him, taking comfort in the fact that 'in the secret shady lanes you are a solitary explorer, face to face with Nature in her prettiest moods, and you realise what a thinly-peopled, wild, woodland country England is outside her great over-grown towns'.[37] These cyclists use their machines to connect with wild spaces where traces of the industrialised society they inhabit can no longer be detected. A communion with the organic world is at the heart of both Thomas's and Bockett's desire to ride and to write, and a rejection of the emblems of industrial progress in favour of a reconnection with the past, 'nature' or 'the wild' is central to their aesthetic.

At the beginning of a new century, these cycle pilgrims looked warily to the future, notably in terms of the interaction between the environment, humans and the various machines spawned by the industrial age. The bicycle allowed these authors access to a peripatetic, Romantic mobility that retains an essential connection to the environment and the past. As Anne Wallace argues, the peripatetic as a literary mode and material practice persisted beyond the first half of the nineteenth century and 'remains a functional but unrecognized mediation of our continuing encounters with technology, speed, and change, contributing to the unwitting perpetuation of Romantic ideology'.[38] Bombarded by rapid technological change, cycle pilgrims used their bicycles to perpetuate a peripatetic engagement with landscape. Thomas pauses in his ride to observe the expanse of Salisbury Plain and 'feel[s] the age of the earth, the greatness of Time, Space and Nature; the littleness of man even in an aeroplane, the fact that earth does not belong to man, but man to the earth'.[39] In contrast to the self-aggrandising train, car and aeroplane, the bicycle encourages a humble awareness of the body's place within the landscape through which it moves. Like the pedestrian, the cyclist adopts an attentive, bodily, mindful approach to movement through spaces, texts and the layers of the past that constitute them.

Cycling and Narrative Structure: H. G. Wells's *The Wheels of Chance* and Maurice Leblanc's *Here are Wings*

Having considered the cyclist's heritage from Romantic walkers, we will now take a closer look at the specific narrative role of the bicycle in fiction written at the time of the widespread adoption of the technology.[40] H. G. Wells's *The Wheels of Chance* (1896) and Maurice Leblanc's *Here are Wings* (*Voici des ailes*) (1898) are two iconic cycling novels written respectively in Britain and France during the 'bicycle boom' of the 1890s. Wells's story recounts the draper Hoopdriver's ten-day cycling holiday in the south of England, while Leblanc's tale relates two Parisian couples' cycling tour over several weeks in Normandy and Brittany. Reading these two texts in tandem will allow us to uncover the ways in which this new form of mobility altered its users' interaction with their surroundings and offered a fresh approach to the act of narration.

The first three chapters of *The Wheels of Chance* are brief, providing momentary glimpses into Hoopdriver's working life. Within these opening sections the narrative gradually begins to focus on the steep learning curve of the aspiring cyclist, at first obliquely (the reader's attention is initially drawn to 'The Remarkable Condition of this Young Man's Legs', which the narrator proceeds to describe with 'the scientific spirit, the hard, almost professorial tone of the conscientious realist')[41] and then explicitly, when we are provided with an impressionistic depiction of Hoopdriver's lessons:

> Behind the decorous figure of the attentive shopman that I had the honour of showing you at first, rises a vision of a nightly struggle, of two dark figures and a machine in a dark road [. . .] a wavering unsteady flight, a spasmodic turning of the missile edifice of man and machine, and a collapse.[42]

So long as the protagonist is unable to ride, the narrative remains at an effective standstill – recounting little else than 'the tale of [Hoopdriver's] bruises and abrasions'[43] while he attempts to mount a bicycle – and the paternal voice of the narrator is loudly heard. The mysterious 'vision of a nightly struggle' provides the interest of the story, a rare glimpse of movement and intrigue in the draper's static, humdrum life. It is only from the fourth chapter – entitled 'The Riding Forth of Mr Hoopdriver' – that the story begins to get into its stride, as the protagonist's voice starts to emerge. The chapters lengthen and the narrator retires, setting aside the judgements of the first three chapters in order to leave front of stage to characterisation and plot.

Similarly, in Leblanc's tale, the opening chapter conveys an impression of stasis and immutability that is connected to the fact that the characters have not yet begun their journey. Two wealthy young couples, Pascal and Régine Fauvières and Guillaume and Madeleine d'Arjols, have come to dine at their club at the Bois de Boulogne, where they engage in the fashionable activity of riding bicycles. Their enthusiasm for the machine is apparent, yet the narrator insists that their main motivation for cycling is to follow society's codes and appear fashionable:

> There are such things as necessary opinions, indispensable pleasures, obligatory shows, and they obeyed all these requirements like good,

submissive children, as anonymous, elegant, frivolous beings with idle souls and sleeping hearts, indentured to fashion, taking exercise for fashion, just as they would have stayed in bed all day if fashion had required it.⁴⁴

Reflecting contemporary French concerns around idleness, decadence and degeneration,⁴⁵ these childless, loveless couples appear as listless automatons mindlessly following the precepts of the social circle to which they belong. Towards the end of the novella, Pascal will reflect that these years were 'my lost years, my years of sleep, torpor, discomfort, hypocrisy!'⁴⁶ Cycling is the activity that rouses Pascal and the other characters from their indifference. When Guillaume suggests riding to Dieppe – where their club is to meet the following week – the idea appears to the women as 'some extraordinary adventure, outside the normal conditions of life, one of those distant and perilous adventures from which there may be no return'.⁴⁷ Although their expectations seem exaggerated, they will in fact correspond to the reality of their journey, which transforms their lives completely. The growing enthusiasm around their departure culminates in the closing line of the first chapter – 'Well then, let's go!'⁴⁸ – which invites us away from the stagnant, bland world of the Parisian club to begin a voyage of discovery. In both novels, then, cycling represents an escape from the monotony of daily life, providing the means by which the characters will embark on an adventure and undergo profound personal transformation.

In the opening chapters of Wells's 'bicycling idyll', the narrator's musings on the nature of fiction and his evocation of the literary style of realism establish a parallel between Hoopdriver's attempts to learn how to ride a bicycle and the mastery of narrative form. Wells was not alone in suggesting a link between the frustration of learning how to ride a bicycle and that of managing to produce a worthy literary text. Mary Kennard (or Mrs Edward Kennard, the name under which she published) wrote a large number of now neglected works of popular fiction and non-fiction on themes such as horse riding, cycling, motoring and sports from 1883 to 1903. In *A Guide Book for Lady Cyclists* (1896), she recounts her own struggle to learn to ride, and makes a telling comparison: 'It was as bad as writing one's first novel, when one set to work secretly and would have died rather than let anybody suspect the task on which one was engaged.'⁴⁹ When she has mastered the skill, however, cycling becomes a writing tool: Kennard recounts how she set out on rides in the morning to clear her head before writing.⁵⁰ As well as mirroring the difficult creative process, cycling could provide inspiration to artists. Edward

Elgar, for instance, rode fifty miles a day in the Malvern hills when he was composing the Enigma Variations in 1899.⁵¹ Like Hoopdriver and the aspiring novelist, Kennard battles in private to acquire a new skill, hiding her imperfect cycling and writing from public view. The fits and starts of the novice author mirrored the covert exertions of these apprentice cyclists.

While Leblanc's characters are already proficient cyclists when the story begins, the second chapter of *Here are Wings* refuses an effortless start to their journey. The characters are seen 'sprawling on the bank of a ditch' while 'the machines lay pell-mell, to the right and left, like cumbersome objects that have been discarded as quickly as possible and not without some resentment'.⁵² Not yet used to the physical difficulties of riding long distances in the heat, the journey and the story get off to an unsure start that has the virtue of introducing an element of humour into an otherwise straight-faced narrative. In various ways, then, both Wells and Leblanc make use of the difficulties of cycle touring, or riding a bicycle itself, in order to get their own narratives into motion, and to mirror the apprentice author's hesitant first steps.

In both novellas, it is the bicycle that physically allows the change of location and the encounter with various characters needed to determine the rest of the story. The bicycle opens up a narrative space and a unique geography in which mobile protagonists cross and recross each other's paths, forming new and unexpected configurations in the process. Marc Augé, one of the rare critics to have considered the literary qualities of the bicycle, provides the following compelling description of the spatial and sensory transformation operated by the machine:

> You slip subtly into another geography which is eminently and literally poetic, since it creates immediate contacts between places that ordinarily could only be visited separately. This geography seems to be the source of spatial metaphors, of unexpected mergings and short-circuits that are aroused by the awakened curiosity of these new ramblers, one pedal stroke at a time [. . .] The bicycle is writing, often free or even wild writing – an experience of automatic writing [. . .]⁵³

What emerges from early cycling literature is a renewed form of human interaction and relation to one's environment which creates its own literary geography. Augé highlights how the cyclists' privileged, immediate contact with their surroundings, combined with the speed that allows them to reconnect places and people that must remain separate for the walker or train traveller, create unexpected couplings that are a direct inspiration for metaphor and poetry. Cycling becomes a form of writing, which in turn can actively shape texts that place this form of locomotion at the core of the narrative.

In *The Wheels of Chance*, in stark contrast to the stasis of the opening chapters (which reflect the immutability of Hoopdriver's working life in London), successive scenes of country life and specifically the intrigue with fellow cyclists Jessie and Bechamel quickly provide rhythm and interest to the narrative. Ellen Gruber Garvey remarks how, 'as a prop or narrative convenience, the bicycle had many of the same attractions for story writers as it did for tourists: riders could ride alone or in pairs or groups; they could stop at will and visit familiar or unfamiliar places'.[54] The bicycle quickly came to fulfil that basic and crucial function of literature: moving characters from place to place and confronting them with new people and landscapes. In Wells's novel, Hoopdriver encounters two upper-class cyclists on the first day of his ride: teenage Jessie, fleeing home, and her tutor Bechamel, who has helped her escape from her overbearing stepmother. The three cyclists' south-bound trajectories repeatedly overlap, resulting in numerous unexpected encounters. In this sense, Wells's cyclists correspond to Tim Edensor's view of rhythmically constituted places, with each character's bicycle becoming 'one rhythmic constituent in a seething space pulsing with intersecting trajectories and temporalities'.[55] These trajectories eventually collide to form a new configuration on the evening in Bognor when Jessie escapes from Bechamel, who has lured her away from home with the intention of seducing her, and cycles off with Hoopdriver. In contrast to collective, timetabled rail travel, the bicycle creates its own subjective time and rhythm in the narrative that allows for confrontations and coincidences that would otherwise seem forced and unlikely. When Hoopdriver takes detours to avoid the couple by whom he feels he is 'haunted', he invariably meets them on the road or in an inn.[56] Ironically, it is when Hoopdriver starts actively pursuing the pair, after he is alerted to Bechamel's attempted and uninvited seduction of Jessie, that he loses their trace. It is as though the bicycle introduces a contingent time that refuses forward planning, constantly confronting the characters with unexpected events to which they must respond spontaneously and ingeniously. Just as previous works 'haunt' texts, in Derrida's terms, these cyclists are on individual journeys that haunt each other, creating points of friction and interaction that weave the texture of the story.[57]

Carsten Meiner points out that chance and contingency were central to literary depictions of coach journeys, and such an outlook is closely connected to the bicycle in Leblanc's pastoral tale.[58] Pascal depicts his new life as 'the good life, full of chance and unexpectedness', and similar terms appear later, when the narrator describes how 'they travelled at random on the roads and at random through life'.[59] In common with Hoopdriver, these cyclists are constantly confronted with unexpected sights and situations, and rejoice in this experience. Towards the end of the novella, Pascal describes how 'Our souls, like our bodies, have flown across the great white roads, through the purity of space [. . .] It even seems that events have come upon us just as [the bicycle] itself rushes across landscapes and horizons.'[60] The bicycle as a form of locomotion is here directly linked to narrative progression; events come suddenly and vividly upon the reader, just as impressions unfold unexpectedly before the mobile cyclist.

All this might seem to point to a lack of agency on the part of the travelling protagonists, but these cyclists do in fact actively participate in determining the rhythm of their journey. In contrast to Wells's tale, no major characters are introduced over the course of Leblanc's narrative; rather, the bicycle journey intervenes to form a new constellation of the four characters we meet at the beginning. Thanks to the different speeds of each cyclist, two new couples form, since 'we always left together, but we invariably arrived in pairs, Guillaume and Régine speeding ahead like lunatics, Mme d'Arjols and Fauvières contenting themselves with a moderate pace'.[61] While the narrator aligns himself with Pascal's perspective from the beginning, the diminishing view of his wife and Guillaume, cycling ahead, effectively removes them from the narrative from this point. The reader stays behind with Pascal and Madeleine who, cycling slowly and making frequent stops, gradually fall in love (as do the speeding pair ahead). It is the personal, subjective nature of travelling by bicycle that makes such a turn of events possible, allowing the continuity of traditional alliances and social constraints to be broken down. Had the four characters been travelling in a collective, passive manner such as by train, there would have been no possibility for privacy and the growth of mutual affection. Cycling brings each character's individuality to the fore, allowing for a reconfiguration of the couples that is more in line with their tastes, outlooks and personalities. The budding desire between Madeleine and Pascal, as well as that implied between Guillaume and Régine, soon merges with the joy of cycling to become the main narrative drive.

The novel form relies on movement from place to place, from one perspective to another, and it is the bicycle that provides the motor and sets the pace for this narrative mobility in both texts. In *The Wheels of Chance*, the speed, flexibility and independence of the bicycle place the characters in a sort of perpetual motion, locating them in a different temporal sphere from the non-cycling characters. Bechamel remains in the narrative only as long as he is a cyclist; once Hoopdriver has stolen his much superior bicycle to escape with Jessie, the narrator leaves him fuming in his hotel room. We hear no more of him and do not find out how or if he returns home to his wife after his botched elopement.[62] It is in the closing chapters of the novel, when Jessie's stepmother and her three admirers are in hot pursuit of the pair, that the bicycle reveals itself as both an exemplary narrative device and a supremely adaptable technology. Jessie's fraught stepmother, Mrs Milton, first hears of her whereabouts from her admirer Widgery, who has been cycle touring in Sussex and rushes to her house to bring her the news.[63] The late hour prevents them from leaving straight away, as there are no more trains; coming only pages after the description of Jessie and Hoopdriver's nocturnal flight from Bechamel, the superior potential of the bicycle for the purpose of escape is thrown into sharp relief.

The subsequent chapters recount the pursuit of the cyclists and repeatedly drive home the superiority of the bicycle over the train; while Mrs Milton and her cohort are held up by late trains and the incomplete railway network, Jessie and Hoopdriver slip effortlessly from their clutches, flitting from one village to the next without a trace. The narrator says, 'the fugitives vanished into Immensity [. . .] there were no more trains';[64] the cycling characters seem to exist in a different dimension to the encaged and dependent train travellers. Dangle eventually catches up with the pair in a horse-drawn dogcart, but – in a further display of the bicycle's supremacy over older forms of transport – the horse is spooked by the bicycles and bolts down the hill, once again allowing the cyclists to escape. The final scene exclusively involves bicycles and tricycles, since the rescue party have mounted 'a remarkable collection of wheeled instruments'.[65] They eventually manage to catch up with the fugitives thanks to the fact that 'downhill nothing can beat a highly geared tandem bicycle'.[66] It is interesting to note that communication as well as transportation technologies play a crucial narrative role in the chase; Jessie is betrayed by the letter she writes to her former teacher Miss Mergle, who immediately alerts Mrs Milton of her whereabouts by telegram.[67] The bicycle was just one of a range of *fin-de-siècle* technologies that allowed authors such as Wells to move characters and information around at will, experimenting with narrative forms that could convey the speed, elasticity and contingency of modern experience.

The culminating chase scene mentioned above typifies Wells's vision of the bicycle as a rapid, modern technology that alters its users' interaction with time and space. In an earlier scene, Hoopdriver rides past Jessie and Bechamel as they are arguing under a bridge. Here, it is the bicycle's unique silence and speed that allows him to '[come] on them suddenly, without the slightest preliminary announcement, and when they least expected it, under the South-Western Railway arch'.[68] Wells draws attention to the cyclist's singular mode of perception by placing the characters in a position where they would be invisible to passengers in passing trains. Riding fast, Hoopdriver receives only 'the impression of a second', but the few words he hears and the body language he glimpses are enough for him to grasp the dangerous nature of the situation Jessie is in. 'It's horrible,' he hears Jessie cry, 'it's brutal – cowardly – .'[69] At this pivotal moment in the story, Hoopdriver realises the pair are not in fact siblings, and hatches the plan of saving the young woman from Bechamel's uninvited advances. Wells's narrative use of the moment is exemplary of what Sue Zemka has termed a late-century 'shift in priorities away from the moment as a vector of emotional pitch and narrative movement to the moment as an opening into or distillation of meanings that are invisible to sight and invite complex interpretative procedures'.[70] While Hoopdriver's moment of insight under the railway bridge does involve visual clues, it is the words he hears (again, inaccessible to the closed-in railway passenger or to the pedestrian, whose gradual approach would have been seen or heard) which allow him to distil the various clues he has received over the preceding days.

This alternative and embodied relationship to time and one's environment is explored at length in *Here are Wings*. After the characters have become accustomed to cycling all day, their relationship to time seems transformed. The narrator describes how 'the hours that had gone by left them with a feeling of beatitude and surprise [. . .] In the heady confusion of their dreams, they felt like fabulous beings that have been touched by a fairy's wand.'[71] It is as though they have entered into a strange cycling time that mirrors the fictional, narrative time in which the reader must suspend belief for the length of the story. Now that the protagonists have left behind the tedium of their old lives, the idea of joining their club at Dieppe seems impossible; indeed, it would mean the end of the journey, and the conclusion of the story. It is the suggestion made by one member of their party, 'What if we carried on in this way, far away, without a plan, towards Brittany?'[72] that allows for the continuation of the narrative. They decide to continue their journey, 'wandering on the high roads, obeying their every whim',[73] again recalling the cyclist's inheritance from walking while suggesting an affinity with the observant, marginal outlook of the *flâneur*, a figure I examine at greater length in Chapter 4. Like Romantic walkers or the *flâneur*, the cyclist seeks the position of an anonymous, slow-paced, mobile observer of the world and rejects the focus on time efficiency and speed that had come to characterise industrial societies. Leblanc's characters challenge the contemporary focus on speed by travelling 'without haste, without a programme',[74] and as such are able to enter into an alternative temporality that permits a closer interaction with their surroundings and, by the end of the novel, allows them to cast off society's moral and behavioural codes completely.

Whether the mobility they offer is efficient or meandering, bicycles do much more than simply move characters from origin to destination. The form of movement they represent in both Wells's and Leblanc's texts is reliant on interruptions, unexpected encounters, stoppages and accidents. In this sense, they share a common lineage with literary depictions of the carriage as theorised by Carsten Meiner, who argues that the nature of the vehicle is 'that of not working, of falling apart and breaking',[75] thus inscribing chance and contingency into the narrative, while reflecting the uncertainties of modern experience. Lukács also notes the important narrative role played by failure, arguing that 'by a strange and melancholy paradox, the moment of failure is the moment of value; the comprehending and experiencing of life's refusals is the source from which the fullness of life seems to flow'.[76] Indeed, the bicycle provides even more opportunity for chance encounters and coincidences than a public coach, as it follows no set route and can change direction or stop according to the rider's will.

The title of *The Wheels of Chance* already gives an indication of the importance of random encounters in the narrative; it is Hoopdriver's repeated, unplanned meetings with the cycling couple Jessie and Bechamel that provide the backbone to the story. Yet in the majority of cases it is the bicycle's dysfunction that allows the characters to actually engage with each other. When the hero first meets Jessie cycling along the Surbiton road, it is his fall (an incident he significantly blames on the bicycle – 'Had the machine a devil?')[77] that allows them to exchange a few words. Some chapters later,

Hoopdriver's first interaction with the dastardly Bechamel occurs while the latter is repairing a puncture on the Ripley road.[78] As such, the mobility provided by the bicycle sets up the context for encounters, but, as with coach travel, it is often when the vehicle breaks down that 'these chance collisions of human beings' (to borrow E. M. Forster's phrase)[79] are able to occur. Indeed, as Forster depicts in *Howards End* (1910), brief encounters between strangers are part and parcel of the experience of modernity, and are a phenomenon that transportation technologies such as the train, car and bicycle helped render commonplace.

It is not only mechanical failures that can cause the cyclist to call a halt. The bicycle is intimately connected to the body that powers it, as well as to prevailing meteorological conditions. Just as earlier authors such as Fielding and Dickens made use of coaching inns as a metaphor for the breaks between chapters, Wells and Leblanc mobilise their cyclists' necessary pauses to eat and sleep in order to structure their narratives. In coaching days, horses were changed at set points during the journey, giving travellers an opportunity for a rest. With the bicycle, however, it is the human rather than the equine body that must be periodically refuelled and rested, and this provides a rich opportunity to add narrative rhythm and structure. Leblanc's heroes listen carefully to their bodies; the narrator recounts how 'They did not exhaust themselves. Two or three hours in the morning, and again at the end of the day, without haste, without a programme. The slightest sign of fatigue led them to call a halt.'[80] Rather than pushing themselves to cover impressive distances or stick to a rigid schedule, the four cyclists adopt the pace their body dictates. This pace is mirrored in the narrative, which alternates cycling scenes with descriptions of the long breaks the two couples take from cycling in picturesque spots or quaint inns.

In the opening chapter of *Here are Wings*, the first words spoken are by Guillaume, who remarks as he gets off his bicycle, 'Let's not lose any time [. . .] I'm starving.'[81] In addition to Pascal's enthusiastic admiration of the bicycles lined up in the stable, it is the cyclists' appetite that provides some sign of life within the stifling environment of the club. Guillaume relishes his meal, stating that 'I know of nothing more delicious than satisfying the hunger that you have earned with your own muscles.'[82] The pleasure he takes in eating after physical exercise prefigures the importance of food in the rest of the narrative. For example, the first premises of the liaison between Guillaume and Régine occur in the following exchange, when the young woman dares to call him by his first name:

'Guillaume, can you see the village that's all the way over there?'
'Yes, that's where we'll have lunch.'
'Well, then! Let's bet I'll be there before you.'[83]

Motivated by the prospect of lunch, the two quicker cyclists shoot off, thus constituting two newly formed couples in separate narrative spaces. In addition to the physical requirements of eating and sleeping, the pace of these cyclists' journeys is also determined by the weather. In contrast to coach, train or car passengers, cyclists are open to the elements, and the rate of their progress depends on factors such as heat, wind and rain. Thus, when rain 'detained them for two days'[84] in a small town, Pascal and Madeleine have the time to discuss and work through the latter's jealous feelings concerning Guillaume and Régine. As such, the physical needs of the body and the weather conditions provide structure to the journey and to the text, interrupting the movement of the narrative to provide necessary moments of reflection and introspection.

In *The Wheels of Chance*, the narrative does not skip over the places where Hoopdriver stops to eat, drink and sleep during his journey; in fact, they are often sites where key encounters or realisations occur. Moreover, the reader is invited to enter into the rhythms of Hoopdriver's body; on the first night of his holiday we share in his sleep by reading an account of his rather surreal dreams.[85] It is as though his bodily rhythms correspond directly to the narrative time, with a journey into his subconscious made possible by the fact he is asleep. On the evening he escapes with Jessie, the narrator explicitly makes use of the time when the young people are sleeping to insert an 'interlude' describing the events occurring at Jessie's home. 'And here,' the narrator informs us, 'thanks to the glorious institution of sleep, comes a break in the narrative again.'[86] At the end of this chapter, the reader is once again reminded that 'this is only an Interlude, introduced to give our wanderers time to refresh themselves by good honest sleeping'.[87] Thus, the narrative is aligned with the sensations, needs, pains and pleasures connected to the body of the central cyclist. The subjective experience of cycling, being intimately connected to the steady rhythms of the body's movement and its physical requirements, invites us to adopt a unified perspective that differentiates itself from the disconnection of rail travel. In-between spaces are revived, taking attention away from departure and destination, or beginning and end, in order to concentrate on the subjective process of the journey as a unified, bodily experience.

Both authors draw on the subjective rhythms of cycling to conclude their narratives. Yoonjoung Choi observes a compelling parallel between Wells's narrative and the act of cycling, observing that '[l]ike cycling, which encourages people's active participation, Wells's cycling romance refuses the final statement; it is a participatory reading in carnivalesque "becoming"'.[88] Choi mobilises Bakhtin's concept of the carnivalesque in order to illustrate how Wells adopts a literary mode that subverts dominant discourses through humour and chaos, while inviting the reader's participation in the narrative. The reader is left to imagine the end of the story, as Hoopdriver returns to his dreary life as a draper in London. Just as Bechamel was eclipsed from the story when his bicycle was stolen, Hoopdriver 'dismounts with a sigh' in the last paragraph of the novella, and so 'vanishes from our ken'.[89] Leblanc's novella 'refuses the final statement' even more categorically; the two newly formed couples simply take separate routes – one pair towards the coast, the other inland – and we are left wondering if they ever attempt to return to their bourgeois, married lives in Paris, or whether they decide to prolong their bohemian existence indefinitely. Thus, just as cyclists cannot be passively carried along by their machines, in both these tales the reader is invited to contribute imaginative energies to the journey's end.

As this analysis illustrates, the cycle journey quickly came to mirror the narrative endeavour and provide a novel framework for it. Both Leblanc and Wells adopted cycling as the structure for their narrative, the new-found mobility of their characters providing the pretext for encounters with successive localities and people. The specific form of mobility provided by the bicycle opened up a new geography based on individual, spontaneous exploration and unexpected encounters. At the same time, progression remained attuned to the needs, limits and desires of the body powering the machine, and subject to interruptions and stoppages that provided rich opportunities for punctuating the narrative.

Adventurous Bicycles: Romance and Detective Fiction

The thrilling chase that ends *The Wheels of Chance* casts a backward glance at the many adventure and detective stories published in the cycling press in the 1880s. Through an examination of a range of stories that appeared in the newspaper *The Irish Cyclist*, Brian Griffin shows that in the early days of cycling the object was closely associated with an imaginary of danger, excitement and sensation.

Griffin quotes the prominent cycling journalist Beatrice Grimshaw, who wrote in 1893:

> I knew, by means of reading all the cycling papers, and the exciting stories therein contained, that it was the commonest thing in the world for ordinary riders of the wheel to be chased by escaped lunatics, railway trains, burglars, etc etc . . . in short, to go through what the eighteenth century would have called 'a thousand vastly diverting adventures'.[90]

The paper's editor, the former racing cyclist R. J. Mecredy, also remarked on the conspicuous association with the adventure genre in the early days of cycling, claiming in 1901 that 'every literary aspirant who had steered a cycle felt capable of making it the ground-work for those slender romances of the late-Victorian magazine style'.[91] Added to the slim format of the books these pioneering cyclists were inspired to produce, the themes selected for treatment were linked to their thrilling pastime. Mecredy noted that

> Those were enthusiastic times, and with all their mock heroics and melodramas they had their charm. We were all younger then, and were not too captious in judging a story with a few bicycles in it. How we thrilled when the hero ran away down the 1 in 5 incline, and held our breath as he neared the inevitable precipice at the duly accredited express speed.[92]

Representing the pinnacle of locomotive technology at this time, the bicycle was well placed to fulfil the colourful role in fiction that car chases or air battles play for contemporary cinema audiences. Griffin identifies an 'adventure phase' in cycling literature during the era of the high-wheeler, when the activity was still an elite and risky pastime and cyclists were largely daring, athletic, well-off young men. The cyclist became the modern-day knight, as Mecredy noted in 1893. 'The hero is depicted on a bicycle,' Mecredy observes, 'instead of a horse, and flourishing a wrench instead of a pistol.'[93]

A corresponding example of this trend is provided in an 1889 novel by Mark Twain (1835–1910), entitled *A Connecticut Yankee in King Arthur's Court*, in which Lancelot comes to the rescue of King Arthur and the novel's hero Hank with 'five hundred mailed and belted knights on bicycles!'[94] As late as 1910, H. G. Wells's cycling hero Mr Polly feels 'like one of those old knights [. . .] who rode about the country looking for dragons and beautiful maidens and chivalresque adventures' when exploring the countryside on his bicycle.[95] Herbert Sussman appraises the bicycle in

Wells's *The Wheels of Chance* as an example of how 'opportunities for courageous action and exotic adventure were not only still possible but actually increased by mechanization'.⁹⁶ Wells recognised this fact not only in his 1896 cycling romance, but also in an 1897 story entitled 'A Perfect Gentleman on Wheels', in which the narrator remarks:

> the bicycle in its earlier phases has a peculiar influence upon the imagination. To ride out from the familiar locality, into strange roads stretching away into the unknown, to be free to stop or go on, irrespective of hour or companion, inevitably brings the adventurous side uppermost.⁹⁷

The capacity of the bicycle to confront its user with unknown people and places, along with the sense of autonomy it provided, helped establish this enduring association between cycling and adventure or detective fiction.

The openness of the bicycle meant that it could not be easily associated with the hidden criminality of the railway compartment.⁹⁸ The forms of deviancy associated with cycling – racers who endangered pedestrians, New Women who challenged societal conventions – were more often socially unacceptable rather than criminal. Yet the bicycle could also offer a means to achieve a measure of anonymity that offered criminals the possibility of escape. In Grant Allen's *Hilda Wade* (1899), a novel that combines elements of New Woman and detective fiction, Mr Le Geyt escapes London on a bicycle after he has murdered his wife. The perspicacious detective Hilda Wade carefully deduces the murderer's plan of action:

> he would buy a new bicycle – a different make from his own, at the nearest shop; would rig himself out, at some ready-made tailor's, with a fresh tourist suit – probably an ostentatiously tweedy bicycling suit; and, with that in his luggage-carrier, would make straight on his machine for the country.⁹⁹

While the railway provides too obvious a means of escape, with many witnesses and set routes that allow pursuers to narrow down the criminal's options, the bicycle allows the wealthy Le Geyt to become a class-ambiguous traveller, and to leave London on one of the many routes that lead to the country. Hilda nonetheless manages to track the culprit down to his native Devon, where she and the narrator Hubert follow him by train and bicycle. When he sees him, even Hubert fails to recognise his good friend Le Geyt, who had the 'loose-knit air of a shop assistant' riding towards the sea on his bicycle.[100] The adaptability and anonymity conferred by the bicycle could thus allow fictional criminals a means of slipping through the net of the justice system.

The bicycle was rarely portrayed as a tool for criminals, however, with writers more often depicting it as a new tool for the detective. In Mc Donnell Bodkin's *Dora Myrl: The Lady Detective* (1900), Dora tracks down a thief who first fled by means of the railway and corners him thanks to a bicycle chase. Although the criminal is also a cyclist, his initial choice of the train and the superiority of Dora's machine single out the bicycle as a propitious tool for the detective. Dora makes a triumphant entry into the local town to hand the thief over to the police:

> There was a wild sensation in Eddiscombe when, in broad noon, the bank thief was brought in riding on a one-pedalled machine to the police barrack and handed into custody. Dora rode on through the cheering crowd to the hotel.[101]

Furthermore, Brian Griffin points out how the short stories in *The Irish Cyclist* often involved 'cyclists discovering organised illegal activity in the countryside'.[102] This reflected the contemporary context, since as Griffin notes elsewhere, Irish policemen were some of the earliest and most enthusiastic converts to the wheel.[103] In fiction and society at large, the bicycle quickly became a privileged crime-solving device.

In the 1897 collection *The Humours of Cycling*, the short story 'My Match with Eileen. A Cycling Adventure in Ireland' by Lawrence Ogden Robbins also deals with the association between cyclists and crime-solving in an Irish context. This story gives us an insight into the specific ways in which the bicycle could become an invaluable tool for the detective. The English protagonist goes on a cycling tour in the north of Ireland, where he is invited to stay in a farmer's home in Antrim. He arrives at the house shortly after a band of thieves have made off with most of his host's possessions – as well as his complicit niece – in a horse-drawn carriage. The hero cycles after them, managing to follow the tracks of the horse called Eileen, paying close attention to various 'clues' that bring him closer to the criminals:

> I tried all three ways for a short distance; not a clue [. . .] I had actually mounted my wheel, and was turning the pedals slowly, still irresolute, when the clue came. There came a brief sound, of the quality of great

remoteness; thud, thud, thus, five or six times, and a faint rumble – so faint, I could have questioned having heard it. Yet I knew it was the sound of a horse and wagon passing rapidly over a loose, wooden bridge: and never have I felt such a thrill of adventure as at that moment.[104]

In tracking down the criminals, the hero makes careful use of his senses, while his bicycle seems to become more attuned to the surroundings and to gain animation; the hero describes how 'I could have framed a eulogy for the bicycle that seemed to take its way under my faulty guidance with a sort of animate intelligence.'[105] The cyclist is mistaken for a 'detective officer' by the keeper of the inn where the thieves stop, recalling a scene in *The Wheels of Chance*, in which Bechamel takes Hoopdriver for a detective, sent to rescue Jessie from his clutches. The cycling draper takes up the bait, acting as 'a detective, a Sherlock Holmes in fact', in order to concoct his plan of helping Jessie flee.[106] This leads to a state of mental and sensory stimulation that mirrors the description provided by Ogden Robbins. The hero of 'My Match with Eileen' reflects, after the event, that he had enjoyed the chase because it had 'all the delight of adventure; the suspense and stealth and that tingling sense that our best daring and wit may be at instant demand'.[107] The excitement of the chase recalls the physical experience of riding a bicycle, when the rider's reflexes and senses are constantly alert. Just as, in Raymond Williams's terms, 'Conan Doyle [. . .] created in Sherlock Holmes a version of pure intelligence penetrating the obscurity which baffled ordinary men',[108] late Victorian cyclists appear as super-sensory beings, capable of interpreting the world with heightened perception and uncovering mysteries as a result.

Alertness and attention to detail are central to the work of a detective, and nowhere is this more explicit than in the Sherlock Holmes stories by Arthur Conan Doyle (1859–1930). Two stories in *The Return of Sherlock Holmes* (1905) integrate bicycles into the narrative as key elements in the solving of the central crime. In 'The Priory School', Holmes's sharp eye, familiar with 'forty-two different impressions left by tyres', is able to distinguish the different tracks of two bicycles across a marsh, one belonging to a young abductee and the other to a teacher from the school who followed the kidnappers in an attempt to save the boy.[109] Indeed, the detective is even able to surmise in what direction the riders were travelling and at what speed from how far the wheels sank into the mud. While clues may be misleading – in this story, for example, the culprits' horses are shod with shoes that mimic cow's hooves – paying close attention to them is key to solving the crime. In another story, 'The Solitary Cyclist', Holmes notices instantly that the governess Violet Smith is a keen cyclist because of 'the slight roughening of the side of the sole caused by the friction of the edge of the pedal'.[110] The detective's attention to detail mirrors the perspective of the perceptive young cyclist, who pays a visit to Holmes after growing wary of a male cyclist following her at a distance each time she rides to the railway station. As in 'The Priory School', it turns out that the cyclist in this story is not the criminal, but rather someone seeking to protect a potential victim, since Violet is being targeted by a pair of men planning to abduct her in a horse and trap. In both stories, the perpetrators' chosen mode of locomotion is a horse. As a modern, adaptable instrument, the bicycle appears much more likely to be associated with detective work than with the activities of criminals in fiction of this time. It is portrayed as the successor to the horse and the train, a vehicle that responds to and enhances the insight and attentiveness of its user.

The bicycle was an ostensible symbol of modernity, and it therefore comes as little surprise that detective and adventure novels should have included it in their heroes' array of gadgets. Tom Gunning takes up Walter Benjamin's insight by arguing that 'the narrative form of the detective story, rather than [serving] simply as an exercise in puzzle-solving, depends explicitly upon the modern experience of circulation'.[111] Gunning describes the opposing positions of 'the criminal, who preys on the very complexity of the system of circulation; and the detective, whose intelligence, knowledge, and perspicacity allow him to discover the dark corners of the circulatory system, uncover crime, and restore order'.[112] Central to the system of circulation, means of transport were frequently portrayed in detective stories. Authors readily associated the bicycle with fictional detectives, who are able to gain access to hidden recesses of knowledge due to their versatile, modern means of transport. Just as James Bond films showcase the latest – real or imagined – technological developments, late Victorian detective writers closely associated recent technologies with their protagonists. Indeed, the detective heroine Dora Myrl, who rides into the novel on a bicycle, recounts that 'within the last year I have been a telegraph girl, a telephone girl, a lady journalist'.[113] She has mastered a wide range of new technologies – telegraph, telephones, typing machines and bicycles – and shaped her life, image and identity around them. In turn, these authors shape their stories around a new technology that radically transformed the way in which we apprehend and move through the world.

The Humours of Cycling

> The attitudes, gestures and movements of the human body are laughable insofar as the body brings to mind a simple mechanism.
>
> Henri Bergson[114]

As well as interacting with detective and adventure fiction, the bicycle became a novel means of weaving humour into texts at the turn of the twentieth century. From their earliest days, writers have found in bicycles a rich source of comic inspiration. As we shall see, this humour relied on a blurring of the established lines between human and mechanical, animate and inanimate, themes which mirrored crucial turn-of-the-century preoccupations. Critically examining humour may seem an impossible task; it escapes any definition we try to pin on it, and often a joke obstinately loses its power once it has been pulled apart for analysis. In his classic treatise *Laughter* (*Le rire*) (1900), Henri Bergson recognised this fact from the outset, but nonetheless insisted on the importance of coming to an understanding of *le comique*, since it can provide important insights into 'the social, collective and popular imagination'.[115] Following Bergson's reasoning, I analyse how and why two-wheeled transportation had the capacity to provoke mirth and provide fresh possibilities for amusement, play and creativity in texts written in the early days of the technology. This will lead us to a closer understanding of the role it came to play in the popular imagination and to appreciate the lasting legacy of the humour associated with cycling.

Bergson's essay provides a compelling critical framework for an examination of humour in cycling texts. It appeared in 1900, during the bicycle craze in France and the UK, and at a time when ideas around humour were evolving as a result of contact with British models. It is not French *humour* – understood as a form of satire – which interests Bergson here, but rather self-deprecating British humour. Judith Stora-Sandor, editor of the review *Humoresques*, makes the following distinction: 'French humour is mockery. Jewish or English humour is self-deprecation.'[116] This eccentric, self-conscious laughter has been called 'l'humour 1900' in France, and is tied to the turn of the century and to French ideas of Britishness, inherited from authors such as Lewis Carroll and Edward Lear. Bergson's text thus enacts the contemporary cultural dialogue between British and French concepts of humour, interestingly mirroring the to-ing and fro-ing of ideas around the technology and the social significance of the bicycle at this time.

This typically British humour is in evidence in *Three Men on the Bummel* (1900) Jerome K. Jerome's sequel to the bestselling comic classic *Three Men in a Boat* (1889). This novel sees the three friends from the earlier work (now older, though not much wiser) heading off on a cycling tour in Germany. As Murray Roston notes, the long-lasting humour of *Three Men in a Boat* relies on Jerome's first-person narration, by means of which 'he created a pseudo-self, a projection of himself seemingly unaware of the foibles, misapprehensions and illusions for which the story lampoons him'.[117] A similar narrative technique is adopted in the sequel, providing a clear example of the kind of self-reflexive British humour that Bergson was describing. Throughout *Three Men on the Bummel*, cycling affords rich opportunities for self-mockery, since the characters come to realise that 'human performance lags ever behind human intention'.[118] As Roston observes, the narrator is 'to be laughed at whenever the gap between his illusions and the reality of his situation is perceived'.[119] Due to fatigue, clumsiness or inattention, the cycling protagonists repeatedly fail to realise their grand aims of rising early and cycling great distances, and instead suffer various minor setbacks and disasters. Indeed, after a drawn-out departure and a leisurely tour by rail around Germany, they only begin their eponymous cycling 'Bummel' in the Black Forest two-thirds of the way through the novel.

Bergson focuses on analysing comic situations at close range, pulling apart funny situations to uncover and reflect on why they make us laugh. He summarises the essential conditions which may provoke laughter in the following terms: 'it seems that humour arises when people in a group direct their attention to one of its members, silencing their sensitivity and calling only upon their intelligence'.[120] This description brings to mind the new sight of cyclists who were navigating the streets at the time Bergson was writing. By adopting this individual means of transport, early cyclists singled themselves out from the group and became a fascinating object for the collective gaze. Going against the grain of the collective paradigm of transport, early cyclists were certainly a spectacle, drawing the attention, fascination or ridicule of those they encountered. Indeed, they continue to be a visible minority on the streets today, where they are also frequently the target of other road users' jokes or derision.

Bergson's first example of a humorous situation is a description of a man in the street who trips and falls, which is easily transposable to the very visible falls and collisions of cyclists.[121] Falling was part and parcel of riding a bicycle, especially in the early period of its adoption. The nature of the high-wheeler or Ordinary bicycle meant

Figure 1.1 R.T.M., 'How to Mount a Bicycle: A Drama in Four Acts', *The Jarvey*, 12 January 1889 (Dublin: Mecredy and Kyle). By permission of National Library of Ireland.

that the rider was placed directly above the front wheel some two metres above ground. While this provided an agreeable lofty sensation, reduced vibration and increased efficiency thanks to the large wheel diameter, falls were frequent and dangerous. Bergson reasons that falls are funny because of a lack of reactivity and adaptability:

> Due to a lack of flexibility, distraction or stubbornness, or through stiffness or acquired speed, the muscles continued to make the same movement when the circumstances required something else. This is why the man fell, this is what makes the passers-by laugh.[122]

He goes on to insist on the mechanical aspect to this stiffness, arguing that laughter is provoked by 'a certain mechanical stiffness where you would expect to find attentive suppleness and the lively flexibility of a human being'.[123] Pedalling cyclists conform very closely to this description. Their movements are not completely free, but rather mechanised by the limits the machine imposes on them; notably, the need to balance, to keep the machine in motion and to continuously turn the pedals. As Bergson notes, what is humorous is the idea that an automatism would keep the cyclist on a forward course, while rationally there is call to stop or steer to avoid the obstacle.

Automatism in human movement is a theme that was often employed to comic effect in turn-of-the-century cycling narratives. The mechanical limits imposed upon the body and its instincts were keenly felt by early cyclists, as Wells reminds us in *The Wheels of Chance*. A novice to cycling, the hero Hoopdriver 'doubted his steering so much that, for the present, he had resolved to dismount at the approach of anything else upon wheels'.[124] When he encounters a cart, he attempts to stop and instead falls off his bicycle, unable to recall quickly enough how to dismount. The author J. W. Allen relates a similar situation in his fictionalised account of cycle touring, *Wheel Magic* (1909):

> I remember once beholding an elderly lady riding slowly and carefully, straight at me. I was well on my proper side of the road. I rang my bell, and she looked at me and came on, as it were fascinated. If I turned out of her way, it seemed likely that she would turn also. I dismounted and stood facing her ten yards away. And still she came on, very slowly and resolutely, still she struck my front wheel and sprawled in the roadway.[125]

In the above examples, it is the mechanisation of the cyclists' actions, their rigidity and lack of adaptability to the current situation, that results in comic effect. Several short stories from the collection *The Humours of Cycling* involve similar scenes, where the rider does not react in the way the reader would have expected, but rather in the way the machine obliges him to, inevitably resulting in a collision.[126]

While mechanising human movements and instincts, the bicycle could provoke humour by requiring its rider to adopt an animal-like posture. The bodily posture of cyclists was held up for ridicule by some of the detractors of the technology, notably in connection with the notorious, eccentric, fast-paced cyclists who were respectively termed 'scorchers' and *vélocipédards* in the UK and France. R. J. Muir's mock-Platonic dialogue *Plato's Dream of Wheels* (1902) describes these pariahs of the cycling world in the following terms:

> Tamias – Indeed, I have seen young men [. . .] strangely curved as to the back, and I have felt impelled to cry onto them in the words of Persius – 'Oh, crooked souls, forever bent to the earth' but they ever flashed past without stopping to listen.
> Eremus – That is true, for they are even as squirrels, *skiouroi*, in their rapid motion and in the clutch of their fore-paws, whence, I fancy, they have derived their names of *skiourchers* or scorchers.[127]

Here Muir paints cyclists as a hybrid of human and animal elements which – again according to Bergson – is as likely to produce mirth as the combination of mechanical and human characteristics. The hunchback position described by Muir is one Bergson refers to as particularly humorous due to its capacity to mimic a facial expression or 'make the body grimace'.[128] The unusual bodily position that the bicycle obliged its rider to adopt was another source of comic inspiration for authors who integrated the technology into their texts.

The bicycle also provides a context for a humorous disruption of the temporal sphere. Bergson describes the situation:

> Let us imagine a certain naive inflexibility of the senses and intelligence, which results in us continuing to see what is no longer there, to hear sounds that have stopped, to say things that are no longer appropriate, to adapt to a past, imagined situation when we should be responding to present reality.[129]

This description could apply to the falling cyclists described above, who seem unable to change their minds about their course of action, in spite of changed circumstances. The sensation of being out of sync with the world is evoked by Allen who, as he falls, wishes for 'a half-minute back from remorseless Time – nay, ten seconds – that is all that one requires [. . .] And the Past is suddenly merged in the acutest of Presents. The misused machine lies prone.'[130] In the description of Hoopdriver's fall in front of a heathkeeper, at least three different temporal spheres are evoked:

He gripped the handles and released the brake, standing on the left pedal and waving his right foot in the air. Then – these things take so long in the telling – he found the machine was falling over to the right. While he was deciding upon a plan of action, gravitation appears to have been busy. He was still irresolute when he found the machine on the ground, himself kneeling upon it, and a vague feeling in his mind that again Providence had dealt harshly with his shin.[131]

Here, narrative time ('these things take so long in the telling') is longer than subjective time ('he was deciding on a plan of action') while objective, scientific time ('gravitation') is the quickest of all, acting to place the cyclist on the ground before he or the reader expect it. We could also infer a fourth, 'providential' time, corresponding perhaps to John Urry and Phil Macnaghten's 'glacial' or 'evolutionary' time, which is 'immensely long and imperceptibly changing'.[132] At a time when thinkers such as Einstein and Bergson were revolutionising contemporary attitudes towards time, novelists such as Wells experimented with the separation and superimposition of discrete temporal spheres for comic effect.[133]

The humour around cycling also relied heavily on the close mingling of human and mechanical elements. In her study of comedy, *The Odd One In* (2008), Alenka Zupančič engages with Bergson's theory of the comic, reasoning that, in Bergson's terms, comedy arises because there is 'something mechanical encrusted on the living'.[134] Yet rather than suggesting that this is a one-way process, Zupančič argues that in comic situations there is a mutual exchange of agency between humans and objects; while the human takes on the inertia of the material world, objects gain animation in turn. In her example of a baron slipping in a puddle, not only does the baron become 'mechanical', but the puddle manifests 'elasticity' and 'changeability'. What we laugh at is humans' sense of self-importance, their desire to control the material world, and their blindness to the agency of objects. Zupančič asks: 'is not the comic precisely the reversal in which we come upon something rigid at the very core of life, and upon something vivid at the very core of inelasticity?'[135]

The intimacy of cyclists' connection to their machines provides a compelling opportunity for a blurring of the living and the non-living, a theme that was used to comic effect from the earliest days of cycling literature.[136] Jerome's cycling novel mobilises the humorous motif of self-deprecation, as we have seen, but it also relies heavily on the comic agency of non-human actors. While in *Three Men in a Boat*, the intelligent dog Montmorency or a stubborn tin of pineapples provide examples of the agency of non-human elements, in the sequel the bicycle allows for a rich comic exploration of the vibrancy of objects. This is well illustrated by a passage in which the exasperated narrator watches an incompetent friend attempt to 'overhaul' his bicycle, which puts up stiff resistance:

> The bicycle, I was glad to see, showed spirit; and the subsequent proceedings degenerated into little else than a rough-and-tumble fight between him and the machine. One moment the bicycle would be on the gravel path, and he on top of it; the next, the position would be reversed – he on the gravel path, the bicycle on him. Now he would be standing flushed with victory, the bicycle firmly fixed between his legs. But his triumph would be short-lived. By a sudden, quick movement it would free itself, and, turning upon him, hit him sharply over the head with one of its handles.[137]

This struggle between man and machine is richly comic since it refuses the conventional distinction between inert objects and active humans. While the man attempts to dismember it, the bicycle fights back, attempting to injure the man in turn. What is funny here is the man's undue sense of self-importance and expertise; the reader observes the struggle alongside the increasingly frustrated narrator, knowing that the man's efforts are in vain. The bicycle mocks the man's stubborn belief in his own agency and his inability to notice that of the non-human elements around him.[138]

Drawing on the lively agency of the objects a cyclist encounters and the uncanny temporal space the technology opens up, Wells makes active use of the comic potential of the bicycle in *The History of Mr Polly* (1910). The bicycle figures in a humorous episode that recalls Jerome's comic technique of depicting a gap between the first-person narrator's illusions and reality. Chatting with his young female cousins, 'Mr Polly struck a vein of humour in telling them how he learnt to ride the bicycle. He found the mere repetition of the word "wabble" sufficient to produce almost inextinguishable mirth.'[139] A disjointed account of running into a pedestrian follows, giving a vivid impression of the jumbled, atemporal impressions received by the cyclist:

> Hears the bell! Wabble. Gust of wind. Off comes the hat smack into the wheel. Wabble. *Lord!* what's going to happen? Hat across the road, old gentleman after it, bell, shriek. He ran into me. Didn't ring his bell, hadn't *got* a bell – just ran into me. Over I went clinging to his venerable head. Down he went with me clinging to him. Oil can blump, blump into the road.[140]

Polly's snappy sentences, which often leave out pronouns and verbs, his exclamations, interrogations, and mixing of present and past tenses provide a colourful retelling of the collision. The humour of this scene relies on the elements we discussed above: the mechanisation of the cyclist's movements, the disruption of the temporal sphere and the agency of inanimate objects. Following the accident, Polly immediately attributes agency and blame to the man's hat – 'I told him he oughtn't to come out wearing such a dangerous hat – flying at things. Said if he couldn't control his hat he ought to leave it at home.'[141] Polly is convinced that this object wilfully caused the accident, something that he claims occurs frequently to cyclists: 'that's the sort of thing that's constantly happening you know – on a bicycle', he observes. 'People run into you, hens and cats and dogs and things. Everything seems to have its mark on you; everything.'[142] Yet what is humorous above all here is Polly's blindness to his own responsibility (and that of his bicycle) in causing the accident. When his cousin sarcastically comments '*You* never run into anything', Polly 'very solemnly' replies, 'Never. Swelpme.'[143] His cousins are laughing at, rather than with, Polly, yet his bicycle allows him to create vital human connections. It provides the means by which he is able to travel to visit his young relatives, while also giving him something to amuse them with once there: 'Mr Polly had never been such a social success before. They hung upon his every word – and laughed.'[144] His popularity with his cousins will lead to his engagement to one of them, reminding us of the importance of humour as a basic building block of social interaction. The bicycle, although usually an individual mode of transport, is nonetheless an inherently sociable instrument that provides rich opportunities for creating connections between people. Wells mobilises the bicycle as a vector of social interaction, a question explored at length in Chapter 2.

While humour is a fundamental building block of humanity, it should not be forgotten that laughter can quickly turn into derision or ridicule. Bergson makes the pertinent remark that laughter is society's 'punishment' for those who fail to conform to what is considered normal or acceptable.[145] In light of this, the laughter that society directed at bicycles may be viewed as a form of social policing, a punishment for non-conformity or eccentricity. Writers who used humour in their sketches of cycling were, in part, reflecting this social reality. Nicholas Oddy examines Victorian cycling-related paraphernalia and comes to the conclusion that 'the machine got off to a derision-laden beginning that characterised its subsequent public perception'.[146] Russell Mills cites an example from a General Motors exhibition in which comic relief was provided in the form of a man crashing his bicycle into a pig pen, and claims that 'bicycles are not ordinarily taken seriously in twentieth-century industrial culture. Jet planes, locomotives, nuclear reactors, and other machines are taken seriously – but not bicycles.'[147] Both Oddy and Mills suggest that the derision connected to bicycles functioned to effectively rule them out as a serious transport technology.

While humour plays a role in many of the works I have been discussing, many authors in fact show evidence of taking the bicycle seriously, as a machine that alters human capacities and our interaction with our environment. It is interesting to note that in Jules Romains's comic novel *Les Copains* (*The Pals*) (1913), one of the only scenes in which a serious, metaphysical and lyrical tone is adopted is that in which the friends set off on a cycle tour. Bénin sincerely declares, 'I love these machines. They do not carry us stupidly. They extend our limbs and let our energy reach its full potential. How silently they go! This loyal silence! This silence that respects everything.'[148] This solemn passage stands in stark contrast to the irreverent, comic tone of the rest of the novel, reminding us that bicycles can provoke not only laughter, but also respect, wonder, gratitude and admiration.

A sense of humour is part of being human, and the fact that bicycles have been so often used to comic effect in literature is, first and foremost, proof of the preponderant place they rapidly came to occupy in human affairs, and of the new opportunities they opened up for play and enjoyment. Their comic potential stems from their ability to combine elements of mechanical and organic, human and animal, past, present and future in one artefact. The bicycle provided writers with a rich new terrain on which to experiment with humour. Yet bicycles have long been subversive and counter-cultural objects, and society's laughter in their early days should not be considered entirely benign in light of this.

Cycling and Publishing

> The highways and byways of literature are given up, so to speak, to the literary bicyclist. He travels in a costume peculiar to himself, and he considers the landscape all his own.
>
> Lord Justice Bowen[149]

As Richard Altick reminds us in his social history of the British reading public, 'few major tendencies in nineteenth-century English life were without their effect. Some stimulated the taste for reading; some inhibited it; some, paradoxically, did both.'[150] While cycling might justifiably be considered a 'major tendency' in this period, it is a difficult task to try to locate the ways in which an individual and active mode of locomotion might have interacted with reading and publishing practices. The impracticality of cycling and reading simultaneously means that the cyclist is rarely associated with reading, in contrast to the idle railway, bus or tram passenger. Some skilful riders of the Ordinary bicycle may have had free use of their hands thanks to being able to steer by leaning one way or the other, as one cyclist recalled in 1892:

> It is both useful and enjoyable to have one's hands free. It allows you to read your guidebook, look at your map, take notes, use your handkerchief, smoke, drink, eat, even take off or put on an item of clothing, all without slowing down. It would be impossible to do this with such ease and safety on any other type of machine.[151]

While hands-free riding might have been a possibility for some riders in the Ordinary era, the steering mechanism and greater speed of the safety bicycle – along with the increased presence of obstacles and other road users – generally meant that cyclists were obliged to keep their eyes on the road ahead and their hands on the handlebars. Cycling, then, is unlike many other modes of transport in that the activity itself seems to be incompatible with reading. It is perhaps for this reason that the bicycle was one of the modern forms of diversion held responsible for contributing to declining reader numbers at the turn of the century. Indeed, cycling and other outdoor activities were seen by some contemporaries as the antithesis of reading, for good or ill. Altick portrays them as a potential threat to the growing popular reading culture:

> The new fashion for participant sports – cycling, rowing, tennis, walking, croquet – offered powerful competition to the reading habit. Thus the spread of leisure both favoured and discouraged the development of the reading public. There was more time to read, but eventually there were also many more things to do with one's spare time.[152]

Given what some saw as the dubious value of contemporary literary output, active pursuits such as cycling were often promoted as a more beneficial use of working people's spare time. Such an opinion is expressed in *New Grub Street* (1891) by George Gissing (1857–1903) – a novel that recounts an author's struggle to write a three-decker novel – when the upper-class invalid John Yule asks:

> Who is it that reads most of the stuff that's poured out daily by the ton from the printing press? Just the men and women who ought to spend their leisure hours in open-air exercise; the people who earn their bread by sedentary pursuits, and who need to *live* as soon as they are free from the desk or the counter, not to moon over small print.[153]

Such arguments effectively placed outdoor pursuits in competition with reading. Yet contemporary accounts suggest that the two practices did in fact influence and interact with each other in subtle ways.

Links between the bicycle and the written word were very quickly established, with cyclists being portrayed as both readers and writers. In the preface to an 1897 collection of cycling songs and poems, *Lyra Cyclus; or the Bards and the Bicycle* (Figure 1.2), Edmond Redmond proclaimed that 'A new school of poesy has arisen to celebrate the tribulations and triumphs of the Bicycling world.'[154] Responding to a novel technology, the songs designed to be sung to the tune of 'well-known and popular airs' drew on a disappearing folk tradition.[155] Club rides, bicycle unions, the cycling press and literature all helped to found a community of the wheel, recalling Anderson's 'imagined community' of the novel and the nation.[156] Bicycle riders identified with each other not only by means of their conspicuous shared activity of cycling, which in Jon Day's words '[taught] people the contours of their own country',[157] but also through the texts that circulated among them. The bicycle boom witnessed a growing taste for reading about cycling, as evidenced by the multiplication of cycling newspapers, magazines and collections of poetry, stories and song. As early as 1880, the *Bicycling and Athletic Journal* was inspired to hold a writing competition among its readers, offering a 'prize machine' to the best short story writer.[158] Twelve stories were subsequently published in a small bound volume, 'dedicated to all lovers of the wheel and those who are interested in bicycling'.[159] These examples foreground the common ground shared by reading and cycling. Both activities fulfilled what Altick has identified as the main function of reading in industrial Britain; that is, to palliate the 'crisis in popular culture' caused by the loss of folk traditions generated by mass migration to cities, while providing a means of 'escape and relaxation' for overworked industrial subjects.[160]

Figure 1.2 Anonymous, cover of Edmond Redmond, *Lyra Cyclus: Or, The Bards and the Bicycle* (Rochester, NY: Bacon, 1897). Public domain.

F. W. Bockett established a natural association between the new mobility offered by the bicycle and the activity of reading, claiming that 'all gentle cyclists ride with a book in their pockets'.[161] Bockett follows in the tradition of Romantic authors by associating an active mode of locomotion with reading and writing. Not only did walking invite introspection and inspiration, it offered an actual opportunity to read; Thomas de Quincey and William Hazlitt both enjoyed reading during their long walks.[162] The physical book is often present in Bockett's descriptions, whether it be a 'little sixpenny edition' of Izaak Walton's *Compleat Angler* (1653), or a book of Abraham Cowley's essays, sent to him by a librarian friend 'because he thought it would go easily into the pocket of my cycling jacket'.[163] Bockett saw cycling as the fair-weather equivalent of reading, and vice versa. On wet days, he advises cyclists to take a rest day and read in a public library (which, he gladly states, are becoming more and more numerous).[164] During his rides he rejoices in coming across second-hand book shops and in finding 'a hostelry for pilgrims on wheels with bookshelves [. . .] What a haven for a rainy afternoon, what an alleviation for a cracked centre bracket!'[165] On fine days, he reads mid-ride in spots connected to his favourite authors.[166] The cyclist's goal, claims Bockett, should be 'building up a healthy mind in a healthy body';[167] the two activities therefore complement each other, and reading is as central to his 'gentle' approach to life as cycling.

The location of books and the manner in which they were consumed were intimately tied to changes in people's everyday mobility. The railway had already participated in 'the placing of books in the main-traveled roads of Victorian daily life',[168] to borrow Altick's phrase. Beaumont and Freeman observe that thanks to the railways, reading 'became less ritualized, and more ordinary [. . .] It was woven into the everyday rhythms of modernity';[169] while Aileen Fyfe contends that 'the railway carriage transformed reading into a public activity' and 'brought the bookshop into the street'.[170] These tendencies were continued and expanded in the era of the bicycle. Roads and coaching inns, neglected since the coming of the railways, were revived by the legions of cyclists who took to them for the daily commute or for weekend rides. Cyclists did not necessarily have to carry a book with them, as they were likely to find one on arrival. In J. W. Allen's *Wheel Magic*, the narrator encounters another cyclist who is absorbed in a book he has come across in an inn, while Miriam in Dorothy Richardson's *The Tunnel* (1919) ends her first day's cycling with a copy of *Robert Elsmere* that she discovers at the hotel at which she is staying.[171] Books were dotted around the thoroughfares of daily life, to be picked up, flicked through and borrowed at will. In this sense, cyclists took one step towards a modern, virtual relationship with text that Sara Thornton characterises as 'a paperless world in which stories and illustrations, text and image, float and travel, materialize in one place and then evaporate'.[172] A decentralised model emerged, in which people's individual mobility and the reduced price and size of books allowed them to carry volumes with them, or go easily to a place where they could be found.

This more mobile paradigm of reading was accompanied by a move towards shorter formats. At the beginning of *The Wheels of Chance*, Wells's narrator makes the claim that Hoopdriver's 'entire life, you must understand, was not a continuous romance, but a series of short stories linked only by the general resemblance of their hero'.[173] This metaphor of the protagonist's life perhaps makes a nod to the serialised form in which the text first appeared, in the journal *Today*. Leblanc's *Here are Wings*, likewise, was first published serially in *Gil Blas* in 1897. Selling weekly instalments to newspapers allowed struggling authors to make a living, while gauging the public's interest in the story. Even authors whose reputation was already established, such as Zola and Dickens, published novels in serial form before they became available as bound volumes. While such practices had been common throughout the century, the taste for short, snappy formats grew during the 'short story age' (as *The Irish Cyclist* editor R. J. Mecredy termed it)[174] at the turn of the century.

A move towards brevity can also be noted in the cycling press. The leading periodical *The Irish Cyclist* began life in 1885 as a text-heavy broadsheet, featuring lengthy articles and relatively few images. By 1894 the format had changed considerably; advertisements and images abounded, and instead of publishing articles, the news appeared 'in brief', summarised to a few snappy sentences and placed under headings such as 'Jottings', 'Cranks' and 'General'. While brevity may have been viewed by some as a form of intellectual penury, it nonetheless contributed to making newspapers and stories accessible to those who were newly literate, in the wake of education reforms that had helped swell the reading population.[175] In Gissing's *New Grub Street*, Mr Whelpdale incarnates contemporary changes in reading habits and publishing choices when he explains his idea for a newspaper as follows:

> I would have the paper address itself to the quarter-educated; that is to say, the great new generation that is being turned out by the Board schools, the young men and women who can just read, but are incapable of sustained attention. People of this kind want something to occupy them in trains, and on 'buses and trams [. . .] what they want is the lightest and frothiest of chit-chatty information – bits of stories, bits of description, bits of scandal, bits of jokes, bits of statistics, bits of foolery.[176]

Whelpdale's newspaper, entitled *Chit-Chat*, clearly parodies the magazine *Tit-Bits*, founded by Georges Newnes in 1881. The choice to publish brief articles and excerpts from fiction was made with a clear awareness of the needs, interests and lifestyles of the magazine's newly literate working- and lower-middle-class readership. John Carey credits publications such as *Tit-Bits* with 'awakening interest in books, arousing curiosity and introducing its readers to new ideas',[177] in contrast to highbrow literary organs such as T. S. Eliot's *Criterion* and F. R. Leavis's *Scrutiny*, which were inaccessible to readers who did not possess the requisite cultural capital. Literary magazines such as *Tit-Bits*, and later *The Strand*, actively encouraged a new readership of clerks and shopkeepers, many of whom were also among the most enthusiastic converts to cycling.

In addition to these shorter formats, publishers appealed to this new readership by reprinting cheap, portable editions of classic literature. This move responded to the growing desire among a new generation of readers to gain access to a wealth of knowledge that had previously been denied them. A clear parallel can be established between the democratisation of mobility by means of the bicycle, and the growing accessibility of the written word, both of which had long been the preserve of the wealthiest in society.

Thanks to the reduced dimensions of books, cyclists could carry them on their journeys. Many publishers issued pocket-sized guidebooks and fiction at the turn of the century, accommodating the needs of space-conscious cyclists. Armstrong and Inglis presented their tiny guide *Short Spins Around London* (1903) as 'a volume of limited dimensions, intended for the pocket'; and Iliffe and Son also issued a 'Nutshell Series', whose books aimed 'to give as much information upon cycling matters as possible in so small a space'.[178] The publisher J. M. Dent primarily issued reprints of classic literature, yet he also published a small number of new titles, particularly travel literature and guides. He is an interesting example of an innovative publisher who sought to respond to evolving reading and lifestyle habits. According to the historian Frank Arthur Mumby, the publisher's first two volumes, Charles Lamb's *Essays of Elia* and his *Last Essays*, 'struck a fresh note in the trade', both in their subject matter and their portable format.[179] F. W. Bockett, whose *Literary Landmarks for Pilgrims on Wheels* was published by Dent, always carried 'a little sixpenny edition in one of the pockets of my jacket' on his rides, and counted Lamb's books among his favourites.[180] Dent's next success was the 'Temple Shakespeare' series, in forty volumes at a shilling each, which Mumby argues convinced the publisher that 'there was a demand for the revival of the pocket classic'. Dent followed up on the success of his 'Temple Shakespeare' by publishing the 'Temple Classics' series and, later, the 'Everyman's Library'.[181] Dent's pocket classics and travel literature in the last years of the century may well have appealed to cyclists, many of whom were not only newly mobile but also newly literate.

Of course, the commercial impetus behind publishing books about the fashionable new activity of cycling should not be overlooked. Ellen Gruber Garvey has shown how magazine fiction of the 1890s functioned to normalise women's cycling, seeking to create a socially acceptable image of the activity in order to sell safety bicycles to a wider market.[182] Most cycling guides from the period, as well as some works of fiction, contain visual advertisements for various brands of bicycles and accessories, the text often acting as an incitement to buy a bicycle or other commodities.[183] One glaring instance of this tendency occurs in Mary Kennard's *Guide Book for Lady Cyclists*, which includes several pages of illustrated advertisements at the beginning and the end of the text.[184] In addition to this overt marketing strategy, in the midst of a description of her first long-distance cycling tour (to visit the Nottingham Raleigh works – a bicycle brand that her guidebook unashamedly advocates), Kennard inserts a personal endorsement of Liebig Company's Beef Tea.[185]

As well as paying authors and publishers for product placement in ostensibly objective guidebooks, bicycle manufacturers often edited a newspaper or magazine themselves. The cycling industry was clearly concerned with promoting the bicycle by means of the written word. The Coventry printer William Isaac Iliffe responded to a demand for written material on bicycles by founding a publishing house in the 1880s, offering a range of guidebooks and fiction on cycling.[186] Coventry was the beating heart of the British bicycle industry, and the fact that a cycling publisher flourished alongside mushrooming manufacturers is further evidence of the close link between the medium of text and the activity of cycling.

Authors, too, were aware of the selling potential of writing bicycles into their texts, as we saw in the analysis of romantic and detective fiction earlier. As a struggling young author, H. G. Wells saw a marketing opportunity in the bicycle. In an 1895 letter to the editor Grant Richards, the fashionable activity of cycling functions as a crucial selling point for his manuscript:

> I have just completed a story of 60,000 words which will appear here serially in Jerome's *Today*. It is a purely humorous work and describes

the sensations and adventures of a draper's assistant during a ten days holiday tour upon a bicycle [. . .] the details of bicycle riding, carefully done from experience and the passing glimpses of characteristic scenery of the south of England, should, I think, appeal to a certain section of the public.[187]

Here Wells promotes his story by means of its association with a new, exciting technology, while inscribing his work within a popular genre of fictionalised travel or history writing. As Jeremy Lewis records, Jerome K. Jerome admitted that he 'did not intend to write a funny book, at first' when he started working on *Three Men in a Boat*, but was rather responding to the contemporary popularity of boating on the Thames. As Lewis notes, 'publishers did brisk business with guidebooks-cum-histories of the river, in which topographical details were interwoven with easily digested snippets of English history'.[188] Wells was undoubtedly aware of the recent popularity of cycling when he made his bid to become one of the first authors to publish a novel on the subject; Jerome would follow suit with *Three Men on the Bummel* in 1900. Such texts responded to the contemporary taste for a guidebook style in fiction while integrating a new technology that aroused widespread public curiosity. The cachet cycling had achieved encouraged writers and publishers to actively mobilise the image of the bicycle to appeal to the public.

Bicycles and books were both part of a dizzying picture of rocketing consumption and multiplying forms of visual and textual stimuli at the end of the century. Bicycle manufacturers viewed books, newspapers and journals as a marketing opportunity, while cyclists also became conspicuous consumers. Targeted by advertisers, cyclists responded to the demands of a society of mass consumption that invited them to find self-fulfilment and a sense of identity in the act of buying and the sentiment of ownership. In opposition to the nineteenth-century, collective, sedentary paradigm of reading enshrined by the bulky three-decker novel, individual mobility along with growing rates of literacy inaugurated a more mobile, modern, decentralised and potentially subversive approach to the written word. Books themselves became mobile, allowing readers to dip in and out of the narrative, or obtain 'passing glimpses' of lives and scenery, to borrow Wells's phrase from his letter to the prospective publisher of *The Wheels of Chance*. Portable, cheap, accessible and thought-provoking books found their way into pockets and saddle-bags, widening people's horizons in a complementary way to the bicycle.

Notes

1. For a modern treatment of the relationship between touring and writing, with ample consideration of the bicycle in the interwar period, see Bertho-Lavenir, *La Roue et le Stylo*.
2. Bockett, *Some Literary Landmarks*, 6.
3. Jarvis, *Romantic Writing and Pedestrian Travel*, 1.
4. Quoted in ibid., ix.
5. See, among others, Robinson, *The Walk*; Solnit, *Wanderlust*.
6. Jarvis, *Romantic Writing and Pedestrian Travel*, ix.
7. Wallace, *Walking, Literature, and English Culture*, 1.
8. Eric J. Leed, *The Mind of a Traveler: From Gilgamesh to Global Tourism* (New York: Basic Books, 1991).
9. Louis Baudry de Saunier, *Ma petite bicyclette: sa pratique* (Paris: Flammarion, 1925), 20.
10. See Hans Erhard, 'Cycling or Roller Skating: The Resistible Rise of Personal Mobility', *Cycle History* 5 (1994), 129–32. The author argues that during the mini Ice Age at the turn of the nineteenth century, the popularity of ice-skating allowed people to grow accustomed to balancing and using human energy for locomotion, conditions that arguably favoured the invention of the draisine at this time.
11. See Brian Rejack, 'Nothings of the Day: The Velocipede, the Dandy, and the Cockney', *Romanticism* 19, no. 3 (2013), 291.
12. Ibid.
13. Ibid., 294.
14. Jarvis, *Romantic Writing and Pedestrian Travel*, 14.
15. E. R. Pennell's travel accounts were published jointly with her husband. However, recent scholarship by Dave Buchanan and analysis of Elizabeth's correspondence point to the strong likelihood of her sole authorship. As such, I refer to Elizabeth alone as the author.
16. Elizabeth Robins Pennell and Joseph Pennell, *Our Sentimental Journey through France and Italy* (London: T. F. Unwin, 1893).
17. Edward Thomas, *In Pursuit of Spring* [1914] (Albany, CA: Berkeley Hill Classics, 2013), 3.
18. Pennell, *Our Sentimental Journey*, xi.
19. Ibid., v.
20. Jarvis, *Romantic Writing and Pedestrian Travel*, 22.
21. Bockett, *Some Literary Landmarks*, 7.
22. Dave Buchanan, 'Pilgrims on Wheels: The Pennells, F. W. Bockett, and Literary Cycle-Travels', in *Culture on Two Wheels: The Bicycle in Literature and Film*, ed. Jeremy Withers and Daniel P. Shea (Lincoln, NE: University of Nebraska Press, 2016), 20.
23. Bockett, *Some Literary Landmarks*, 111.
24. Ibid., 211.
25. Pennell, *Our Sentimental Journey*, xiii.

26. Ibid., xi.
27. See Dave Buchanan, 'Cycling and the Picturesque: Illustrated Cycle-Travel Writing of the 1880s', *Cycle History* 19 (2008), 67–72.
28. Ibid.
29. Pennell, *Our Sentimental Journey*, 38.
30. However, as Dave Buchanan notes, cycling could become a 'picturesque-immersion-travel-experience' for middle-class travellers. In the 1880s' cycle travel writing of Thomas Stevens, Charles Edward Reade and others, cycling is conceived as a form of 'tramping'. See Buchanan, 'Cycling and the Picturesque'. Buchanan quotes Elizabeth Pennell, who complained that some landlords 'do not understand that men and women of leisure and means can find amusement in putting on rough clothes and tramping or wheeling it up hill and dale'; Elizabeth Robins Pennell, 'From Coventry to Chester on Wheels', *The Century Magazine*, September 1884, 653.
31. Thomas, *In Pursuit of Spring*, 42.
32. Buchanan, 'Cycling and the Picturesque', 70.
33. Thomas, *In Pursuit of Spring*, 14.
34. Ibid., 60.
35. The bicycle paradoxically helped to promote urban sprawl by allowing workers to live further from polluted urban centres.
36. Thomas, *In Pursuit of Spring*, 22.
37. Bockett, *Some Literary Landmarks*, 64.
38. Wallace, *Walking, Literature, and English Culture*, 9.
39. Thomas, *In Pursuit of Spring*, 82. It is interesting to note that Anne Wallace points to the crucial role of the pedestrian narrator in Wordsworth's 'Salisbury Plain' poems. Wallace, *Walking, Literature, and English Culture*, 1.
40. An earlier version of this research was published as 'Cycling and Narrative Structure: H. G. Wells's *The Wheels of Chance* and Maurice Leblanc's *Voici des ailes*', in *Mobilities, Literature, Culture*, ed. Marian Aguiar, Charlotte Mathieson and Lynne Pearce (New York: Palgrave Macmillan, 2019), 237–57.
41. H. G. Wells, *The Wheels of Chance: A Bicycling Idyll; The Time Machine* [1896] (London: J. M. Dent, 1935), 5.
42. Ibid., 7.
43. Ibid., 8.
44. Maurice Leblanc, *Voici des ailes* [1898] (Vierzon: le Pas de côté, 2012), 14.
45. For a discussion of the degeneration debate in the context of the cycling craze, see Christopher Thompson, 'Regeneration, Dégénérescence, and the Medical Debate about Bicycling in *Fin-de-Siècle* France', in *Sport et santé dans l'histoire/Sport and Health in History*, ed. Thierry Terret (Sankt Augustin: Academia, 1999), 339–46.
46. Leblanc, *Voici des ailes*, 87.

47. Ibid., 15.
48. Ibid., 16.
49. Kennard, *A Guide Book for Lady Cyclists*, 3.
50. Ibid., 23.
51. Nye, *A bicyclette: anthologie*, xxv.
52. Leblanc, *Voici des ailes*, 17.
53. Marc Augé, *Éloge de la bicyclette* (Paris: Payot & Rivages, 2008), 55–6.
54. Ellen Gruber Garvey, *The Adman in the Parlor: Magazines and the Gendering of Consumer Culture, 1880s to 1910s* (New York: Oxford University Press, 1996), 124.
55. Tim Edensor, 'Rhythm and Arrhythmia', in *The Routledge Handbook of Mobilities* (Abingdon: Routledge, 2014), 164
56. Wells, *The Wheels of Chance*, 36.
57. Jacques Derrida, *Spectres de Marx: l'état de la dette, le travail du deuil et la nouvelle Internationale* (Paris: Galilée, 1993).
58. Meiner, *Le carrosse littéraire*.
59. Leblanc, *Voici des ailes*, 30, 50.
60. Ibid., 87.
61. Ibid., 26.
62. Wells, *The Wheels of Chance*, 95.
63. Ibid., 105.
64. Ibid., 137.
65. Ibid., 186.
66. Ibid., 181.
67. Ibid., 187.
68. Ibid., 53.
69. Ibid.
70. Sue Zemka, *Time and the Moment in Victorian Literature and Society* (Cambridge: Cambridge University Press, 2011), 65.
71. Leblanc, *Voici des ailes*, 22.
72. Ibid.
73. Ibid., 23.
74. Ibid., 26.
75. Meiner, *Le carrosse littéraire*, 221.
76. György Lukács, *The Theory of the Novel: A Historico-Philosophical Essay on the Forms of Great Epic Literature*, trans. Anna Bostock (Cambridge, MA: MIT Press, 1971), 126.
77. Wells, *The Wheels of Chance*, 21.
78. Ibid., 31.
79. E. M. Forster, *Howards End* [1910] (London: Penguin, 2000), 21.
80. Leblanc, *Voici des ailes*, 26.
81. Ibid., 5.
82. Ibid., 9.
83. Ibid., 25.

84. Ibid., 70.
85. Wells, *The Wheels of Chance*, 48–51.
86. Ibid., 102.
87. Ibid., 107–8.
88. Yoonjoung Choi, 'The Bi-Cycling Mr Hoopdriver: Counter-Sporting Victorian Reviving the Carnivalesque', *Critical Survey* 24, no. 1 (2012), 112.
89. Wells, *The Wheels of Chance*, 197.
90. Brian Griffin, 'The Romance of the Wheel: Cycling, Fiction and Late Nineteenth-Century Ireland', *Sport in History* 29, no. 2 (2009), 285.
91. Quoted in ibid., 292.
92. Quoted in ibid., 293.
93. Quoted in ibid.
94. Mark Twain, *A Connecticut Yankee in King Arthur's Court* [1889] (New York: Bantam Classics, 1983), 267.
95. H. G. Wells, *The History of Mr Polly* [1910] (London: Pan, 1963), 88. A cyclist named Mr Warspite also plays a detective role in a mysterious episode at the end of *Mr Polly*, when he discovers Polly hiding from his armed aggressor, Uncle Jim, in a ditch. Mr Warspite, the narrator informs us, 'takes that exceptionally lively interest in his fellow-creatures which constitutes so much of the distinctive and complex charm of your novelist all the world over, and he at once involved himself generously in the case' (203–4).
96. Sussman, *Victorians and the Machine*, 164.
97. H. G. Wells, 'A Perfect Gentleman on Wheels', in *The Humours of Cycling* (London: James Bowden, 1897), 8.
98. On the association between criminality and the railways, see Schivelbusch, *The Railway Journey*; Beaumont and Freeman, *The Railway and Modernity*; Adrienne E. Gavin and Andrew F. Humphries (eds), *Transport in British Fiction: Technologies of Movement, 1840–1940* (Basingstoke: Palgrave Macmillan, 2015).
99. Grant Allen, *Hilda Wade, A Woman with Tenacity of Purpose* [1900] (New York: Jefferson, 2015), 46.
100. Ibid., 48.
101. Matthias Mc Donnell Bodkin, *Dora Myrl: The Lady Detective* (London: Chatto and Windus, 1900), 56.
102. Griffin, 'The Romance of the Wheel', 285.
103. Brian Griffin, *Cycling in Victorian Ireland* (Dublin: Nonsuch Publishing, 2006), 75–84.
104. Lawrence Ogden Robbins, 'My Match with Eileen. A Cycling Adventure in Ireland', in *The Humours of Cycling* (London: James Bowden, 1897), 36.
105. Ibid., 37.
106. Wells, *The Wheels of Chance*, 72.
107. Ogden Robbins, 'My Match with Eileen', 39.

108. Raymond Williams, *The Country and the City* (Oxford: Oxford University Press, 1973), 229.
109. Arthur Conan Doyle, *The Return of Sherlock Holmes* [1905] (London: Penguin, 2011), 142.
110. Ibid., 97.
111. Tom Gunning, 'Tracing the Individual Body: Photography, Detectives, and Early Cinema', in *Cinema and the Invention of Modern Life*, ed. Leo Charney and Vanessa R. Schwartz (Berkeley, CA: University of California Press, 1995), 20. Walter Benjamin located the origin of the modern detective story in the 'obliteration of the individual's traces in the big city crowd' allowed by the modern environment. See Walter Benjamin, *Charles Baudelaire: A Lyric Poet in the Era of High Capitalism*, trans. Harry Zohn (London: NLB, 1973), 43.
112. Ibid.
113. Bodkin, *Dora Myrl*, 6.
114. Henri Bergson, *Le rire: essai sur la signification du comique* (Paris: PUF, 1981), 22–3.
115. Ibid., 2.
116. Judith Stora-Sandor and Nelly Feuerhahn, quoted in *Le Monde*, 'Le rire sans éclats', 23 March 2013.
117. Murray Roston, *The Comic Mode in English Literature from the Middle Ages to Today* (London: Continuum, 2011), 198.
118. Jerome K. Jerome, *Three Men on the Bummel* [1900] (London: Penguin, 1994), 139.
119. Roston, *The Comic Mode in English Literature*, 198.
120. Bergson, *Le rire*, 6.
121. Ibid., 7.
122. Ibid.
123. Ibid., 8.
124. Wells, *The Wheels of Chance*, 14.
125. Allen, *Wheel Magic*, 40–1.
126. See G. B. Burginthere, 'Some Emotions and – No Morals; Or, How to Learn "to Bike"', in *The Humours of Cycling* (London: James Bowden, 1897), 26; Fred Wishaw, 'Pogeley's Ride Down Town', in *The Humours of Cycling*, 22.
127. Robert James Muir, *Plato's Dream of Wheels; Socrates, Protagoras, and the Hegeleatic Stranger; with an Appendix by Certain Cyclic Poets* (London: T. F. Unwin, 1902), 7–8.
128. Bergson, *Le rire*, 18.
129. Ibid., 8.
130. Allen, *Wheel Magic*, 39–40.
131. Wells, *The Wheels of Chance*, 14.
132. Phil Macnaghten and John Urry (eds), *Contested Natures* (London: Sage, 1998), 147.

133. See, for instance, Henri Bergson, *Durée et simultanéité. À propos de la théorie d'Einstein* (Paris: Librairie Félix Alcan, 1929).
134. Alenka Zupančič, *The Odd One In: On Comedy* (Cambridge, MA: MIT Press, 2008), 111.
135. Ibid., 115.
136. A later example of the comic agency of bicycles is provided in Flann O'Brien's *The Third Policeman* (1967), in which the policeman Sergeant Pluck develops an 'Atomic Theory' about the exchange of molecules and agency between cyclists and their bicycles.
137. Jerome, *Three Men on the Bummel*, 41.
138. As in his earlier novel, Jerome frequently portrays the agency of animals as well as machines in *Three Men on the Bummel*. For instance, the narrator describes an encounter with a German horse that takes an instant dislike to them, possibly because they are foreigners and/or cyclists. The narrator describes how the horse 'turned his head, and looked me up and down with a cold, glassy eye [. . .] I have never known a horse that could twist himself as this horse did. If I had seen his eyes looking at me from between his own hind legs, I doubt if I should have been surprised' (ibid., 92).
139. Wells, *Mr Polly*, 81.
140. Ibid., author's italics.
141. Ibid.
142. Ibid.
143. Ibid. Wells thus phonetically transcribes the phrase 'So help me.' Author's italics.
144. Ibid., 82.
145. Bergson, *Le rire*, 15–16.
146. Nicholas Oddy, 'Cycling in the Drawing Room', *Cycle History* 11 (2001), 175.
147. Russell Mills, 'Thinking about Thinking about Cycles', *Cycle History* 5 (1995), 11.
148. Jules Romains, *Les Copains* (Paris: Gallimard, 1922), 88.
149. Lord Justice Bowen, in a lecture on popular education at the Working Men's Club, February 1894. Reproduced in his obituary in *The Spectator*, 14 April 1894.
150. Richard D. Altick, *The English Common Reader: A Social History of the Mass Reading Public, 1800–1900* (Chicago: University of Chicago Press, 1957), 3.
151. *La vélocipedie pour tous, par un vétéran* (Paris: Libraries-imprimeries réunies, 1892). Quoted in Thiesset and Thomasset, *Les bienfaits de la vélocipédie*, 12.
152. Altick, *The English Common Reader*, 88.
153. George Gissing, *New Grub Street* [1891] (London: Penguin, 1968), 55.
154. Edmond Redmond, *Lyra Cyclus; Or, The Bards and the Bicycle* (Rochester, NY: Bacon, 1897), preface.

155. One song from this period that has stood the test of time is Harry Dacre's 1892 'Daisy Bell', which includes the refrain 'you'd look sweet upon the seat of a bicycle built for two'.
156. Benedict R. Anderson, *Imagined Communities: Reflections on the Origin and Spread of Nationalism* (London: Verso, 1991).
157. Jon Day, *Cyclogeography: Journeys of a London Bicycle Courier* (London: Notting Hill Editions, 2015), 140.
158. T. Harris et al., *On Wheels!!! By Twelve Spokes* (London: Cricket and Football Times, Bicycling and Athletic Journal, 1880), 7.
159. Ibid., 1.
160. Altick, *The English Common Reader*, 4.
161. Bockett, *Some Literary Landmarks*, 117.
162. Robinson, *The Walk*, 44.
163. Bockett, *Some Literary Landmarks*, 266, 136.
164. Ibid., 34.
165. Ibid., 45, 224.
166. Ibid., 266.
167. Ibid., 228.
168. Altick, *The English Common Reader*, 305.
169. Beaumont and Freeman, *The Railway and Modernity*, 23.
170. Aileen Fyfe, *Steam-Powered Knowledge: William Chambers and the Business of Publishing, 1820–1860* (Chicago: University of Chicago Press, 2012), 136.
171. Allen, *Wheel Magic*, 52; Dorothy M. Richardson, *The Tunnel* [1919] (London: Virago, 2002), 236.
172. Sara Thornton, *Advertising, Subjectivity, and the Nineteenth-Century Novel: Dickens, Balzac and the Language of the Walls* (Basingstoke: Palgrave Macmillan, 2009), 172.
173. Wells, *The Wheels of Chance*, 42.
174. Griffin, 'The Romance of the Wheel', 292.
175. Government Education Acts in the 1870s provided for the establishment of 'Board Schools' which made education more affordable. Primary education between the ages of 5 and 10 became mandatory at a small fee in 1881, before becoming free of charge in 1891.
176. Gissing, *New Grub Street*, 496.
177. John Carey, *The Intellectuals and the Masses: Pride and Prejudice among the Literary Intelligentsia, 1880–1939* (New York: St Martin's Press, 1993), 109.
178. Arthur C. Armstrong and Harry Robert Gall Inglis, *Short Spins Round London* (London: Gall and Inglis, 1903), preface; Charles William Brown, *Cycling* (London: Iliffe and Son, 1895), preface.
179. Frank Arthur Mumby, *Publishing and Bookselling* (London: Cape, 1974), 279.
180. Bockett, *Some Literary Landmarks*, 266.
181. Mumby, *Publishing and Bookselling*, 280.

182. Garvey, *The Adman in the Parlor*, 106–34.
183. For example, W. J. Coppen, *Romances of the Wheel: A Collection of Romantic Cycling Tales* (Coventry: Iliffe and Son, 1880); Kennard, *The Golf Lunatic and his Cycling Wife*.
184. This was common practice in Victorian publishing, as shown by Thornton in *Advertising, Subjectivity, and the Nineteenth-Century Novel*.
185. Kennard, *A Guide Book for Lady Cyclists*, 76.
186. Titles included Henry Sturmey, *The 'Indispensable' Bicyclists' Handbook, A Complete Cyclopædia on the Subject* (Coventry: Iliffe and Son, 1880); Coppen, *Romances of the Wheel*; F. J. Erskine, *Tricycling for Ladies, Or, Hints on the Choice & Management of Tricycles: With Suggestions on Dress, Riding & Touring* (London: Iliffe and Son, 1885); A. J. Wilson, *The Pleasures, Objects, and Advantages of Cycling* (London: Iliffe and Son, 1887); George Douglas Leechman, *Safety Cycling* (London: Iliffe and Son, 1895); F. J. Erskine, *Bicycling for Ladies* (London: Iliffe and Son, 1897); Thomas W. Girling, *Cycles and the Trade* (London: Iliffe and Son, 1898).
187. H. G. Wells, *The Correspondence of H. G. Wells*, ed. David C. Smith (London: Pickering and Chatto, 1998), I, 256, letter to Grant Richards, 6 November 1895.
188. Jeremy Lewis, 'Introduction', in Jerome K. Jerome, *Three Men in a Boat* (Oxford: Oxford University Press, 2000), vii.

Chapter 2

Liberation on Two Wheels: Class, Gender and the Bicycle in Literature

> Free people must travel the road to productive social relations at the speed of a bicycle.
>
> Ivan Illich[1]

Cycling participated actively in the momentous social changes that took place at the turn of the twentieth century. By providing mobility to disadvantaged groups, the bicycle became a political symbol closely associated with the growing demands of the working class and women for equality. Yet such movements were by no means uncontested, and strenuous attempts were also made to contain the potentially subversive image of working-class or women's cycling within certain codes formulated by bourgeois, patriarchal society. This analysis of the class dimension of the bicycle focuses on three novels by H. G. Wells, an author who made extensive use of cycling as a symbol of social ascendancy or alternatively of a rejection of the British class structure. I expose how the bicycle stands for a democratisation of mobility and knowledge, and suggests an alternative to the tenets of capitalist society. The second part of this chapter engages with a debate that has received much attention in recent years: the bicycle's role in women's emancipation. Through an exploration of works of British fiction, I explore how the bicycle gave women concrete new freedoms, while exposing how society simultaneously attempted to constrain women cyclists within the reductive stereotypes of the New Woman and the lady cyclist. The final section crosses the Channel in order to examine what is perhaps the bicycle's most important contribution to debates on both class and gender. As Proust's use of the bicycle in his portrait of Albertine shows, cycling helped challenge social and gender categories by exposing their cultural and temporal contingency. Cycling was an activity that allowed individuals to begin to formulate alternative identities that eroded the distinctions established by their oppressors. The bicycle was thus a technology that pointed to an alternative, counter-hegemonic organisation of society.

Bicycles and Class

Democratising Travel

At the close of Chapter 1, I pointed to the connection between the bicycle's democratisation of mobility and a broadening of the country's intellectual life through higher rates of literacy and changing tendencies in publishing. At the end of the nineteenth century, 'clerking culture' was associated with, among other things, bicycles and lowbrow literature; objects that directly challenged the monopoly of knowledge by a social elite. As John Carey observes, at the turn of the century the term 'suburban' was 'distinctive in combining topographical with intellectual disdain',[2] enshrining an attempt by the elite to keep the masses on the periphery of both geographical and intellectual spaces. Within this context, the extensive use of the bicycle in the fiction of working- or lower-middle-class authors such as H. G. Wells, Jerome K. Jerome and Grant Allen points to its role in helping to formulate what Carey calls an 'alternative culture' to which the newly literate masses could relate.[3] As Carey points out, at the turn of the century 'a new culture of socialism, cycling, free thinking and the flouting of respectable norms was flourishing among the clerks, teachers, shop assistants, telegraphists and other white collar youth. Cycling was important in extending the clerks' experience and interests.'[4] The bicycle was one democratising force in both society and fiction that helped to challenge the boundaries drawn between social classes, allowing for a more creative exploration of both spaces and texts.

The bicycle made longer distance travel accessible to any ablebodied person, transforming mobility from an exploitative into an empowering activity. Mobility had long been the preserve of the upper strata of society, while the working class had always been complicit with and essential to this privilege; they were the grooms, the stable boys, and later, the signalmen and the train and cab drivers. This dominant paradigm of mobility, built on harnessing the time and energy of the working class for the benefit, comfort and convenience of the upper class, manifested itself in the various human-powered vehicles developed across Europe prior to the draisine. David Herlihy has explored the neglected early history of human-powered transport, documenting how throughout the eighteenth century inventors patented designs for four-wheeled passenger vehicles powered by servants, who actioned a mechanical drive with their hands or feet. In 1813, Karl Drais's first design for a vehicle – a four-wheeler accommodating two to four passengers and powered by a servant – conformed to the principle that it was inappropriate for the wealthy to provide their own locomotive energy.[5] Nonetheless, Drais's stubborn search for greater efficiency and speed led to the invention of the two-wheeled draisine in 1818, a machine that, according to Herlihy, 'transformed the very nature of the human-powered vehicle. It was no longer a mechanical "chariot" carrying multiple passengers, but rather a single "horse" that obeyed only one master.'[6] Crucially, it was the first machine that required energy input from the person being transported, rather than extracting energy from an external power source, an animal or another human being. The draisine and its various descendants throughout the nineteenth century thus made the radical statement that the idle upper class could supply their own energy for locomotion, and consequently that the working class could also use their energy to power their own movement, rather than that of somebody else.

Of course, the passenger paradigm was not overcome by this technology; the train was modelled on it, and early motor car owners employed drivers and mechanics for their machines, just as their predecessors had employed staff in their stables. Our current reliance on fossil fuels for locomotion may be viewed as a continuation of a model that relies on the exploitation of human and natural resources. Some have made the link between the end of the slave trade in the nineteenth century and the beginning of the oil era, with profit-driven exploitation of human lives and energy being replaced by a dependence on oil extracted mainly from former colonies, which had previously supplied slaves, and consumed at great cost to both humans and the planet. In contrast, the self-sufficiency of human-powered locomotion by its very nature challenged the idea that the energy of the many should be used for the profit of the few. As such, the bicycle might be considered a *de facto* levelling device that refused distinctions of class by requiring all able bipeds to pedal. This stood in sharp contrast to the railway's reinforcement of class differences through first, second and third class carriages, and the motor car, which was reserved exclusively for the rich and, like the train, ran on fossil fuels that generated human exploitation and environmental pollution. Cycling stood apart from this paradigm of travel, and this was perhaps one of the reasons why it forged links with political non-conformism at the turn of the century. As well as becoming an emblem of women's struggle for suffrage, as we shall see later in this chapter, it was quickly transformed into a tool for spreading socialism. Tom Groom made an explicit connection between the two pursuits at the founding of the socialist *Clarion* newspaper's cycling club in 1894, when he argued that 'We are not neglectful of our Socialism, as the frequent contrasts a cyclist gets between the beauties of nature and the dirty squalor of towns make him more anxious than ever to abolish the present system.'[7] As Groom's statement underlines, the geographical mobility and change of outlook permitted by cycling encouraged a more critical outlook on the organisation of society.

For middle- or upper-class cyclists, encounters with fellow road users also provided insights into other people's lives. F. W. Bockett argued that 'one good thing about ambling on a bicycle is that it brings you into contact with all sorts and conditions of men', making visible 'social contrasts' between town and city, rich and poor.[8] Bockett's choice of the verb 'ambling' reinforces the link to his walking ancestors, whose example he consciously seeks to emulate. 'Social contrasts' are arguably more visible to cyclists than to walkers, since they move more rapidly through city, suburbs and countryside, while retaining a close connection to their surroundings. Just as a link was established between non-conformism and rambling at the turn of the nineteenth century (John Thelwall's *The Peripatetic* [1793] being perhaps the best known example),[9] cycling also acquired a political dimension at the turn of the twentieth century.

Historical accounts of the class spread of the bicycle generally present a trickle-down effect, in which the technology first became available to the aristocracy, before mass production and falling prices made it affordable to the middle class and eventually the working class in the early twentieth century.[10] While this interpretation might appear plausible from our current standpoint, we should remain cautious of adopting teleological, top-down interpretations of the spread of the bicycle. I am influenced by Bijker et al.'s SCOT model of the history of technology, which encourages a networked rather than a linear outlook. Various meanings were debated and negotiated during the period of the machine's 'interpretative flexibility', which for the bicycle is defined as the years from 1879 to 1898.[11] Contemporary texts allow us to come into contact with these debates, exposing diverging interpretations of the technology and its social spread. One example of this complicated picture of the class spread of the bicycle may be found in Mary Kennard's *Guide Book for Lady Cyclists*. In clear contrast to current perspectives on bicycle history, this upper-class author affirms that hers was not the first social group to adopt the bicycle:

> Ah! Yes, for those in the so-called upper classes, who cycle with open eyes, attentive ears and receptive minds, there is much – very much – to be learnt. We have no right to be impatient, and if now and again the cyclist of many years is apt to treat us with a touch of derisive scorn – depend upon it, we deserve it. They discovered the beauties of the pastime long before we did.[12]

Kennard's advice to novice upper-class cyclists in the mid-1890s highlights the fact that the pastime was not associated exclusively with the aristocracy at this time. Although Kennard is unclear about which social group 'the cyclist of many years' belongs to, she is undoubtedly referring to a lower class than her own; perhaps to the middle class, working-class racers, or those who made a living thanks to their bicycle. The illustration in Figure 2.1, published in the same year as Kennard's *Guide Book* and Wells's *The Wheels of Chance*, also suggests that the working class (and not only racers) were among the first to make use of bicycles in the mid-1880s, with upper-class cyclists appearing in the boom years of the 1890s (when, the artist suggests, the working-class man turned to the formerly aristocratic pursuit of horse riding). The rapid development of the technology in the 1880s and 1890s meant that new, improved models appeared every few years, and outdated bicycles were sold on at greatly reduced prices, allowing lower earners access to the technology.[13] It should also be recalled that the bicycle created new forms of employment; many people found work in the flourishing bicycle trade, delivering telegraphs or goods, or as professional bicycle racers.[14] In addition, the socialist bicycle clubs set up across Britain up by the *Clarion* newspaper supplied their users with machines at a discount.[15] By various means, then, working-class people could gain an early footing on the mobility ladder. As these examples show, contemporaries did not necessarily experience the technology in a straightforward manner, and the meanings attached to it diverge according to geographical, social and political factors. Rather than providing a linear view of the class spread of the technology, an examination of literature allows us to appreciate the vehicle's specific role in transgressing and blurring class boundaries, democratising movement and knowledge along the way.

Figure 2.1 Frederick Pegram, 'A Contrast', *Punch, or the London Charivari*, 4 May 1895, 207. By permission of TopFoto.

H. G. Wells and the Bicycle

H. G. Wells was the son of a small shopkeeper and a domestic servant, and spent his early years employed as a draper's assistant. He achieved a measure of financial independence after winning a scholarship to study science and becoming a teacher, before turning to writing to earn a living. Although he suffered from poor health as a result of a football accident in his twenties, he was a keen cyclist from the 1890s. Wells found some of his earliest literary inspiration in cycling; he recorded that while living in Woking in 1895,

> I learnt to ride my bicycle upon sandy tracks with none but God to help me; he chastened me considerably in the process, and after a fall one day I wrote down a description of the state of my legs which became the opening chapter of *The Wheels of Chance*.[16]

Cycling was an interest he shared with a number of other writers and friends, including Jerome K. Jerome and Bernard Shaw; his autobiography includes a humorous account of teaching George Gissing to ride in a bid to improve his health.[17] Often drawing on autobiographical details in his fiction, Wells manifests a persistent concern with portraying and interrogating the complexities of the English class system. He mobilises various means of transportation in his fiction as metaphors for movement through the strata of English society, a strategy that he makes explicit towards the end of *Kipps: The Story of a Simple Soul* (1905), when the narrator invites the reader to

> imagine fleeing through our complex and difficult social system as it were for life, first on foot and severally to the Folkestone Central Station, then in a first class carriage [. . .] then in a four-wheeler, a long, rumbling, palpitating, slow flight through the multitudinous swarming London streets.[18]

In this instance, as we shall see, Kipps's flight marks the beginning of his downward spiral after being rocketed into the upper echelons of British society. The various means of transport evoked give a sense of the importance for Wells of locomotion in individuals' relations with class structures, and also in determining the character of societies to come.

As Wells underlined in *Anticipations* (1900), an essay predicting future developments in society, 'upon transport, upon locomotion, may also hang the most momentous issues of politics and war'.[19] While he concluded that 'the nineteenth century [. . .] will, if it needs a symbol, almost inevitably have as that symbol a steam engine running upon a railway',[20] Wells looked forward in his fiction and non-fiction to the new and emerging paradigms of transport and society that would come to define the twentieth century. Bicycles feature in Wells's vision of future methods of locomotion, commerce and warfare. Like other turn-of-the-century writers, Wells conceived of cycling as a possible antidote to urban degeneration, allowing workers access to the cleaner air of the countryside while providing a precious opportunity for exercise. Yet he recognised the obstacles encountered by cycling city-dwellers; in one passage of *Anticipations* he imagines what a historian from the future would conclude about cycling in his own time in the following terms:

> 'Just where the bicycle might have served its most useful purpose,' he will write, 'in affording a healthy daily ride to the innumerable clerks and such-like sedentary toilers of the central region, it was rendered impossible by the danger of side-slip in this vast ferocious traffic.' And, indeed, to my mind at least, this last is the crowning absurdity of the present state

of affairs, that the clerk and the shop hand, classes of people positively starved of exercise, should be obliged to spend yearly the price of a bicycle upon a season-ticket, because of the quite unendurable inconvenience and danger of urban cycling.[21]

Despite the danger of cycling on congested London streets, Wells firmly believed in the economic and health-giving benefits of the bicycle, especially for the 'sedentary toilers' to whose ranks he had once belonged. Five years later, in *A Modern Utopia* (1905), Wells predicted that 'cycle tracks will abound in Utopia'.[22] This well-known excerpt is often quoted out of context, for Wells enumerates various mechanised modes of transport before imagining these utopian cycle tracks 'following beside the great high roads, but oftener taking their own more agreeable line amidst woods and crops and pastures'.[23] Indeed, Wells had a diversified vision of locomotion in the ideal future society. In his outlook, the bicycle would play a key role as a cheap, health-giving means of transport that allowed a privileged connection to rural environments and a practical means of transport in well-planned cities.

My reading of several of Wells's social novels examines the bicycle's fascinating role in the author's vision of class relations. His use of the bicycle and other machines in his fiction conforms to Herbert Sussman's observation that 'primarily the machine appears in those Victorian writers most directly concerned with immediate social problems'.[24] The choice to group these three texts together corresponds to a strain in Wells's own thinking about his fiction. As Simon J. James points out, some thirty years after its first publication Wells described *The Wheels of Chance* as one in a 'series of close studies in personality', adding characters such as Lewisham, Kipps, Mr Polly and Ann Veronica as further examples of 'personalities thwarted by the defects of our contemporary civilisation'.[25] Wells – briefly a member of the Fabian society, and a lifelong socialist – used his fiction to directly attack Victorian class structures. As became evident in his feud with his former friend Henry James, he refused the idea that art should be autonomous from society. Rather, he believed in 'the necessity for art to engage directly in creating the utopia that he saw as the only alternative to mankind's self-destruction'.[26] Indeed, Wells's social novels share in common with his science fiction their utopian stance. In a 1905 letter to the editor of the *Fortnightly Review*, Wells maintained that

> the proper method of approach to sociological problems is the old, various and literary way, the Utopian way, of Plato, of More, of Bacon, and

not the nineteenth century pneumatic style, not by its constant invocation to biology and 'scientific' history and its incessant unjustifiable pretension to exactitude and progress.[27]

Even if he here claimed to reject a 'scientific' approach to societal issues, Wells's early writing is heavily influenced by contemporary scientific, economic and social theories. As Sussman observes:

> throughout his early writing, his Darwinism and his Marxism coincide. For the evolutionary fantasy becomes a means not only of expressing the physical and psychological results of mechanization but also of depicting the more generalized effects of the class struggle.[28]

Particularly in his science fiction, Wells explored possible other worlds in order to draw attention to the contradictions and the injustices of the world in which he was living. In his social novels, the bicycle operates to open up a utopian space not dissimilar to the world into which Wells's Time Traveller is projected by his conspicuously bicycle-like time machine.[29] The three novels I examine all mobilise cycling as a means to propel their characters into another social, rather than temporal, reality; and for each of Wells's heroes the bicycle becomes a means of subversively and creatively exploring the byways of the social hierarchy.

Wells's early novel *The Wheels of Chance* provides a useful point of entry into the author's thinking on the interrelation between class issues and the bicycle, alongside a short story published shortly after, 'A Perfect Gentleman on Wheels'. Analyses of *Kipps: The Story of a Simple Soul* and *The History of Mr Polly* allow us to trace the complex symbolism of the bicycle as means for Wells's heroes to negotiate or subvert the baffling English class system. All three novels share in common a young draper hero who aspires for more from life than selling fabric to his social superiors. Hoopdriver channels his desire for a better life into a cycling holiday, while Kipps and Mr Polly unexpectedly inherit money. In the latter two novels, cycling does not provide the backbone of the narrative, yet bicycles frequently recur in the story in connection with the characters' ascendant or declining social status. The temporal span of these three novels, from the height of the bicycle boom to the beginning of the motor car era, permits us to examine the evolution of the technology's class significance in the period. While Hoopdriver and Kipps mimic the attitude of gentlemen cyclists, Mr Polly takes to cycling as part of a rejection of the concept of social climbing. In Wells's novels, the bicycle is an amorphous symbol that refuses to be associated with a single category. It takes us on a meandering, subversive ride through the intricate and often infuriating social reality in which his characters dwell.

Class Transgression in The Wheels of Chance

In *The Wheels of Chance* Wells makes extensive use of the bicycle as an outward sign of modernity and social climbing. Vehicles had long played this role in literature; Carsten Meiner points out how the coach was used as symbol of social ascendancy in eighteenth-century *romans de parvenus* such as Anne Claude de Caylus's *Histoire de Guillaume, cocher* (1740), for example.[30] In late nineteenth-century fiction the bicycle performed a corresponding symbolic function. For Wells's heroes, ownership of a bicycle is generally associated with real or imagined ascendant class status, even if its symbolism might gradually grow more complicated as the narrative progresses. The novel's hero Hoopdriver mobilises the bicycle as a means to transgress the boundaries of the social class to which he belongs. On the first morning of his ten-day cycling holiday, the cyclist is called a 'bloomin' Dook'[31] by a sarcastic heathkeeper who witnesses him falling off his bicycle. Even if insulted, Hoopdriver is buoyed up by being mistaken for a member of the aristocracy, an impression he is successfully able to convey thanks to his machine and his new cycling suit. Cycling southwards through the London suburbs allows him to play the role of 'a gentleman, a man of pleasure, with a five-pound note, two sovereigns, and some silver at various convenient points of his person. At any rate as good as a Dook, if not precisely in the peerage.'[32] The young man is acutely conscious of his new image, and soon after the encounter with the heathkeeper he takes great pleasure in hearing a nursemaid remark to her charge 'Look at the gentleman wizzer bicitle.'[33] Hoopdriver's bicycle, on the first day of his trip, seems to magically transform him from a lowly draper on a hard-earned annual holiday into a leisured gentleman.

Hoopdriver's masquerade is taken to the next level when he encounters Jessie fleeing her stepmother's home along with her ill-intentioned tutor, Bechamel. Perhaps benefiting from Jessie's naivety, Hoopdriver invents an identity as a colonial Englishman once he has helped the young woman flee from Bechamel's sexual advances. As Simon James shows in his insightful analysis of the novel, 'the plot depends on Jessie's misreading of Hoopdriver's clothing, language, culture and class', and concentrates on the 'democratising effects both of new styles of clothing alongside another class-levelling, cheaply mass-produced technological innovation, the safety bicycle'.[34] Jessie misinterprets Hoopdriver's class because of his ambiguous clothing; unlike flat caps or bowler hats, the apparel associated with cycling did not signal a specific class identity, and thus allowed a certain freedom within the restrictive social reality of late Victorian Britain.

Yet the transformation is not a complete success; the upper-class cyclist Bechamel, for one, initially identifies his rival as a 'greasy proletarian', before later taking him for a private detective.[35] Indeed, Hoopdriver's outdated bicycle, wan physical appearance and Cockney accent provide fairly obvious clues to his origin, and the mere fact of riding a bicycle did not automatically denote upper-class status. In fact, cycling was an activity that was actively encouraged among urban workers at the time; Hiroshi So examines how Wells's cycling romance participated in larger medical and political discourses around the health benefits of cycling for working-class Londoners.[36] It is also important to recall that the bicycle was mobilised as a means to enforce conformity to the norms of bourgeois society, which relied on an efficient, compliant working class. In the realm of cycle racing, Christopher Thompson shows in his history of the Tour de France how the fashioning of bicycle racers as 'pedalling workers' represented 'an attempt to shape working class identity in ways that would improve the moral and material condition of the laboring masses and in so doing calm middle class fears about the challenges those masses posed to the social order'.[37] Since the salaries, speed, fame and attitudes of these professional cyclists went counter to the criteria that distinguished bourgeois cyclists from *vélocipédards* (a denigrated category of inelegant, often working-class cyclists), the race organisers 'sought to effect their social redemption through repeated references to elegance, distinction, intelligence and nobility',[38] and by heavily policing the conduct of cyclists both during races and in their day-to-day lives. Similarly, in the context of turn-of-the-century Canada, Philip Gordon Mackintosh identifies 'domestic bicycling' as 'a bourgeois attempt to control the public use of the bicycle'[39] by defining the contexts in which the technology could be used and the appropriate behaviour and dress which could be associated with it. By adopting the dress and demeanour of a gentleman on a bicycle, then, Hoopdriver is in many ways conforming to a bourgeois discourse that sought to defuse the dangerous prospect of an active, mobile, independent proletariat able to define its own codes and identity.

Hoopdriver's foray into the life of a gentleman can never be more than fleeting. Despite Jessie's trustfulness and the hero's repeated attempts to disguise his origins, he is betrayed by his body language (bows and hand rubbing suggestive of a draper) and his locution (his Cockney accent, and calling Jessie 'Miss'), before eventually admitting the truth. Material considerations also oblige him to end the subterfuge; his meagre savings are rapidly exhausted as a result of paying for two rooms in the best hotels with Jessie. Thus, while the bicycle affords Hoopdriver the opportunity to temporarily masquerade as a member of the leisured upper class during his holiday from the drapery emporium, his escape is only temporary. His flight with Jessie must come to an abrupt end, and the closing pages of the novel see both young people firmly reprimanded and brought back into the fold of their respective classes.

At first glance it might seem that the established social structure emerges unscathed at the end of the novel. Yet Hoopdriver's incursion into upper-class life is significant at both the individual and the societal level. As the cyclist returns to his life as a draper, an important change has occurred in his outlook: 'Tomorrow, the early rising, the dusting, and drudgery, begin again – but with a difference, with wonderful memories and still more wonderful desires and ambitions replacing those discrepant dreams.'[40] Crucially, Jessie promises to send him books in order to encourage his attempts at 'self-education'.[41] Hoopdriver returns a changed man, armed with the physical and intellectual means to question his subservience. In addition to Jessie's promise of books, he has a new bicycle; the outdated machine he departed with has been replaced by Bechamel's brand-new model (stolen in order to rescue Jessie), now repainted in grey. In our final glimpse of Hoopdriver disappearing through the gates of the drapery emporium, the new bicycle he holds acts as a visual emblem of the changes he has undergone, while also pointing to the small chip he has made in the social edifice. In emulating the upper class, and finally making off with a vehicle and a reading list from two of its members, Hoopdriver makes an incursion into the codes of the social hierarchy. As Yoonjoung Choi argues, Wells effectively mobilises cycling in this novel to embody a Bakhtinian carnivalesque spirit, with the bicycle as an ideal means for 'breaking class and gender boundaries'.[42] Bakhtin employs the concept of the carnivalesque to refer to a literary mode that subverts the beliefs of the dominant group through humour, absurdity and chaos.[43] Hoopdriver's temporary foray into the upper class uncovers the absurdity of a system delineated by an arbitrary set of codes, activities and clothes. Society as a whole retains its oppressive class structures, but the bicycle becomes a tool for opening up a liminal, utopian space, in which fresh possibilities of social organisation might be explored, challenging the prevailing social order.

Wells's cycling romance might be compared to a short story written shortly after, which appeared in the collection *The Humours of Cycling* (1897). In 'A Perfect Gentleman on Wheels', Wells effectively retells *The Wheels of Chance* from another perspective; here it is an aristocratic gentleman who is humbled by a bicycle journey. The vain, arrogant young hero is ridiculed from the start; both he and his machine are described as 'overdressed', his bicycle being 'chocolate enamelled' and its rider wearing a cocked hat and trousers 'to distinguish himself from the common cycling cad'.[44] While Hoopdriver is called a 'bloomin' Dook' by a heathkeeper, a cabman calls 'New Woman'[45] after Mr Crampton, an insult that underlines his effeminate appearance while drawing attention to the gender- and class-blurring capabilities of the bicycle. As in *The Wheels of Chance*, Crampton's bicycle ride to Brighton brings him into contact with another social class than his own; yet he refuses to talk to the working-class 'bounder' who makes friendly conversation with him on the road. He stops to help a young woman with a puncture mainly because she is 'noticeably pretty'.[46] But having no mechanical knowledge (his 'man' had oiled his machine before he left), he leaves her bicycle in a worse state than when he began, growing more irritable and unpleasant as his ineptitude becomes increasingly apparent. To the young woman's exasperation, he proudly refuses the assistance of a number of well-meaning passers-by, until she insists on accepting help from the very 'bounder' Crampton had snubbed earlier.

As an engine fitter, the working-class cyclist is able to tell that Crampton has 'been pretty near knocking all the quality out of a vally'ble machine'. Crampton angrily responds that 'I'm quite prepared to pay for any damage I've done', thus attempting to gain the upper hand on the mechanic by invoking his superior economic position.[47] Yet what counts for these cyclists on a lonely road is not how much money or status each of them have, but their practical skills, physical capabilities and empathy for one another. Crampton's reference to his financial capital is absurd, as what is needed is mechanical knowledge and a genuine desire to help, rather than to simply seduce or impress. Crampton ends the day by abandoning the pair and catching a train to Brighton, details he omits when relating his journey to his family that evening. The narrator describes how 'An acute realisation of the indescribable vulgarity of cycling came into his mind. A dirty, fatiguing pursuit that put one at the mercy of every impudent Cad one met.'[48] This gentleman has fallen out of love with cycling because it has stripped him of his pretensions and exposed him for what he is; an insincere, vain, selfish, incompetent man. In his dealings with other human beings Crampton shows no proof of being the eponymous 'perfect gentleman', in spite of outward appearances. The bicycle brings him down to the level of common humanity; his lack of compassion and mechanical know-how and his failure to ride all the way to Brighton strip him of his airs and graces. The engine fitter's set of skills – his friendly, frank manner, consideration for others and mechanical knowledge – emerge triumphant from the story, pointing to alternative means of judging social worth, while challenging the notion that class distinctions rest on certain character traits. Where Hoopdriver transgresses class boundaries by dressing up as a gentleman cyclist, Crampton's fashionable clothes and bearing do not prevent the bicycle from bringing him crashing down to earth. In both these tales, the bicycle overlooks worldly trappings and connects its riders to their common humanity.

Sociable Cyclists, Contingency and Upward Mobility in Kipps

Kipps provides us with a further compelling case study of Wells's use of the bicycle in his social fiction.[49] In contrast to *The Wheels of Chance*, the bicycle's role in *Kipps* has been largely overlooked by critics. Indeed, the symbolism of the bicycle in this novel is more subtle than in Wells's first cycling romance, as the object is rarely associated with the main protagonist; rather, it is his contact with other cyclists that most often plays a crucial narrative role. In this account of Artie Kipps's rags-to-riches return trip, the bicycle recurrently crops up in the narrative as a symbol of opportunity, chance and contingency, all of which might lead protagonists up or down the social ladder. The bicycle provides a means of re-reading this well-known novel, providing a perspective that allows us to come into fresh contact with the text. Above all, the bicycle affirms the importance of values such as spontaneity, empathy and sociability while incarnating both a refusal of and an alternative to stifling Victorian class codes.

The bicycle makes its first appearance in the novel in a description of the young Artie Kipps, who 'by inherent nature [. . .] had a sociable disposition. When he was in the High Street he made a point of saying "Hallo!" to passing cyclists.'[50] In the humdrum world of New Romney, where Kipps is brought up by his aged aunt and uncle, the enterprising and enthusiastic young boy is drawn to the adventure and opportunity incarnated in the rare sight of cyclists who pass through the village. His spontaneous friendliness is given an outlet through interacting with the riders of this quintessentially sociable vehicle, which Marc Augé has credited with 'the reinvention of amicable, light-hearted social relations, which are perhaps fleeting but nonetheless convey *joie de vivre*'.[51] While Augé's reflection was made in the context of car-congested twenty-first-century cities, the bicycle functioned in a similar way in Wells's era by reinstating roads and villages as spaces of encounter in the wake of the railway age. By reviving the possibility of roadside meetings from coaching days, the bicycle instated a new, ephemeral paradigm of interpersonal interaction, based on brief meetings between strangers from various social strata. Kipps's spontaneous interaction with these cyclists contrasts sharply with the description of his aunt and uncle some lines earlier, who 'never received visitors' and, fearing mixing with their social inferiors or superiors, '"kept themselves to themselves," according to the English ideal'.[52] The young boy's irreverence towards the strictures of the English class system is thus incarnated in the image of the passing cyclists he greets in the opening pages of the novel.

Some ten pages later, the bicycle reappears when the adolescent Kipps is told a secret by his friend Sid. Sid confides he has a 'girl', and Kipps is taken aback on discovering her identity, since

> Maud Charteris was a young person of eighteen and the daughter of the vicar of St. Bavon's – besides which, she had a bicycle – so that as her name unfolded, the face of Kipps lengthened with respect. 'Get out,' he gasped incredulously. 'She ain't your girl, Sid Pornick.'[53]

Kipps's incredulity is well-founded, for Maud's age and class make her inaccessible to the haberdasher's son Sid, who in fact can only dream of being involved with this young cyclist. This second occurrence of the bicycle in the account of Kipps's formative years points to its potent symbolic link to the superior social class into which the young man is to ascend over the course of the novel. Although Sid does not become romantically involved with the vicar's daughter, he leaves home at fourteen to be apprenticed in a bicycle shop. At the same time, the carefree young Kipps (who has meanwhile fallen in love with Sid's younger sister, Ann) starts his apprenticeship as a draper in Folkestone.

The difference between the friends' career paths is patent, as Sid gradually rises through the ranks and is eventually able to open his own shop, while Kipps remains on the bottom rung of the ladder in the drapery emporium, becoming a mere cog in the capitalist machine. 'Dimly he perceived the thing that had happened to him,' the typically condescending narrator relates, 'how the great stupid machine of retail trade had caught his life into its wheels, a vast, irresistible force which he had neither strength of will nor knowledge to escape.'[54] Kipps's predicament recalls the characterisation of the modern urban subject by Georg Simmel in *The Metropolis and Mental Life* (1903), where he observes that 'the individual has become a mere cog in an enormous organisation of things and powers which tear from his hands all progress'.[55] In contrast to the senseless, exploitative wheels of retail, the bicycle is portrayed as a machine that allows Sid to achieve a certain autonomy and to navigate an individual route through the unfriendly waters of commerce. While Sid's star rises in his London bicycle shop, the machine plays a key role in the radical change that occurs in Kipps's fortunes thanks to his chance encounter with the playwright Chitterlow, a character whom the critic Michael Draper describes as 'an amusingly disruptive figure whose vitality is associated with rule-breaking and intoxication'.[56] Walking through Folkestone one evening, dreaming about his desirable but unattainable woodcarving teacher Helen Walshingham 'in a state of profound melancholia [. . .] Fortune came upon him, in disguise and with a loud shout [. . .] followed immediately by a violent blow in the back'.[57] A series of confused sensations ensues, until Kipps is helped up from the ground and finds himself 'confronting a figure holding a bicycle'. 'The bicyclist' – as Chitterlow is metonymically called during the whole four-page scene – proceeds to excuse himself, alternately blaming the accident on his handlebars, the hill he was descending, or his own lack of skill. The sympathy of the cyclist is perhaps spurred by the approach of a policeman (who could fine him for 'scorching', knocking over a pedestrian and having no lamp), and he offers to bring Kipps to his house so he can clean his wounds and repair his ripped trousers. 'Accidents *will* happen,' he remarks as they walk to his home, 'especially when you get *me* on a bicycle.'[58] Chitterlow thanks Kipps for pretending there had been no accident in the policeman's presence, prophetically telling him 'You acted like a gentleman over that slop.'[59] As we shall see, this collision does in fact have the unlikely result of transforming the humble Kipps into a gentleman.

Once he has served Kipps a glass of whisky, Chitterlow remarks:

> It's curious how one runs up against people bicycling! [. . .] half an hour ago we didn't know we existed. Leastaways we didn't know each other existed. I might have passed you in the street, perhaps, and you might have passed me.[60]

This central scene highlights the contingency of modern experience, and the paradoxical role played by transportation and communication technologies in both hindering and facilitating human encounters. In an increasingly anonymous, fast-paced urban environment, Simmel observed, human contact is sidelined or limited to monetary exchange; we cultivate 'a necessary indifference to those around us'.[61] As Chitterlow's remark 'we didn't know we existed' suggests, the high-speed metropolis also dulls the human sensorium through overstimulation, leading to a certain loss of our sense of self.[62] Cycling participated in the acceleration of urban environments, yet its individual nature and its openness to its surroundings meant that it was also a propitious vehicle for encouraging human contact. It is significant that this crucial meeting takes the form of an accident. As I discuss further in Chapter 3, many critics point to the importance of technological shocks in the constitution of the modern subject, and the bicycle was one of many technologies that made such shocks more commonplace. For Kipps, the bicycle plays a very different role than it did for the newly mobile draper Hoopdriver, or for the enterprising mechanic Sid. It is an external force that acts upon him, a point of entry into another social reality unchosen by him. The bicycle acts as an intermediary, unexpectedly allowing a well-educated if struggling playwright's path to cross with that of a lowly draper's assistant.

The pair stay up drinking until morning; Kipps arrives late to work and consequently receives his dismissal. Yet two days later Chitterlow calls on the despondent Kipps with a cutting from a newspaper, which he fishes out from his pocket along with 'a bicycle pump' – an object recalling the context of their first encounter – and various other paraphernalia.[63] The barely literate Kipps struggles to understand the meaning of the advertisement, and Chitterlow is obliged to explain to him that 'It means [. . .] that you're going to strike it Rich.'[64] With Chitterlow's help, and after some hesitation, Kipps responds to the letter and discovers that his grandfather (who, as an illegitimate child, he never knew) has bequeathed him a house and an income of twelve hundred pounds a year. The advertisement about Kipps's inheritance, placed in a newspaper read by the higher social classes, was unlikely to be read by Kipps nor by any of his circle, a fact that uncovers the closed nature of the social and economic establishment, where information is only circulated between the initiated. It is the draper's fortuitous collision with the cycling playwright that tears the fabric of this unjust logic, allowing Kipps access to the carefully guarded higher echelons of society.

As Kipps gradually comes to appreciate the implications of the wealth he has acquired, he associates the bicycle with an almost medieval idea of social hierarchy, thinking 'Over a thousand a year made him an Esquire, didn't it? [. . .] In which case, wouldn't he have to be presented at court? Velvet breeches, like you wear cycling, and a sword!'[65] His flights of fancy about possible purchases include 'a motor-car' and 'a bicycle and a cyclist suit', and he soon begins a course of private cycling lessons.[66] As Kipps is rocketed into Folkestone high society, he is mentored in etiquette, elocution and reading by a certain Mr Cootes, but his social shortcomings are painfully clear to the new company he keeps. Cootes looks benevolently upon Kipps's interest in cycling, while insisting on the importance of continuing his education in manners, literature and other subjects. When Mrs Walshingham observes that 'He's going in for his bicycle now', Cootes replies, 'That's all right for summer [. . .] but he wants to go in for some serious intellectual interest.'[67] As a new member of the upper class, it is now expected that Kipps will demonstrate intellectual and cultural capital. Rather than aiming to genuinely extend Kipps's range of experience, however, his tutor simply tries to make him appear cultivated, to enable him to convincingly play the role of a member of the leisured upper class. Recalling the Bahktinian carnivalesque use of the bicycle as an external marker of social status in *The Wheels of Chance*, Kipps's attempts to emulate the accent, habits and intellectual pursuits of the upper class only reveal the arbitrariness of such a system, inviting a critical outlook on class markers.

One morning, soon after Kipps has become a rich man, Chitterlow calls on him, acting as 'a reminder of a world quite outside those spheres of ordered gentility'[68] in which he has been strenuously attempting to immerse himself. Although he had planned to spend the day reading 'a precious little volume called *Don't* that Coote had sent round for him – a book of invaluable hints, a summary of British deportment' and attempting a 'difficult exercise called an Afternoon Call', Chitterlow takes him for 'a great walk, not a long one, but a great one', into 'a wilderness of thorn and bramble, wild rose and wayfaring tree', suggestive of 'Alpine adventure'.[69] The playwright, meanwhile, waxes lyrical on his art, and urges his friend to buy a half-share in his next play. After their walk, they enjoy a 'simple but sufficient meal [. . .] distributed with careless spontaneity' by Mrs Chitterlow.[70] Their Romantic ramble and simple repast could not contrast more sharply with the idle, superficial lifestyle that Kipps is vainly attempting to emulate. Although at the end of the day Kipps finds himself slightly irritated by his friend's intrusion – and especially his financial request, to which he nonetheless eventually agrees – it is clear where the narrator's sympathies lie, as he steps forward to beg the reader's indulgence, advising 'You must not think too hardly of him.'[71] It will be some time before Kipps, greatly relieved, is forced to climb back down the social ladder, but Chitterlow's frank, simple presence at this early stage in his social ascendancy acts as a foil to the disingenuous nature of upper-class life. Although it was the cyclist who initially pointed Kipps's way out of enslavement to the vast 'machine of retail trade',[72] the route he suggests is a very different one from that encouraged by the superficial world into which Kipps has just been projected.

In the fourth chapter, entitled 'The Bicycle Manufacturer', Kipps hires a motor car to make his first trip back to his home town after coming into his inheritance, ostensibly to tell his aunt and uncle about his engagement to Helen Walshingham. In New Romney, he bumps into his childhood friend Sid, now a successful bicycle manufacturer who boasts that he produces the 'best machine at a democratic price in London. No guineas and no discounts – honest trade. I build 'em – to order. I've built [. . .] seventeen. Counting orders in 'and . . .'[73] When Kipps reveals that he has inherited money, a house, and is engaged to educated, upper-middle-class Helen, Sid is both surprised and indignant. He points to the hypocrisy of a system that pays most to the most idle in society, affirming 'I'm a Socialist, you see.'[74] Sid offers his frank opinion on 'the Present distribution of Wealth',[75] suggesting an alternative organisation of society; he imagines that if he came into such money, he would 'start an Owenite profit-sharing factory perhaps. Or a new Socialist paper.'[76] He exhibits 'disgust' at the price Kipps paid to hire his motor car, and as he watches his friend drive off the narrator remarks, 'The young mechanic had just discovered that to have manufactured seventeen bicycles, including orders in hand, is not so big a thing as he had supposed, and such discoveries try one's manhood.'[77]

Sid, the self-made bicycle manufacturer, is of course participating in a profit-driven system, drawing revenue from the sale of an object in high demand. Overproduction and falling prices during the bicycle boom provoked a financial crisis in 1898, most keenly felt in the USA, and bicycle manufacturers such as Alexander Pope developed mass-production techniques on a proto-Fordian model.[78] In addition, the manufacture of bicycles relied on colonial rubber extracted at the cost of many lives in central Africa.[79] On a global scale, then, bicycle production can hardly be seen as establishing a socialist paradigm, yet the mushrooming of bicycle manufacturers often revived flagging local economies and suggested alternative forms of economic organisation.

The prime example in the UK was Coventry, where bicycle manufacture took over from the production of watches and sewing machines as the new cottage industry; by the 1890s, 248 different cycle manufacturers employed approximately 40,000 workers in the city.[80] Glen Norcliffe characterises the bicycle industry in Coventry as creative and collaborative, consisting of an 'interconnected network of "actors" and innovative firms [. . .] a pool of skilled entrepreneurs and workers' in which 'ideas were shared, and the actors, although competitive, were also to a degree cooperative'.[81] Sid's small-scale production of bicycles in Hammersmith enshrines a refusal of the generation of surplus value through large-scale mechanised production. Sid's seventeen hand-built bicycles stand in silent, humble opposition to Kipps's noisy motor car and the fortune that lies behind it. The manual skills required for the construction of bicycles, on which Sid builds his modest living, contrast sharply with the suddenly idle Kipps, who is able to abandon manual trade because of his wealth. The self-perpetuating wealth the hero has inherited recalls his hired motor car, as both rely on complex, capitalist processes (extracting rent from the poor; extracting oil from the ground). Sid and his bicycles propose a more transparent model of mobility and economy, founded on a non-exploitative use of human labour and energy.

The opening pages of chapter 6 relate Kipps's first bicycle journey, and are rich in details that explore the bicycle's complex and somewhat paradoxical effect on an individual's interaction with environment and society. While Chitterlow's and Sid's bicycles have thus far acted as external forces on the protagonist, respectively helping him to discover his fortune and suggesting an alternative economic model, Kipps's own experience of cycling forces him to consider the subjective impact of his sudden change in status. He rides to New Romney in a second attempt to inform his family of his engagement (and his corresponding social ascendancy, including a change of name from Kipps to Cuyps), something he had neglected to do on his previous visit. The chapter begins:

> One day Kipps set out upon his newly mastered bicycle to New Romney, to break the news of his engagement to his uncle and aunt – positively. He was now a finished cyclist, but as yet an unseasoned one [. . .] ever and again he got off and refreshed himself by a spell of walking.[82]

His slow-paced approach to his home town invites significant insights about 'the atmosphere of New Romney', which had 'some faint and impalpable quality that was missing in the great world of Folkestone'.[83] The 'homeliness' and 'familiarity' Kipps senses are certainly linked to the fact that he grew up in these surroundings, yet the close observation permitted by his chosen forms of locomotion (cycling and walking) allows for a specific, nostalgic engagement with place, as illustrated in the following passage:

> He had noted as he passed that old Mr Clifferdown's gate had been mended with a fresh piece of string. In Folkestone he didn't take notice, and he didn't care if they built three hundred houses [. . .] It was fine and grand to have twelve hundred a year; it was fine to go about on trams and omnibuses and think not a person on board was as rich as oneself [. . .] but yet there had been a zest in the old time out here, a rare zest in the holidays, in sunlight, on the sea beach, and in the High Street, that failed from these new things.[84]

Modes of locomotion come to the fore as Kipps begins to gain awareness that wealth will not bring him fulfilment. It is by slowing his movement to a walking or cycling pace, and being observant of small details in his surroundings, that this crucial realisation – inaccessible to the unobservant, passive tram or omnibus passenger – comes to him.

On the road into New Romney, Kipps bumps into his childhood sweetheart Ann Pornick, who is now employed in domestic service. He neglects to mention his change in status to her, and they walk companionably together, talking 'with remarkable ease to one each other'.[85] Ann incarnates the nostalgia in which Kipps had been absorbed before meeting her, and he is deeply moved by the encounter – so much so that he once again forgets to share the news of his engagement with his aunt and uncle. On his journey back to Folkestone, the bicycle's role is transformed; it becomes a vector of his social distance from the people and places he knew as a child. In the following description, cycling engenders a fragmented, subjective interaction with place that brings to mind modernist narrative technique:

> The south-west wind perhaps held him back; at any rate he found himself through Dymchurch without having noticed the place. There came an odd effect as he drew near Hythe. The hills on the left and the trees on the right seemed to draw together and close in upon him until his way was straight and narrow. He could not turn round on that treacherous half-tamed machine, but he knew that behind him, he knew so well, spread the wide vast flatness of the Marsh shining under the afternoon sky. In some way this was material to his thoughts. And as he rode through Hythe, he came upon the idea that there was a considerable amount of incompatibility between the existence of one who was practically a gentleman and of Ann.[86]

Kipps's skills of close observation have now evaporated: the machine and his incomplete mastery of it – he is not yet a proficient enough cyclist to look over his shoulder while riding – give him tunnel vision, making him oblivious to the localities he passes through. The regular, rhythmic sentences of this passage reflect the cyclist's steady movement on his machine. The claustrophobic atmosphere of the landscape is reflected in the syntax, with phrases drawing to an abrupt end rather than opening out on to a wider vista. This closed-in vision is contrasted to 'the vast flatness' which Kipps imagines behind him but is unable to see. Kipps's concentration on pedalling denies him a view of the Marsh he knew in his childhood, and the straight and narrow road on which he is travelling reflects the constraints of his new-found social superiority and the yawning gap between himself and the servant Ann.

The depiction of the landscape as an emanation of Kipps's psychological and social reality suggests an affinity with the emerging modernist narrative technique, which sought to portray subjective experience rather than objective reality. It is the bicycle's liminal position between corporeal and mechanical means of locomotion that allows it to play an equivocal role in this sequence. On his slow-paced, observant journey to New Romney, the bicycle encourages Kipps to reconnect with his past and question the value of his new life as a gentleman. Yet on the return trip, his bicycle provides a means by which he accelerates into his new lifestyle, away from the people and places of his childhood. It is important to note that a condition of this latter function is Kipps's inability to fully control his bicycle, leaving him at the mercy of the 'treacherous' machine. Unable to turn around to glance at the landscape that vividly recalls his past, Kipps feels the machine has taken over, negating his own agency as its rider. Although none of his further bicycle rides are related in any detail in the novel, it is fair to presume that as the cyclist becomes a more proficient rider and gains mastery over the machine, he may find a balance between the extreme observant/nostalgic and unobservant/progressive ways of seeing both evoked in connection with the bicycle in this chapter.

Following this visit to New Romney, Kipps feels increasingly ill at ease and out of place in his new social circle in Folkestone. He returns to see Ann, and is unable to face Helen Walshingham, but nonetheless writes to his aunt and uncle to inform them of his engagement to her. On receiving the reply that they are coming directly to Folkestone to meet his fiancée, Kipps takes flight to London, fearing the coming collision between his old world and the new one, which he imagines would be 'a hideous, impossible disaster'.[87] London provides Kipps with a comforting temporary anonymity, but even there his ambiguous social identity is a source of constant anxiety; unsure that his table manners are up to the task, he avoids dining at the Royal Grand Hotel, yet he feels too well dressed to go into a fish shop. While wandering hungrily through the streets, he meets his old friend Sid, who invites him home for mutton. They travel third class on the Underground to Sid's shop in Hammersmith, 'a practical-looking establishment, stocked with the most remarkable collection of bicycles and pieces of bicycle that [Kipps] had ever beheld'.[88] The bicycle shop acts as the setting for what the critic Ivan Melada has seen as an important instance of overt socialist propaganda in Wells's novels.[89] Here, Kipps meets Sid's lodger Masterman, an impoverished socialist intellectual suffering from tuberculosis.[90] His conversation with Kipps acts as a moment of epiphany for the unenlightened protagonist, whom the narrator has consistently depicted as the eponymous 'simple soul'. Masterman asks Kipps how it feels to be rich, and goes on to argue that individual and collective happiness cannot be achieved by the accumulation of wealth. 'As for happiness,' Masterman maintains, 'you want a world in order before money or property or any of those things have any real value, and this world, I tell you, is hopelessly out of joint.'[91] Masterman's judgement is illustrated by Kipps's dilemma; although he has found wealth, he is far from happy, as he feels out of place in his new social circle. Masterman illustrates his conviction that people are essentially similar through a transport metaphor, arguing that 'your cads in a bank holiday train, and your cads on a two thousand pound motor, except for a difference in scale, there's not a pin to choose between them'.[92] These modes of transport function as markers of distinction between people and shape people's behaviour and outlook. Masterman decries the senseless waste in the current application of technology, arguing that 'God gives [the rich] a power like the motor-car, and all they can do with it is to go careering about the roads in goggled masks killing children and making machinery hateful to the souls of men!'[93] Occurring within the confines of Sid's bicycle shop, Masterman's speech is an invitation to a more sober, compassionate way of life that makes rational use of technology without pushing it to destructive extremes.

On returning to Folkestone, Kipps breaks off his engagement with Helen, marries his childhood sweetheart Ann and settles down to 'a quiet little life' with her, occasionally making trips to New Romney by bicycle.[94] Finally, in a familiar Wellsian trope (partly based on the author's own biography), Kipps loses most of his fortune as a result of speculation by Helen's brother and by undertaking to build a grand house. In the closing pages of the novel, the couple have set up a bookshop and are raising their first born, receiving occasional cheques from Chitterlow thanks to Kipps's share in his play, which turned out to be a great success. Thus, the eccentric cyclist who first announced Kipps's change in status makes an understated return as the novel draws to a close. Rather than bringing a great fortune, he makes a modest contribution to their sober, happy lifestyle.

Thus, in both *The Wheels of Chance* and *Kipps* the bicycle plays a key role in freeing lower-middle-class protagonists from the drudgery of a life of servitude. While Hoopdriver manages to blur and question class boundaries on his cycling holiday, in *Kipps* the bicycle plays the role of a counter-cultural, subversive force, actively rejecting a profit-driven outlook in order to question what constitutes human happiness. Indeed, the bicycle accompanies Kipps's ultimate rejection of the exploitation inherent in both his role in a drapery emporium and as a wealthy gentleman, suggesting that individual freedom is paramount in achieving fulfilment. It is this aspect of the bicycle's symbolism that comes to the fore in the figure of a final Wellsian cyclist, Mr Polly.

Alternative Routes to Happiness in The History of Mr Polly

In *The History of Mr Polly*, the activity of cycling participates in a broader rejection of a wealth-driven, capitalist organisation of society. By the time Wells wrote *Mr Polly* in 1910, the bicycle was no longer a status symbol but potentially a means for critiquing high capitalist society. Alfred Polly does just this, not by backing any definite social or political programme, but by championing sociability, creativity, spontaneity and happiness over the pursuit of wealth. Although he does not learn to ride a bicycle in his youth, the machine plays a background role in Polly's life from its beginning, since his retired father had run a 'music and bicycle shop'.[95] While Polly's education, like that of Kipps, has left him with little more than a confused jumble of ideas, he is a sensitive and intelligent character who loves literature and 'dreamt always of picturesque and mellow things'.[96] Indeed, as Michael Draper points out, Polly combines Kipps's 'comic rebelliousness' with Chitterlow's 'transforming imagination', resulting in 'Wells's most heroic, most memorable and least patronised character'.[97] Polly is still patronised to an extent, and John Carey groups him together with Wells's 'lower-middle-class types – Polly,

Hoopdriver, Kipps', towards whom Wells has an equivocal stance: 'Wells's attitude to them [. . .] is divided. He feels for them, but does not quite treat them as men.'[98] In spite of the persistence of a somewhat condescending narrative tone, the portrait of Polly contains much more psychological detail than that of his predecessors. The bicycle plays an important role in his characterisation, contributing to both the imaginative and rebellious aspects of his personality.

Polly seems to have a disposition that is singularly unsuited to the demeaning work of shopkeeping; yet just like Hoopdriver and Kipps, he trained as a draper and works in an emporium. Disgusted at the violent dismissal of his friend Parsons (for his over-creative decorating of a shop window), he quits his stable job in the emporium; then follows a period of unemployment and various short-term jobs, which leave him feeling like a rabbit 'in a net'.[99] All this changes on the death of his father, when Polly inherits a modest three hundred and fifty pounds, thanks to an insurance policy and his father's savings.[100] It is his small inheritance that frees him from life as an employee, allowing him to begin to reflect on different ways of living. The bicycle, as we shall see, plays a key role in Polly's period of exploration.

Polly leaves his job in London and goes to stay with his cousin Harold Johnson in the fictional suburban town of Easewood, where he 'translated his restless craving for joy and leisure into Harold Johnsonese by saying that he meant to look about him for a bit before going into another situation'.[101] Indeed, the advice from his family is to marry and invest his capital in the purchase of a draper's shop at the earliest possible opportunity. Polly, however, delays his decision: his first purchase with his new capital is 'a safety bicycle which he proposed to study and master in the sandy lane below the Johnson's house', soon followed by 'a number of books'.[102] The bicycle and books stand as emblems of Polly's resistance to the profit-centred attitude he is being encouraged to adopt. They allow him to reconnect with the adolescent 'Joy de Vive' he had experienced during long walks in the countryside with his friends from the drapery emporium. We are told that during Polly's youth, 'the bicycle was still rare and costly, and the motor-car had yet to come and stir up rural serenities'.[103] As it lost its status as a luxury item, however, the bicycle increasingly began to take on the counter-cultural symbolism that rambling had enshrined for certain writers in the Romantic era.

The bicycle was mobilised in various other contemporary narratives as an anti-capitalist symbol; J. W. Allen's cycle touring account *Wheel Magic; or, Revolutions of an Impressionist* contains a chapter about a character who, rather than investing an inheritance he comes into, quits his job, buys a bicycle and begins a life as a cycling nomad. To him it is the society around him that seems insane:

> It amuses me [. . .] to think of all the nonsensical advice that was dumped on me then. I was told how I could double my capital in two years! [. . .] I didn't mean to shut myself up in a poky business. What on earth should a sane man do such things for?[104]

Polly adopts a similar attitude, making the most of the freedom he is suddenly able to enjoy rather than seeking to perpetuate the system that had imprisoned him as a toiling draper. Rather than taking up the advice of those around him to invest in a shop, Polly begins to travel through the local vicinity on 'exploratious meanderings',[105] experiences that allow him to reflect creatively on his surroundings and develop a healthier relationship with his emotions and his body after long years of confinement on the shop floor:

> He did not ride at the even pace sensible people use who have marked out a journey from one place to another, and settled what time it will take them. He rode at variable speeds, and always as though he was looking for something that, missing, left life attractive still, but a little wanting in significance. And sometimes he was so unreasonably happy he had to whistle and sing, and sometimes he was incredibly, but not at all painfully, sad. His indigestion vanished with air and exercise [. . .][106]

Wells's prose here mirrors the meandering approach to life favoured by Polly, with the accumulation of successive sub-clauses reflecting an ongoing search rather than a journey with a clear beginning and end. The free, winding path followed by the sentences mirrors Polly's erratic bicycle riding, which refuses the idea of departure, destination and uniform speed encouraged by other means of transport. Rather, Polly sets his own speed, performing an active, present engagement with his surroundings, constantly 'looking for something', and ever willing to enact an open exchange with the world. As the texture of the writing suggests, Polly actively questions the dominant model of society based on acceleration, accumulation and efficiency.

By means of his bicycle rides Polly begins to lead a 'double life', telling his cousin he is 'looking for an opening' and in fact going to enjoy the company of his three young female cousins in a nearby town.[107] One day he discovers a picturesque wood, where he surprises a young girl, Christabel, attempting to climb over the stone wall marking the boundary of her boarding school. Polly falls in love at first sight, feeling 'like one of those old knights [. . .] who rode about the country looking for dragons and beautiful maidens and chivalresque adventures'.[108] The first thing Christabel notices about Polly is his bicycle – she tells him that she cycles, too – and the object (as well as his complicity with her part-flight from school) at once allows them to establish a certain intimacy. Like Jessie in *The Wheels of Chance*, upper-class Christabel is initially unable to ascertain Polly's social class, and she uses the bicycle in an attempt to do so:

> 'I say,' she said, in the pause that followed, 'why are you riding about the country on a bicycle?'
> 'I'm doing it because I like it.'
> She sought to estimate his social status on her limited basis of experience.[109]

The leisure time that Polly disposes of hints at a superior class status, yet Christabel's questions 'probed ever nearer to the hateful secret of the shop and his normal servitude'.[110] Nonetheless, they continue to meet at the same spot for the next ten days, Christabel remaining in limbo on the wall with Polly admiring her from below. The liaison ends abruptly when school term starts again, wrenching Polly from 'the happy dream in which he had been living, of long, warm days, of open roads, of limitless, unchecked hours, of infinite time to look about him'.[111] Polly's life as a cycling *flâneur* comes to a sudden end when he takes stock of his dwindling inheritance and conforms to society's expectations by marrying his cousin Miriam and investing what remains of his capital in a shop. His bicycle, however, allows him to make one last imaginary and geographical flight south 'towards the tropics and the equator and the south coast of England', where he finally takes a shop in the little village of Fishbourne 'to escape the doom of Johnson's choice' in Easewood.[112]

For the next fifteen years, Polly leads a miserable life as the owner of a business, managing to find occasional release from daily drudgery in cycling and reading:

> on summer evenings he would ride his bicycle about the country, and if he discovered a sale where there were books, he would as often as not waste half the next day in going to acquire a job lot of them haphazard [. . .][113]

Yet his overall mood is despondency, which is clearly linked to his lack of physical activity. The narrator intervenes here in an attempt to provide a structural justification for Polly's discontent, citing a certain fictitious social theorist who has developed the concept of 'collective intelligence' in opposition to individualism.[114] He 'quotes' this imaginary thinker for a number of pages, developing the following bodily metaphor of a sick society:

> A rapidly complicating society [...] which as a whole declines to contemplate its future or face the intricate problems of its organisation, is in exactly the position of a man who takes no thought of dietary or regimen, who abstains from baths and exercise and gives his appetites free play. It accumulates useless and aimless lives as a man accumulates fat and morbid products in his blood, it declines in its collective efficiency and vigour and secretes discomfort and misery.[115]

Polly here becomes 'a microcosm of society' and a 'rather crude political symbol',[116] as Michael Draper observes, functioning to throw the ailments of society into sharp relief. Wells insists on the parallel between social organisation and our individual relationship to our bodies. One of the reasons the bicycle stands in opposition to the contemporary organisation of society is that it encourages us to reconnect with our bodies, our surroundings and others, encouraging a vision of society that is more far-sighted and humane, in contrast to the individualistic, profit-seeking society in which Polly finds himself trapped.

The final straw for Polly comes when he crashes his bicycle into his neighbour's ironmongery stall. Estranged from all his other neighbours, he had developed a friendship with Mr Rusper the ironmonger, but this collision leads to insults and a physical fight. The cause of the accident is explained thus:

> His bicycle was now very old, and it is one of the concomitants of a bicycle's senility that its free wheel should one day obstinately cease to be free. It corresponds to that epoch in human decay when an old gentleman loses an incisor tooth. It happened just as Mr Polly was approaching Mr Rusper's shop, and the untoward chance of a motor car trying to pass a waggon on the wrong side gave Mr Polly no choice but to get on to the pavement and dismount.[117]

The bicycle's senility mirrors the lamentable physical and mental state of its owner. Due to the machine's jammed freewheel, Polly's attempt to dismount causes him to crash into his neighbour's goods, which sparks off an argument. Where, in his youth, Polly had used the bicycle as a tool for exploring more interactive, collective, non-materialist ways of being in the world, he has now become a taciturn, unwilling victim of the capitalist system. Just as the bicycle's freewheel refuses to function, Polly has become incapable of free, independent thought, imprisoned in a life he resents. Although this scene relies on the malfunctioning of the machine, the bicycle displays evidence of agency here, forcing a crisis that makes Polly face up to his reality and take action.[118]

Following the bicycle accident, Polly sinks deeper into depression and decides to commit suicide. He makes a plan to burn down his house, in order to make his death look accidental. Once he sets his house alight, however, a sudden survival instinct takes over. Polly manages to escape from his burning house, but the fire spreads to the rest of the town. The unexpected result of Polly's attempted suicide is a rare pulling together of Fishbourne society in an attempt to extinguish the blaze and save lives. Previously the pariah of the town, Polly becomes a local hero by saving an old woman from a burning house; as a result of this turn of events, 'everyone thought well of him and was anxious to show it, more especially by shaking his hand painfully and repeatedly'.[119] As well as drawing the community together, the blaze brings the perverse nature of capitalism into sharp focus; those who have lost their shops and homes in the fire will in fact be better off thanks to their insurance policies. 'It's cleared me out of a lot of old stock [. . .] that's one good thing',[120] Mr Wintershed remarks, highlighting the skewed logic of an economic system built on ever-renewed commodities and capital.

The fire changes Polly's life in a very different way; it leads him to the discovery that 'if the world does not please you, *you can change it*'.[121] Rather than cashing in on his insurance policy (which he leaves to his wife), he makes the resolution to 'walk and loiter by the way [. . .] and get an odd job here and there, and talk to strange people'.[122] This phase of the middle-aged man's life recalls his cycling phase soon after receiving his inheritance, when his bicycle offered him the means of temporarily delaying his integration into the world of commerce and matrimony. The correlation between Polly's youthful meanderings by bicycle and his adoption of the life of a tramp in middle age is emphasised by the fact that his wandering on foot soon leads him back to the very same 'lichenous stone wall' to which he had cycled to meet the schoolgirl Christabel many years previously.[123] Just as the bicycle had encouraged him to adopt a more attentive relationship to his body, the environment and others, walking allows him to lead 'a healthy human life, living constantly in the open air [. . .] After a lapse of fifteen years he rediscovered this interesting world, about which so many people go incredibly blind and bored.'[124]

The contrast between Polly's nomadic, pastoral existence and the general tendency of society is underlined by the evocation of modern means of transport. He is woken from his sleep on a pile of brushwood 'by the distant rattle of a racing motor-car breaking all the speed regulations',[125] and he is described from the perspective of a car driver in the following terms:

> A tramp sat by the roadside, thinking, and it seemed to the man in the passing motor-car he must needs be plotting for another pot of beer. But, as a matter of fact, what the tramp was saying to himself over and over again, was a variant upon a well-known Hebrew word.[126]

Polly is reflecting on the biblical term 'Itchabod', translated as 'the glory has departed'. With this word Polly solemnly bids farewell to the conventional life he had struggled to adopt from his youth. The senseless acceleration of the motor car Polly hears, and the warped, erroneous viewpoint of the passing driver, stand in sharp contrast to the human-powered, contemplative existence the hero has finally chosen.

The bicycle, then, has quite a straightforward symbolism in *Mr Polly*, in contrast to its more equivocal portrayal in *The Wheels of Chance* and especially *Kipps*. Wells's final cyclist hero uses the vehicle as a means to engage in a peripatetic, alternative lifestyle, actively refusing the tenets of the capitalist society he inhabits. His bicycle rides during his youth act as an apprenticeship in liberty, a foretaste of the life he will eventually adopt as a tramp, where he rejects possessions in order to engage actively with the world and the people he encounters. All of these novels share in common their vision of the bicycle as a technology that serves humanity instead of distorting our relationship to people and the environment. Wells's heroes use the vehicle to engage more meaningfully with their bodies, their surroundings and others. Marc Augé wonders 'whether, in the end, the use of the bicycle could allow us to invent a third way, between liberalism and socialism, which concerns itself principally with the happiness of individuals'.[127] It would seem that for Wells, whatever the political role of the bicycle, it is above all a means to find personal fulfilment and happiness. And what better basis for a just society?

Women's Cycling in British Literature

> The lady novelist of today resembles the 'literary bicyclist' so delightfully satirised by the late Lord Justice Bowen. She covers a vast extent of ground, and sometimes her machine takes her along some sadly muddy roads, where her petticoats – or her knickerbockers – are apt to get soiled.
>
> Hugh Stutfield[128]

The bicycle has been credited with radically changing women's lives. While many critics have examined women's adoption of cycling from the 1890s, Glen Norcliffe reminds us that women's general accession to the activity actually began around 1880, with the appearance of the tricycle, alongside the still popular high wheeler.[129] Eugen Weber recalls how at an international feminist congress in Paris in 1896, Maria Pognon, the president of the French League for Women's Rights, raised her glass in a toast to the 'egalitarian and levelling bicycle' that was in the process of liberating her sex.[130] In the same year, the North American feminist Susan B. Anthony also famously deemed the bicycle an agent of women's emancipation, arguing that

> [the bicycle] has done more to emancipate women than anything else in the world. It gives women a feeling of freedom and self-reliance. I stand and rejoice every time I see a woman ride by on a wheel [. . .] the picture of free, untrammeled womanhood.[131]

Women's cycling contributed to momentous changes in female clothing and mobility, helping to challenge the prevailing patriarchal cast of society while stoking the emerging movement for women's suffrage.[132] At the same time, women's sudden ability and demand to wear more practical clothing and move freely aroused furious debates over the moral and health dangers of cycling. As Christopher Thompson and Fiona Ratkoff argue, in France many observers 'saw women cyclists as the source of fatal social chaos' and held the bicycle responsible for *fin-de-siècle* spectres such as degeneration or depopulation.[133] Here I examine this compelling moment in the history of feminist struggles in the UK and France through the lens of contemporary fiction. Both bicycles and the New Woman novels I examine interacted with contemporary debates about the changing place of women in society.[134] My study presents a nuanced view of the complex and equivocal role the bicycle played in alternately liberating women and reinforcing their subordination in a society that remained decidedly patriarchal.

A significant cultural icon at the turn of the century, the New Woman was widely discussed and written about in newspapers and fiction of the period; it has been estimated that between 1883 and 1900 over a hundred novels were written about the figure.[135] Part caricature, part reflection of the new lifestyles being adopted by certain women, she was depicted in novels such as Grant Allen's *The Woman Who Did* (1895) as someone who cast off Victorian conventionality in order to seek education, reject marriage and gain an independent living. Sally Ledger writes that 'the New Woman was a very *fin-de-siècle* phenomenon [. . .] she was part of that concatenation of cultural novelties which manifested itself in the 1880s and 1890s'.[136] Another cultural novelty, the bicycle, rapidly became associated with this image of mobile, emancipated women in literature. Here I take a fresh look at New Women awheel in a British context by examining fictional works by a panel of authors including H. G. Wells, Grant Allen, George Gissing, Arthur Conan Doyle, Mc Donnell Bodkin, Mary Kennard and Ada L. Harris. This literary examination highlights some of the unexpected ways in which cycling changed the lives of women, while drawing attention to the limits of this redefinition of women's place in private and public spheres.

New Women: Appropriating Mobility

The bicycle has powerful symbolic value in New Woman literature. As Chris Willis observes:

> Popular fiction of the time often uses the figure of the female cyclist as a paradigm of the New Woman. If a character makes her first appearance on a bicycle, it is almost inevitable that she will turn out to be single and well-educated, with strong views on women's rights.[137]

Indeed, many New Woman authors are keen to associate their emancipated female characters with the bicycle in their opening pages, even if it only plays a minor role in the rest of the narrative. For example, an image of a female cyclist is placed prominently on the cover of Mc Donnell Bodkin's *Dora Myrl*, and the lady detective also makes her appearance on a bicycle on the first page. Similarly, the title of Harris's *A Widow on Wheels*, the cover illustration of the eponymous lady on her bicycle and the lively discussion of cycling at a ladies' sewing circle recounted in the opening pages draw attention to the activity of cycling, even though the bicycle subsequently plays a very minor role in the novel. The eponymous widow Mrs Gresham

Green rides her bicycle 'in the face of outraged local propriety, which was inclined to regard a widow on wheels as almost as great an anomaly as one of the visionary creatures mentioned in Ezekiel'.[138] In H. G. Wells's New Woman novel *Ann Veronica* (1913), the bicycle briefly figures as a symbol of the eponymous young woman's perceived liberation. When she tells her father she feels 'cooped up' at home, he protests, asking 'Did I stand in the way of your going to college? Have I ever prevented you going about at any reasonable hour? You've got a bicycle!'[139] It is as though the mere mention of a woman's bicycle were sufficient to denote the extent of her perceived freedom from the traditional authority of her husband or father.

Other texts provide more detail and insight into the manifold ways in which cycling brought real changes to women's lives in this period. A crucial aspect of this was clothing, since the physical and mechanical requirements of the bicycle rendered Victorian corsets and heavy skirts even more inhibiting. This gave crucial impetus to the dress reform movement which had been gradually gaining momentum since the 1850s. In British fiction of the time, the image of female cyclists' 'rational dress' is often used by male authors as an emblem of women's controversial challenge to societal codes. Wells's hero Hoopdriver in *The Wheels of Chance* is transfixed by the 'Young Lady in Grey' he beholds cycling towards him on the Surbiton road, while 'strange doubts possessed him as to the nature of her nether costume. He had heard of such things of course – French perhaps.'[140] On closer inspection he realises that 'the things were – yes – *rationals*!', a discovery which leads him to lose control of his bicycle and fall off.[141] The barmaid in an inn they stay at is equally shocked by Jessie's dress, remarking on its lack of gender specificity: 'There'll be no knowing which is which in a year or two.'[142] Even though Hoopdriver later learns Jessie's name, she is referred to as the 'Young Lady in Grey' throughout the narrative. The metonymic designation of the novel's heroine draws attention to the importance of Jessie's unconventional clothing as a symbol of her refusal of the traditional role society reserves for her. Yet, as we shall see in due course, the stress placed on Jessie's clothes is also symptomatic of the strict codification of women's cycling clothing, which allowed only a limited measure of comfort and mobility.

In various novels of the period, clothing associated with cycling enshrines female resistance to patriarchal authority. Mary E. Kennard provides a portrait of an upper-class woman's love affair with the bicycle in her novel *The Golf Lunatic and his Cycling Wife* (1902), in which Cynthia asserts that 'truly it may be said that woman a-wheel is woman emancipated'.[143] When Cynthia, on returning from a bicycle tour of several weeks, is asked by her unfaithful husband to entertain his new love interest, she hesitates between two outfits. One denotes submission to, the other rejection of, her subordinate position as a cheated wife:

> I debated whether to put on my oldest clothes and go out bicycling, or to dress myself nicely and do as my husband had bidden me. I was racked by indecision. I [. . .] descended to my room in order to don my cycling skirt.[144]

Here Cynthia expresses resistance to her tyrannical husband's demeaning request through her choice of clothing, which enshrines either acceptance or refusal of women's subordinate position. Grant Allen's heroines also employ their cycling wear as an outward symbol of liberation, donning cycling costumes in unexpected contexts. In *The Type-Writer Girl* (1897), Juliet wears her 'cycling suit in the fields, and laboured like a man' at an anarchist settlement, while in *Miss Cayley's Adventures* (1899), Lois remarks that in India 'my short bicycling skirt did beautifully for tiger-hunting'.[145] The stereotypically masculine activities in which these women participate while wearing cycling costumes draw attention to the symbolically loaded potential of the bicycle. Women's discovery of mobility gave them the possibility to venture beyond the domestic sphere, providing access to areas of work and recreation previously reserved for men.

While cycling apparel gave women the chance to move more freely, the activity itself is presented as a lesson in autonomy for women by certain authors. Moving alone through city streets and country roads was a novel and emancipating experience for women. Juliet notes in *The Type-Writer Girl*: 'A woman on a bicycle has all the world before her where to choose; she can go where she will, no man hindering.'[146] Mary Kennard similarly insists on the importance of this new-found mobility in her *Guide Book for Lady Cyclists*, arguing that

> [a bicycle] widens the general vista in a most extraordinary manner, and enlarges the limitations by which ordinary women are surrounded. It thrusts back the prison walls, and gives her freedom and independence, such as she had never even dreamed of. Instead of a two-mile area, she can now rejoice in one of forty or fifty miles.[147]

While opening up a new geography, especially for those living in rural areas, cycling allowed women to cultivate new physical and mental capacities. In Emile Zola's *Paris* (1897), Marie claims that cycling allows women to 'learn to navigate through life'.[148] Discussing the matter with the priest Pierre, she makes a strong case for the transformation cycling can bring about in women's habits, minds and outlooks:

> Think of those girls whose mothers bring them up sheltered under their skirts. They are taught to be afraid of everything, they are forbidden from taking any initiative, their judgement and willpower are never called upon, so that they do not even know how to cross the street, paralysed by the idea of obstacles . . . Put a young girl upon a bicycle, and set her free on the roads: she will have to open her eyes, to see and avoid the pebble, to turn at the right moment and in the right direction, when a bend in the road appears [. . .] Overall, is this not a continual apprenticeship in willpower, an admirable lesson in conduct and defence? [. . .] I mean that those who can avoid the pebbles, who turn at the right moment on the road, will also know how to overcome difficulties and make the best decisions in their social and emotional lives, with a clear, honest, solid intelligence.[149]

Marie here makes a compelling association between the physical negotiation of obstacles on the road and the ability to carve out an individual path in the world. Her confident tone, rhetorical questions and frequent use of imperatives provide a vivid illustration of her argument, revealing that she herself is a self-reliant and intelligent young woman. She clearly recognises that women's subservience is socially conditioned, starting from infancy when young girls are taught to be afraid of obstacles rather than attempt to overcome them. As Marie recognises, the physical mobility offered by the bicycle had crucial psychological implications; it provided women with a practical means to cast off their dependent role and learn to make autonomous choices.

Similarly, for Allen's Miss Cayley, the ability to ride a bicycle is closely linked to an enterprising approach to life. This is clear in the heroine's introductory description of herself:

> having large dark eyes, with a bit of a twinkle in them, and being as well able to pilot a bicycle as any girl of my acquaintance, I have inherited or acquired an outlook on the world which distinctly leans rather towards cheeriness than despondency.[150]

In addition to giving her good humour, cycling has taught Lois Cayley how to be savvy, resourceful and independent. Indeed, at the start of the novel she is able to make the decision to 'Put on my hat and walk out'[151] into London in search of opportunity as a result of the sense of adventure and self-reliance cycling has taught her. As we shall see in Chapter 3, the bicycle is unique among other transportation technologies in that it enhances rather than diminishes faith in the body's abilities. New Women cyclists in literature tend to express a sense of physical and intellectual empowerment; they remain keenly connected to their bodies while reaping the benefits of a machine that optimises their locomotive capacities.

In contemporary societies, just as in the Victorian era, cycling gives women the opportunity to feel secure and legitimate in potentially hostile environments. The bicycle effectively functions as a weapon of self-defence, allowing women to travel safely and rapidly away from localities where they might otherwise be at risk. In Wells's *The Wheels of Chance*, when Bechamel makes uninvited sexual advances towards Jessie, the young woman's bicycle allows her to flee from him in order to avoid sharing his hotel room for the night.[152] In Allen's *The Type-Writer Girl*, the male members of the anarchist settlement initially use the bicycle lessons offered to them by Juliet as a means to 'entice [her] away from the common field towards remoter lanes where occasions for private talk were more easily obtained'.[153] Yet the bicycle ultimately acts as her way out of this potentially dangerous situation. The men's unwanted attention motivates her decision to leave, at which point the community attempts to confiscate her bicycle. Juliet flatly refuses and hastily cycles off, in a vivid demonstration of the vehicle's potential to allow women to distance themselves from would-be aggressors. Allen's other cycling heroine, Lois Cayley, also makes a getaway from an unknown male cyclist who begins pursuing her. Despite his opening remark when he finally corners her – 'you're a lady of considerable personal attractions'[154] – her pursuer's motives turn out to be economic rather than sexual; he is impressed by her skill as a cyclist and offers her a job racing a machine he has invented at a promotional event.

While the bicycle could offer women the means to protect themselves, some authors also depicted female cyclists as fearless knights in shining armour, physically and mentally equipped to rescue their lover where he had once rescued her.[155] One example of this trope may be found in *Miss Cayley's Adventures*, in a scene where Lois rescues her lover Harold after he has fallen over a precipice. In her rush to reach him, Lois does not heed her more conventional friend Elsie's advice to 'hurry down on our cycles to Lungern and call some men from the village to help us'.[156] Instead, she rescues him herself, descending down a sheer cliff face on a rope wearing her 'dog-skin bicycling gloves', and thus proving her belief that 'women are almost always brave in the great emergencies'.[157] In the story 'A Fin de Cycle Incident' (1897) by Edna C. Jackson from the United States, another melodramatic woman-rescues-man scene takes place. The young cycling heroine Renie Raine resolves to give up cycling for the sake of her fiancé Horace Waldon, who harbours very conventional ideas about suitable female conduct and dress. However, on what Renie decides will be her last ride before her marriage, she overhears some men in a wood plotting to rob and kill her betrothed during his journey home by horse. In order to reach him before the robbers, she casts off her 'encumbering skirt' and rides speedily in bloomers along the railway tracks. She manages to get ahead of the robbers by taking a short cut through a railway tunnel, jumping off her bike at the last minute before it is crushed by a train arriving behind her. Although the bicycle's ritual sacrifice at the end of the story might appear to suggest a definitive end to cycling for Renie, in fact this rescue scene changes Harold's outlook on women and cycling. Following their marriage, the couple enjoy bicycle rides together, with the wrecked bicycle being kept as 'a precious relic in Mr Waldon's library'.[158] These examples point to the bicycle's symbolic role in transforming the spheres of activity that were traditionally associated with women.

Cycling also affords precious moments of female homosociality within the space of these novels.[159] As Virginia Woolf (1882–1941) remarked in *A Room of One's Own* (1929), representations of women in fiction throughout history have consistently reduced them to their role as wives and mothers, neglecting to portray ties of friendship or love between women. 'All these relationships between women [. . .] are too simple. So much has been left out, unattempted', Woolf argues.[160] She goes on to observe that 'almost without exception they are shown in their relation to men [. . .] all the great women of fiction were, until Jane Austen's day, not only seen by the other sex, but seen only in relation to the other sex'.[161] Wells and Allen generally omit scenes of female bonding from their New Women novels; in fact, female characters are more often portrayed as having antagonistic relationships with each other, as we shall see. Moreover, each of their heroines conforms to patriarchal expectations by either directly or implicitly heading for matrimony at the end of the novel. However, the female authors Mary Kennard and L. T. Meade both draw attention to the empowering women-only spaces that bicycles helped foster. Kennard draws on autobiographical details from a journey with her sister[162] in order to narrate Cynthia and her friend Dora's cycle trip to Scotland, which leaves them 'proud of the muscles and the energy which in six days had accomplished a distance of over three hundred miles'.[163] On arriving at their destination, Cynthia asks, 'After that, who will dare affirm that women can't get on together, and are helpless without a man to look after them?'[164]

Cycling was thus a practical means for women to create ties beyond the domestic sphere and carve out a role in society independent of their relationship to men. Systems of mutual support were fostered by the activity of cycling, allowing women to liberate themselves from their traditional reliance on their fathers or husbands. In Meade's *The Cleverest Woman in England* (1898), a New Woman novel brimming with scenes of female bonding bordering on the erotic, the bicycle plays a minor but significant role. When her maid Lucy is unwell, the feminist campaigner Dagmar prescribes cycling as 'one of the grandest cures for indigestion', and makes sure her protégée is able to acquire a bicycle.[165] Dagmar's recommendation is particularly significant in the context of the contemporary medical debate around the bicycle, which saw some outspoken male doctors maintaining that cycling could provoke various health disorders for women. Although this advice eventually results in Lucy's dismissal – since Dagmar's mother-in-law is scandalised to see their maid on a bicycle – it provides a significant instance of women cutting themselves free from the male-dominated medical establishment in order to seek new modes of female sociability and support. The bicycle facilitated this by providing the means for women to socialise independently, fostering relationships beyond the family sphere.

A final instance of the bicycle's positive role in transforming the lives of women is the fact that it could provide new sources of paid employment. In 1896, the cycling periodical *The Hub* published an article entitled 'How Some Wheelwomen Earn Money', which included interviews with female bicycle mechanics and cycle instructors.[166] Mary Kennard's cycling heroine Cynthia earns money by testing out and reviewing bicycles for a magazine.[167] Matthias Mc Donnell Bodkin places his female detective on wheels in *Dora Myrl: The Lady Detective*, while Ada L. Harris's *A Widow on Wheels* and Mrs Westmacott in Arthur Conan Doyle's *Beyond the City* provide further portraits of financially autonomous cycling women.[168] Allen's Lois Cayley is an independent globe trotter who manages to make her living first from bicycle racing, and subsequently by becoming a cycle saleswoman.[169] As such, the bicycle was portrayed in literature as a technology – among many others at the turn of the century – that accompanied and facilitated women's gradual accession to the sphere of paid employment.

In many ways, then, literature reflects the bicycle's role in bringing real changes to the lives of women. Yet it should not be forgotten that the bicycle, as well as the New Woman, played a role in emerging commodity culture, and could be manipulated to serve certain ends. As Chris Willis argues, at the turn of the century 'the New Woman had become a marketable novelty figure whose presence in a story increased its chance of good sales'.[170] As we saw in Chapter 1, the inclusion of the fashionable bicycle in literature could function as a sales pitch, drawing readers' attention to a specific book because of the desirability and novelty of the object it displayed. Moreover, the cycling New Woman has been viewed by Andrew Shrimpton as 'perfectly attuned to the demands of a mass consumption economy', in that she is a glamorous woman, well patronised by advertising, who uses consumer goods for the purposes of self-fulfilment, to express her own 'individuality' along lines that are considered 'daring' or 'risqué'.[171] The bicycle was one of the most conspicuous means by which the New Woman expressed her identity, thus performing the role of the consumer that the twentieth century held specially in store for housewives. While many lively descriptions of liberated, adventurous young cycling women may be found in literature, the majority of these intrepid heroines are heading for matrimony, motherhood and domesticity by the end of the story. I shall now turn my attention to the attempt made to contain the dangerous spectre of the liberated female cyclist within another stereotype: that of the lady cyclist.

Domesticated Mobility: The Lady Cyclist

Friedrich Kittler argues that around 1900, the image of woman as sexual object and mother was replaced in the cultural imagination by woman as information worker: typist, telegraphist, secretary. He points out how the character Mina Harker in Bram Stoker's *Dracula* (1897), for instance, becomes 'the central relay station of an immense information network' which is largely controlled by men.[172] Kittler's example goes to show that new technologies were not necessarily liberating; depending on the uses to which they were put, and the meanings given to them, they might become means of bolstering patterns of domination.[173] In society as well as in literature a domesticated, ladylike paradigm of female cycling emerged, seeking to defuse the threat of overly liberated women. Ellen Gruber Garvey's examination of a number of fictional portrayals of female cyclists in newspapers and periodicals in the USA in the 1890s reveals that such literature, alongside contemporary advertising and journalism, functioned to foster an acceptable image of female cycling, one which reaffirmed rather than challenged the prevailing social order:

> Because the fears women's bicycling raised were primarily social, fiction, with its articulation of social relationships, was better suited than medical articles or other coverage to take the sting out of those fears. It reconfigured the relationships the bicycle seemed to be changing and assigned new meanings to those changes. Fiction carried the burden of instructing readers in the complexities of the bicycle's social meaning, investing it with romance and glamour, and reassuring readers that riding would not disrupt the social order.[174]

Indeed, behind the emancipatory image of the bicycle lurked deep misgivings about women's evolving status, and a desire to assign meanings to such changes that would not threaten the established order. Garvey shows how the bicycle manufacturing industry in the 1890s (which was closely tied to cycling newspapers and magazines) was keenly interested in doubling its market by selling its wares to women, but in order to do so it was obliged to tackle contemporary fears around the health and moral dangers of the activity. Some doctors maintained that reproductive capacities would be jeopardised, while others claimed that women would experience sexual pleasure on their bicycles. As Garvey argues, these debates both mirrored and masked the revolutionary potential of autonomous mobility for women:

> the medicalized masturbation metaphor was a particularly compelling one because both the bicycling woman and the masturbating woman were out of male control, possibly doing damage to 'the race' [. . .] Of course the real issue at stake was not masturbation but women's mobility and independence.[175]

Garvey points out how, in order to foster an acceptable image of female cycling, specialised saddles, frames and clothes were marketed to women, with both fiction writers and the press actively seeking to cultivate a respectable image of the activity. Zack Furness takes up Garvey's observation and similarly argues that

> This period functioned as a 'test drive' not only for the type of marketing techniques eventually used to sell women both automobiles and a consumption-based idea of liberation but also for men to utilize popular

media as a tool for disciplining women's transportation habits and their mobility more broadly.[176]

This perspective sheds new light on the questions of dress and mobility already discussed in the previous section. While the clothing associated with cycling could allow women more physical comfort, it could also coerce them into respecting a very rigid set of cultural codes. By placing excessive emphasis on the question of clothing, writers contributed to the perpetuation of the male gaze and, along with the medical debate, shrouded the real issue at hand: that of women's mobility. Many cycling periodicals from this period contain columns on 'Cycling for Ladies', which are predominantly concerned with the subject of fashion. In the first edition of the successful periodical *The Cycling World Illustrated*, for instance, the ladies' column was titled 'Arrayed like one of these', a title that hints at the still controversial status of women's cycling dress.[177] The column dealt solely with the question of clothing, and promoted a markedly conservative approach. The renaming of the column as 'Array yourself becomingly' in the following month is indicative of an explicit injunction to women cyclists to adhere to society's dress codes, rather than choose the most practical or comfortable outfit for their activity.[178] Indeed, the pinched waists, long skirts and complicated hats recommended by *The Cycling World Illustrated* do not suggest that practicality was the main concern. Rather, women's priority was to continue to appear graceful and ladylike, in spite of their indulgence in this novel physical activity.

In Virginia Niles Leeds's 1897 story 'A Coast and a Capture', the narrator Josephine describes how, on donning her brother's trousers for a clandestine nocturnal bike ride, she is finally able to benefit from a freedom of movement that would have been impossible in a heavy ankle-length skirt:

> Oh, the luxury of jumping on! The words convey nothing to those who, like myself, have always had to wait until the right pedal is just exactly at a certain angle; then, placing one foot upon it, have had to balance in mid-air, as it were, while we divided our skirt and wriggled into position on the saddle. Nothing of that now. I gave the machine a little shove-off first, then I hopped on as easily as you please, and I felt as I fancy the slaves must have felt after the Emancipation Act.[179]

This precise description of the difficulty of mounting a bicycle in a long skirt (even if it was a divided one, designed for cycling) and the contrasting ease of 'jumping on' in trousers provides a clear illustration of the tangible changes that dress could make in women's experience. The simplicity and delight of riding in trousers is reflected in the opening exclamation, while the complex syntax of the following sentence mirrors the difficulty of mounting a bicycle in a heavy skirt. It is important to note that in the above story the heroine must wait for the cover of darkness in order to secretly don her brother's clothes and take his bicycle out for a ride. Indeed, bloomers remained taboo in many places into the twentieth century, and the majority of early female cyclists in Britain wore either specially adapted skirts or the more daring 'rational dress', consisting of knickerbockers, leggings and a long coat.[180] Even this costume was hotly contested; in 1898 Lady Harberton, president of the Rational Dress Society, took the proprietor of a coffee room to court for refusing her service on account of her dress. In Dorothy Richardson's *The Tunnel* (1919), which is examined at length in Chapter 3, Miriam's progressive friends Jan and Mag confide that 'We went out – last night – after dark – and rode – round Russell Square – twice – in our knickers.'[181] Although they do also ride bicycles in the daytime, they are unable to enjoy the experience fully due to the restrictive clothes and demure attitude they are required to adopt. As with Josephine, it is only the cover of darkness that allows these women to fully experience the true 'freedom of movement' that comes from riding a bicycle in loose, practical clothes that were still thought of as 'unfeminine'.

Mary Kennard's *Guide Book for Lady Cyclists* includes two chapters on 'The Great Dress Question'. Kennard offers a number of practical suggestions, including how to make one's own cycling skirt,[182] yet ultimately she remains compliant with the late Victorian society in which she lives, and rejects the still controversial rational dress. She advises:

> The female cyclist is wise to make concessions to public opinion [. . .] If it were the fashion in this country for ladies of good standing and position to wear knickerbockers, and if they could appear as freely in them as in France, without shocking the non-cycling portion of the community, then, no doubt much might be adduced in their favour [. . .] The English are essentially a modest nation, and the male portion of the community are, as a rule, particular about their womenkind. Men like them to be feminine and lady-like in appearance, and more especially so, when they begin to intrude a little on what they have hitherto considered their province.[183]

Here Kennard puts her finger on the real issue at hand: the fact that bicycles allowed women to 'intrude' on the male province of mobility.

In response to this threat, a larger discourse established a domesticated image of female cyclists by defining the clothes they were and were not permitted to wear. Kennard later emphasises that

> the wheel-woman of the upper class should do everything in her power to conciliate, and prove that she does not desire to rival man, but only to enjoy a delightful and exhilarating sport in a quiet, unobtrusive and ladylike fashion.[184]

Clothing that aligned with the expectations of patriarchal society was one of the main means by which cycling women were constrained to adopt a heavily gendered version of mobility. Rather than empowering them, cycling could be used to deny women the physical comfort enjoyed by men while reinforcing their objectified role. Alongside discourses on acceptable cycle clothing for women, bicycle manufacturers adapted the vehicle itself to traditional women's clothing in order to foster a respectable image of the activity. Nicolas Oddy has examined the precocious gendering of the bicycle, noting that the concept of differentiated men's and women's bicycles was established in the late nineteenth century and has persisted to the present day. This is in spite of the fact that the 'assumptions about women's clothing which were current a century ago [. . .] are now severely out of date if not completely irrelevant'.[185] As we have seen, even at the time assumptions about women's clothing were being radically questioned, and the fact that bicycles were designed to accommodate long, bulky skirts tells us much about the bicycle industry's perpetuation of social norms.

The dropped frame marketed at women (and priests) was weaker and heavier than the standard diamond frame, a fact well recognised by Kennard. It is worth quoting her opinion on the subject at length, once again taken from her *Guide Book for Lady Cyclists*:

> A great many ladies prefer the dropped or rounded frame, which consists of one or two curved tubes. They are supposed to give more room for the dress, and beginners find them easier for mounting and dismounting. Otherwise it is hard to account for their preponderance. At this year's National Show, I was surprised at the number exhibited, and on enquiring the reason of several manufacturers, was informed that the frames were so constructed in compliance with the demand for them which had arisen in fashionable circles. In every instance, however, the makers deprecated the design, considering that, if extra comfort were gained, it was obtained at the expense of strength and rigidity. Now, if any lady once mounts a gentleman's machine, she will be surprised at the ease with

which she propels it in comparison with her own. It runs much more lightly. This, in great measure, is attributable to the diamond-shaped frame. The dropped frame is structurally weak, in spite of all the stays that have been devised to add to its support. It is also comparatively heavy.[186]

Despite the mechanical superiority of the diamond frame, the demand in 'fashionable circles' to keep women in skirts took precedence over considerations of efficiency and comfort. Moreover, Garvey shows how the medical discourse around the 'risk' of clitoral stimulation from the saddle condemned the forward-leaning, racing position, strongly encouraging women to adopt an upright posture on a dropped frame.[187] The weight and design of women's bicycles made them more difficult to ride as quickly as men's machines, encouraging women not to 'scorch' and to respect the feminine ideal of slow, graceful riding.

Kennard admits, when discussing the dress question, that 'there is one point which the divided style of costume undoubtedly possesses; it enables the rider to ride a diamond-framed machine'.[188] In Kennard's fiction, female characters gladly cast off social conventions in order to ride their bicycles. Cynthia, for instance, describes how she 'loved wandering about alone, looking at sky and earth, not as a dressed-up puppet afraid of spoiling her clothes, but as an unconventional individual'.[189] When Cynthia becomes a cycling correspondent for a magazine, she tests out a light, high-geared machine. Many readers' letters respond to her positive review, allowing Cynthia to discover 'that a very large section of the feminine element liked going a good pace, and being able to keep up with their husbands and brothers. In fact, they showed a considerable hankering after speed.'[190] However, in spite of certain women's equal desire for light, efficient and robust machines, the bicycle industry continued to produce ladies' models which mainly responded to the criterion of respecting established codes on female dress and behaviour. The determination to keep women riding at a moderate pace in traditional clothing led to the promotion of a model that refused women the ease with which men piloted their machines, and offered them a compromised vehicle which, incongruously, is still thought of as a 'ladies' bicycle' to the present day. Thus, even if cycling women gained a measure of equality with men, it should not be forgotten that some cyclists were more equal than others.

These discourses around clothing and the machine itself emerged alongside certain decorative, ladylike uses of the bicycle. Philip Gordon

Mackintosh has illustrated how a 'domesticating' and 'womanly' discourse was constructed around cycling in Canada at the turn of the century.[191] This was effected by such means as bicycle gymkhanas and parades, during which the machines and their riders were decorated with flowers, ribbons and banners, and various games were played. Images and accounts of such events frequently recurred in the British cycling press, especially in those publications aimed at women, such as *The Cycling World Illustrated*. While Mackintosh focuses on the class issue, portraying such events as manifestations of 'a bourgeois attempt to control the public use of the bicycle',[192] this discourse also had an important gender dimension. It promoted a purely decorative image of an object that had the potential to widen women's limited sphere of activity. Such ornamental use of the bicycle contrasts sharply with the masculine ideal of cycle racing being developed at this time. While women's velocipede races had been organised in Paris as early as 1868, female competitive cycling was a marginalised, taboo or ridiculed activity, and women were strongly sanctioned against fast riding in general. As Claire Simpson observes, women's cycle racing at the turn of century was often used as humorous entertainment or a publicity stunt, giving men the opportunity to enjoy the sight of scantily clad women. Simpson records how 'women's races were routinely staged between acts at the theatre and music hall, or on the programmes of freak shows, commercial advertising shows, acrobatics exhibitions and so forth'.[193]

Echoes of such an attitude may be traced in literature. Grant Allen's heroine Lois Cayley, for instance, is hired as a racing cyclist purely due to the selling power of her gender and physical appearance, as the inventor frankly admits in his strangely transcribed American accent: 'ef a female wins, it makes success all the more striking and con-spicuous. The world to-day *is* ruled *by* advertizement.'[194] He later emphasises 'It ain't only your skill, you see [. . .] It's your personal attractiveness as well that I go upon.'[195] Moreover, the political meaning attached to the activity could be heavily circumscribed by specific groups. For instance, Linda Walker notes that the Conservative Party established a cycling group for women in the 1890s called the Primrose Cycling Corps. Walker quotes the Duke of Malborough, who noted that 'if women were out canvassing for the Conservative Party in the 1895 election, we can safely assume that by then the bicycle had become an acceptable expression of femininity'.[196] When mobilised by the party ruling the country at the time, one that held an ambivalent attitude to women's suffrage and promoted a domesticated view of women's responsibilities, the revolutionary image of cycling could indeed be radically curtailed.

Literature reflected society's ambivalent attitude towards the new freedoms cycling could afford women, with some authors seeking to defuse the threat of emancipated female cyclists. In contrast to the positive images of female friendships fostered by cycling offered by Kennard and Meade, the male authors in our corpus more often portray antagonistic relationships between female cyclists and other women. A case in point is the relationship between Jessie and her stepmother Mrs Milton in Wells's *The Wheels of Chance*. When the novel's protagonist Hoopdriver first encounters her, Jessie has fled her stepmother's stifling home and is travelling around the south of England in order 'to come out into the world, to be a human being – not a thing in a hutch'.[197] Yet the home she has left is that of an independent widow, and a New Woman novelist to boot. Jessie's desire for freedom, the novel makes clear, emerged from her reading of the type of literature her stepmother produces. 'Her motives are bookish,' the narrator affirms, 'written by a haphazard syndicate of authors, novelists, biographers, on her white inexperience.'[198] Yet her stepmother claims that her books have been 'misunderstood, misapplied' by young women such as Jessie, who take their message too literally. 'I want people to *think* as I recommend, not to *do* as I recommend,' Mrs Milton maintains, arguing that unlike her wayward stepdaughter, the heroine of her most famous novel 'never flaunted her freedom – on a bicycle, in country places'.[199] The dispute between Jessie and her stepmother suggests that even those women who claim to be working for emancipation are unable to agree on the degrees and forms of freedom women should be accorded. In Wells's novel the bicycle thus functions as a marker of the tension between the theoretical and practical applications of women's liberation.

A similar clash between the opinions of a cyclist and those of women with a more traditional outlook occurs in Arthur Conan Doyle's *Beyond the City* (1891). The boisterous widow Mrs Westmacott is an identikit New Woman: she smokes, drinks stout and distributes posters for meetings on the enfranchisement of woman from her tandem tricycle (piloted along with her compliant nephew). Her widower neighbour Mr Walker admires her, and professes to share her opinions on the equality of the sexes. Yet when his more conservative daughters fear that he is planning to propose to Mrs Westmacott, they devise a cunning plan to prevent the union, which they think would be doomed to failure. These once demure young women begin to conduct science experiments, think up career plans, dress in rational costume, smoke and hold dinner parties with young men. On witnessing this transformation in his darling daughters, their father is appalled. Seeing he is upset, Mrs Westmacott advises cycling as a calmant ('You should come with me for a ten-mile spin upon the tandem'), before firmly reminding him that 'You must live up to your principles – you must give your daughters the same liberty as you advocate for other women.'[200] Yet Mr Walker instead abandons the idea of proposing to Mrs Westmacott, ordering his daughters to 'forget these odious notions which you have imbibed [. . .] dress and act as you used to do before ever you saw this woman'.[201] Even Mrs Westmacott, who sees through the sisters' ruse, admits to them after they have given up their act that 'really I think I like you better as you are'.[202] Like Wells, Doyle stages a confrontation between those who profess a belief in gender equality and those who boldly put it into action, with the female cyclist clearly designating the latter category. Both authors use the bicycle as a means to demonstrate the conviction that women's liberation cannot work in practice, either because society at large is not yet ready for it, or because people will never agree on the degrees of freedom women should enjoy.

To return to *The Wheels of Chance*, Jessie's attempt to liberate herself is initially portrayed as an admirable undertaking, yet the narrative effectively functions to disqualify her bid for freedom. Jessie's confident flight from the villas of Surbiton mirrors the somewhat more hesitant 'Riding Forth of Mr Hoopdriver' a few chapters earlier, and her desire to create a new identity for herself as a liberated woman clearly parallels Hoopdriver's wish to reinvent himself beyond class divisions. The draper goes on a cycling holiday in order to refuse 'being put in the cage', a phrase that foreshadows Jessie's later description of her condition as 'a thing in a hutch'.[203] However, Wells finally foregrounds Hoopdriver's struggle for class equality over Jessie's attempt to emancipate herself. Jessie and Hoopdriver are only able to remain on the run from Mrs Milton and her various male admirers as long as their funds last. This realisation comes as a surprise to the young woman: '"Money!" said Jessie. "Is it possible – ? Surely! Conventionality! May only people of assured means Live their own Lives? What a curious light – !"'[204] As Lena Wanggren has pointed out, the capitalisation of Jessie's phrases stresses her perceived naivety: 'Like the capitalization of the initial letters of New Woman, the initial capital letters here [. . .] signify these as concepts, abstract ideas, more than concrete objects and occupations.'[205] The reader is already under the impression that Jessie's ideas of freedom are vague and ill informed, but her aspirations are dealt the final death-blow by her admission in the closing pages of the novel, following an upbraiding by her stepmother, a clergyman and a former teacher. 'Women write in books about being free, and living our own life, and all that kind of thing,' Jessie remarks, but she concludes: 'No one is free, free even from working for a living, unless at the expense of someone else. I did not think of that.'[206] As Simon J. James notes, Wells's revisions to *The Wheels of Chance* in 1901 and 1925 silenced Jessie's proto-Woolfian plea for female equality.[207] Whereas in the original 1896 edition Jessie only agrees to return home on her stepmother's acceptance of certain demands – 'I want a room of my own, what books I need to read, to be free to go out by myself alone'[208] – in the final cut she silences her appeal and plainly states that economic realities come before considerations of gender equality. Similarly, in Wells's dramatic adaptation of his novel, *Hoopdriver's Holiday* (1904), Jessie manages to escape her stepmother to live with a more liberal aunt, yet Hoopdriver gets the final word, making a lengthy closing speech about class inequalities.[209] In this tale Wells displays a clear interest in the feminist cause, but his class focus effectively establishes a hierarchy in which patriarchy may only be overthrown after capitalism, rather than reflecting on the ways in which the two struggles might converge. Thus, while appearing to recognise and integrate contemporary women's demands for equality in the figure of the cyclist, Wells's cycling novella (especially in the revised version from 1901) functions to disqualify Jessie's appeal for liberty.

In George Gissing's story 'A Daughter of the Lodge' (1901), the bicycle is also mobilised as a means to point to the supremacy of the class struggle over gender considerations. When the women's rights campaigner May Rockett returns to visit her parents, the keepers of the lodge for the aristocratic Shale family, her class difference from the Shales' daughter Hilda is accentuated by the latter's possession of a bicycle. 'It's a pity the machines can't be sold cheaper',[210] Hilda remarks condescendingly, in order to draw attention to May's inferior class at a social gathering where one of the main topics is women's emancipation. May, who 'would have long ago bought a bicycle had she been able to afford it',[211] leaves the gathering angrily and, on reaching home at the same time as Hilda, refuses to open the gate for the upper-class cyclist. This lack of respect for her parents' employers leads to a crisis in which the Rocketts are almost evicted, but May's grovelling apology saves them from disaster at the last minute. Gissing's tale, like those of his contemporaries Wells and Doyle, complicates the bicycle's role in emancipating women. In common with Wells, Gissing suggests that considerations of class are paramount. Both May and Hilda are battling for gender equality, yet their diverging classes prevent them from cooperating, and the bicycle acts as an outward symbol of the antagonism between them. It is interesting to recall here that in Wells's first novel, *The Time Machine* (1895), the Time Traveller travels on a bicycle-like time machine to a nearly genderless future, where, however, class divisions have become tragically salient. 'In costume, and in all the differences of texture and bearing that now mark the sexes from each other, these people of the future were alike',[212] the Time Traveller remarks of the idle Eloi, before he discovers that they are both looked after and preyed upon by the subterranean worker Morlocks. It appears that for authors such as Wells, sexual inequality would organically disappear or resolve itself in the future, while the class struggle would have to be actively fought in order to reach the desired conclusion.

While cycling allowed women a certain degree of autonomy, discourses around the activity were heavily influenced by the patriarchal society in which these newly mobile women lived. A focus on fashion, the design of the 'ladies' frame', vehement medical debates and the promotion of certain ornamental interpretations of women's cycling all attempted to exclude women from enjoying the full benefits of this levelling form of transport. In literature, the bicycle became a symbol of women who went 'too far' in their demand for equality; cyclists like Jessie became stereotypes of the overly liberated woman, who eventually returned to the fold of society and matrimony with her tail between her legs. Yet even if the bicycle could become an outward symbol of women's conspicuous consumption, and of their subordination, it is interesting to note that the actual experience of cycling could encourage an ascetic outlook that went counter to this tendency. In Mary Kennard's novel *The Golf Lunatic and his Cycling Wife*, during a cycling tour the heroine's friend Dora has to renounce her desire to go shopping because of the limited space in their luggage. The narrator is grateful that

> Fortunately, any increase in our luggage was an impossibility. She was therefore forced to refrain from blouses, hats, jackets and all the rest of it. Bicycling has that advantage. You cannot spend money on personal attire, and the ordinary female when touring saves considerably in this direction alone. It is good for her, too, to exercise self-control. To admire without possessing is a salutary lesson for some of the sex.[213]

The sparing, practical tone of Kennard's writing here mirrors the outlook of the touring cyclist, who must refuse any superfluous elements in her luggage. While it was itself a consumer object, the bicycle placed a limit on the number of personal effects one could transport, encouraging a more sober approach than that being encouraged by consumer society at the time, especially as promoted to women. Ultimately, although women cyclists faced many obstacles, they could use their bicycles to navigate subversive routes beyond the consumerist, patriarchal thrust of the societies in which they lived.

Albertine the Cyclist: A Queer Feminist Bicycle Ride through *In Search of Lost Time*

We have thus far been considering the bicycle's interaction with issues of class and gender principally in a British context. I now propose to turn to French literature in order to examine the bicycle's crucial role in allowing its users to transgress social and sexual boundaries and formulate radical new identities.[214] The previous section showed how problematic it is to view the bicycle purely as a 'freedom machine' for women, as society formulated a heavily gendered interpretation of the activity, continuing to circumscribe women to a restrictive, domestic role. In examining Proust's use of the bicycle, I explore what was perhaps the technology's most important interaction with questions of gender and class: its ability to blur the very distinctions that constitute these categories. As we have seen throughout this chapter, the clothes that cyclists wore and the attitudes they adopted as a result of contact with this new technology boldly declared that gender and class were not fixed states, but fluctuating social constructions.

The period of the bicycle boom in France corresponds chronologically with the events of *In Search of Lost Time* (published 1913–27). The seven novels are set in the period spanning c. 1879 to 1919, and given Proust's commitment to reviving every detail of a lost world, it comes as little surprise that the then hugely popular machine features in his masterpiece. The bicycle makes its first appearance towards the end of the second volume, *Within a Budding Grove* (1919), pushed along the beach by the young woman who will remain central to much of the rest of the work, Albertine. This emblematic scene has been examined by several critics, but until now little attention has been given to subsequent appearances of cyclists, notably in *Sodom and Gomorrah* (1921–22), *The Prisoner* (1923) and *The Fugitive* (1925).[215] By following the bicycle's complex itinerary through the universe of *In Search of Lost Time*, I unravel the machine's rich contribution to the ever-shifting portrait of the novel's heroine, a woman who dares to challenge the strict moral codes of bourgeois society. Albertine's bicycle is mobilised in order to trace the outlines of a radical new social order, one which would embrace not only new gender and class identities, but also subversive sexual orientations.

The Apparition of a Cyclist

As was the case in Britain, the USA and elsewhere, the bicycle played an important role in the struggle of early French feminists, who saw in it both the symbolic and the actual means to achieve freedom in clothing, movement and lifestyle. Yet in the politically and socially strained context of *fin-de-siècle* France, many saw the rapidly evolving position of women as a sign of social decay, with traditional family and societal values being dangerously eroded. Detractors of the bicycle railed against women's newly discovered freedom to roam, deplored their adoption of the bloomers (*culottes*) required to ride the machine comfortably, and published articles on the supposed health dangers posed to women cyclists, claiming that bicycle saddles afforded women masturbatory pleasures or reduced their fertility.[216] In a society that still considered the main function of women to be reproductive, female cycling habits were partly held responsible for the country's falling birth rate.[217] Theories of social degeneration, influenced by social Darwinism and eugenics, helped spread the fear that the decadent bourgeois nation was on the decline.[218] As Christopher Thompson and Fiona Ratkoff have convincingly argued, the panic around degeneration 'became focused on the female cyclist',[219] an emblematic figure whose unexpected arrival in urban and rural France was indeed a striking symbol of the new zeitgeist.

The loaded symbolism of women's cycling is effectively conveyed in the memorable scene in which Albertine and her friends make their first appearance in *In Search of Lost Time*. There is no doubt in Proust's young narrator's mind, as he stands before the Grand Hôtel in the stylish French seaside resort of Balbec, that the young women he suddenly beholds striding across the beach are an entirely unknown and fascinating phenomenon. In this masterful sequence that resembles an impressionist painting, the group first appears as a moving blur and gradually acquires detail as the narrative progresses, as though the viewer were slowly stepping back from a canvas. One of the first observations the narrator makes about the indistinct group is that 'One of these strangers was pushing in front of her, with one hand, her bicycle.'[220] The anonymous cyclist is Albertine, and it is her bicycle that will repeatedly be used as a means to identify her, until her name is learned some time later. As Marie-Agnès Barathieu notes in her excellent study of the semantics of journeys in *In Search of*

Lost Time, Proust constitutes 'a metalanguage around and starting from the bicycle' in the characterisation of Albertine.[221] The bicycle stands defiantly at the end of the first phrase describing the protagonist, and will return in subsequent layers added to her portrait. As we shall see, her unconventional clothing, rough language and robust body are all connected to her identity as a cyclist.

The young women make their dramatic entry at the moment of the day when the bourgeois hotel guests are taking their daily stroll on the beach, and the awkward gestures of the latter (described as 'unharmonious') could not stand in greater contrast to the graceful, purposeful movement of the youthful 'flock of seagulls' clothed in their 'special outfits' designed for playing sports.[222] These women are clearly at ease in their 'beautiful bodies with beautiful legs, beautiful hips, healthy and calm faces, which looked agile and clever' as they move effortlessly across the beach.[223] Although they are walking, their bold, almost mechanised movements recall those of speedy cyclists: rather than avoiding obstacles, 'They [. . .] forced stationary people to move aside as though a machine were advancing.'[224] The young women move much more quickly than the stuffy bourgeois walkers, and one of them even leaps over a terrified old man as he sits on his deckchair.[225] The transfixed narrator overhears the loud conversation between the women: 'slang words which were so uncouth and cried so loudly . . . (amongst which I nonetheless made out the unpleasant phrase "live my own life")'.[226] This battle-cry of young womanhood instantly convinces the narrator that these women must have an even deeper involvement in the world of cycling than he had previously imagined. Abandoning the hypothesis that they are of a bourgeois background, he remarks, 'I concluded rather that all these young women belonged to the population which frequents velodromes, and must be the very young mistresses of racing cyclists.'[227] Thompson and Weber both point out that French cycling clubs and velodromes were increasingly frequented by the working class in the 1890s.[228] The narrator thus connects these young women with the social class at the polar opposite from his own, adding to his fascination with these strange creatures. As it turns out, however, they belong to 'the very wealthy petite bourgeoisie, from the world of business and industry'.[229] This increasingly wealthy middle class sought to mimic the habits of the upper class, thus explaining the young women's presence in the chic resort of Balbec.[230] Yet their irreverent behaviour as they cross the beach implies an audacious challenge rather than conformity to the dominant social hierarchy. Their erroneous association with working-class racing cyclists establishes them as radical, subversive elements in a carefully guarded social reality.

This evocative sequence, central to the rest of the work since it introduces Albertine, provides a compelling portrait of the changes being wrought in contemporary French society, and it is fitting that Proust should place 'the young woman with the bicycle' at its centre.[231] Siân Reynolds points to the British affectations in the speech and mannerisms of Albertine and her friends to argue that the New Woman was chiefly a cultural construct in the USA and Britain, maintaining that attempts to import her to France were forced and unsuccessful.[232] However, I would argue that such behaviour was typical of the climate of anglomania in *fin-de-siècle* France and does not necessarily imply that the French only inherited a copycat version of feminism. Albertine's bicycle, pushed in front of the group, acts as a banner announcing the birth of a new society. Françoise Gaillard points out that 'the young woman with the bicycle is an unstoppable force that not only shakes up strolling holidaymakers, but also social barriers, cultural codes and generational relations'.[233] By means of their daring behaviour, dress and language, the figures on the beach produce their own social space and provide a triumphant portrait of *la femme nouvelle*, a figure alternatively respected or reviled but at all events recognised as an important presence in turn-of-the-century France.

While certain contemporary commentators held that the bicycle contributed to social degeneration through its adverse effects on fertility and by facilitating women's freedom of movement, others argued that this new technology could play an important role in the regeneration of the declining nation through physical activity. Dr Just Lucas-Championnière argued that 'The bicycle represents women's accession to physical exercise; and physical exercise for women means the future regeneration of that part of the nation doomed to degeneration.'[234] The supreme feats of physical endurance accomplished by early racing cyclists even led some to imagine that a new race of superhumans would result from the invention of the bicycle, as we shall see in the analysis of Alfred Jarry's novel *Le Surmâle* in Chapter 3. Though Albertine does not win a 10,000-mile race against a steam train like Jarry's hero, she does pit herself against a machine, boasting that she can ride to the races at la Sogne three times faster than the tram.[235] In a rare manifestation of physical vigour, even the sickly narrator finds the energy to accompany the young women on their cycling day trips.[236] Thus, while presenting a challenge to conservative bourgeois society, Albertine and her friends also reflect the contemporary view

Desirable, Androgynous Cyclists

As the narrator gradually grows closer to Albertine, the bicycle continues to be mobilised as a means of identifying her and in order to symbolise the budding desire of the young man. The bicycle makes a passing appearance earlier in *Within a Budding Grove*, when the machine is first glimpsed by the narrator from the seat of Madame de Villeparisis's carriage, ridden by an anonymous, desirable 'farm girl', a 'shopkeeper's daughter' or an 'elegant young lady'.[237] These initial evocations bring the object into the narrator's field of vision, associating it with desire and fleeting visions of feminine beauty but attributing it to no one character in particular.[238] Its specific role becomes more concrete in the passage just examined, where the bicycle serves as a point of reference in a moving mass, and is subsequently used to identify Albertine in her different degrees of individualisation. As Barathieu observes, 'The label of cyclist is a practical means of differentiating [Albertine] from the others, and at the same time, this metonymic designation confirms the characteristic element enacted by the dynamics of the text.'[239] Indeed, the metonymic identification of Albertine as a cyclist provides us with a microcosmic example of Proust's aesthetics of perception, in which phenomena are first apprehended by their outward features, before gradually acquiring definition and meaning. Proust's writing seeks to mirror this accumulative and deceptive process of perception which constantly presents us with optical illusions ('optical errors'), since the object itself is ever changing; when 'we think we are catching up on it, it moves again'.[240] This description of perception itself vividly recalls the fragmentary visual perspective of a passing cyclist.

It is within this moving field of perception that desire takes root. Indeed, Albertine's identity as a fleeting, unattainable cyclist is key to her attraction. When she is finally introduced to her admirer in the painter Elstir's studio – seated in a 'silk dress' – the narrator finds her merely 'mediocre and touching' compared with the ravishing 'bicycling bacchante' he had glimpsed on several occasions in Balbec.[241] Later, in *The Prisoner*, the narrator will characterise Albertine as 'a fugitive being' and repeatedly recall her 'flying by on her bicycle' when trying to get to the root of his desperate jealousy and desire for her.[242] Thus, an appreciation of her beauty cannot simply rely on the fact of her physical attractiveness, but must also take into account her movement through space, her dynamism and speed. The connection between desire and movement is recalled in a further portrait of cyclists in *The Prisoner*, when the narrator and Albertine make an outing to the fashionable bois de Boulogne. The narrator describes how 'three young women were sitting beside the immense arch of their bicycles which stood next to them, like three immortals leaning on a cloud or on a fabulous steed on which they made their mythological journeys'.[243] These 'Goddesses'[244] provide their admiring onlookers with a glimpse into another realm, and the classical imagery suggests a fascination with a mythical past. Observing these beings, the narrator reflects on 'the similarities between desire and travel',[245] two themes wonderfully represented by the bicycles against which the women are leaning.

Elsewhere in the park, we are provided with a rare portrait of a cyclist in movement:

> Further along another young girl was kneeling near her bicycle, fixing it. Once the repair was finished, the young racer got on her bicycle, but without straddling it as a man would have done. For an instant the bicycle swayed, the young body seemed to have grown a sail, an immense wing; and soon we saw the young creature, half-human, half-winged, angel or peri, disappearing at full speed, continuing her voyage.[246]

This glimpse of a self-sufficient cyclist, who repairs and then mounts her bicycle before disappearing into the distance, provides an evocative illustration of women's new social horizons. The flight and bird metaphors used in this passage also echo turn-of-the-century literature and advertising posters, which frequently connected cycling to flight, often through images of winged young women (see Figure 2.2).[247] This part-human, part-bird, part-machine cyclist subversively merges the categories she belongs to. She could belong to Donna Haraway's cyborg world, in which 'people are not afraid of their joint kinship with animals and machines, not afraid of permanently partial identities and contradictory standpoints'.[248] Haraway emphasises how 'in retelling origin stories, cyborg authors subvert the central myths of origin of Western culture',[249] notably finding a way to reinvent the vulnerable, exploited image of femininity through contact with non-human elements. Proust's depiction of a winged female cyclist participates in a radical rethinking of the boundaries of both gender and the human by means of an intimate partnership with the machine.

Figure 2.2 Georges Massias, advertising poster for Cycles Gladiator, c. 1895. Public domain.

At a time when, according to Michel Foucault, medical authorities were attempting to rigidly classify sexuality according to fixed categories and repress any deviant forms of sexual desire,[250] Proust's narrative provides a subtle, subversive and very modern portrait of a fluid spectrum of gender and sexual identities. Rather than attempting to establish boundaries, Proust carefully points to new modes of identification through various characters and symbols. The bicycle proves to be a productive symbol for the author, as from its earliest days it was a technology that aroused suspicions of gender-blurring. It is interesting to note that in French there are at least two words for 'bicycle', one of which is feminine, *bicyclette*, and the other, *vélo*, masculine.[251] Although there are historical reasons for this, and there is some variation in their meaning (the former often alludes to old-fashioned town bicycles while the latter is used more generally and also applies to racers), they are essentially interchangeable and refer to the same object. Yet the bicycle's lack of gender specificity is more than just a linguistic quirk. Some nineteenth-century observers were particularly alarmed by the degendering of female cyclists. Sarah Bernhardt and Stéphane Mallarmé, for example, both deplored the adoption of bloomers by women cyclists, claiming that such a practice necessarily entailed a loss of femininity.[252] An article in the newspaper *l'Auto-Vélo* in 1897 satirically announced the birth of a new species: 'the bicycle-woman, who seems to have both male and female traits, without having any clearly defined sex'.[253] These fears highlighted the social contingency of the very concept of femininity, which was purely defined by the activities, clothes and attitudes that women were encouraged to adopt.

Albertine offers us a vision of a character who exhibits both male and female traits, using her bicycle to perform the less conventional sides of her personality. A masculine woman also features in Leblanc's *Here are Wings*, in which Pascal admires Madeleine's 'boyish looks' and later describes her 'male silhouette which dissipated the harmony of her gestures'.[254] Writing in the early 1920s, when communities of cross-dressing women or 'inverts' had, according to Judith Halberstam, 'developed into visible and elaborate subcultures',[255] Proust looks back to the world in which such identities were just beginning to crystallise, helped by activities such as cycling. Both Proust's and Leblanc's narratives take place amid what Halberstam terms 'the momentous negotiations about gender that took place at and around the turn of the century', which 'played a part in untangling once and for all the knots that appeared to bind gender to sex and sexuality in some mysterious and organic way'.[256] Albertine represents for the narrator 'a new variety of female beauty',[257] but one that goes beyond the boundaries of the conventionally feminine and is instead one of the myriad manifestations of what Halberstam terms 'female masculinity'.[258]

Signs of Albertine's masculinity are already present when we first encounter the young woman using slang, wearing a sports outfit, 'pushing a bicycle and walking with a swagger' along the beach in Balbec.[259] In the painter Elstir's studio, when the narrator catches a glimpse of 'the young cyclist' framed in the window like one of the impressionist paintings hanging on the walls, she greets the painter mid-ride, 'without stopping', provoking a flurry of desire in the narrator.[260] Burning to follow Albertine but waiting for Elstir to accompany him outside, the young hero paces impatiently around the studio until he discovers a portrait of 'a young actress from another time half-dressed as a man'.[261] The pleasure the narrator derives from looking at this portrait is a result of the subject's fluid, ambiguous gender:

> the gender seemed to be on the verge of admitting that it was that of a slightly boyish girl, then it evaporated and appeared again later, giving the impression of a depraved, pensive and effeminate young man, then fleeing again, it remained elusive.[262]

Although he does not recognise her, the portrait is of a young Madame Swann, who is an object of the narrator's desire in the first part of *Within a Budding Grove*. The discovery of this gender-ambiguous portrait and the pleasure the narrator takes in it are directly connected to the fleeting glimpse he has just had of the androgynous young cyclist through the window.

This association between mobile cyclists and fluctuating gender reoccurs in *The Prisoner*. The narrator, watching the morning traffic from his window, first mistakes a male pedestrian for 'an inelegant woman'.[263] This instance of gender confusion is immediately followed by a description of speeding, blurred, sexless cyclists, at one with their machines: 'the winged hunters, in changing hues, sped towards the stations, their bodies hugging their bicycles'.[264] This image is in turn reflected in *The Fugitive*, when the narrator recalls a memory of Albertine as an androgynous cyclist-warrior, 'leaning over her mythological bicycle wheel, on wet days shrouded in her rubber warrior's tunic that defined the curve of her breasts'.[265] As in the earlier portrayal of cyclists in the bois de Boulogne, this description integrates mythical, masculine and feminine traits into the portrait of Albertine. The ambiguity surrounding cyclists' gender is one of the reasons why the bicycle is such a productive image for Proust, a writer for whom an individual's identity is not a fixed state but a constant dialogue. It is as elusive as any of our impressions and as fleeting as a passing cyclist.

Bisexual Bicyclists

While contributing to the destabilisation of gender divisions, the bicycle plays a compelling role in expressing queer desire for Proust.[266] In Balbec, the narrator is jealous of Albertine's visits to female friends, and links her illicit desire to her incessant bicycle riding. It is only after her sudden death that he receives evidence of her sexual encounters with women, in the form of a letter from Aimé, the *maître d'hôtel* at the Grand Hôtel in Balbec. Aimé confirms that Albertine had bribed staff so that she could bring many different women with her into the shower.[267] In the jealous confusion that follows this discovery, the narrator tortuously imagines her walking and cycling from one lover's house to the next: 'Albertine had lived in one place, walked to the next and ridden her bicycle to the next.'[268] While the narrator and Albertine are living together in *The Prisoner*, he recounts how she 'would tell me in the vaguest of terms, as though it were a secret, about her bicycle rides in Balbec'.[269] Although she does not divulge what was secret about her bicycle rides, she goes on to admit being propositioned in a carriage by the narrator's childhood friend, Gilberte, and clandestinely staying at a female friend's house for three days, only emerging on to the street once, 'disguised as a man, just for fun'.[270] In this rare moment of honesty between the narrator and Albertine, we are provided with a glimpse of the lives of turn-of-the-century, cross-dressing, cycling lesbians; a lively portrait which reflects the emergence of female cross-dressers in Europe by the early 1920s. Living in a society which shunned queer desire, Proust's characters must come up with their own lifestyles and languages to express it. When referring to desire between women, the narrator employs the term 'gomorrhéen' (from the biblical city of Gomorrah, destroyed by God for its sinfulness), while Albertine uses the euphemism 'mauvais genre', translating either as 'bad taste' or 'wrong kind/gender'.[271] Along with this coded language and cross-dressing, the bicycle plays a key role in Albertine's attempts to explore and communicate her sexuality.

The bicycle is also used to point to this unnameable sexuality in the depiction of the novel's other queer hero, baron de Charlus. The violent dispute overheard between Charlus and his lover Jupien which opens the fourth volume, *Sodom and Gomorrah*, contains a telling mention of 'a very nice cyclist' who makes deliveries for the pharmacist.[272] As Barathieu points out, Ghislain de Diesbach explains with reference to Proust's correspondence that male delivery cyclists acquired an unexpected role at this time, being occasionally solicited to meet the sexual demands of rich men.[273] We may therefore presume that Charlus's reference to a 'nice' delivery cyclist is an attempt to arouse Jupien's jealousy. Moreover, in *The Prisoner*, a young dairywoman's offhand reference to her plans to go cycling that afternoon acts as a trigger for the narrator's fit of jealousy about Albertine's desire for women. On the mention of cycling, he suddenly catches sight of a newspaper advertisement that informs him that the actress Léa (known to have relationships with women) is performing in the play which Albertine has gone to see that morning.[274] Panicked, the narrator sends his servant to retrieve her from the theatre, and a bicycle once again plays a role in carrying a message from Albertine to her jealous lover: 'I am on my way, though slower than this cyclist whose bike I would gladly take so I could be at your side sooner.'[275] Although in this second instance the cyclist is carrying an apparently devoted message, the context of the bicycle's two appearances here – framing the jealous outburst – reveals its symbolic role as a vehicle for the expression of Albertine's unutterable sexuality. It is significant that while Albertine pedalled freely to see women in Balbec, in her performed role of a bourgeois heterosexual woman in Paris she cannot ride a bicycle back to her lover's house, but is instead confined to a carriage.

The narrator appears to be appalled by Albertine's queer desire. However, it is thanks to his recognition of the slippage between queer and straight relationships that the artist comes to an appreciation of the variegated continuums that exist in human experience and that are reflected in art. A fluctuating spectrum of sexuality is depicted in the scene where the narrator recounts Charlus's discovery of the actress Léa's sexually explicit letter to his lover Morel. This letter undermines Charlus's preconceptions about strictly defined sexualities, as he realises that his potential rivals for Morel's love include 'not just those he had thought, but an entire, huge part of the planet, made up of women as well as men, of men who loved not only men but also women'.[276] In this way, Charlus comes face to face with 'the sudden insufficiency of a definition'[277] when it comes to attempting to characterise sexuality or indeed any aspect of human nature. Attending Madame Verdurin's salon, the narrator is racked by jealousy over Albertine's potential desire for Mademoiselle Vinteuil's lover, the woman who has brought to life the unfinished last work of the great composer Vinteuil. As the narrator is transported by the septet he is hearing for the first time performed by the violinist Morel, Charlus's lover and protégé, he gains a crucial insight: it is thanks to two queer relationships – characterised as 'impure elements'[278] – that this major work has at last seen the light of day.

Albertine is ultimately too radical for the society in which she lives. Indeed, the second time the narrator catches sight of her at the seaside, it is as she is being marched home by her English governess, 'her head bent like an animal being made to go back into the stable against its will'.[279] It is only thanks to her trademark machine – 'she was pushing the same bicycle' – that the narrator is able to recognise the independent young woman he beheld on the beach, now under the yoke of 'an authoritarian figure'.[280] This scene prefigures the narrator's own sequestration of Albertine in his Paris home in *The Prisoner*. Finally it is the narrator, as a representative of the conservative bourgeois class that the young woman is challenging, who will be responsible for the tragic transformation of his lover. He himself notes the striking contrast between 'this Albertine shut up in my house' and the young woman whom 'everybody used to follow, whom I had such difficulty catching up on, flying by on her bicycle'.[281] In Judith Butler's terms, he actively encourages her to 'perform' femininity once under his roof; that is, to dress and behave in the manner expected of well-to-do young women.[282] Rejecting her cycling clothes of old, he goes to great lengths and expense to acquire fashionable new dresses for Albertine. He seeks very precise advice from his aristocratic neighbour, the duchesse de Guermantes, on the most appropriate styles and materials in which to clothe his captive.[283] Albertine's new status as a 'tamed wild animal'[284] is brought vividly to mind in a scene in the narrator's bedroom where, asked to play the pianola, the movements of her limbs both recall and deform those which previously she had employed to ride her bicycle. The pianola is described as 'a magic scientific lantern' whose music, like the bicycle, allows its listeners to be transported in space and time.[285] This instrument, however, is first and foremost a symbol of her sequestration. Her legs, which had 'turned the pedals of a bicycle throughout her adolescence', now compliantly action a mechanical piano.[286] Examining her hands, the narrator is once again reminded of a cyclist's pose: 'Her fingers, which had previously been familiar with handlebars, now lay upon the keys like the fingers of a Saint Cecilia.'[287] The narrator and the society in which he lives have broken this once vigorously independent cyclist. She has become an incarnation of the virgin patron saint of music, constrained to perform and to conform to Christian, bourgeois norms.

On the final page of *The Prisoner*, the narrator discovers that Albertine has disappeared. His desperate attempts to find her at the start of the sixth volume, *The Fugitive*, are in vain as she is soon killed in a riding accident. Some critics have pointed out that this death mirrors that of Alfred Agostinelli, Proust's driver and secretary, who died in a plane crash in 1914.[288] It is significant that it is a horse and not a modern vehicle such as a bicycle, a car or a plane that is to blame for Albertine's death. A symbol of the old world, of both the aristocracy and the wealthy and aspiring bourgeoisie, the horse comes to deal the *coup de grâce* (after the blows dealt by the narrator himself) to this radical new cyclist who dared to challenge distinctions of gender, sexuality and class. Yet Albertine's challenge to conservative identities would not be forgotten in the twentieth century's re-exploration of gender and sexuality that people like her helped pioneer.

In turn-of-the-century France and Britain, bicycles – and especially the female cyclist – were intimately tied to contemporary debates. Cycling was attacked and praised with equal fervour and held up alternately as a symbol of social progress or decay. Just as a spinning bicycle wheel gives the illusion of remaining static, during this period radical change was occurring beneath a veneer of stasis. In Proust's evocation of a lost world, the bicycle proves to be an extremely productive metaphor not only thanks to its incarnation of the conflicting forces shaping modernity, but also because of the way in which it reflects fragmentary perception and evokes the fluctuating nature of desire and gender. Proust, along with British authors such as Wells and Allen, mobilises the bicycle to illustrate how, through contact with a new technology, and in spite of conservative resistance to change, fixed ideas of class, gender and sexuality can gradually be eroded. As Pamela Thurschwell notes of this period, 'cultural imaginings of technologically uncanny contact are intertwined with an expanding sense of sex and gender flexibility'.[289] The uncanny contact with technology that I examine in the next chapter opens up a space for the formation of diverse new subjects, who explore new means of identifying with people and machines.

Notes

1. Illich, *Energy and Equity*, 12.
2. Carey, *The Intellectuals and the Masses*, 53.
3. Ibid., 58.
4. Ibid., 59.
5. Herlihy, *Bicycle*, 21.
6. Ibid., 24.
7. Denis Pye, *Fellowship Is Life: The National Clarion Cycling Club, 1895–1995* (Bolton: Clarion, 1995), 16.
8. Bockett, *Some Literary Landmarks*, 123, 21.
9. See Robinson, *The Walk*, 52.
10. David Herlihy points out that 'the bicycle, in fact, did not truly complete its transition from a rich man's toy to a poor man's carriage until the early part of the twentieth century'. Herlihy, *Bicycle*, 7.
11. Bijker, *Of Bicycles, Bakelites, and Bulbs*, 20.
12. Kennard, *A Guide Book for Lady Cyclists*, 23.
13. This is how the draper Hoopdriver comes to acquire an outdated, solid tyre, cross-bar machine in Wells's *The Wheels of Chance*.
14. See Ritchie, *Quest for Speed*.
15. Herlihy, *Bicycle*, 274.
16. H. G. Wells, *Experiment in Autobiography*, vol. II [1934] (London: Jonathan Cape, 1969), 543.
17. Ibid., II, 568.
18. H. G. Wells, *Kipps: The Story of a Simple Soul* [1905] (London: Collins, 1961), 231.
19. H. G. Wells, *Anticipations of the Reaction of Mechanical and Scientific Progress Upon Human Life and Thought* [1901] (Auckland, NZ: Floating Press, 2008), 3.

20. Ibid., 4.
21. Ibid., 24–5.
22. H. G. Wells, *A Modern Utopia* [1905] (Lincoln, NE: University of Nebraska Press, 1967), 47.
23. Ibid.
24. Sussman, *Victorians and the Machine*, 3.
25. Simon J. James, 'Fin-de-Cycle: Romance and the Real in *The Wheels of Chance*', in *H. G. Wells: Interdisciplinary Essays*, ed. Steven McLean (Newcastle upon Tyne: Cambridge Scholars Publishing, 2008), 34.
26. Ibid.
27. Wells, *Correspondence*, II, 79.
28. Sussman, *Victorians and the Machine*, 174–5.
29. H. G. Wells, *The Time Machine* [1895] (London: Book Club Associates, 1980), 22–4.
30. Meiner, *Le carrosse littéraire*, 56.
31. Wells, *The Wheels of Chance*, 16.
32. Ibid., 17.
33. Ibid., 25.
34. James, 'Fin-de-Cycle', 41.
35. Ibid., 32.
36. Hiroshi So, '*The Wheels of Chance* and the Discourse of Improvement of Health', *The Wellsian: The Journal of the H. G. Wells Society* 29, no. 1 (2006), 37–47.
37. Thompson, *The Tour de France*, 142.
38. Ibid., 166.
39. Phillip Gordon Mackintosh, 'A Bourgeois Geography of Domestic Bicycling: Using Public Space Responsibly in Toronto and Niagara-on-the-Lake, 1890–1900', *Journal of Historical Sociology* 20, no. 1–2 (2007), 144.
40. Wells, *The Wheels of Chance*, 196.
41. Ibid., 193.
42. Choi, 'The Bi-Cycling Mr Hoopdriver'.
43. See Mikhail M. Bakhtin, *Rabelais and His World*, trans. Hélène Iswolsky (Bloomington, IN: Indiana University Press, 1984).
44. Wells, 'A Perfect Gentleman on Wheels', 6.
45. Ibid.
46. Ibid., 10.
47. Ibid., 13.
48. Ibid.
49. An earlier version of this research was published as 'Liberation on Two Wheels: Social Change and the Bicycle in H. G. Wells's *Kipps* and *The History of Mr Polly*', *The Wellsian* 41 (2018), 5–27.
50. Wells, *Kipps*, 9.
51. Augé, *Éloge de la bicyclette*, 36.
52. Wells, *Kipps*, 9.

53. Ibid., 19.
54. Ibid., 37.
55. Georg Simmel, 'The Metropolis and Mental Life' [1903], in *The Sociology of Georg Simmel*, trans. Kurt H. Wolff (London: Free Press, 1950), 422.
56. Michael Draper, *H. G. Wells* (London: Macmillan, 1987), 77.
57. Wells, *Kipps*, 59.
58. Ibid., 60.
59. Ibid.
60. Ibid., 63.
61. Simmel, 'The Metropolis and Mental Life', 415.
62. Ibid., 410.
63. Wells, *Kipps*, 83.
64. Ibid.
65. Ibid., 116.
66. Ibid., 103, 134.
67. Ibid., 167.
68. Ibid., 118.
69. Ibid., 123, 120.
70. Ibid., 122.
71. Ibid., 123.
72. Ibid., 37.
73. Ibid., 154.
74. Ibid., 155.
75. Ibid.
76. Ibid., 156.
77. Ibid., 157.
78. Herlihy, *Bicycle*, 290.
79. See Woodruff, *The Rise of the British Rubber Industry*.
80. See Geoffrey Williamson, *Wheels within Wheels: The Story of the Starleys of Coventry* (London: Bles, 1966); Glen Norcliffe, 'The Rise of the Coventry Bicycle Industry and the Geographical Construction of Technology', *Cycle History* 15 (2004), 41–58.
81. Norcliffe, 'The Rise of the Coventry Bicycle Industry', 55. In this article, Norcliffe offers a critique of Bijker et al.'s SCOT model of socio-technological change.
82. Wells, *Kipps*, 173.
83. Ibid.
84. Ibid.
85. Ibid., 174.
86. Ibid., 176.
87. Ibid., 188.
88. Ibid., 194.
89. Ivan Melada, 'Review of *Socialist Propaganda in the Twentieth Century British Novel*, by David Smith', *Studies in the Novel* 12, no. 1 (1980), 95.

90. We may presume that Wells named this character after his contemporary, the socialist writer C. F. G. Masterman, who wrote *The Condition of England* in 1909.
91. Wells, *Kipps*, 198.
92. Ibid., 199.
93. Ibid., 201. This mirrors Masterman's view of motor cars as an 'extravagance of wealth and waste'. See C. F. G. Masterman, *The Condition of England* (London: Methuen, 1909), 23.
94. Ibid., 235.
95. Wells, *Mr Polly*, 45.
96. Ibid., 49.
97. Draper, *H. G. Wells*, 82.
98. Carey, *The Intellectuals and the Masses*, 144.
99. Wells, *Mr Polly*, 53.
100. Ibid., 55.
101. Ibid., 77.
102. Ibid., 77.
103. Ibid., 31.
104. Allen, *Wheel Magic*, 62–3.
105. Wells, *Mr Polly*, 79. Mr Polly's speciality is inventing words.
106. Ibid., 78.
107. Ibid., 85.
108. Ibid., 88. This is an instance of the connection between cycling and the adventure and romance genres, as discussed in Chapter 1.
109. Ibid., 90.
110. Ibid.
111. Ibid., 103.
112. Ibid., 106, 123.
113. Ibid., 126.
114. Ibid., 129.
115. Ibid., 130.
116. Draper, *H. G. Wells*, 87.
117. Ibid., 140.
118. As I showed in Chapter 1, the bicycle often plays its most crucial narrative role when it malfunctions.
119. Wells, *Mr Polly*, 162.
120. Ibid., 164
121. Ibid., 167, author's italics.
122. Ibid., 168.
123. Ibid., 171.
124. Ibid., 169.
125. Ibid., 170.
126. Ibid., 171.
127. Augé, *Éloge de la bicyclette*, 80.
128. Hugh Stutfield, 'Tommyrotics', *Blackwood's Magazine* 157 (June 1895), 833–45.

129. Norcliffe, *Critical Geographies of Cycling*, 5; there are also some accounts of women velocipedists, and Denis Johnson issued a ladies' draisine as early as 1819. See Herlihy, *Bicycle*, 38.
130. Weber, *France, Fin de Siècle*, 203.
131. Susan B. Anthony, quoted in Nellie Bly, 'Champion of her Sex', *New York World*, 2 February 1896, 9–10.
132. An exception is Anita Rush, 'The Bicycle Boom of the Gay Nineties: A Reassessment', *Material Culture Review / Revue de La Culture Matérielle* 18 (June 1983), 1–12. This article claims that the importance of the bicycle in social movements has been exaggerated, and that it reflected rather than sparked feminist and socialist struggles.
133. Christopher Thompson and Fiona Ratkoff, 'Un troisième sexe? Les bourgeoises et la bicyclette dans la France fin de siècle', *Le mouvement social* 192 (September 2000), 36.
134. This area of study is already amply furnished; see, for example, Gail Cunningham, *The New Woman and the Victorian Novel* (London: Macmillan, 1978); Carolyn Christensen Nelson (ed.), *A New Woman Reader: Fiction, Articles, and Drama of the 1890s* (Orchard Park, NY: Broadview Press, 2001); Angelique Richardson and Chris Willis (eds), *The New Woman in Fiction and in Fact: Fin de Siècle Feminisms* (Basingstoke: Palgrave, 2001); Macy, *Wheels of Change*.
135. Ann L. Ardis, *New Women, New Novels: Feminism and Early Modernism* (New Brunswick, NJ: Rutgers University Press, 1990), 4.
136. Sally Ledger, *The New Woman: Fiction and Feminism at the Fin de Siècle* (Manchester: Manchester University Press, 1997), 1.
137. Chris Willis, 'Heaven Defend Me from Political or Highly-Educated Women! Packaging the New Woman for Mass Consumption', in *The New Woman in Fiction and in Fact: Fin de Siècle Feminisms*, ed. Angelique Richardson and Chris Willis (Basingstoke: Palgrave, 2001), 53.
138. Ada L. Harris, *A Widow on Wheels* (London: Hutchinson, 1896), 3–4.
139. H. G. Wells, *Ann Veronica* [1913] (London: J. M. Dent, 1962), 24.
140. Wells, *The Wheels of Chance*, 20.
141. Ibid., 21, author's italics.
142. Ibid., 74.
143. Kennard, *The Golf Lunatic and his Cycling Wife*, 71.
144. Ibid., 307–8.
145. Grant Allen, *The Type-Writer Girl* (London: C. Arthur Pearson, 1897), 74; Grant Allen, *Miss Cayley's Adventures* (Kansas City, KS: Valancourt Books, 2008), 157.
146. Allen, *The Type-Writer Girl*, 50.
147. Kennard, *A Guide Book for Lady Cyclists*, 22.
148. Emile Zola, *Œuvres complètes. Paris fin de siècle, 1897*, ed. Henri Mitterand, Jacques Noiray and Jean-Louis Cabanès, vol. XVII (Paris: Nouveau Monde, 2008), 236.

149. Ibid.
150. Allen, *Miss Cayley's Adventures*, 6.
151. Ibid., 4.
152. Wells, *The Wheels of Chance*, 92.
153. Allen, *The Type-Writer Girl*, 76–7.
154. Allen, *Miss Cayley's Adventures*, 45.
155. While Grant Allen made use of the trope of the female knight, both of his New Women cyclists are also 'rescued' by modern-day male knights in the course of these novels. In *The Type-Writer Girl* (p. 90), Juliet is saved by a 'St George' in a dog-cart after a bicycle accident, and in *Miss Cayley's Adventures* (p. 44) the American inventor is termed 'St George' when he intervenes with a policeman to save Lois from paying a fine for not having a licence for her bicycle.
156. Allen, *Miss Cayley's Adventures*, 83.
157. Ibid., 86, 88.
158. Edna C. Jackson, 'A Fin de Cycle Incident', in *The Humours of Cycling* (London: James Bowden, 1897), 56–65.
159. In sociology, homosocial refers to same-sex non-sexual relationships, such as friendship. The term was popularised by Eve Sedgwick in her discussion of male homosocial relationships, which often perpetuate patterns of male dominance. See Eve Kosofsky Sedgwick, *Between Men: English Literature and Male Homosocial Desire* (New York: Columbia University Press, 1985).
160. Virginia Woolf, *A Room of One's Own* [1929] (London: Penguin, 1992), 82.
161. Ibid.
162. See Kennard, *A Guide Book for Lady Cyclists*, 70–84.
163. Kennard, *The Golf Lunatic and his Cycling Wife*, 207.
164. Ibid., 210.
165. L. T. Meade, *The Cleverest Woman in England* (London: J. Nisbet, 1898), 101.
166. 'How Some Wheelwomen Earn Money', *The Hub*, 12 September 1896.
167. Kennard, *The Golf Lunatic and his Cycling Wife*, 69.
168. Arthur Conan Doyle, *Beyond the City* (London: George Newnes, 1921).
169. Allen, *Miss Cayley's Adventures*.
170. Willis, 'Heaven Defend Me from Political or Highly-Educated Women!', 64.
171. Shrimpton, 'The Cultural Significance of Cycling', 43.
172. Kittler, *Discourse Networks*, 354.
173. Similarly, some have argued that the array of household gadgets marketed at women throughout the twentieth century, rather than liberating them from domestic chores, in fact reinforced their role as housewives.
174. Garvey, *The Adman in the Parlor*, 123–4.

175. Ibid., 117.
176. Zack Furness, *One Less Car: Bicycling and the Politics of Automobility* (Philadelphia, PA: Temple University Press, 2010), 22.
177. Virginia, 'Arrayed like one of these', *The Cycling World Illustrated*, 18 March 1896, 20.
178. Virginia, 'Array yourself becomingly', *The Cycling World Illustrated*, 29 April 1896, 19.
179. Virginia Niles Leeds, 'A Coast and a Capture: A Bicycling Story', in *The Humours of Cycling* (London: James Bowden, 1897), 87.
180. In France, however, *culottes* were popular with female cyclists from the 1890s.
181. Richardson, *The Tunnel*, 148.
182. Kennard, *A Guide Book for Lady Cyclists*, 39–54. As Kat Jungnickel shows in her book *Bikes and Bloomers: Victorian Women Inventors and their Extraordinary Cycle Wear* (London: Goldsmiths Press, 2018), a number of women invented patents for cycle wear, and making your own cycling skirt from a pattern was quite common.
183. Ibid., 44.
184. Ibid., 52.
185. Nicholas Oddy, 'Bicycles', in *The Gendered Object*, ed. Pat Kirkham (Manchester: Manchester University Press, 2006), 66. Oddy is here partly quoting an unpublished conference paper by Paul Rosen.
186. Kennard, *A Guide Book for Lady Cyclists*, 27.
187. Garvey, *The Adman in the Parlor*, 115.
188. Kennard, *A Guide Book for Lady Cyclists*, 44.
189. Kennard, *The Golf Lunatic and his Cycling Wife*, 73.
190. Ibid., 69.
191. Mackintosh, 'A Bourgeois Geography of Domestic Bicycling', 126.
192. Ibid., 144.
193. Claire S. Simpson, 'Capitalising on Curiosity: Women's Professional Cycle Racing in the Late-Nineteenth Century', in *Cycling and Society*, ed. Dave Horton, Paul Rosen and Peter Cox (Aldershot: Ashgate, 2007), 51.
194. Allen, *Miss Cayley's Adventures*, 50.
195. Ibid., 51.
196. Linda Walker, 'Party Political Women: A Comparative Study of Liberal Women and the Primrose League, 1890–1914', in *Equal or Different: Women's Politics, 1800–1914*, ed. Jane Rendall (Oxford: Blackwell, 1987), 179.
197. Wells, *The Wheels of Chance*, 99.
198. Ibid., 66.
199. Ibid., 140.
200. Doyle, *Beyond the City*, 100, 101.
201. Ibid., 114.
202. Ibid., 191.

203. Wells, *The Wheels of Chance*, 12, 99.
204. Ibid., 178.
205. Wanggren, 'The Freedom Machine', 132.
206. Wells, *The Wheels of Chance*, 188.
207. James, 'Fin-de-Cycle', 43.
208. H. G. Wells, *The Wheels of Chance, A Bicycling Idyll* (New York: Macmillan, 1896), ch. 39.
209. H. G. Wells, *Hoopdriver's Holiday* [1904], ed. Michael Timko (Lafayette, IN: Purdue University, 1964); see also Simon J. James, *Maps of Utopia: H. G. Wells, Modernity and the End of Culture* (Oxford: Oxford University Press, 2012).
210. George Gissing, 'A Daughter of the Lodge' [1901], in *The House of Cobwebs, and Other Stories* (London: Constable, 1906), 183.
211. Ibid.
212. Wells, *The Time Machine*, 35.
213. Kennard, *The Golf Lunatic and his Cycling Wife*, 200.
214. An earlier version of this research was originally published as 'Albertine the Cyclist: A Queer Feminist Bicycle Ride through Proust's *In Search of Lost Time*', in *Culture on Two Wheels: The Bicycle in Literature and Film*, ed. Jeremy Withers and Daniel P. Shea (Lincoln, NE: University of Nebraska Press, 2016), 116–35.
215. See Anne-Marie Clais, 'Portrait de femmes en cyclistes ou l'invention du féminin pluriel', *Les cahiers de médiologie 5*, no. 1 (1998), 69–79; Siân Reynolds, 'Albertine's Bicycle, or: Women and French Identity during the Belle Epoque', *Literature & History* 10, no. 1 (2001), 28–41; an important exception is Agnès Barathieu, *Les mobiles de Marcel Proust: une sémantique du déplacement* (Villeneuve d'Ascq: Presses universitaires du Septentrion, 2002). This volume provides a rich discussion of bicycles in Proust's work, and my research is much indebted to it.
216. See, for example, Ludovic O'Followell, *Bicyclette et organes génitaux* (Paris: Baillière, 1900), 63–4.
217. See Thompson and Ratkoff, 'Un troisième sexe?', 13.
218. See Daniel Pick, *Faces of Degeneration: A European Disorder, c.1848–c.1918* (Cambridge: Cambridge University Press, 1989), 35–59; Thompson, 'Regeneration, Dégénérescence, and the Medical Debate about Bicycling in Fin-de-Siècle France', 339–46.
219. Thompson and Ratkoff, 'Un troisième sexe?', 10.
220. Marcel Proust, *À la recherche du temps perdu II. À l'ombre de jeunes filles en fleurs. Le côté de Guermantes. Esquisses* (Paris: Gallimard, 1988), 146.
221. Barathieu, *Les mobiles de Marcel Proust*, 174.
222. Proust, *À la recherche du temps perdu II*, 146–7.
223. Ibid., 149.
224. Ibid.

225. Ibid., 150. For some contemporary portraits of and reactions to *vélocipédards*, see Thiesset and Thomasset, *Les bienfaits de la vélocipédie*, 161–5.
226. Proust, *À la recherche du temps perdu II*, 151.
227. Ibid.
228. See Thompson and Ratkoff, 'Un troisième sexe?', 32; Weber, *France, Fin de Siècle*, 200.
229. Proust, *À la recherche du temps perdu II*, 200.
230. For a compelling discussion of the social significance of bourgeois leisure and sports, with consideration of *À la recherche*, see Alain Corbin (ed.), *L'avènement des loisirs: 1850–1960* (Paris: Aubier, 1995).
231. Ibid., 186.
232. Reynolds, 'Albertine's Bicycle', 36.
233. Françoise Gaillard, 'A l'ombre des jeunes filles en vélo ou l'invention de la jeunesse', *Les cahiers de médiologie 5*, no. 1 (1998), 84.
234. Just Lucas-Championnière, *La Bicyclette* (Paris: L. Chailley, 1894), 47, author's italics.
235. Proust, *À la recherche du temps perdu II*, 231.
236. Ibid., 251.
237. Ibid., 71.
238. Barathieu shows how the bicycle is also used to introduce Jean, a character desired by the narrator in Proust's first novel, *Jean Santeuil* (1895, published 1952). See Barathieu, *Les mobiles de Marcel Proust*, 122.
239. Ibid., 126.
240. Proust, *À la recherche du temps perdu II*, 226.
241. Proust, *À la recherche du temps perdu II*, 228.
242. Marcel Proust, *À la recherche du temps perdu III. Sodome et Gomorrhe. La Prisonnière. Esquisses* (Paris: Gallimard, 1988), 600, 576.
243. Ibid., 675.
244. Ibid.
245. Ibid., 677.
246. Ibid., 677–8.
247. See Nadine Besse and André Vant, 'A New View of Late 19th Century Cycle Publicity Posters', *Cycle History 5* (1994), 117–23.
248. Donna Haraway, *Simians, Cyborgs, and Women: The Reinvention of Nature* (New York: Routledge, 1991), 154.
249. Ibid., 175.
250. Michel Foucault, *Histoire de la sexualité*, vol. 1: *La volonté de savoir* (Paris: Gallimard, 1976), 9–22.
251. There are also several informal words for the bicycle, including *bécane* (f), *biclou* (m) and *petite reine* (f). For an etymological consideration of these various words, see Odon Vallet, 'Vélo, bicyclette: histoire des mots', *Les cahiers de médiologie 5*, no. 1 (1998), 15–18; for a more philosophical reflection on the difference between *bicyclette* and *vélo*,

see Philippe Delerm, *La première gorgée de bière et autres plaisirs minuscules: récits* (Paris: Gallimard, 1997), 88–9.
252. Thiesset and Thomasset, *Les bienfaits de la vélocipédie*, 110–14.
253. Ibid., 105–6.
254. Leblanc, *Voici des ailes*, 9, 27.
255. Judith Halberstam, *Female Masculinity* (Durham, NC: Duke University Press, 1998), 75.
256. Ibid., 48.
257. Proust, *À la recherche du temps perdu II*, 165.
258. Halberstam, *Female Masculinity*, 1–43.
259. Proust, *À la recherche du temps perdu II*, 151.
260. Ibid., 199–200.
261. Ibid., 204.
262. Ibid., 205.
263. Proust, *À la recherche du temps perdu III*, 643.
264. Ibid., 644.
265. Marcel Proust, *À la recherche du temps perdu IV. Albertine disparue. Le temps retrouvé. Esquisses* (Paris: Gallimard, 1989), 70.
266. It is interesting to note that in French, *pédale* is not only a part of a bicycle but also a slang term for a queer man.
267. Proust, *À la recherche du temps perdu IV*, 97.
268. Ibid., 99–100.
269. Proust, *À la recherche du temps perdu III*, 886.
270. Ibid., 878, 838.
271. Ibid., 592, 878.
272. Ibid., 11.
273. Ghislain de Diesbach, *Proust* (Paris: Perrin, 1991), 418.
274. Proust, *À la recherche du temps perdu III*, 651.
275. Ibid., 663.
276. Ibid., 720–1.
277. Ibid., 721.
278. Ibid., 769.
279. Proust, *À la recherche du temps perdu II*, 185.
280. Ibid.
281. Proust, *À la recherche du temps perdu III*, 576.
282. Judith Butler, 'Performative Acts and Gender Constitution: An Essay in Phenomenonology and Feminist Theory', *Theatre Journal* 40, no. 4 (1988), 519–31.
283. Proust, *À la recherche du temps perdu III*, 541.
284. Ibid., 884.
285. Ibid., 883.
286. Ibid., 884.
287. Ibid, author's italics.
288. Barathieu, *Les mobiles de Marcel Proust*, 192.
289. Pamela Thurschwell, *Literature, Technology, and Magical Thinking, 1880–1920* (Cambridge: Cambridge University Press, 2001), 4.

Chapter 3

The Body and the Machine: The Sensory Discoveries of the Cyclist

> Of course [humans] aren't things, but things aren't things either [...] Anyone who has looked at machines knows how unmechanical they are.
>
> Bruno Latour[1]

The bicycle offers a mechanised yet embodied experience of movement – in contrast to the disembodied, vision-focused experience of travelling by train and in motorised vehicles – that vividly enacts the exchange between human and non-human actants. Throughout the nineteenth century, the dividing line between humans and machines, the organic and the mechanical, seemed to grow more and more salient. Raymond Williams points out that 'mechanic' and 'organic' were near synonyms before the industrial era, when Romantic poets began to formulate opposing definitions of the two.[2] At the end of the nineteenth century, with the multiplication of new technologies, this question was of particular pertinence. Mark Seltzer suggests that turn-of-the-century discourses on bodies and machines were articulated around four main concepts: machines replacing bodies, people becoming more machine-like, technologies creating bodies, and finally the possibility of an intimate coupling of bodies and machines.[3] As we shall see in the course of this chapter, elements of all of these possibilities recurred and overlapped in literature about cycling in the period. Cycling went some way towards mechanising human movements and perception, industrialising the body's motion while exposing it to the possibility of shock and injury. Yet the bicycle also offered an intense sensory journey, reconnecting its users to an embodied experience of movement in the wake of the railway era and providing a means of achieving a unique synthesis of human and mechanical elements. The bicycle was technology on a human scale, capable of reconnecting its users with their senses, while encouraging a porous, reciprocal exchange with the landscapes, people and objects encountered by the mobile subject. In this way it was an industrial machine that offered a means of escape from the pitfalls of industrial civilisation.

In examining the cyclist's relationship with the machine, it is particularly useful to integrate materialist criticism that has focused on the exchanges between subjects, objects and their surroundings. Gilles Deleuze and Félix Guattari's concept of assemblages, the actor-network theory of Bruno Latour, Bill Brown's research into how things have shaped the modern subject and Jane Bennett's work on vital materialism all influence my readings of texts that express an intimate dialogue between people and their bicycles, with the senses acting as an interface between the two. Bicycles are compelling objects for thing theorists. Ian Hodder cites the example of a man riding a bicycle as emblematic of 'human-thing entanglement',[4] while Jane Bennett claims that the concept of an assemblage 'is perhaps best understood on the model of riding a bicycle on a gravel road'. Bennett expands the metaphor, explaining that 'one can throw one's weight this way or that, inflect the bike in one direction or toward one trajectory of motion. But the rider is but one actant operative in the moving whole.'[5] The attitude of early riders towards their machines provides a compelling illustration of Bennett's idea of 'the vitality of matter' or Latour's concept of 'actants', where both human and non-human elements actively shape the world around us.[6] The bicycle seems to offer a subtle compromise between the nightmare of technology with a life of its own and the alienation inherent in a completely devitalised idea of matter. The steel and rubber of the machine cannot operate independently, but are capable of responding to and collaborating with human energy. It is the tightly bound human–machine–world cluster described by cycling authors that makes the bicycle such an important avatar of modernity.

Mechanised Motion

> The bicycle is almost unique among human-powered machines in that it uses human muscles in a near-optimum way.
>
> David Gordon Wilson, Jim Papadopoulos and Frank Rowland Whitt[7]

Many of the first cyclists found learning to ride a bicycle a very uncanny experience. Cycling comes as second nature to most European adults nowadays; mastering the skill is a symbolic rite of passage in early childhood, meaning that the learning process itself is often quickly forgotten. It is therefore difficult for contemporaries to appreciate the strangely mechanised bodily sensations that nineteenth-century cyclists must have experienced. Yet at the time of the appearance of the technology, writers vividly described disciplining their bodies in order to learn how to ride a bicycle. Apprentice cyclists discovered the idiosyncrasies of the machine and integrated them into their own reflexes in order to master the basic skills required to cycle: steering, balancing and pedalling. As such, many authors on cycling bore witness to a sense of bodily mechanisation resulting from close engagement with a complex technology. Considering the industrial legacy of the bicycle presented in various texts will allow us to come into fresh contact with a now familiar object that asked the body to do very unfamiliar things.

Cycling as a means of progression takes a considerable amount of training to learn, and the first cyclists made surprising discoveries about balancing on two wheels. Mary Kennard explains in the opening pages of her *Guide Book for Lady Cyclists* that 'To recover the balance when riding a bicycle, the rider should always steer on the falling side.'[8] Although this gesture becomes instinctive once learned, it is one that takes many weeks or months of practice to achieve, as it is contrary to the balancing instinct learned from walking. In his essay 'Taming the Bicycle' (1886), Mark Twain expressed his surprise on discovering that

> the big wheel must be turned in the direction in which you are falling. It is hard to believe this, when you are told it. And not merely hard to believe it, but impossible; it is opposed to all your notions [. . .] The intellect has to come to the front, now. It has to teach the limbs to discard their old education and adopt the new.[9]

Twain's humorous account of learning to cycle describes how the novice cyclist has to disregard his innate reflexes in order to train his body to act in the way the machine requires. Moreover, in contrast to bipedal stability, balance on a bicycle is coupled with rapid forward movement rather than immobility. Reflecting on this paradox encountered by early cyclists, François Rachline notes:

> the cyclist not only had to accept imbalance when stationary, but also admit that balance would result from movement. He therefore had to turn familiar logic on its head, the logic that rules all celestial bodies, according to Newton, and even the social 'body', according to economic

theory. In other words, the cyclist had to act against his intuition. He had to fight against the obvious. Slowness became the enemy of balance. Stability on the ground, normally a given when at rest, came from rapid movement.[10]

Both Twain and Rachline bear witness to a baffling, counter-intuitive experience when mounted on two wheels. Our instinctive sense of balance, achieved when stationary and by leaning away from the side towards which we are falling, was suddenly turned on its head. An unfamiliar equilibrium of the the rider–bicycle assemblage had to be sought, which required the integration of new, mechanised instincts.

From a Marxist perspective, a parallel may be established between the repetitive, counter-intuitive action of pedalling a bicycle and the meaningless, alienating gestures of factory workers, who are restricted and subordinated to the machines they operate. 'The worker's continued repetition of the same narrowly defined act and the concentration of his attention on it teach him by experience how to attain the desired effect with the minimum of exertion,' Marx argues, thus transforming him into 'the living mechanism of manufacture'.[11] These terms recall passages from 1890s cycling guides, explaining the exact bodily gestures cyclists should adopt in order to action the machine in the most efficient manner. R. J. Mecredy, for example, gives meticulous instructions about the optimal placement of the saddle, commands his reader to breathe only through his nose, and explains his 'ankle action' technique, which allows cyclists to achieve an 'enormous increase of power'.[12] Such discourses effectively codified cyclists' gestures, disciplining the body to make it conform to the optimum working of the machine. Like the worker, the cyclist might be seen as someone who repetitively 'performs the same simple operation' and thus 'converts his body into the automatic, one-sided implement of that operation'.[13] Authors such as Wells and Alfred Jarry suggested that while such machine dependency might make new feats of strength and endurance possible, this might also have negative repercussions on the human body and society at large.

These newly mechanised sensations provided inspiration to certain authors, some of whom saw learning to ride a bicycle as a sort of return to an original state, rather than a distortion of human instincts. The Scottish classicist R. J. Muir, for instance, made humorous use of the uncanny experience of apprentice cyclists in a story entitled *Plato's Dream of Wheels* (1902). Muir retells the chariot allegory from Plato's *Phaedrus* (c. 370 BCE), but rather than representing the soul as a pair of winged horses driven by a charioteer, Muir's fictional

Socrates reinvents the myth: 'Originally the souls of men lived in the outermost sphere of the highest heavens. There, moving round and round, swiftly and regularly, upon two wheels, they enjoyed great felicity.'[14] According to Muir, it was the ability to master the bicycle's steering mechanism – that is, steering towards the falling side – that allowed these souls to remain spinning around heaven, as the philosopher explains: 'the former wheel, being turned cunningly towards the side on which there was an inclination to fall, supported the soul and kept it upright'.[15] Whereas Plato's original souls fell to earth on losing their wings, in Muir's version it is the inability to steer and balance correctly that leads to the fall of the celestial beings. These erring souls then became men, and lost all knowledge of 'circular motion': 'therefore they move awkwardly upon two pins, moving first the one and then the other, so vilely are we fallen away from our former glorious condition. But it seems that in these latter days the human race is to have an opportunity of attaining again to circular motion.'[16] Muir depicts the cyclist's motion as an ideal form of innate human mobility; an original state to which we now have the possibility of returning, thanks to technology. It is easy to imagine why Plato's celestial incarnation of the soul – a charioteer and horses – composed of human, animal and mechanical elements, became a cyclist in Muir's retelling, since the figure was a striking amalgam of the technical and the corporeal working together in tight collaboration. The strangeness of learning to steer towards the falling side – while turning one's legs in circles in order to move forward and achieve balance – certainly implied a certain mechanisation of the human body's own movement. Yet as Muir's story reminds us, though mechanised, the new instincts learned by cyclists paradoxically seemed to provide a perfected, innate form of balance and motion.

Once early cyclists had taught their bodies to steer and balance, they could experiment with the unusual sensation of moving smoothly across land on two wheels. In spite of its long association with human civilisation, the wheel had only recently been disassociated from animal traction. In the early days of rail travel, James Adamson noted some important differences between mechanised and animal-powered locomotion on wheels. Schivelbusch quotes the following passage from Adamson's 1826 work:

> Even in walking and running one does not move regularly forward. The body is raised and depressed at every step of our progress; it is this incessant lifting of the mass which constitutes that drag on our motions which checks their speed, and confines it within such moderate

limits [. . .] With machinery this inconvenience is not felt; the locomotive engine rolls regularly and progressively along the smooth tracks of the way, wholly unimpeded by the speed of its own motions; and this, independent of its economy, is one of the great advantages it possesses over animal power.[17]

Wheeled transportation thus implies a smooth and economical locomotive experience, in contrast to the wearisome and inefficient task of placing one foot (or hoof) in front of the other. Wheels carry our weight and remove the need to spend energy balancing on two feet. Bicycle wheel technology made great leaps forward from the 1870s, resulting in highly sophisticated wheels by the late century. With the addition of ball bearings and tangent, wire-spoked wheels in the 1880s, cyclists were mounted upon light, robust and efficient machines that could be ridden along roads of better and better quality.

The counter-intuitive experience of balancing on wheels, along with the novelty and sophistication of the technology, helped construct a mechanical imaginary around the bicycle. The simple word 'machine' was sufficient to denote a bicycle at this time and, as Jeremy Withers argues, 'to most Victorians the word bicycle was synonymous with sophisticated machinery and technology'.[18] Many writers of this period synecdochically referred to a bicycle as a 'wheel' while simultaneously placing emphasis on the artificiality of this mechanism and its distance from the 'organic' or 'natural'.[19] In *The War of the Worlds* (1898), for instance, H. G. Wells's narrator observes while surveying the machines brought to earth by the Martians:

> And of their appliances, perhaps nothing is more wonderful to a man than the curious fact that what is the dominant feature of almost all human devices in mechanism is absent – the *wheel* is absent; among all the things they brought to earth there is no trace or suggestion of their use of wheels. One would have at least expected it in locomotion. And in this connection it is curious to remark that even on this earth Nature has never hit upon the wheel, or has preferred other expedients to its development.[20]

In a scathing attack on human invention, Wells's narrator points to the wheel's glaring absence from the animal and plant kingdom on earth, as well as from the impressive array of devices from Mars. Contributing to what Jeremy Withers terms 'the novel's overall project of undercutting humanity's smugness regarding its own accomplishments',[21] this passage suggests that the technology of the wheel is evolutionarily inferior.

Wells's contemporary G. K. Chesterton muses in a similar vein in his short essay 'The Wheel', in which he remarks that 'the wheel, as a mode of movement, is a purely human thing'.[22] He insists on the lack of wheels in the animal kingdom, noting that

> wings, fins, flappers, claws, hoofs, webs, trotters, with all these the fantastic families of the earth come against us and close around us, fluttering and flapping and rustling and galloping and lumbering and thundering; but there is no sound of wheels.[23]

In this wonderfully sonorous portrayal of modes of locomotion, Chesterton contrasts the consonantal, vibrant, organic sounds of the animal kingdom with the eerily mute wheel. The silence of wheels reflects both their absence among animals or plants and their soundless rotation on bicycles. Chesterton also points to the strangeness of steering as a means of determining direction, noting that 'man is the only thing to steer; the only thing to be conceived as steering'. As we discussed earlier, the experience of steering bicycles contributed to transforming walking man into 'the Man at the Wheel', whom Chesterton characterises as a central modern figure. In this period heavily influenced by Darwin's theory of evolution and discoveries in prehistory, the remark that wheels were not to be found among animals constituted a direct attack on man's achievements, seen as futile attempts to better nature's (or, for authors such as Chesterton, God's) designs.[24] Wells and Chesterton remind us how contemporaries vividly experienced the newness and artificiality of the central component of the bicycle, the wheel, noting its uncanny effect on mechanising human movement.

These meditations on the distance between the realm of nature and that of human invention reflected contemporary debates about the possible effects of the close collaboration between the cyclist's body and the machine it powered. Such concerns found their way into literature: in *The War of the Worlds*, Wells considered the possibility of the mechanisation of the body as a result of prolonged contact with technology. The invading Martians have extended their bodily capabilities by means of technology, and nearly succeed in wiping out humans as a result:

> Yet though they wore no clothing, it was in the other artificial additions to their bodily resources that their great superiority over man lay. We men, with our bicycles and road-skates, our Lilienthal soaring-machine, our guns and sticks and so forth, are just in the beginning of

the evolution that the Martians have worked out. They have become practically mere brains, wearing different bodies according to their needs just as men wear suits of clothing and take a bicycle in a hurry or an umbrella in the wet.[25]

While the narrator derides the futility of human inventions when compared with the deadly fighting machines constructed by the Martians, he nonetheless recognises that a technology such as the bicycle is part of the self-same drive to mechanise and improve the limited capacities of the body. Although the aliens gain the upper hand in the war at first, their bodies have become vulnerable as a result of over-dependency on machines, and the whole invading force is rapidly annihilated through contact with a virus that is harmless to humans. Wells's Darwinian outlook leads him to imagine the potential negative evolutionary repercussions of integrating technology into the innate functions of the human body.

Although the bicycle does not physically encage its rider like the car, the train or the Martians' fighting machines, authors do convey a certain sense of restriction associated with this new technology. In Wells's *The Wheels of Chance*, Hoopdriver has a series of strange dreams after his first day's cycling. In one dream, he is prevented from chasing his rival, Bechamel, 'by the absurd behaviour of his legs. They would not stretch out; they would keep going round and round the treadles of a wheel, so that he made the smallest steps conceivable.'[26] These subconscious imaginings hint at the bicycle's potential to deform the movements of the human body by forcing it to adapt to the demands of mechanism. In a scene recalling Hoopdriver's dream, J. W. Allen recounts a nightmare he had after a day spent cycling, in which his bicycle morphs into a merry-go-round:

> It was like a crowded London street; except, indeed, that all the vehicles and people were moving in the same direction [. . .] Suddenly I asked myself 'Where am I going? Where is this all going?' [. . .] I felt I must stop. I was full of protest. The motion of the machine merely took on a new quality, and the handle-bars went from me. I found myself in a sort of chair and still moving forward, faster than ever, on a sort of circular track. Apparently it was an enormous merry-go-round I had got into.[27]

Although the narrator is initially riding a bicycle, the description of the vehicle suggests that in the course of the dream it transforms into a vehicle resembling a car. He loses control over the machine ('the handlebars went from me'), and we can presume that he is no longer powering it, since he describes how the motion 'took on a new quality'. This loss of autonomy intensifies the impression of senseless, rapid movement on a 'sort of circular track', going nowhere. The narrator, 'full of protest', is carried away by the vehicle, and the abrupt syntax conveys a feeling of helplessness and of being confronted with a series of disorienting impressions. As Allen's dream suggests, it is when mechanism takes over from human power that a sense of control is lost, and that human will and life are jeopardised.

Such concerns about the damaging effects of mechanism and industrial civilisation on the human body were reflected in contemporary scientific discourses. The author of an 1899 article, for instance, argued that the bicycle was part of a regression to quadrupedal motion, claiming that 'The cycle [. . .] will produce an inability to undertake bipedal locomotion.'[28] This outlook was parodied in the illustration by Edward Tennyson Reed in Figure 3.1. As well as decrying its negative effects on women's fertility, some doctors theorised the concept of 'bicycle face', a condition that was seriously discussed in medical journals and the press from 1895. In an article on the 'hidden dangers of cycling' published in *The National Review* in February 1897, a straight-faced Dr A. Shadwell argues:

> With set faces, eyes fixed before them, and an expression either anxious, irritable, or at best stony, they pedal away, looking neither to the right nor the left, save for an instantaneous flash, and speaking not at all, except a word flung over the shoulder at most. It is this strange and unhuman gravity which excites the ridicule and hostility of the street cad and of the dull-witted rustic alike.[29]

Doctors such as Shadwell suggested that such an expression could become a permanent feature, leaving cyclists with a disagreeable physiognomy. While discussed with gravity by some of the bicycle's detractors, those who adopted the bicycle were largely of the opinion expressed by A. W. Rumney that 'The face argument is absurd.'[30] Nevertheless, the development of such a discourse points to contemporary fears around the mechanisation of the body as a result of prolonged contact with technology.

As Jeremy Withers argues, 'the narrator's (and Victorian society's in general) overinfatuation with the bicycle appears to be, for Wells, a step in the direction of being displaced and disabled by one's own technological achievements'.[31] Wells's *War of the Worlds* suggests that over-dependence on machines for locomotion and other needs will result in weakened, fragmented bodies, which are no longer able to function without mechanical appendages. In this light, the bicycle might be thought of as a 'prosthesis'. Tim Armstrong employs this term to

Figure 3.1 Edward Tennyson Reed, 'A Warning to Enthusiasts', *Punch, or the London Charivari*, 6 July 1889, 5. By permission of TopFoto.

point to the dual potentialities of modern technologies: extending and perfecting the body's capabilities, while limiting and fragmenting the body itself.[32] Paul Virilio similarly underlines the potentially disabling effect of technologies, writing of 'the urbanisation of the body, plugged into diverse interfaces' which effectively transform 'the over-equipped able-bodied person [into] the near equivalent of the equipped disabled person'.[33] Many theorists have focused on the car as the ultimate expression of a disabling prosthesis, and Zack Furness argues that the cyclist effectively foreshadowed the car passenger's experience of automobility through 'the development of an entire meaning system around personal transportation, and the disciplining of bodies and the environment in the service of an autonomous mobility'.[34] The cyclist, he goes on to claim, 'effectively previews the emergence of the driver-car or the car-driver, a "hybrid" assemblage'.[35] John Urry coined the term 'automobility' to describe the car driver's subordination to the machine: 'The driver's body is itself fragmented and disciplined to the machine [. . .] The body of the car provides an extension of the human body, surrounding the fragile, soft and vulnerable human skin with a new steel skin.'[36]

While the bicycle might also be considered as an extension of the human body, it leaves its rider open to the elements and does not encase its rider in a new steel skin like the car or train. Elements of cyclists' mechanised experience of mobility certainly prefigured the experience of the car driver and participated in contemporary discourses concerning the displacement of the body by the machine, expressed by authors such as Wells. Yet the rider–bicycle assemblage is unique in its ability to knit together human and mechanical elements without overriding either. Despite the fears outlined above, I argue that the bicycle does not become a prosthesis, nor does it relegate the body to second place, weakening and displacing it. Rather it is the cyclist's strength, balance and intelligence that animate the otherwise inert machine. As we shall see, this mingling of human and machine offered both an intense sensory experience and a means to forge a meaningful interaction with machines.

The Aesthetics of Mechanics

Cyclists were confronted with mechanised experiences when in the saddle, but also when taking apart, building or repairing their bicycles. Whereas the majority of nineteenth-century inventions required highly specialised knowledge and tools for repair, fixing a puncture or oiling a chain was accessible to anyone who was willing to get their hands dirty. Becoming a cyclist required gaining a certain level of mechanical know-how and autonomy, as breakdowns could occur at any point along the road, far from help. This was a feature of cycling from the very earliest days of the pursuit; as Andrew Ritchie points out, cycling guides in the late 1860s 'often explained how to make velocipedes as well as how to ride them'.[37] I argue that this democratic proximity to the machine's working parts invited an active, rewarding relationship with technology. As the following examples show, the bicycle was an industrial technology that democratised the spanner. The working parts of a machine were made accessible to anyone who manifested an interest in them, regardless of sex and class.[38] This encouraged a relationship with technology that was meaningful and empowering rather than alienating and disabling.

A transformation in contemporary attitudes to the machine is given expression in two books on cycling by Mary Kennard. In her non-fiction *Guide Book for Lady Cyclists*, Kennard insists on the importance of acquiring mechanical knowledge of the bicycle in addition to mastering the actual skill of riding. 'If you are really fond of your cycle and take an interest in it,' she advises her readers, 'the only plan is never to neglect an opportunity of learning things connected with its construction.'[39] She argues that 'there is no reason why any person (even in the upper classes) gifted with ordinary intelligence, should not master a few simple details connected with the care and repair of the cycle'.[40] She herself takes real pleasure in this aspect of cycling, recounting how she and her local bicycle mechanic

> toiled away in friendly comradeship, he all black and stained [. . .] I, hot and dusty from my ride, brushes and cloths in hand, worshipping on my knees at the shrine of the beloved cycle. I never could polish it enough.[41]

It is the bicycle that provides the pretext for this moment of 'comradeship' between a working-class man and an upper-class woman, a fact that recalls the levelling potential of the technology.

In Kennard's novel *The Golf Lunatic and his Cycling Wife*, which recycles several autobiographical scenes from the *Guide Book*, the heroine Cynthia is meticulous about cleaning (and talking to) her mount every evening, no matter how tired or hungry she may feel after her ride. 'I cleaned my Raleigh religiously,' she recounts, 'and as I cleaned it I inwardly said to it: "O, little wheel, I am grateful to you."'[42] One evening when she arrives at her destination wet and exhausted after a rainy ride into the night, she privileges cleaning her bicycle over taking care of herself, much to her host's alarm: 'my host was so concerned at my neglecting myself in order to polish my mount, that he offered to give it a final rub'.[43] When not cycle touring, Cynthia spends her time learning mechanics or testing the latest bicycles in order to write reviews for the cycling press. Like Kennard herself, Cynthia 'haunted the workshop of our High Barby repairer, and picked up a good deal of practical knowledge which stood [her] in good stead'.[44] This experience in mechanics allows Cynthia to repair her bicycle as well as those of her husband and her friend on subsequent cycling tours.

Kennard is not alone in suggesting that cyclists must learn both to ride and repair their vehicles; mechanical scenes complement riding scenes in a great number of cycling narratives. In Jerome K. Jerome's *Three Men on the Bummel*, the three friends check that their machines are in working order before leaving for a cycling tour in the Black Forest. The narrator is suspicious of 'overhauling', after witnessing a traumatic scene in which a friend pulled his bicycle to pieces in a botched attempt to repair it, and concludes: 'There are two ways you can get exercise out of a bicycle: you can "overhaul" it, or you can ride it.'[45] In spite of Jerome's binary outlook, most accounts bear witness to a close interrelation of the two activities. Both riding and repairing bicycles are forms of tacit, practical, sensory knowledge that cannot be easily explained in words or writing, but can only be learned empirically. Moreover, they both require an intimate, reciprocal relationship with and understanding of the machine. F. W. Bockett humorously connected cyclists' passion for mechanics and maintenance to pre-industrial belief systems:

> The philosophers of the future will write many learned treatises on the influences of the bicycle in that reversion to fetishism which is one of the queer characteristics of the present day. They will point out how the daily lubricating of the bearings developed into a sacred offering accompanied by mystic rites, and they will draw fancy pictures of men and maidens decorating their 'wheels' with flowers with a view to persuading the tyres not to indulge in punctures.[46]

Bockett terms this a '"reversion to a primitive type", as the scientists put it',[47] yet it is paradoxically predicated on an intimate connection with an industrial artefact. In Bockett's description, machinery acts as the means for reconnecting with a primitive, ritualistic outlook in the context of a highly industrialised present. By encouraging a close interaction with mechanism, the bicycle encouraged a perspective that took stock of the primitive heritage of humanity while incorporating the vitality of objects into the cyclist's worldview.

In engaging with the machine's mechanism, cyclists entered into an intimate relationship with the materials that made up the object. Jane Bennett recalls the central thesis of Cyril Smith's *A History of Metallography* (1960), which posits that

It was metalworkers' intense intimacy with their material that enabled *them*, rather than (the less hands-on) scientists, to be the first ones to discover the polycrystalline structure of nonorganic matter. The desire of the craftsperson to see what a metal can *do*, rather than the desire of a scientist to know what a metal *is*, enabled the former to discern *a* life in metal and thus, eventually, to collaborate more productively with it.[48]

Repairing bicycles, like riding them, provides a means of physical interaction with the steel, rubber and leather that make up the machine. Cyclists discovered life in their machines, reflected in the frequent tendency to portray the bicycle as the successor of the horse, a companion that required daily care and cleaning. It was common for early cyclists to vaunt the superiority of the low-maintenance bicycle over animal-powered locomotion.[49] Nonetheless, the bicycle appears to have inherited patterns and habits of care from its equine ancestor. The attention shown to these cherished machines was cited by Bijker et al. as an indicator of their social status in the 1890s.[50] They quote Charles Darwin's granddaughter Gwen Raverat, who recalls:

> How my father did adore those bicycles! Such beautiful machines! They were as carefully tended as if they had been alive; every speck of dust or wet was wiped from them as soon as we came back from a ride; and at night they were all brought into the house.[51]

In A. C. Pemberton's *Cycling and Society* (1897), this solicitous contemporary attitude towards bicycles – in evidence in the *Punch* illustration in Figure 3.2 – is reflected in the fact that they are housed indoors, in pride of place:

> In the marble hall of Chelsea House [. . .] and most other palatial mansions, the bicycle-stand is now a matter of course, and many people [. . .] are careful not to leave their machines exposed to the damp air and to dust.[52]

Bockett notes that many women took special care with their bicycles when transporting them by train; they 'swathe handle-bars, frame and even spokes with wonderful bands of linen, for all the world like the swaddling clothes of a week-old baby'.[53] The care shown to bicycles in this period not only reflects the fact that they were expensive, luxury items; it hints at a relationship with technology that recognised the vitalism of the object itself.

154 The Alternative Modernity of the Bicycle

DIVISION OF LABOUR.
It is not the business of Ducal Footmen to Clean the Family Bicycles. The Ladies Ermyntrude and Adelgitha have to do it themselves.

Figure 3.2 Anonymous, 'Division of Labour', *Punch, or the London Charivari*, 24 January 1896, 6. By permission of TopFoto.

These contemporary attitudes towards bicycles anticipated what Flann O'Brien famously termed 'the humanity of the bicycle' in his novel *The Third Policeman* (1967).[54] O'Brien provides perhaps the most memorable and humorous literary incarnation of a concept that had been in circulation from the earliest days of cycling: the idea that bicycles could pick up human traits as a result of close contact with their riders. The 'Atomic Theory' explained by Sergeant Pluck holds that cyclists and their bicycles exchange atoms, with the result that the humans become part bicycle, and bicycles part human. Alfred Jarry's *The Supermale*, which we will examine at length later in this chapter, experiments with the idea of porosity between human and machine, as both adopt elements from the other in his narrative. Wells, too, played with the idea of bicycles and humans adopting patterns of behaviour from each other. When young Hoopdriver encounters the attractive cyclist Jessie, the narrator blames the moral quality of his bicycle (which he puts down to its depraved previous owner) for the panic and fall that ensue. 'No one who has ever ridden a cycle of any kind but will witness that the things are unaccountably prone to pick up bad habits – and keep them', the narrator remarks, before describing the physical symptoms the bicycle exhibits: 'it became convulsed with the most violent emotions directly the Young Lady in Grey appeared. It began an absolutely unprecedented Wabble.'[55] This attribution of human characteristics to a machine points to a vibrant exchange and dialogue between riders and their bicycles, which led to a re-examination of the limits of both the human and the mechanical.

The Human Motor: Mechanising the Body in Alfred Jarry's The Supermale

As a human-powered machine, the bicycle was uniquely placed to play a role in contemporary debates around the mechanisation and perfecting of the capacities of the human body. This concern was epitomised in an obsession with testing the limits of human endurance. Around the time that the first commercially available velocipedes appeared in Paris, a body of medical writing emerged examining the efficiency of the human body. In *The Human Motor*, Anson Rabinbach surveys a vast body of writing concerned with human work and fatigue, noting that whereas 'before 1860 almost no medical or scientific studies of fatigue are recorded', there appeared a 'new medical discourse in the 1870s charting the topography of fatigue, especially in France but also in other European countries'.[56] 'Fatigue' was defined by certain medical authorities as a malfunctioning of the human motor, to be overcome by various means, such as diet, stimulants and training. The body was subjected to the logic that scientists and engineers had been applying to machines throughout the industrial era. It became a means for transforming energy into work, and was examined in terms of its input, output and efficiency. Such an outlook was characterised in the UK by works such as Arnold Bennett's 1908 *The Human Machine*, which encouraged its readers to view their body as a mechanism that could be controlled with careful training.[57] While Rabinbach fails to consider the bicycle in his study, it was a technology that offered an ideal means to mechanically test the physical capacities of the body. As contemporaries recognised, this highly efficient mechanism powered solely by human energy was an exemplary technology for testing and quantifying human endurance.

As the technology of the bicycle was fine-tuned from the mid-1880s, incredible tests of performance were thought up to push the human–machine assemblage to its limit. Andrew Ritchie outlines how competitive cyclists at the turn of the century covered ever greater distances at faster and faster speeds:

> 'Gigantism' and the pursuit of superlative records occurred in both sport and the development of technology, especially around the turn of the century. Both phenomena were fundamental expressions of an industrialised

society, in which outstanding and hitherto unrealized achievements became the objective of all human endeavours.⁵⁸

At a time when faith in technological and athletic achievement was at its apogee, racing cyclists were pushed to feats that would shock present-day athletes and audiences. At hugely popular six-day track races, considered to be one of the first mass spectator sports, cyclists continually raced around a circuit for six days and nights, stopping only when absolutely necessary. These cyclists pushed their bodies to incredible extremes. In 1897 Charlie Miller covered the record distance of 2088.35 miles (3360.87 km) in a New York six-day track race, averaging a speed of 14.5 mph (23.3 km/h) and sleeping for only 4.5 of the 9.75 hours he spent off his bicycle.⁵⁹ Watson and Gray describe these 'grim feats' as accomplished by riders who by the end of the race were 'begging for sleep, dazed by their efforts, hallucinating or hypnotized by what the press liked to call "the race to nowhere"'.⁶⁰ A similar drive to stage extreme feats of endurance was observed in French road races. For instance, the Bordeaux–Paris bike race, first held in 1891, was 577 kilometres long, and in the Paris–Brest–Paris race, inaugurated the same year, cyclists covered 1,196 kilometres, carrying their own food and supplies. Soon after the French champion cyclist Charles Terront won the inaugural Paris–Brest–Paris race in a time of 71 hours 22 minutes (six days ahead of a petrol-powered Peugeot Type 3 quadricycle driven by Auguste Doriot and Louis Rigoulot), he rode over three thousand kilometres from St Petersburg to Paris in just over fourteen days. Such heady distances are still attempted in a small number of present-day races – such as the self-supported European Transcontinental Race – but this drive to what Ritchie terms 'gigantism' has largely disappeared from contemporary cycle racing. The 'outstanding and hitherto unrealized achievements' society was witness to at the turn of the century were an outcome of the encounter with a novel technology that seemed capable of transforming the body into an unstoppable machine.

Alfred Jarry's *The Supermale* (1902) provides a memorable literary incarnation of this contemporary obsession with testing human endurance and fatigue. Jarry himself was an enthusiastic cyclist who bought a luxury Clément racing bicycle in 1896, never managing to pay off the debt he had incurred in making the purchase before his untimely death. Published a year before the first Tour de France, this self-styled 'modern novel' mobilises the bicycle as a symbol of society's obsession with mechanically and chemically augmenting the body's capacities. As Marieke Dubbelboer observes, '[Jarry] recognises all the fashionable motifs and ideas circulating about the machine, but in order to mock and subvert them'.[61] While ridiculing contemporary fads such as the long-distance cycling feats described above, the novel also reflects a strain in Jarry's own thinking about the perfectibility of human strength through mechanical invention. In his 1896 review of the *Cyclo-Guide Miran* he describes the bicycle as 'an external skeleton' which has developed independently of human evolution.[62] Quoting other contemporary authors on cycling, Jarry remarks that 'the Rosny brothers have already called the bicycle a new organ; above all it is a mineral extension which, being born of geometry, is almost infinitely perfectible'.[63] In *The Supermale*, Jarry both explores and satirises the concept of the mechanical perfectibility of the human body when coupled with machines.

Set in a near future (c. 1920), the narrative centres around the exploits of the aristocratic André Marcueil, who provocatively asserts at the beginning of the novel that 'Love is an insignificant act, since you can indulge in it endlessly.'[64] This bold statement is founded on a firm belief in the possibility of attaining a form of perpetual motion, the holy grail of engineers for centuries. Justifying himself to his audience – the doctor Bathybius, the engineer Arthur Gough and the chemist William Elson – Marcueil uses a cycling metaphor to make his point:

> Complex muscular and nervous systems benefit from complete rest, it seems to me, while their 'other half' is working. It is well known that each leg of a cyclist rests and even enjoys an automatic massage, as restorative as any embrocation, while the other one is working.[65]

This image reinforces the link with perpetual motion machines – such as the overbalanced wheel – whose inventors sought to harness the force of gravity, one half rising as the other fell. Moreover, Marcueil's description highlights the bicycle's unique role as a machine that accompanies the body's effort, facilitating an almost perfected expenditure of energy. Since the body recovers strength and energy when at rest, the alternate pedalling action of a cyclist's legs leads Marcueil to imagine that a person on a bicycle could achieve perpetual motion, never needing to rest. Such an outlook was fostered by mid-nineteenth-century discoveries in thermodynamics, whose first law stated that energy in an isolated system is constant; therefore energy can neither be created nor destroyed. Yet the second law of thermodynamics asserts that entropy in a system will always increase, reducing the ability of energy to do work.

These discoveries in physics proved the theoretical impossibility of the holy grail of perpetual motion while contributing to the debates around fatigue and degeneration that characterised the late century. A fear of limits coexisted alongside an optimistic belief in endless human potential, as Rabinbach observes:

> The concepts of energy and fatigue reflected the paradox of this social modernity, at once affirming the endless natural power available to human purpose while revealing an anxiety of limits – the fear that the body and psyche were circumscribed by fatigue and thus could not withstand the demands of modernity.[66]

The bicycle and the imaginary that came to surround it in late industrial Britain and France contributed to the emergence of discourses that presented the human body as a machine to be tested and perfected. Yet the spectre of the dissipation of human energy loomed large, suggesting that the body could not cope with the demands that machine culture placed on it.

In the opening pages of *The Supermale*, Marcueil is described as a 30-year-old 'ordinary man' who, judging from his frail physique, seems to be 'remarkably weak'.[67] Unmarried and physically decrepit, he represents the type of degenerate subject that certain commentators believed would bring about the imminent depopulation and decline of the nation. Yet a subsequent chapter recounting Marcueil's youth informs the reader that he is not the feeble man he appears to be; he has hidden his superhuman strength and sexual energy all his life, in order to appear normal. It is his desire to prove his conviction that 'human strength has no limits'[68] that motivates him to eventually want to test his own body, although he continues to veil his true identity. Marcueil's first attempts to measure his physical might are carried out on machines built specifically for that purpose. Jarry's narrative parodies the contemporary invention of just such devices, including the ergograph and the aesthesiometer.[69] Marcueil then turns to cycling, covertly taking part in a 10,000-mile race between five cyclists on a quintuplet and a steam train, from Irkousk to Paris.[70] American chemist William Elson travels on the train while the team of cyclists race a tandem for five days and nights at speeds of up to 300 km/h, fed only on Elson's 'Perpetual Motion Food'. Like the Tour de France – first held in 1903 as a publicity event for a sports newspaper, *L'Auto* – the race is thought up as a means of promoting Elson's product while proving that, when augmented by this stimulant, 'the human motor [is] superior to mechanical motors'.[71] Marcueil, on the other hand, takes part in the race in order to test his belief in 'the infinite nature of human strength', unaided by performance-enhancing drugs.[72]

The long central chapter recounting the race is narrated by an American cyclist riding the quintuplet, Tom Oxborrow.[73] One of his fellow cyclists, Jewey Jacobs, dies from overexertion during the race. Oxborrow, referring to the body of his deceased team mate, describes how his limbs 'seized up', adding that 'this term, which applies to friction in machines, described the corpse perfectly'.[74] The trainers share this mechanised, commodified view of the racer's body, deciding against removing the corpse since Jacobs is still under contract until the end of the race. Instead, they order the remaining four cyclists to pedal harder to reanimate their departed team mate, whose corpse starts pedalling again furiously. The cyclists take the lead as the train runs out of fuel, but when they approach the finish line they are outrun by a mystery solo cyclist who – though his friends don't recognise him – is none other than Marcueil. When he first appears, Oxborrow takes him for a novice, inept cyclist, known at the time as a *pédard*.[75] Remarking on his poor technique and outdated clothing, the narrator fully expects the mysterious cyclist to be run over by the steam train at any minute: 'He was wobbling so much that it looked like he had been cycling for barely three hours [. . .] He was dressed in a frock coat and wearing a dusty grey top hat.'[76] This image of an old-fashioned cyclist remains 'photographed in his retina',[77] yet just a few moments later his first impression proves to be false:

> It was not a dream: a strange cyclist was in front of the locomotive. But he was not riding a town bicycle with solid tyres! He was not wearing elastic boots! His bicycle wasn't squeaking [. . .] His swelling muscles had split his shorts apart at the thighs! His bicycle was a racing model the like of which I had never seen, with microscopic tyres, and with a ratio higher than that on the quintuplet.[78]

Before the narrator's eyes, the outdated *pédard* becomes a supermodern scorcher. An absurd nineteenth-century apparition is transformed into a vision of the future, an optimised human body mounted on a perfected machine. This detailed portrait of an old-fashioned cyclist reminds us that the frenetic pace of technological development meant that even by 1902 – with the appearance of the automobile and the beginnings of aviation – the cyclist was something of an archaic apparition. Yet the portrait of the futuristic cyclist drives home the persistent modernity of an artefact that provided an optimised means to test, push and develop the limits of the human body. The clothes, muscles and bicycle of the supermale mingle into one striking, futuristic image of a body perfected by technology.

After winning the race, Marcueil returns home to accomplish his next feat: while disguised as an 'Indien', he has sex a record eighty-two times in 24 hours with Ellen Elson, William's daughter. Ellen, a keen driver, wears driving goggles during the experiment in order to conceal her identity from the independent observer, Dr Bathybius.[79] While the couple attempt to test the limits of their sexual capacity, the inclusion of this symbolic accessory points to the mechanical outlook on the body fostered by contact with technologies such as the automobile. At the end of the experiment the astonished Bathybius exclaims, 'He is not a man, he is a machine.'[80] In order to inspire love for Ellen in Marcueil, the engineer Arthur Gough then invents a machine that shocks him with 11,000 volts. The desired effect is not achieved, however; it is the machine that falls in love with the man, as Marcueil's strength is superior to that of the electric shock machine. Seeing the result, the doctor remarks:

> but it's so natural, after all! [. . .] now that metal and mechanism are all powerful, in order to survive man must become stronger than machines, just like he overpowered animals . . . Simply adapting to his environment . . . this is the first man of the future . . .[81]

In the closing pages of the novel, this evolutionary explanation for Marcueil's superhuman strength focuses the reader's attention on the risks posed by a society in which humans constantly interact with machines. In order to survive, the doctor claims, humans must overcome machines, becoming machine-like and losing their humanity (in Marcueil's case, the capacity for love) in the process. Marcueil's death at the end of the novel is a reminder of the necessary limits of such a mechanistic view of human potential: he breaks free from the electric shock machine and impales himself on the iron railings of his château. The final description of his corpse, 'twisted round the railings, or the railings round the body',[82] provides a grotesque image of a body deformed by the inert metal it sought to imitate, and finally indistinguishable from it.

As Corry Cropper has argued, Jarry's novel is not simply an irreverent, humorous tale: it is a response to contemporary attitudes about the relationship between humans and machines, a 'cautionary prophecy about the negative consequences of speed and technology, a warning of positivism's hubris'.[83] Jarry instrumentalises the bicycle in this novel as one in a string of real and imaginary inventions that incarnate the ominous drive to industrialise and mechanise the human body. Marcueil is the man of the future who, through prolonged contact with technology, has learned to treat his body as a machine to be tested, pushed and optimised. As Bettina Knapp observes, Jarry's novel highlights 'the fragility of the human species' and offers a negative view of the machine age and its increasing power over individuals and societies.[84] Jarry suggests that while machines might allow us to overcome certain limitations of the body, such limitations are necessary, natural, and constitute what it means to be human. Overlooking them by treating the body purely as a machine leads to the destruction of the body, alongside a loss of fundamentally human sentiments such as love and compassion. While the bicycle race plays a central role in Jarry's cautionary tale, it would seem that it is above all the organisers' attitude that is to blame for the suffering (and death) of those involved. Ultimately, when used 'in moderation', the bicycle stands apart from other technologies in providing a balance of mechanised and corporeal sensations that promotes an empowering interaction with the machine.

Speed, Shock and the Sublime

We have seen how cycling, in certain contexts, could engender a mechanisation of human instincts, muscles and movement. The close contact with a machine also exposed cyclists to the experience of speed in a way that was entirely new to the human sensorium. While trains could boast greater velocity, rapid movement across land had rarely been experienced in the immediate, bodily manner the bicycle allowed. Even today, when cars and planes transport us at hundreds of miles an hour, the thrill of fast cycling persists. As Watson and Gray observe of cycling, 'these sensations make speed real in a way that only occurs in a modern car at over eighty miles an hour [. . .] they give cycling an intensity and an immediacy often lost to the driver'.[85] This intense contact with speed was central to the experience of early cyclists, and widely written about in literature. The speed of the bicycle left people open to the potential of shocks, collisions and accidents – experiences that were predicated on a close proximity to mechanism, and that have been seen by several critics as constitutive of the experience of modernity. Paul Virilio quotes Marc Bloch, who links speed and the accident, arguing that both are central to the fabric of contemporary societies:

> One feature, the most distinctive of all, pits contemporary civilization against those that have preceded it: speed. The metamorphosis occurred

in the space of a single generation, the historian, Marc Bloch, noted in the 1930s. This situation involves a second feature in turn: the accident. The gradual spread of catastrophic events not only affects the reality of the moment but causes anxiety and anguish for generations to come.[86]

For Virilio, technological progress is necessarily accompanied by its dark underbelly; the threat of violence. He writes elsewhere: 'When you invent electricity, you invent electrocution [. . .] Every technology carries its own negativity, which is invented at the same time as technical progress.'[87] The cyclist's physical presence amid motorised, pedestrian and equine traffic subjected the body not only to fresh sensations, but also to new kinds of trauma. While the mid-nineteenth century witnessed a panic around railway deaths, Sydney Aronson recalls that in the United States at the turn of the twentieth century, 'so many [bicycle] accidents occurred that a new obituary column entitled "Death by the Wheel" appeared in newspapers'.[88]

Accidents on bicycles were especially frequent in the early period of their use, when expressions to describe specific types of falls were coined, including 'come a cropper' and 'do a header' (since Ordinary bicycle riders were likely to fall head first). R. J. Mecredy gave this practical advice to cyclists in 1890:

> An Ordinary bicycle is the most dangerous [. . .] If no hedge or hawthorn bush is near, throw your legs over the handlebars and put the brake hard on, and you will shoot forward and alight on your feet, when you must make every effort to keep on your feet and run as hard as you can, for your bicycle is in eager pursuit, and a stroke from it may place you *hors de combat*.[89]

While falls became less perilous with the appearance of the safety bicycle, they were by no means abolished. Crashes and collisions were taken up as motifs in both fiction and non-fiction writing throughout the period; W. J. Coppen's 1880 *Romances of the Wheel*, for instance, features both a frontispiece and a story entitled 'A Spill' (Figure 3.3), and the final story, 'Willie's Last Ride', recounts a father's grief at losing his son in a bicycle accident. Kennard, Wells and Jerome all describe fictional falls in comic or gruesome detail, while in J. W. Allen's metaphysical ode to the bicycle, *Wheel Magic*, a whole chapter is dedicated to the various sorts of crash a cyclist might be exposed to. On the other side of the Channel, Frédéric Régamey in *Vélocipédie et automobilisme* (1898) included several lively pages of textual and visual illustrations of the various accidents a cyclist

"A SPILL."—(PAGE 48.)

Figure 3.3 Anonymous, 'A Spill', from W. J. Coppen, *Romances of the Wheel* (Coventry: Iliffe and Son, 1880), frontispiece. Public domain.

might be unlucky enough to experience.[90] This technology thus confronted people with new forms of physical trauma and shock which fascinated writers not only because of their comic or dramatic effect, but because of their importance in constituting the outlook of the modern subject.

Walter Benjamin characterised the psychological impact of new modes of transport, describing a subject's movement through a busy city street:

> Moving through this traffic involves the individual in a series of shocks and collisions. At dangerous intersections, nervous impulses flow through him in rapid succession, like the energy from a battery [. . .] Thus technology has subjected the human sensorium to a complex kind of training.[91]

As Benjamin reminds us, the late nineteenth-century street was an increasingly hazardous space, criss-crossed by swarms of people, animals and vehicles. Benjamin is here describing the shocks experienced by a pedestrian, yet he focuses on the new technologies of the industrial era as the source of the 'nervous impulses' that transform the urban subject. Present-day critics continue to focus on the centrality of speed, shock and trauma to modern experience. Hartmut Rosa claims that the temporal structure of modernity was defined by a general impression of 'social acceleration' as a result of the impact of various transport and communication technologies from the turn of the century.[92] Sue Zemka focuses on the modern subject's exposure to shock and injury while in contact with these new technologies in traffic or on the factory floor.[93] Recalling Virginia Woolf's assertion that modern life is inherently traumatic, Zemka argues that 'modern shock does not begin with trench warfare, but rather with rapid industrialization'.[94] Nicholas Daly examines the staging of railway accidents in sensation dramas of the 1860s, arguing that the appeal of replaying crashes reveals a paradox; while industrial modernity is 'predicated on the intellectual separation of people and machines [. . .] the corollary of this is a modernity that obsessively replays the meeting of the two'.[95] Like the recurrent motif of train collisions which Daly describes, turn-of-the-century representations of the bicycle consistently returned to the potential of this technology for harm. Although the non-motorised nature of the bicycle made this technology considerably less hazardous than trains or cars, it should not be forgotten that it nonetheless exposed cyclists and those around them to new forms of shock, trauma and injury.

Accidents were rarely an enjoyable experience, yet several authors depicted the thrill of constantly being faced with the potential of danger while riding a bicycle. J. W. Allen draws attention to the pleasurable risk factor experienced by cyclists, whose safety is largely reliant on independent mastery of the machine:

> One of the finest qualities of cycling is just that it involves an element of difficulty and even danger. Our ordinary comings and goings are sadly lacking in this ingredient of happiness. There is a certain danger in railway travelling; but on the railway, so far as you are personally concerned, you are almost completely at the mercy of brute chance. On a bicycle it is your own skill and coolness and power that must overcome difficulties and carry you in safety. You are braced not only to energy, but to prudence and foresight and nice balance.[96]

Cyclists stand apart from dominant, collective and mechanised modes of transport; autonomous in the midst of the traffic, they have a greater degree of agility and flexibility than bulkier vehicles. Moreover, the danger to which they are visually exposed (unlike the train passenger, who is blind to potential obstacles on the line and, as

Allen points out, unable to take action to avoid them) gives them what could be termed a sublime experience of the street, where a fear of destruction is constantly balanced by the faith in their own ability to avoid the obstacle. When moving at speed or in darkness – especially in an urban environment – the cyclist may be involved in a collision at any moment, and this experience can be rewarding as well as terrifying. Allen's sentiment is mirrored in Virginia Niles Leeds's 1897 short story 'A Coast and a Capture', in which the heroine is exhilarated by a close brush with death:

> I shoved off with utter recklessness, drew my feet up on the fork, and proceeded to coast. How the wheel flew! Everything swam before me from the rapidity of my flight, and every moment I expected to be dashed to destruction [...] Just as I reached the rails, around the rock-bound curve came the midnight train. A dark, looming, quivering phantom, shaking the earth as it thundered along, and bearing down with menace and fury upon all venturesome atoms that should stand in its way.[97]

In this bicycle-versus-train scene, the swift cyclist manages to ride over the tracks before the passing night train prevents her pursuers from following her. This episode inherits the trope of the closely avoided railway disaster, which Daly has examined as a means of 'training' subjects to 'accommodate the shocks of mechanical modernity'.[98] Yet potential bicycle collisions involve a crucial extra element of individual skill, intelligence and mastery of the machine. The bicycle was a technology that invited daring riders to experience exhilaration and risk more directly than railway passengers, while allowing a close collaboration with a machine that provided affirmation of riders' capacity to avoid danger. This was a further means by which the bicycle offered an empowering, human-centred and even sublime interaction with technology, in opposition to the debilitating and disabling sensations that result from the experience of motorised modes of transport.

Beyond Vision: Stimulating the Senses

While providing a striking instance of the meeting and interaction of man and machine, turn-of-the-century cyclists attested to a renewed sensory experience in the saddle. As we shall see, many early cyclists claimed that their sensory impressions were sharpened rather than impoverished by their experience awheel, in contrast to other transport technologies. The unique quality of the bicycle is its capacity to knit the mechanical and corporeal together without overriding either. The bicycle leaves its rider open to the environment and requires sustained physical effort to achieve motion. The effect of this is a stimulation and mingling of the senses and muscles, occurring alongside and in interaction with the mechanised sensations we have thus far been exploring. Early cycling authors bear testament to an embodied engagement with their environment, in contrast to the previous paradigm of visually focused and disembodied rail travel. Wolfgang Schivelbusch described the cultural impact of the 'panoramic view' engendered by the railways, with passengers prevented from hearing, smelling, touching or looking closely at objects passing nearby, obliging them to contemplate distant, sweeping vistas.[99] Cyclists, on the other hand, enjoy a sensorily rich experience of place that shares much in common with pedestrian travel, relying not only on vision but also on hearing, smell and touch to interpret their surroundings. They may set their own pace, travelling at speed or slowly, changing direction, walking or stopping at will. Cyclists are conscious of the people, animals and things around them, actively interacting with the landscape through which they move.

W. S. Beekman from the USA reflected on the changes he felt had occurred in his sensory organs on learning to cycle in his autobiographical touring account *Cycle Gleanings* (1894): 'Once possessing a machine, see the effect. The entire system is stimulated, the mind strengthened, purified and quickened [. . .] One can never forget the sensations experienced during the time acquiring the art of riding.'[100] Beekman here combines a sensory, corporeal register (the imperative 'see', 'the entire system', 'the mind', 'the sensations') with verbs suggesting mechanical precision and optimisation (stimulate, strengthen, purify, quicken). This unique machine appeared able to harness the benefits of industrial innovation while simultaneously providing a means of escape from industrial civilisation by offering a fully embodied experience. At once mobile and attentive, cyclists were key players at a moment when, in Jonathan Crary's terms, vision was 'taken out of the incorporeal relations of the camera obscura and relocated in the human body'.[101] Not only vision, but all the other human senses were combined with mechanised movement to create one compelling incarnation of the 'unstable attentive subject' of modernity theorised by Crary.[102]

Bodily Progression: Effort and Reward

Central to the cyclist's multi-sensory experience is the energetic input required from the body. Where the energy needed for progression was constantly in evidence in coaches or on horseback, railways and other fuel-powered transport had occulted energetic input, making forward motion seem effortless. While many hailed the machine's negation of the need for human or animal labour as a victory of industrialisation, others saw it as a fundamental distortion of human experience. John Ruskin (1819–1900) famously asserted that 'all travelling becomes dull in exact proportion to its rapidity',[103] and elsewhere railed against mechanical aids to locomotion, arguing that 'nothing in the training of the human mind with the body will ever supersede the appointed God's ways of slow walking and hard working'.[104] While Ruskin vociferously denounced the bicycle along with other modes of transport, many early cyclists in fact shared his views on the value of hard work and slow, attentive progress while travelling. The sociologist of sport Michel Bouet recognises the bicycle's ability to reconnect the body to its own capacities, arguing that

> One of the specific pleasures of cycling is feeling endowed with multiplied strength, but which nonetheless remains our own, that of our body. We do not have to pay for our exaltation with a loss of autonomy, as is the case when we annex natural energy, such as that of the wind or an animal (on horseback), or extract energy from a car's engine.[105]

The loss of autonomy inherent in motorised (or, according to Bouet, even equine) travel is the price paid for the exhilaration of fast, effortless, disembodied movement. Cyclists, on the other hand, reap the benefits of a mechanism that optimises their motion without robbing them of their energetic autonomy. In *Here are Wings*, Maurice Leblanc's hero Pascal attributes the specific joy of cycling to this direct correlation between bodily energy and movement: 'joyfully we create speed and impressions that are the equivalent of the energy and hopes we have put in. We progress because we are strong and supple, and we see beautiful things because we are capable of going to see them.'[106] Cycling allows people to feel empowered solely by their own energy output. The latent capacities of the body are revealed and enhanced by the machine.

The bicycle was a child of the Industrial Revolution, yet thanks to the fact that the energy input came from its human rider, cycling rapidly became associated with the sensory register built up around pre-industrial modes of transport, such as walking or coach travel. In his essay 'The English Mail-Coach' (1849), written in the early days of rail travel, Thomas de Quincey argued that mechanised travel results in a distorted and alienating experience of movement:

> Seated in the old mail-coach, we needed no evidence out of ourselves to indicate velocity [. . .] The vital experience of the glad animal sensibilities made doubts impossible on the question of our speed; we heard our speed, we saw it, we felt it as a thrilling; and this speed was not the product of blind insensate agencies, that had no sympathy to give, but was incarnated in the fiery eyeballs of the noblest among brutes, in his dilated nostril, spasmodic muscles, and echoing hoofs [. . .] But now, on the new system of travelling, iron tubes and boilers have disconnected man's heart from the ministers of his locomotion.[107]

The cyclist shares in common with the horses pulling the mail coach – and, according to de Quincey, its passengers – a keen, bodily sense of the energy being spent in order to move. De Quincey insists on the rich sensory experience of coach travel, describing how travellers heard, felt and saw their speed, and thus mingled their senses and bodies with their forward movement on the machine. This is contrasted to the 'blind, insensate' experience of rail travel, where passengers' bodies are 'disconnected' from the means of locomotion. Coach travellers did not directly furnish locomotive energy, yet they were complicit with the horses' effort; de Quincey goes on to stress that their speed, though provided by the horses, 'had yet its centre and beginning in man'.[108] Not only did the passengers directly witness their effort and exhaustion, they would get out of the coach and walk on uphill stretches in order to relieve the animals. Moreover, de Quincey's justification of his preference for riding on the top of the mail coach – 'The air, the freedom of prospect, the proximity to the horses, the elevation of seat [. . .] but, above all, the certain anticipation of purchasing occasional opportunities of driving'[109] – prefigures the aesthetic pleasure of cycling, where the rider is directly exposed to the elements and directs the vehicle independently. The cyclist, like the horse and its passengers, enjoys a direct, transparent relationship to forward motion; kinetic energy is not drawn from invisible 'tubes and boilers', from complex unseen processes such as the extraction of coal or oil, or, in a modern context, from the manufacture of lithium batteries and the production of the electricity to charge them.

Writing in the 1970s, Ivan Illich echoed Ruskin's and de Quincey's impression of the alienation implicit in mechanised travel, describing how the habitual passenger, '[a]ddicted to being carried along [. . .] has lost control over the physical, social, and psychic powers that reside in man's feet'.[110] Sustained work is required from the cyclist to make progress, and the journey is synonymous with physical fatigue or suffering, yet also with a sense of purpose. As Eric Leed recalls, medieval pilgrims did not travel for pleasure, but in order to subject their bodies to the epic ordeal of walking great distances to reach holy sites; a meaning 'explicit in the original English word for travel, *travail*'.[111] The hard work required from the cyclist's body might be exhausting, but it is also a source of meaning and empowerment. By putting effort into movement, the non-motorised traveller is rewarded with a rich sensory experience (described by Beekman and de Quincey) and physical, social and psychic validation (depicted by Illich). The bodily connection to forward movement specific to the walker and the cyclist is the source of a multi-sensory connection to space that, in an industrialised world, proposes an alternative connection to the machine and a human-centred approach to travel.

The human-powered bicycle cast a backward glance to a pre-industrial paradigm, when exchanges occurred mainly at a local level, with energy being generated through human and animal labour in addition to the harnessing of natural resources such as wind and water. Karl Marx noted how mechanised transport had been a crucial motor of capitalism, with its 'constant flinging of capital and labour from one sphere of production into another, and its newly-created connections with the world market'.[112] Mechanised transport created the new geographies required for globalised capitalism and imperialism, systems that rely on the exploitation of the many by the few. The bicycle, on the other hand, proposes a localised, human-scaled geography that makes the 'constant flinging of capital and labour' unthinkable. Once set on the road, no complex processes of extraction, exploitation and pollution underlie the cyclist's movement, in contrast to vehicles powered by fossil fuels or the array of electric-powered modes of locomotion grappling for space on present-day streets. The enthusiastic uptake of cycling by diverse groups in the late nineteenth century was connected to the subversive thrill of rediscovering the power and potential of the human body and its senses, in the context of a highly industrialised, globalised, alienating and commodified present. At the turn of the twentieth century, when imperialist capitalism was at its apogee, the bicycle suggested an alternative route for modernity, one that turned its back on the dizzying pursuit of wealth and mechanisation and reinstated human energy as society's basic currency and the five senses as our interface with the world.

Multi-sensory Movement

Having reconnected to the body as a source of energy and empowerment, cyclists were able to engage in a renewed relationship with all of their senses. Michel Bouet describes the effect of physical effort on the senses in the following terms: 'The activation and intensification of the body's motor functions corresponds to an awakening and an enriching of sensoriality, particularly through kinaesthesia.'[113] This 'muscular sense' was first observed by H. C. Bastian in 1887, just as cycling was beginning to become a popular pursuit. Bastian coined the term kinaesthesia to describe the perception of body position and movement, a sense that was distinct from the five senses observed since Antiquity.[114] Early cyclists were certainly well placed to observe this awareness of their own muscular movements, while actively engaging their other sensory organs. As Justin Spinney observed in an ethnographic study of present-day cyclists in London, cycling is a deeply multi-sensory experience. Spinney illustrates how 'in an embodied practice such as cycling [. . .] vision is shown to be re-embodied alongside the other senses as part of a multi-sensory construction of the experiences and meanings of place'.[115] Although their motion was optimised by mechanism, cyclists' vision was no longer framed by the train window, and their openness to their surroundings allowed them to engage their hearing, smell and touch in their new negotiation of the environment.

Edward Thomas bears witness to the uncanny in-betweenness of cycling in his travelogue *In Pursuit of Spring*:

> Motion was extraordinarily easy that afternoon, and I had no doubts that I did well to bicycle instead of walking. It was as easy as riding in a cart, and more satisfying to a restless man. At the same time I was a great deal nearer to being a disembodied spirit than I can often be. I was not at all tired, so far as I knew. No people or thoughts embarrassed me. I fed through the senses directly, but very temperately, through the eyes chiefly, and was happier than is explicable or seems reasonable. This pleasure of my disembodied spirit (so to call it) was an inhuman and diffused one, such as may be attained by whatever dregs of our life survive after death.[116]

This striking portrait captures the liminal stance of the cyclist, who is at once passenger and means of locomotion. Unlike the walker, Thomas feels 'disembodied', as though he were riding in a vehicle; yet he is not restless, as his legs are pushing the pedals, and his senses are stimulated. Thomas bears witness to a strange alienation from his ego and his body, describing the pleasure he feels as 'inhuman', and comparing it to deathly peace. The bicycle mechanises his movements, while the steady rhythm of the machine seems to stimulate his senses (which he uses 'directly, but very temperately') and his mental state.

Many authors bear witness to a new and privileged sensory experience awheel. Human senses and the opportunities offered by mechanism combined to produce new aesthetic possibilities, as Beekman notes:

> What is more pleasing to the senses than the delicate odor of sweet flowers? [...] And it is only a machine that will so quietly carry you along among such situations; coming so rapidly and silently upon them that they are not wafted away by the vibration of the air before you reach them.[117]

Cycling, Beekman recognised, is characterised as much by its mechanical side as its bodily or natural aspect. It is in the hybridisation of these two previously opposed registers that the cycling aesthetic may be located, as he notes later:

> The language of Nature is to be heard throughout all the length and breadth, and is not drowned out by the rapid whirl of the resilient tires. One can hear it in the delicate swish of the individual blades of grass, the rustling of the leaves, the humming of the insects, the bowing of the boughs, the singing of the birds, and the purring tones of the babbling brooks. One and all keep up an ever-changing accompaniment to the rapid and cheerful click of the endless sprocket-chain.[118]

Here, the ambient smells and noises experienced by the cyclist (which would be inaccessible to the passenger of a train or car) combine with the pleasing sounds of the parts of the bicycle. Beekman willingly mingles the pastoral description of 'the language of Nature' with the 'whirl of the resilient tires' and the 'cheerful click of the endless sprocket-chain', thus aestheticising the mechanical noises of the bicycle and including them in the varied soundscape experienced by the cyclist.

The potential wealth of sensory experience available to the cyclist led some writers to condemn 'scorchers' who sped by without paying any heed to their surroundings. Bockett, for instance, insists that 'when you see a nice view, you must: stop, fill up your pipe and digest the prospect',[119] making it cyclists' moral imperative not to rush by – even if they have the capacity to do so – but to dismount and fully 'digest' a view when it presents itself. Bockett condemns the tendency to 'scorch', arguing that cyclists who focus purely on speed are missing the point. The US cycling advocate Maria Ward also criticised speed-crazed cyclists, claiming that 'The scorcher sees little, hears little, and is conscious only of the exhilaration of the moment.'[120] These critics imply that high-speed cyclists forgo the possibility of rich sensory engagement.

The attack on scorchers by both cycling advocates and detractors is symptomatic of concern about the effects of this new and exhilarating experience. The vigorous efforts made by cycling apologists to discourage 'scorching' betray the fact that the speed of the bicycle created shock waves in society at large. The journalist and writer A. W. Rumney wrote in an evangelistic vein when he added the following preamble to the account of a scorcher who had discovered the joy of cycle touring: 'It is the custom of missionaries to tell of conversions. As my mission in life is to encourage cycle touring, I give the following testimony.'[121] The ex-scorcher in question then expresses himself in terms that recall a religious awakening, describing how 'From that point my eyes were opened, as it were, to a new world [. . .] When I reached home I had given up all idea of any more scorching.'[122] Such language bears testimony to the real attempts being made by middle-class cyclists to promote a gentle, slow-paced and observant approach to cycling over the contrasting paradigm based on speed and exhilaration, and associated mainly with the working class. Bockett makes no secret of his determination to raise cycling to the status of a 'Gentle Art' for 'gentle folk'. He traces the contours of a cycling etiquette, relating to dress, diet and behaviour, formulating certain rules on the 'ethics of coasting' and consistently reminding readers that the cyclist 'is also a gentleman'.[123] His sworn enemy is the speed-crazed cyclist, who is 'a scorcher and not a cyclist, and [. . .] before long he will be as extinct as the old bone-shaker'.[124] He generously forgives scorchers for exulting in the new 'power of flying'[125] which cycling has suddenly bestowed upon them. However, he makes a firm case for establishing a gentlemanly, respectable image of his favourite pastime.

The desire of cycling authors to rise above the negative stereotype of the scorcher was motivated by both social and aesthetic factors; they did not wish to be taken for working-class racers or delivery boys, and they believed that a slow-paced approach to cycling offered a fuller sensory experience. Scorchers fail to adopt a 'gentle' approach; they miss out on the details of the journey by failing to pay attention and rushing to their destination. The focus of these writers on the damaging effects of fast riding is symptomatic of a contemporary concern about the effects of speed on the human body and senses.

The importance of all five senses to early cyclists is testified to in the frequent recurrence of accounts of night-time cycling. These descriptions at once vaunt the merits of a vehicle that allowed its users to travel regardless of timetables, and challenge the visual-focused railway traveller's outlook. Deprived of visual signals, cyclists attest to a heightened, multi-sensory experience of their surroundings. In his autobiographical account of cycle touring, J. W. Allen reflects on his preference for nocturnal rides, noting:

> At night we see the world as it is: vast, phantasmal, nebulous, dark. The sun makes it difficult to believe in the absolutely invisible. At night we know better [. . .] One realises the immensity of things and how unimportant humanity is, even on its own planet.[126]

Allen's verb progression – from 'seeing' to 'believing' to 'knowing' to 'realising' – hints at a subtle questioning of visual discourses, and a widening of the cognitive net to other means of interpreting the 'invisible' world. H. G. Wells's heroes in *The Wheels of Chance* rejoice in the exhilarating experience of cycling at night, when the road – which had been an aggressive visual and tactile presence during the day – becomes principally an aural (albeit silent) element in the nocturnal scene:

> The road that was a mere rutted white dust, hot underfoot, blinding to the eye, is now a soft grey silence, with the glitter of a crystal grain set starlike in its silver here and there [. . .] And in silence under [the moon's] benign influence, under the benediction of her light, rode our two wanderers side by side through the transfigured and transfiguring night.[127]

These cyclists' interaction with the spaces they move through allows them access to a realm beyond the visual. Their multi-sensory, synaesthetic experience is highlighted by the mingling of tactile, visual and aural elements in descriptions such as 'soft grey silence', and a sense of reciprocal exchange with the environment is suggested by the repetitive rhythm at the end of the extract. It is as though the darkness awakens all of the previously dormant senses, taking attention away from the predominance of sight and allowing for an interaction with space that, in Wells's terms, is mutually transfiguring, for both subject and object.

This fantastic register surrounding nocturnal rides was echoed by several other authors. The journalist A. W. Rumney, for instance, enjoyed riding 'on Welsh mountains on a moonlit night, and amongst the weirdness of the solemn hills at the witching hour'.[128] The supernatural tone recurrent in such accounts of night-time riding communicates these riders' hyper-sensory, hypnotic experience. There is a keen aesthetic pleasure, too, in the ghostly atmosphere associated with the night, one that directly linked cyclists to their Romantic forebears. As Edmund Burke observed, darkness confronts us with the fear of injury or death, which is at the root of the experience he terms the sublime:

> in utter darkness, it is impossible to know in what degree of safety we stand; we are ignorant of the objects that surround us; we may every moment strike against some dangerous obstruction; we may fall down a precipice the first step we take.[129]

Darkness acts as an adversity to cyclists, obscuring unknown dangers and making the journey challenging and risky. Yet cyclists' ability to overcome these challenges and the thrill of travelling into the unknown augments their sense of adventure and enjoyment in the journey. While anchored in a keen corporeal awareness, these accounts of nocturnal riding also bear witness to a certain out-of-body experience. It is as though bodily effort and the engagement of all the senses allow cyclists to transcend both the machine and their own physicality, giving them access to a spiritual, immaterial world.[130]

Maurice Leblanc's *Here are Wings* pays close attention to the subtle changes that cycling can operate at the level of the human sensorium. At the beginning of their journey through Brittany and Normandy, the four cyclists are described as being out of touch with their senses and bodies, yet gradually they begin to perceive things afresh:

> They hardly looked at things; their eyes and their minds were closed off to the charm of spectacle. They did not know how to perceive the music of silence, the song of the leaves and the harmony of water. But all this penetrated them through new channels and infused them with an unfamiliar sense of wellbeing.[131]

The narrator first concentrates on the visual register, drawing attention to the characters' closed eyes and minds. It is as though this blindness were a necessary stage on the cyclists' journey, allowing them to distance themselves from the dominant visual paradigm in order to discover 'new channels' for sensory engagement. The description of barely audible ambient noises, which they do not yet 'know how to perceive', points to the crucial role that the other senses will come to play in these cyclists' renewed relationship with their bodies and their environment. After a difficult start to their journey under a glaring sun, the four protagonists first discover the joy of cycling when they continue riding after nightfall, as in the previous examples:

> The silhouettes of things were fading. They moved through the ghosts of trees and blurry hedges. And the further they went, the more it seemed to them that they were gifted with energy and agility, and that they could go on forever, like the water that flowed untiringly along beside them, ever alert, ever joyful and continually refreshed.
> The night engulfed them. The two couples lost sight of each other.[132]

Here, darkness permits the cyclists to establish a mystical, sublime connection with their environment, while also providing the first opportunity for the two newly formed couples to lose sight of each other. Leblanc's syntax mirrors the revitalising experience of nocturnal cycling; two brief sentences convey the effect of the diminishing light, before a long, lyrical sentence composed of several rhythmic phrases reflects the regular motion and the kinaesthetic sense of the cyclists. By the end of the novel Pascal is able to proclaim to Madeleine that, thanks to the bicycle, their senses are more acute: they feel 'liberated in our quickened bodies, in our sharpened senses, in our ears that can hear and our eyes that can see'.[133] Recalling the above description of the cyclists' closed senses – 'They did not know how to perceive'[134] – Pascal bears witness to an awakening of the senses, having learned to perceive the surrounding sights, smells and sounds thanks to the experience of travelling on two wheels.

Several days into the journey, Pascal begins to take stock of the changes that are occurring in his sensorium. He describes his impressions using the following metaphor:

> It seems to me that until now I was imprisoned in a glass case, and that all outside spectacles, sounds and smells, came to me through the glass, watered down and cold, as it were . . . and now it seems that the glass is breaking, bit by bit, and that warm and almost painful sensations come to me directly.[135]

The glass envelope from which Pascal begins to break free recalls the window of a car or train; while transparent, it acts as a filter between the moving subject and the sense data he interprets. This filter implies an absence of involvement in the scene on the part of the subject, and the visual register predominates at the expense of dulled sounds, smells and feelings. As the glass shatters, Pascal discovers a more comprehensive sensory experience, with even the sense of touch being solicited so that he experiences 'warm' and 'painful' sensations. He directly attributes this sensory activation to the bicycle, while (through a world play on *sens*, translating as either 'meaning' or 'sense') he claims that this sensory reconnection gives meaning to life: 'You only need to stimulate the sense/meaning of life within yourself, and that is enough to make you happy, nobly, generously happy, with a feeling of justice and certitude. And we have this little steel object to thank for that.'[136] Pascal characterises the cycling aesthetic as a holistic one; rather than focusing on the details as a walker would, the cyclist achieves a sweeping, multi-sensory engagement:

> When walking you inhale the smell of this plant, you hear the song of this bird. On a bicycle you breathe, admire, hear nature itself. The movement produced extends our nerves to their maximum intensity and gives us a sensitivity we had not known until now.[137]

The machine's movement and speed, Pascal claims, sharpens and intensifies our sensory experience, allowing access to a new sensibility.

The nature of Leblanc's cyclists' new interaction with the world prefigures aspects of Henri Bergson's concept of *élan vital* (formulated in 1907), as well as the phenomenology and materialism of more recent theorists such as Maurice Merleau-Ponty, Deleuze and Guattari, Bill Brown, Bruno Latour and Jane Bennett.[138] All of these thinkers posit that the lines between humans and things, subjects and objects, living and inert, are shifting and fluid. The further Pascal rides, the more convinced he becomes that, rather than being separate from the objects surrounding him, his body mingles with them ('we melt into these very things').[139] This belief is founded on a sensory dialogue with his environment; as Merleau-Ponty argues, in the act of sensory interaction, the sense organ becomes integrated into the fleshy world of objects:

> the hand that touches [. . .] takes up a place amongst the things that it touches, is in some sense one of them, and finally gives access to a tangible greater essence of which it is also a part. Through this overlapping of the touching and the touchable, its own movements are integrated into the universe it is engaging with and are written onto the same map as it.[140]

Prefiguring Merleau-Ponty's thinking, Pascal attests to a sense of belonging to a vibrant world, where his newly awakened senses are the interface with the objects around him. 'My skin itself strikes the outside world,' Pascal affirms, 'my senses are shocked and my brain resonates and stirs.'[141] Pascal's description mirrors Merleau-Ponty's concept of *chair*, a fleshy essence that mediates the sensory interaction between subject and object. By opening themselves up to this direct sensory experience, Leblanc's cyclists merge with their environment: '[they] became parcels of nature, instinctive forces, like clouds drifting by, like rolling waves, like smells wafting in the air, like echoing sounds'.[142] By engaging the senses fully and through close interaction with the bicycle, cyclists become part of the clouds, smells and sounds surrounding them, and enter into dialogue with the vibrant world.

Vibrant Interactions in Dorothy Richardson's The Tunnel

Dorothy Richardson's modernist novel *The Tunnel* (1919) is the fourth instalment in her 13-volume *Pilgrimage* series (1915–38). Set in the 1890s, this semi-autobiographical novel provides an account of the protagonist Miriam's experience of learning to ride a bicycle. Chapter 26, coming two-thirds of the way through the book, relates Miriam's first solo ride, a 60-mile trip from London to Malborough. In the space of this brief, intense chapter, Richardson provides us with a microcosmic vision of the cyclist's unique sensory experience. The account of this journey provides a means to examine the sensory engagement of the cyclist more closely while reflecting on its connection to the narrative technique of the modernist novel. As Sara Danius argues in *The Senses of Modernism*, in modernist literature 'the machine invariably appeared in the same thematic cluster as the corporeal, the sensory and the aesthetic'.[143] Cycling provides Richardson with a means to present an epiphanic moment of subjective, sensory engagement with objects and others. Drawing on Merleau-Ponty's phenomenological approach, I examine at close range the reciprocal processes behind the cyclist's movement and perception. By cooperating in a very direct way with their machines, cyclists performed an active exchange between subject and object, mingling their gestures and movements with those of the bicycle.

Miriam is introduced to the bicycle when she receives a gift of two cycling lessons from an upper-class acquaintance, Miss Szigmondy. The young woman struggles with the learning process; her first lesson leaves her feeling 'shamed and helpless',[144] yet she is determined to master the skill, convinced as she is that cycling will utterly change her life. Remembering her teacher's demonstration, she reflects:

> To be able to go down the quiet street and on into the squares – on a bicycle ... I must learn somehow to get my balance. To go along, like in that moment when he took his hands off the handle-bars, in knickers and a short skirt and all the summer to come ... Everything shone with a greater intensity. Friends and thought and work were nothing compared to being able to ride alone, balanced, going along through the air.[145]

This passage reveals how Miriam's ambition to ride a bicycle is founded on a desire for a novel sensory experience, freedom of movement, comfortable clothing, agency and solitude. The infinitives that open the first two sentences and the use of ellipsis between one reflection and the next draw attention to the dreamlike, virtual nature of Miriam's thoughts, which represent an idealised future rather than present reality. The accumulative nature of the phrases describing cycling reflect the enthusiasm of the protagonist, for whom cycling seems to open the door to a new life. Yet the patriarchal society that Miriam inhabits does not make the learning process easy for her; after her humiliating experience at the cycling school, her male work colleagues make patronising remarks about her attempts to ride a bicycle: '"You'll never learn cycling like *that*," said Mr Leyton, with the superior chuckle of the owner of a secret.'[146] These men subsequently offer her ineffectual lessons that merely provide pretexts for showing off their own speed and skill, further humiliating the apprentice cyclist.

In spite of this discouraging start, Miriam continues to recognise the potential of the mobility that she is gradually acquiring, remarking to her forward-thinking female friends Jan and Mag:

> To be able to bicycle would make life utterly different; on a bicycle you feel a different person; nothing can come near you, you forget who you are. Aren't you glad you are alive today, when all these things are happening?[147]

By gradually appropriating the activity, she makes inroads on a masculine domain, becoming 'a different person' in the process. This prefigures her literary ambition, which gradually takes shape and affirms itself throughout the *Pilgrimage* series. Yet Miriam faces not only social ridicule but economic difficulties in acquiring a machine and the clothing associated with it. She remarks on this subject: 'But aren't clothes awful, anyhow? I've been four and eleven on my knickers and I can't possibly get a skirt till next year if then, or afford to hire a machine.'[148] Miriam's reflection draws attention to the difficult financial choices faced by women who earned their own living. She professes a disregard for stylishness, yet admits that the necessary expense of clothes prevents her from spending her money in other ways, such as hiring a bicycle. Jan and Mag, who also work but are better off than Miriam, are able to advise:

> Why don't you ask them to raise your salary? [. . .] If I were you I should tell them. I should say 'Gentlemen – I wish for a skirt and a bicycle.' [. . .] *They* would benefit by your improved health and spirits. Jan and I are new women since we have learned riding. *I* thinking of telling the governor I must have a rise to meet the increased demands of my appetite.[149]

Miriam's friends' use of the term 'new women' highlights the precocious association of this figure with the bicycle and they clearly recognise the physical, mental and social benefits that cycling brings to women. Yet the barriers Miriam encounters before adopting this new form of transport are significant, as they reflect the hesitancy of society at large to encourage women and the working class to adopt this freeing means of transport.

We saw earlier in this chapter how the novice cyclist not only learned to ride the bicycle, but also to repair it, both of which provided stimulating sensory experiences. Miriam exhibits a keen interest in learning about how the machine works. Responding to her brother-in-law Gerald's suggestion that she tighten up the bolts on her hired bicycle before her upcoming trip, she says 'I will if you'll show me where they are. I've got a lovely spanner. Did you look in the wallet?'[150] The unusual choice of the adjective 'lovely' points to Miriam's growing aesthetic pleasure in the machine, based on a tactile, sensory engagement with its working parts. The epithet is repeated some lines later in the description 'there's a little oil can in the wallet, wrapped up in the rag. It's lovely; perfectly new.'[151] Gerald's offer to help Miriam check the nuts and bolts of her machine points to a participatory attitude towards bicycle mechanics; although Miriam has hired the machine, it is her own responsibility as its rider to tend to its needs, in much the same way that a hired horse would be regularly fed and cleaned.

Furthermore, Richardson neatly ties mechanical and corporeal registers together in this scene by staging the discussion in the presence of Miriam's heavily pregnant sister, Harriett. To begin with, the sisters prudishly avoid talking directly about the pregnancy, but when Gerald starts testing Miriam's bicycle, Harriett's thoughts on childbirth are overlain with her husband's and sister's remarks on the machine:

> 'I simply don't think about it. You don't think about it, except now and again when you realize you've got to go through it, and then you go hot all over.'
> 'The head's a bit wobbly,' said Gerald riding around the lawn.
> 'Does that matter?'
> 'Well, it doesn't make it any easier to ride, especially with this great bundle on the handle-bars. You want a luggage-carrier.'[152]

This interesting parallel diagnostic of the bicycle and the body knits mechanical and corporeal registers together, refusing a clear distinction between one and the other. Moreover, Miriam's front-loaded bicycle vividly brings to mind her heavily pregnant younger sister, whose figure the narrator refrains from directly describing. Although Miriam has had to hire rather than buy her bicycle, her meagre savings have allowed her to invest in a saddle, 'a Brooks B40; about the best you can have. It's my own, and so's the Lucas's Baby bell.'[153] Her choice of bell establishes a further parallel with her sister, whose baby will be cared for and admired like Miriam's bicycle. Furthermore, Miriam's ownership of a saddle and bell reminds us that the bicycle, like any object, organism or system, is a collection of heterogeneous parts. In fitting a saddle and a bell, or taking apart a chain, the cyclist interacts with a carefully engineered yet simple machine, entering into a mechanical dialogue with the object.

When Miriam finally sets off from London by bicycle before dawn, she feels 'so strong riding through London, everything dropping away, nothing to think of; off and free, the holiday ahead, nothing but lovely, lonely freedom all round one'.[154] This exploration beyond London's limits corresponds to the spatial structure of the text identified by Elisabeth Bronfen, who argues that Miriam constantly seeks a balance between interior and exterior spaces, often respectively represented as her room and the various 'islands' to which she journeys.[155] The movement beyond the privileged space of her room in London represents an outward impulse by means of which Miriam tries to come to a closer understanding of her relation to other people, places and objects. The beginning of her cycle ride acts as a foil to the sentiment of alienation expressed during her apprenticeship of cycling, as she establishes a frank and easy contact with the spaces and people around her. Her first remark to a fellow cyclist, 'Is this Reading?' (a question to which she already knows the answer), gives her a rare sense of communion with others: 'If she had yelled Have you got a *soul*, it would have been just the same. If everyone were on bicycles all the time you could talk to everybody, all the time, about anything . . .'[156] The rhetorical nature of Miriam's real and imagined questions suggests that she has gained a clear awareness of the existence of her fellow cyclist's soul, which leads her to formulate a rare expression of a belief in frank communication between people. The day's ride gives her a keener sense of the communion between herself, others and the objects surrounding her. As Pamela Thurschwell notes, physical or spiritual communion between people was a question that preoccupied *fin-de-siècle* thought. This was given impetus both by technological innovation and a growing interest in the occult, since 'talking to the dead and talking on the phone both hold out the promise of previously unimaginable contact between people'.[157] The bicycle, like the telephone, was a technology that made possible this previously unimaginable contact, notably between strangers of different genders and social classes, as we saw in Chapter 2. Here Miriam mobilises the bicycle as a levelling device, one that makes possible a free and frank exchange between people.

The effort of cycling as far as Reading in the morning dew gives Miriam a sense of disconnection from her own tired and damp body, leaving her feeling 'a draggled person that was not her own'.[158] As we have already seen in the case of nocturnal cyclists such as Leblanc's protagonists, there is a paradoxical impression of gaining an out-of-body experience as a result of soliciting the body and the senses. In achieving an altered state of being in the world, our conception of our own body is also fundamentally changed; as William Cohen argues in the case of Victorian literature, 'A fundamental aspect of the human turns out to be the strangeness to itself of the fleshy matter that composes it.'[159] Miriam's body, made unfamiliar to her by physical effort, seems to become capable of establishing a more direct connection with the ground she crosses: she notices how 'The earth throbbed beneath her with the throbbing of her heart.'[160] Vision is the sense that is most consistently described; yet it is a mobile vision, and one that overlaps and interacts with the other senses. Earlier in the novel, before she has learned to cycle, Miriam remarks on the alienating, purely visual aspect to rail travel. While waiting for a train at a station, she remarks that 'The landscape was dead [. . .] Staring at the landscape she felt the lifelessness of her face; as if something had brushed across it and swept the life away, leaving her only sight. She could never feel anymore.'[161] As we shall see, cycling allows Miriam to move beyond the predominant visual paradigm in order to be able to 'feel' with her other senses and be more fully present in the world. During her day's cycling, a drawing-in of vision is depicted; the panoramic views of the railway traveller are refocused on close-up objects that line the road: 'She closed her eyes upon the dazzling growing distances of blue and white, and felt the horizon folding down in a firm clear sweep round her green cradle. Within her eyelids fields swung past green, cornfields gold and black . . .'[162] The bold primary colours evoked here root the sensory experience firmly in the visual. Yet the shift from the celestial colours of blue and white to earthy green, gold and black leave no doubt as to the close-range nature of the cyclist's vision, contrasting with the distancing, panoramic view of the train traveller. Moreover, the view is no longer dazzling, distant, aggressive and alienating; it is 'within her eyelids', integrated into her body itself.

Just like Leblanc's cyclists, Miriam gains a sense of belonging to the scene which she is sensing. As Merleau-Ponty insists, 'the world is not seen "in" my body, and my body is not ultimately "in" the visible world [. . .] there is reciprocal insertion and interlacing between the two'.[163] Where the train or car window frames views in a similar way to a cinema screen or television, here it is the cyclist's eyelids that limit the scene, suggesting that she enacts a direct, bodily engagement, no longer mediated by means of locomotive machines. Visual impressions succeed each other, yet they mingle with the other senses; the 'hard hot light'[164] acquires tactile qualities, and then becomes tinged with auditory elements:

> eyelids were transparent. It was light coming through one's eyelids that made that clear soft buff; soft buff light filtering through one's body . . . little sounds, insects creeping and humming in the hedge, sounds from the grass. Sudden single quiet sounds going up from distant fields and farms, lost in the sky.[165]

The light that penetrates Miriam's closed eyelids also suffuses her whole body. Sensory perception is decentralised from the eyes and spreads through the body, which is crossed and broken up by the light that traverses it, becoming part of the scene it is sensing. Crucially, this kinaesthetic perception and a renewed sense of the subject's place in the world lead Miriam to a rare state of mastery and well-being: 'I've got my sea-legs . . . this is *riding* – not just straining along trying to forget the wobbly bicycle, but feeling it wobble and being able to control it . . . being able to look about easily . . .'[166] Calm control of the machine, now integrated into Miriam's body as though a part of it, allows the unique combination of speed and close-up vision that makes possible the embodied, mobile perception of the cyclist.

Despite her joyous exchange with the other cyclist early in the morning, and her confident belief in the existence of an egalitarian community of cyclists, Miriam panics when she comes across a lone pedestrian on a country road in the twilight. This scene provides a striking representation of the reality of the female cyclist's experience. For Miriam, the presence of this menacing figure appears as a grim necessity, a reality check after a joyous day of freedom: 'She recognized the figure the instant she saw it. It was as if she had been riding the whole day to meet it.'[167] Alone in the half-light, Miriam's hearing remains attuned to her bicycle – 'there was no sound of anything coming along; nothing but the squeak squeak of her gear-case', while 'her eyes [were] fixed on the far-off spaces of the world she used to know'.[168] By forcing her vision into the distance, she attempts to negate her involvement in the scene in which she has found herself. After having experienced a sense of intimate communion with her surroundings, Miriam is not yet ready to enact 'a supernatural erotics of bodily transmission' with another human being, to borrow Thurschwell's phrase.[169] Up close, Miriam realises that the man is drunk and talking to himself and she passes him without incident. She instantly upbraids herself for her fear, which she attributes to her gender, reflecting that 'A man would not have been afraid.'[170] This powerful yet anti-climactic encounter with the Other gains its intensity and meaning from the male gaze and associated threat to which the young woman is subjected. The bicycle at once places Miriam in a dangerous situation and provides her with the means to travel through it unmolested, a feature of other accounts of women's cycling discussed in Chapter 2. Miriam's ability to steer a safe course through hostile waters results in an empowering interaction between woman and machine.

As twilight turns to night, Miriam experiences a visceral and tangible connection with the dark which, as we have seen, became an important trope in cycling literature. Riding through a dark forest, she experiences a keen pleasure in the lack of visual signals: 'Stronger than fear, was the comfort of the dense darkness. Her own darkness by right of riding through the day. Leaning upon the velvety blackness she pushed on.'[171] This tactile dimension to darkness recalls a scene earlier in the novel when, while walking home in London, Miriam remarks on the physical quality of the night: 'The pavement was under her feet and the sparsely lamplit night all round her. She restrained her eager steps to a walk. The dark houses and the blackness between the lamps were elastic about her.'[172] Both urban walking and rural riding (especially at night) are experiences that give Miriam a sense of the solidity of the objects around her; she feels she is touching and interacting with them as she progresses. This provides a vivid illustration of Merleau-Ponty's theory that 'vision is touching with the eyes',[173] pointing to a mutual imbrication of the body, the senses and the world.

The idea of porosity between the senses, and also between the sensing subject and sensed objects, gained currency in late nineteenth-century Britain. William Cohen points out how the scientist Herbert Spencer concluded that 'eyes are essential dermal structures',[174] thus establishing the idea of a continuum between optical and tactile experience. Cohen goes on to argue that 'Spencer is representative of Victorian practice in placing the organs of sensation and ingestion midway between inner and outer aspects of being, both physical and mental.'[175] Richardson's novel provides a compelling illustration of the notion shared by late Victorians and twentieth-century phenomenology that 'my body shapes things and things shape my body'.[176] Descriptions such as 'Miriam sipped her hot tea. The room darkled in the silence. Everything intensified'[177] are characteristic of Richardson's will to illustrate a circular sensory experience, in which the body and the objects surrounding it form part of an uninterrupted continuum of sensation. This connection becomes more accessible in nocturnal settings, when the predominance of sight is curtailed, allowing for a broader range of sense data to come into play.

In Marlborough, a flat tyre obliges Miriam to stop short of her destination and stay the night at a hotel. As we saw in previous examples, it is thanks to the machine's dysfunction that the character gains insight and access to a deeper realm of meaning or experience. For Miriam, staying a night alone in an unknown town is the ultimate expression of her new-found freedom as a young woman, and one that she could not have hoped for without both the bicycle and its mechanical failure, since she was expected to arrive at her sister's house that night. Staying alone in a strange town is an entirely new experience for her, and the joyous experience of liberty is vitally linked to her impression of being part of 'the little crowded world'[178] of the unfamiliar objects that surround her. A sense of interaction between her body and the place it inhabits, intensified by her day's cycle, is conveyed in descriptions such as

> The throbbing of her heart shook the room. Something was telling the room that she was the happiest thing in existence. She stood up, the beloved little room moving as she moved, and gathered her hands gently

against her breast, to . . . get through, through into the soul of the musty little room.[179]

The room's response to her heartbeat and her mobility, 'moving as she moved', mirrors the sense of reciprocity with her surroundings that Miriam achieved during her ride, when 'The earth throbbed beneath her.'[180] These descriptions mirror Merleau-Ponty's assertion that 'my movements and my eye's movements reverberate in the world [. . .] with each blink of my eyelids, a curtain is drawn down and lifted up'.[181] In Miriam's attempt to commune with the objects around her, she looks 'from thing to thing'[182] and names them, thus engaging the voice which, for Merleau-Ponty, is the ultimate expression of sensory experience.[183] Miriam senses the vitality of these objects, to which she attempts to communicate the exhilarating feeling of her own freedom. As she falls asleep, she reflects:

> I'm alive and alone in a strange place. Everything's alive all round me in a new way [. . .] The more she relinquished the idea of harm and danger, the nearer and more intimate the room became . . . No one can prevent my being alone in a strange place, nearer to things and loving them.[184]

Miriam feels newly alive within the space she inhabits because of her sense of being at one with the objects around her. The continuum between subject and object is emphasised by the narrative oscillation between the first and third person, where we experience Miriam's impressions from both an internal and an external perspective. As Elisabeth Bronfen notes, 'Interior space is felt to be protective as long as it permits a sense of belonging there. In spite of its actual enclosure, it appears porous and open to Miriam when it becomes the site of a transcendental experience.'[185] This scene in the hotel room is emblematic of Richardson's spatial aesthetic, which constantly opposes external and internal spaces, gradually moving towards a transcendence of both. The day's cycling gives Miriam a sense of being part of a vibrant world, both within walls and outside them. Her pleasant bodily fatigue reminds her of the empowering physical journey she has accomplished that day, which has given her a new sense of the nature of her interaction with the world of objects and other people.

By adopting cycling Miriam occupies a liminal position, recalling her earlier description of herself as 'somehow between two worlds, neither quite sheltered, nor quite free . . .'[186] Moreover, cycling is an activity by means of which 'Miriam synthesises the polarity between the sexes by assuming a third position, in between', to borrow Bronfen's terms.[187] The alternation of cycling scenes with Miriam's bitter reflections on men's domination of intellectual life functions to present the bicycle as a possible antidote to this state of affairs. Miriam's apprenticeship and appropriation of cycling allow her to find a genuine place and voice in society, vividly prefiguring her emerging vocation as a writer. Throughout *Pilgrimage*, Miriam struggles to find a means of female expression that avoids simply mimicking masculine behaviour and speech, a characteristic she resents in her liberated friends Jan and Mag. As Donna Haraway argues, 'we can learn from our fusions with animals and machines how not to be Man, the embodiment of Western logos'.[188] By collaborating closely with a machine, Miriam explores fresh means of formulating an individual identity beyond established boundaries.

Human–Machine Synthesis

The range of texts we have been examining points to the fact that the cyclist aesthetic was predicated on a reciprocal relationship between bodies and machines. The speed and subjective mobility offered by the bicycle encouraged multi-sensory engagement with the environment while providing the mechanical means for the subject to be continuously and unexpectedly stimulated or shocked. In this final section I explore the ways in which the bicycle–rider assemblage helped overcome ingrained dichotomies in contemporary attitudes towards technology. The question of the human body's interaction with the machines spawned by industrial society preoccupied much nineteenth-century thought, from Mary Shelley to Marx to H. G. Wells. Yet as Herbert Sussman observes, many Victorian writers 'shied away from confronting the mechanized world',[189] while others referred to machines only in order to explicitly oppose them to the organic or the pastoral. Sussman's survey of seven Victorian authors who believed that 'the tangible fact of mechanization shapes the intellectual, aesthetic, and emotional life of their time' highlights the fact that 'only later in the century does there emerge, in H. G. Wells and Rudyard Kipling, prose fiction that celebrates technology and scientific speculation'.[190] Susmann contrasts this to the strong anti-machine feeling of earlier authors such as Thomas Carlyle, William Morris and John Ruskin.

The bicycle was a technology that encouraged the breaking down of the antithesis between humans and machines, the organic and the industrial, the aesthetic and the mechanical. Turn-of-the-century authors who integrated the bicycle into their fiction focused on the unique synthesis of human and mechanical elements it offered while casting it as an object eminently worthy of literary attention. Thanks to its liminal status as a human-powered machine, the bicycle offered an alternative paradigm for defining technology, seen as a partner rather than a threat to human strength and intelligence.

The Nightmare of the Machine: Reimagining Technology

In the technology-filled reality of the early twentieth century, there was an urgent need to recast the relationship between humans and their creations. Mary Shelley's *Frankenstein* (1818) – written during the First Industrial Revolution – was perhaps even more relevant by the end of the nineteenth century, when a plethora of new transport and communication technologies flooded streets and homes. Where Frankenstein's creature murders its inventor's loved ones, transport technologies – and particularly the motor car – caused alarming numbers of deaths at the turn of the century. Today we have become blandly accustomed to the death toll of the automobile, despite the fact that some 27,000 people are still killed or seriously injured on roads in Britain each year, and road traffic accidents remain the leading cause of death among people aged 15–29.[191] Rudyard Kipling, despite being an early motoring enthusiast, was shocked at the loss of life on the roads at the turn of the century, providing the following macabre image in his correspondence: 'in England the dead, twelve coffin deep, clutch hold of my wheels at every turn, till I sometimes wonder that the very road does not bleed'.[192] This grim vision highlights the dark underbelly of human invention and the capacity of technology to harm its creators. As a human-powered machine, the bicycle stood apart from motorised vehicles, posing minimal threat to human or animal life or the environment. As such, it offered a means of reconciling humans with their creations and imagining a new relationship with technology.

In *Dora Myrl: The Lady Detective*, a New Woman novel by Mc Donnell Bodkin, the cyclist heroine's suitor Ernest invents a flying machine that adopts a definition of technology as fundamentally grounded in the human, contrasting it to the other technologies he sees emerging around him.[193] He explains:

> I was resolved to give my man wings, and teach him how to use them for his own pleasure, not his neighbour's misery. My notion was to make

him his own flying machine and his own muscles the sole motive power of his flight [...] A man is not as strong as a steam or gas engine of course, but he is an infinitely more perfect machine.[194]

The power inherent in technology can easily be turned to violent ends, but Ernest suggests this can be avoided by designing a machine actioned by and built around the 'perfect machine' of the human body. Central to Ernest's idea are the concepts of pleasure, speed and efficiency, combined with concern for others' welfare, aspects that were conspicuously absent in attitudes to mechanised transport, where death and injury were often viewed as necessary if unfortunate collateral damage on the march to progress. The First World War would soon become the tragic proof of the ability of the machine to inflict death and suffering on a vast scale.

In order to avoid 'his neighbour's misery', Ernest invents a machine directly inspired by the bicycle, a technology that manages to miraculously multiply human strength, in spite of the doubts of its early detractors. Ernest recalls the disbelief of some early critics of the bicycle in the following terms:

> You cannot put more strength, they said, than a man has into a machine. If it carries him faster than he can walk or run it must be at the cost of a greater exertion. In a word, he cannot go far if he goes fast. We know how their wisdom worked out in practice. A man is able to do twenty miles an hour on a bicycle for a week at a stretch in spite of the tremendous drag of the track's friction against the wheel pressed down with the combined weight of rider and machine. My man-bird, with no friction to stop him, should do sixty at the least.[195]

Ernest imagines a form of conveyance that takes as its blueprint the physical dimensions, capacities and energy of the body in order to rationally optimise human locomotion by means of a machine. Written at a moment when inventors across Europe and the USA were vying to master the secrets of flight, the image of a human-powered aeroplane that Bodkin selects to close his novel suggests an alternative vision of technology. It is an outlook that encourages us to rediscover faith in our own bodies and cultivate a reciprocal, respectful and beneficial relationship with the machine. As Watson and Gray argue:

> the cycle represents a subtle compromise between the demands of engineering and those of our bodies. Indeed, its evolution has been more

intimately bound up with our own physical capacities and dimensions than that of any other machine one can think of.[196]

The political implications of such a perspective are far-reaching. Lukács, quoting Marx, proclaimed that the proletariat must recognise its divested power and create a society where 'man' would be the 'driving force'.[197] Imagining technologies reliant on human power means not only rediscovering faith in human capacities, but taking a step away from the alienation inherent in a non-vital idea of mechanism. Once mechanism becomes vitalised, a collaborative, interactive and empowering paradigm of society might begin to take shape.

In Leblanc's *Here are Wings*, Pascal also develops a corporeal aesthetic of the machine. He contrasts the bicycle with the 'ugly' motor car, a machine that 'hides its organs as though it were ashamed'.[198] Pascal, like Ernest, argues that the machine must mirror the human body it is designed to serve. The beauty of the bicycle, Pascal reflects, can be explained by the fact that it conforms to and mirrors the proportions of the body. He asks:

> Can anything suggest the idea of speed more than these two equal wheels, with tensed spokes vibrating like nerves, like two legs without a beginning or an end? Can anything be thought of as more stable, more solid than this steel body, these rigorous ribs, this device made of logical and necessary muscles?[199]

The corporeal lexicon repeatedly employed to describe the machine's working parts points to the close interaction it invites with the body and the senses. Several days into their transforming bicycle trip, Pascal no longer compares the human body to the bicycle but, like Jarry, depicts it as a culmination of human potential, no longer distinguishable from the body but an outgrowth of it: 'Man is now in possession of all his capabilities [. . .] The bicycle perfects the body itself, completes it one might say [. . .] There is not a man and a machine. There is a quicker man.'[200] For Pascal, even the sounds of the machine directly recall those of the human body: 'the regular clicking of the chain is the beating of the heart, the discreet sound of the wheels on the ground is the blood pulsing through the veins'.[201] Pascal's praise of the object's conformity to the proportions of the human body suggests an affinity with a humanist outlook, which took the human body as the model for architecture and technology. It casts an eye back to Leonardo da

Vinci's Vitruvian Man, which presented the human body as a geometrically perfect object whose proportions should be mirrored in human inventions.

G. K. Chesterton also stressed the need to maintain a connection to human capacities in our relationship with technology. In his essay 'The Free Man and the Ford Car' (1925), he satirises the car industry and those behind it. Chesterton underlines the importance of moving beyond the contemporary obsession with mechanism, paradoxically suggesting that we can use machines in order to achieve this aim. He condemns the mass production of cars since it transforms thousands of factory workers into 'cogitating cog[s]', 'born to make [. . .] small bits of cars'.[202] He scathingly associates the much-vaunted standardisation of Ford cars with various literary and social phenomena, such as the uniform nature of 'magazine stories' and the fact that 'American millionaires all look exactly alike', with interchangeable noses and chins.[203] The only use of machines, Chesterton continues, is to 'create a psychology that can despise machines'; in order to illustrate this, he depicts an imaginary car driver who, on reaching the open countryside, will 'proceed joyfully to break up the car with a large hammer', naturally coming to view it as an 'antiquated absurdity' now that he has reconnected with nature.[204] For Chesterton, humanity has been incarcerated by technology, yet mechanism might perhaps provide a way of returning to a former condition: he observes that 'It is only because the man has been set into exile in the railway-train that he has to be brought back home in a motor-car.'[205]

Chesterton's concept of using 'modern machinery to escape from modern society'[206] is a compelling one in relation to early cyclists, many of whom pedalled their modern machine in a bid to reconnect with pre-industrial, pre-capitalist landscapes and ways of life. Indeed, Chesterton uses the image of a bicycle to illustrate his point at the start of this essay:

> If [. . .] we find that some machine enables us to escape from an inferno of machinery, we cannot be committing a sin though we may be cutting a silly figure, like a dragoon rejoining his regiment on an old bicycle.[207]

The bicycle may have invited ridicule from disciples of never-ending technological progress, yet it was a machine that invited its riders to reconnect to their bodies and surroundings while forging a more reciprocal and empowering relationship with technology.

Human Technology: The Bicycle as a Tool

> The computer [. . .] is the most remarkable tool that we've ever come up with. It's the equivalent of a bicycle for our minds.
>
> Steve Jobs[208]

In the midst of the digital revolution, Steve Jobs, who almost named his Macintosh computer 'Bicycle',[209] recognised the importance of creating tools that accompany human effort and intelligence rather than providing substitutes for them. During the Industrial Revolution in the nineteenth century, Marx reflected on the difference between a machine and a tool; two concepts which, Raymond Williams informs us, were only distinguished from each other in the eighteenth century.[210] Marx cites thinkers who describe a machine as that which has an external source of energy, and a tool as a human-powered implement, before complicating this dichotomy by arguing that a machine is composed of many tools operating at once, and may in fact be powered by a human. Yet Marx maintains that the role of 'the machine, which is the starting point of the Industrial Revolution', is to replace the worker by usurping his tools and giving him 'the merely mechanical role of acting as the motive power'.[211] The machine thus takes over from human skill, dexterity, intelligence and experience. Indeed, Marx maintains that it is the act of taking agency away from the human that results in the machine taking on an ominous life of its own, as the following description suggests: 'As soon as tools had been converted from being manual implements of man into implements of a mechanical apparatus, of a machine, the motive mechanism also acquired an independent form, entirely emancipated from the restraints of human strength.'[212]

The machine, therefore – whether powered by human, animal, wind or steam energy – takes the tools from the worker's hands and becomes a sort of autonomous force that no longer respects the limitations that human strength can place on it. The tool, on the other hand, is intimately tied to the body; it relies on the person using it both to power and direct it. For Marx, the tool gives workers a sense of meaning and satisfaction in their work, while the machine is no more than 'a means for producing surplus-value',[213] alienating workers from production and siphoning off capital to the rich.

While Marx was writing about manufacturing machines and tools, his observations might be applied at a broader level to transport technologies. The bicycle stands apart from other vehicles in that it may be defined as a tool, since it is entirely dependent on human energy and skill to function. As Michel Bouet observes, human-powered machines such as the bicycle enhance the body's power rather than sidelining it:

> The fact that the athlete uses and identifies with a 'machine' should not be interpreted as the marginalisation of the body but rather as its amplification. Among other animals, the human body distinguishes itself by its ability to build tools whose mechanism does not mechanise the body, and which, remaining at his disposition without becoming obligatory, may become second bodies which become incorporated into the original body.[214]

Bouet recognises tool building as a fundamentally human activity that optimises the body's innate capacities. In this sense the bicycle is quintessentially a tool; it does not mechanise the body, but enhances its potential, and acts as a 'second body' intimately incorporated into that of its user.

Heidegger formulates a definition of a tool as 'the ready to hand', observing that the tool does not assert itself, but acts as an extension of the will of the person using it.[215] Drawing on Heidegger's essay 'The Question Concerning Technology' (1954), Margaret Linley recalls the Greek origin of the term technology: *techne*, the name for 'the activities and skills of the craftsman' as well as for 'the arts of the mind and the fine arts'.[216] Technology, for Heidegger, is inherently a manual and artisanal endeavour. Pushing this argument further, Marcel Mauss claimed in 1936 that even the most basic human activities, such as eating, walking or talking, deserved the status of 'techniques' insofar as they had been learned and were embedded in a particular collective context.[217] Indeed, this historical and essential link appeared to have been severed in the industrial age, when technology and humans were often depicted as polar opposites, with only a small number of skilled people being able to operate increasingly sophisticated machines. However, the literary imaginaries surrounding the bicycle went some way to repairing this schism, insisting on the continuity and interaction between these machines and the humans who imagined, built, repaired and powered them.

Technology designed around the body provides a beneficial, perennial augmentation of human capacities. Lewis Mumford pointed to the inherent paradox of modern technology in *Art and Technics* (1952), where he argued that the 'perversion of technics in our time naturally saps the vitality of real art', enslaving rather than freeing its users.[218] At the root of this alienating relationship with technology is 'style obsolescence', or the constant search for new consumer objects. Rather than seeking to be continually renewed, useful technology should change little, as Mumford argues: 'Once established and perfected, type objects should have a long period of use. No essential improvement in the safety pin has been made since the bronze age.'[219] Although many models of bicycle appeared in rapid succession in the late nineteenth century, each claiming to be superior to the last, the standard safety design has hardly changed at all since 1885. Twentieth-century attempts to 'improve' the bicycle with aluminium and carbon frames, or electric components and motors, have only resulted in less robust machines with a shorter lifespan, conforming to capitalism's demand for obsolescence and continued consumption. Industrial manufacture is required for the bicycle's construction, yet once built it can last a lifetime and generates no pollution. The enduring design of the bicycle, like that of the safety pin, at once proves its useful role in society and invites a more fulfilling relationship with technology. The bicycle's simplicity, the stability of its design and its correspondence to the dimensions of the human body all set it apart as a technology that has been developed to accompany and extend rather than distort human capacities. Bicycles are tools that permit us to break down a binary separation of the organic and the mechanical, allowing for an optimisation of human locomotive potential. Rather than threatening to overpower or destroy their creator, bicycles follow humans' lead while offering their riders a new vista on the world.

A Literature of the Machine

In performing this active, creative exchange with a machine, cyclists and writers aestheticised an activity that had been portrayed as ugly and degrading throughout the industrial period. By taking pleasure in their interaction with a mechanical object, cyclists turned the previously demeaning act of machine tending into a meaningful task accessible to all and worthy of literary attention. Sussman argues that while Rudyard Kipling sought to develop 'new literary forms that could include the fact of the machine', he ultimately failed because of the exceeding technical complexity of the objects he sought to portray.[220] In stories such as 'The Bridge Builders' (1893), Kipling attempted to expand the literary use of the technological idiom, but his effort was thwarted by the necessity to write a comprehensible and interesting story, not a civil engineering manual. Sussman observes that 'The main reason for the success, and for the limitations, of Victorian writers on the machine is that, mystified by technology, they were forced to stay within the bounds of what they, and the layman, could understand.'[221] In contrast to other increasingly complex technologies emerging at the time, the bicycle was an exceptionally simple machine whose working parts could be seen and easily understood.

Grant Allen experimented with introducing vocabulary from the realm of bicycle mechanics in his novel *Miss Cayley's Adventures*. When the heroine first meets a North American inventor who has patented a new chainless bicycle, she humorously misinterprets his use of the technical term 'eccentric':

> 'Oh, I knew you were an eccentric,' I said, 'the moment I set eyes upon you.'
> He surveyed me gravely. 'You misunderstand me, miss,' he corrected. '*When* I say eccentric, I mean a crank.'
> 'They are much the same thing,' I answered, briskly. 'Though I confess I would hardly have applied so rude a word as *crank* to you.'
> He looked me over suspiciously, as if I were trying to make game of him, but my face was sphinx-like. So he brought the machine a yard or two nearer, and explained its construction to me. He was quite right: it *was* driven by a crank. It had no chain, but was moved by a pedal, working narrowly up and down, and attached to a rigid bar, which impelled the wheels by means of an eccentric.[222]

Even though she is unfamiliar with this precise system of transmission, Miss Cayley is quickly able to understand the modification the inventor has made to the standard design of the bicycle. The reader, too, is able to grasp the basic working of this chainless bicycle, and appreciate the joke.[223] Allen can count on his readership to laugh at his wordplay with bicycle parts, supposing the public to be familiar with the terms he employs. The simple nature of a bicycle's mechanism, the relatively small number of parts it comprised (compared to, say, a steam engine or a motor car) and their visibility to the naked eye meant that writers such as Kennard, Jerome, Richardson and Allen could write metaphorically or humorously about bicycle mechanics in their novels, and expect to be understood. In this sense the bicycle offered a unique means for imagining a literature of the machine, avoiding Kipling's paradox as theorised by Sussman. Thanks to the simple and human-scaled nature of the technology, writers were able to avoid technological jargon while making creative use of bicycle terminology in their texts.

Significantly, the experience afforded by this new mobility could stimulate the very urge to write. The following description by J. W. Allen focuses on the novel sensory experience and interaction with the machine as the root of the creative impulse:

> We needed to babble of our vision of the wonderful country-side, all clothed with miraculous, live, green things, over-hung with incredible blue, quivering in a golden glory, inhabited, too, by mysterious creatures like ourselves, full of memories, full of anticipations. We would babble of this machine that had brought us to this vision – not with much knowledge nor with too nice an accuracy – but with a great sense of joy.[224]

This vivid description conveys the cyclist's sense of being one actant in an active, vibrant world. The bicycle opens his eyes to the 'live, green things' that surround him and allows him to come to a fresh appreciation of the 'mysterious creature' he himself is. The verb 'babble' stresses the author's instinctive, childlike, joyous reaction to his discovery of these places and sensations. The equal need he feels to babble of 'our vision' and 'this machine' reminds us of the cyclist's hybridised experience, where sharp sensory awareness is coupled with close collaboration with a machine. Moreover, the cyclist here is equivocally placed between past and future, being 'full of memories, full of anticipations'. As I will show in Chapter 4, the ability to look both backwards and forwards was crucial in allowing cyclists to formulate an alternative worldview.

The hybrid of corporeal and mechanical elements offered by the bicycle placed turn-of-the-century cyclists in a liminal space. In pedalling their bicycles, they performed resistance to a binary corporeal/mechanical classification that continues to pose problems in our contemporary relationship to technology. The first cyclists rediscovered the importance of the senses and the body in the wake of the railway era and in opposition to the emerging automobile paradigm, while simultaneously training their bodies to control and interact with a machine that afforded them a rapid, spontaneous and subjective experience of travel. This particular synthesis of the body's capacity for multi-sensory interaction and the machine's speed and agency introduced a unique aesthetics founded on the combination of these two registers and a redefinition and transcendence of both. The next and final chapter will consider how the cyclist's aesthetic uniquely managed to integrate technology into an empowering, human-centred vision of space, time and progress.

Notes

1. Latour, *Nous n'avons jamais été modernes*, 189.
2. Raymond Williams, *Keywords: A Vocabulary of Culture and Society* (London: Fontana, 1988), 201.
3. Seltzer, *Bodies and Machines*, 12.
4. Hodder, *Entangled*, 110.
5. Bennett, *Vibrant Matter*, 38.
6. Ibid., vii; Bruno Latour, *Reassembling the Social: An Introduction to Actor-Network Theory* (Oxford: Oxford University Press, 2005).
7. Wilson, Papadopoulos and Whitt, *Bicycling Science*, blurb.
8. Kennard, *A Guide Book for Lady Cyclists*, 5.
9. Mark Twain, 'Taming the Bicycle' [1886], in *Collected Tales, Sketches, Speeches & Essays, 1852–1890* (New York: Literary Classics of the United States, 1992), 893–4.
10. François Rachline, 'Le vélo du baron', *L'Économie Politique* 38, no. 2 (2008), 105.
11. Karl Marx, *Capital: A Critique of Political Economy*, trans. Ben Fowkes, vol. I (London: Penguin/New Left Review, 1990), 458.
12. Mecredy, *The Art and Pastime of Cycling*, 57–63.
13. Marx, *Capital*, I, 458.
14. Muir, *Plato's Dream of Wheels*, 41–2.
15. Ibid., 42–3.
16. Ibid., 44.
17. James Adamson, *Sketches of Our Information as to Railroads* (Edinburgh: Constable, 1826), 51–2.
18. Jeremy Withers, 'Bicycles, Tricycles, and Tripods: Late Victorian Cycling and Wells's *The War of the Worlds*', *The Wellsian* 36 (2013), 42.
19. This was especially the case in the USA. The terms 'wheeling' and 'wheelman/wheelwoman' were also widely used.
20. H. G. Wells, *The War of the Worlds* [1898] (London: Penguin, 2012), 135.
21. Withers, 'Bicycles, Tricycles, and Tripods', 39.
22. G. K. Chesterton, 'The Wheel', in *Delphi Complete Works of G. K. Chesterton*, vol. I (Hastings: Delphi Classics, 2013), 260.
23. Ibid.
24. Chesterton was a Christian, though not a creationist, and questioned Darwinism. He thought the theory stifled debate and oversimplified more complex processes. See 'Doubts about Darwinism' [1920], in *Collected Works*, vol. XXXII (San Francisco: Ignatius Press, 1989), 55–9.
25. Wells, *The War of the Worlds*, 134–5.
26. Wells, *The Wheels of Chance*, 51.
27. Allen, *Wheel Magic*, 17.
28. Sydney Savory Buckman, 'Cycling: Its Effects on the Future of the Human Race', *The Medical Magazine* 8, no. 2 (1899), 269.

29. A. Shadwell, 'The Hidden Dangers of Cycling', *The National Review*, February 1897.
30. Abraham Wren Rumney, *A Cyclist's Note Book* (Edinburgh: W. and A. K. Johnston, 1901), 18.
31. Withers, 'Bicycles, Tricycles, and Tripods', 49.
32. Tim Armstrong, *Modernism, Technology, and the Body: A Cultural Study* (Cambridge: Cambridge University Press, 1998).
33. Paul Virilio, *La vitesse de libération: essai* (Paris: Galilée, 1995), 23.
34. Furness, *One Less Car*, 17.
35. Ibid., 25.
36. John Urry, 'The "System" of Automobility', *Theory, Culture & Society* 21, no. 4–5 (2004), 31.
37. Ritchie, *Quest for Speed*, 24.
38. Of course, the long-established association between mechanics and working-class men did not disappear, and is still very much with us in the twenty-first century. Even if the bicycle is a technology that invites a more inclusive approach to repair, the domain of mechanics remains decidedly hostile to women and girls.
39. Kennard, *A Guide Book for Lady Cyclists*, 35.
40. Ibid., 36.
41. Ibid., 31.
42. Kennard, *The Golf Lunatic and his Cycling Wife*, 211.
43. Ibid., 242.
44. Ibid., 67.
45. Jerome, *Three Men on the Bummel*, 31.
46. Bockett, *Some Literary Landmarks*, 95.
47. Ibid., 96.
48. Bennett, *Vibrant Matter*, 60, author's italics.
49. One contemporary example is Pierre Giffard and Albert Robida, *La Fin du cheval* (Paris: Armand Colin, 1899).
50. Bijker, *Of Bicycles, Bakelites, and Bulbs*, 94.
51. Gwen Raverat, *Period Piece: A Cambridge Childhood* (London: Faber and Faber, 1952), 240.
52. A. C. Pemberton et al., *The Complete Cyclist* (London: Innes, 1897), 55.
53. Bockett, *Some Literary Landmarks*, 96.
54. Flann O'Brien, *The Third Policeman* [1967] (London: Paladin, 1988), 89.
55. Wells, *The Wheels of Chance*, 19, 20.
56. Anson Rabinbach, *The Human Motor: Energy, Fatigue, and the Origins of Modernity* (Berkeley, CA: University of California Press, 1990), 20, 38.
57. Arnold Bennett. *The Human Machine* [1908] (Auckland, NZ: Floating Press, 2009).
58. Ritchie, *Quest for Speed*, 351.
59. Watson and Gray, *The Penguin Book of the Bicycle*, 232.
60. Ibid.

61. Marieke Dubbelboer, 'Un univers mécanique: la machine chez Alfred Jarry', *French Studies* 58, no. 4 (2004), 483.
62. Alfred Jarry, *Ubu cycliste: écrits vélocipédiques*, ed. Nicolas Martin (Toulouse: Le Pas d'Oiseau, 2007), 33.
63. Ibid.
64. Alfred Jarry, *Le Surmâle: roman moderne* [1902] (Paris: Mille et une nuits, 1996), 7.
65. Ibid., 13.
66. Rabinbach, *The Human Motor*, 12.
67. Jarry, *Le Surmâle*, 9.
68. Ibid., 11.
69. Rabinbach, *The Human Motor*, 23. The ergograph measures the strength of a muscle, while the aesthesiometer quantifies the degree of tactile sensitivity of the skin.
70. The metric distance of the Irkousk–Paris race is given as 1,693 km, which is smaller by a factor of ten. As one person present remarks that 'numbers like that don't mean anything anymore', we may infer that Jarry is poking fun at the length of contemporary bicycle races by absurdly inflating it, before diminishing it in the next line. Jarry, *Le Surmâle*, 13.
71. Ibid., 53.
72. Ibid., 54.
73. The cosmopolitan atmosphere of the novel, which features American scientists and doctors, reflects the international exchange between the USA, France and the UK at the time. The presence of English bicycle terminology such as 'toe-clip' (ibid., 59) and 'ankle play' (p. 60) further testifies to the global construction of discourses around cycling and other technologies.
74. Jarry, *Le Surmâle*, 61.
75. Ibid., 71.
76. Ibid., 72.
77. Ibid.
78. Ibid., 74.
79. Ibid., 98.
80. Ibid., 127.
81. Ibid., 130.
82. Ibid, 134.
83. Corry Cropper, 'Like a Furnace: Alfred Jarry's *The Supermale*, Doping and the Limits of Positivism', in *Culture on Two Wheels: The Bicycle in Literature and Film*, ed. Jeremy Withers and Daniel P. Shea (Lincoln, NE: University of Nebraska Press, 2016), 106; see also Bettina L. Knapp, 'Jarry's "The Supermale": The Sex Machine, the Food Machine, and the Bicycle Race: Is It a Question of Adaptation?', *Nineteenth-Century French Studies* 18, no. 3/4 (1990), 492–507; Philip G. Hadlock, 'Men, Machines, and the Modernity of Knowledge in Alfred Jarry's "Le Surmâle"', *SubStance* 35, no. 3 (2006), 131–48.

84. Knapp, 'Jarry's "The Supermale"', 492.
85. Watson and Gray, *The Penguin Book of the Bicycle*, 34.
86. Paul Virilio, *The Original Accident*, trans. Julie Rose (Cambridge: Polity, 2007), 3.
87. Paul Virilio and Philippe Petit, *Politics of the Very Worst: An Interview by Philippe Petit*, trans. Sylvère Lotringer (New York: Semiotext[e], 1999), 89.
88. Sidney H. Aronson, 'The Sociology of the Bicycle', *Social Forces* 30, no. 3 (1952), 311.
89. Mecredy, *The Art and Pastime of Cycling*, 65.
90. Frédéric Régamey, *Vélocipédie et automobilisme* (Tours: A. Mame et fils, 1898).
91. Walter Benjamin, 'On Some Motifs in Baudelaire', in *Illuminations*, ed. Hannah Arendt, trans. Harry Zohn (London: Fontana, 1992), 175.
92. Hartmut Rosa, *High-Speed Society: Social Acceleration, Power, and Modernity*, trans. William E. Scheuerman (University Park, PA: Pennsylvania State University Press, 2009), 10.
93. Zemka, *Time and the Moment*, 215.
94. Ibid., 216.
95. Daly, *Literature, Technology, and Modernity*, 2.
96. Allen, *Wheel Magic*, 47.
97. Niles Leeds, 'A Coast and a Capture', 89.
98. Daly, *Literature, Technology and Modernity*, 33.
99. Schivelbusch, *The Railway Journey*.
100. Beekman and Eric, *Cycle Gleanings*, 3.
101. Jonathan Crary, *Techniques of the Observer: On Vision and Modernity in the Nineteenth Century* (Cambridge, MA: MIT Press, 1990), 16.
102. Jonathan Crary, 'Unbinding Vision: Manet and the Attentive Observer in the Late Nineteenth Century', in *Cinema and the Invention of Modern Life*, ed. Leo Charney and Vanessa R. Schwartz (Berkeley, CA: University of California Press, 1991), 68.
103. John Ruskin, *The Works of John Ruskin*, ed. Edward Tyas Cook and Alexander D. O. Wedderburn (Cambridge: Cambridge University Press, 2009), V, 370.
104. John Ruskin, 'Letter on Cycling', *Tit-Bits*, 31 March 1888, 399.
105. Michel Bouet, *Signification du sport* (Paris: Editions universitaires, 1968), 190.
106. Leblanc, *Voici des ailes*, 40.
107. Thomas de Quincey, 'The English Mail-Coach' [1849], in *Confessions of an English Opium-Eater and Other Writings* (Oxford: Oxford University Press, 1998), 193–4.
108. Ibid., 194.
109. Ibid., 186.
110. Illich, *Energy and Equity*, 25.
111. Leed, *The Mind of a Traveler*, 6.
112. Marx, *Capital*, I, 506.

113. Bouet, *Signification du sport*, 25.
114. H. C. Bastian, 'The Muscular Sense: Its Nature and Cortical Localisation', *Brain* 10, no. 1 (1887), 1–89.
115. Justin Spinney, 'Cycling the City: Non-Place and the Sensory Construction of Meaning in a Mobile Practice', in *Cycling and Society*, ed. Dave Horton, Paul Rosen and Peter Cox (Aldershot: Ashgate, 2007), 41.
116. Thomas, *In Pursuit of Spring*, 116–17.
117. Beekman and Eric, *Cycle Gleanings*, 14.
118. Ibid., 44.
119. Bockett, *Some Literary Landmarks*, 18.
120. Maria E. Ward, *Bicycling for Ladies* (New York: Brentano, 1896), 79.
121. Rumney, *A Cyclist's Note Book*, 14.
122. Ibid., 16.
123. Bockett, *Some Literary Landmarks*, 37.
124. Ibid., 5.
125. Ibid.
126. Allen, *Wheel Magic*, 91.
127. Wells, *The Wheels of Chance*, 96.
128. Rumney, *A Cyclist's Note Book*, 70.
129. Edmund Burke, *A Philosophical Enquiry into the Origin of Our Ideas of the Sublime and Beautiful* [1757] (Oxford: Oxford University Press, 1990), 130.
130. Such a register recalls the efforts of Thomas Carlyle or Rudyard Kipling to reconcile machinery with vitalism through a transcendental perspective. See Sussman, *Victorians and the Machine*, 197.
131. Leblanc, *Voici des ailes*, 20.
132. Ibid., 21.
133. Ibid., 92.
134. Ibid., 20.
135. Ibid., 31–2.
136. Ibid., 30.
137. Ibid., 39.
138. See Henri Bergson, *L'évolution créatrice* [1907] (Paris: PUF, 1948).
139. Leblanc, *Voici des ailes*, 63.
140. Maurice Merleau-Ponty, *Le visible et l'invisible*, ed. Claude Lefort (Paris: Gallimard, 1964), 174.
141. Leblanc, *Voici des ailes*, 48.
142. Ibid., 52.
143. Danius, *The Senses of Modernism*, 1.
144. Richardson, *The Tunnel*, 144.
145. Ibid., 146.
146. Ibid., 171.
147. Ibid., 149.
148. Ibid., 150.

149. Ibid., 151, author's italics.
150. Ibid, 226.
151. Ibid., 227.
152. Ibid., 227.
153. Ibid., 227.
154. Ibid., 224.
155. Elisabeth Bronfen, *Dorothy Richardson's Art of Memory: Space, Identity, Text*, trans. Victoria Appelbe (Manchester: Manchester University Press, 1999), 27.
156. Richardson, *The Tunnel*, 230, author's italics.
157. Thurschwell, *Literature, Technology, and Magical Thinking*, 3.
158. Richardson, *The Tunnel*, 230.
159. William Cohen, *Embodied: Victorian Literature and the Senses* (Minneapolis, MN: University of Minnesota Press, 2009), xvi.
160. Richardson, *The Tunnel*, 230.
161. Ibid., 109.
162. Ibid., 230.
163. Merleau-Ponty, *Le visible et l'invisible*, 180.
164. Richardson, *The Tunnel*, 231.
165. Ibid.
166. Ibid.
167. Ibid.
168. Ibid, 232.
169. Thurschwell, *Literature, Technology, and Magical Thinking*, 3.
170. Richardson, *The Tunnel*, 232.
171. Ibid., 233.
172. Ibid., 74.
173. Ibid., 175.
174. Quoted in Cohen, *Embodied*, 3.
175. Ibid.
176. Merleau-Ponty, *Le visible et l'invisible*, 171.
177. Richardson, *The Tunnel*, 232.
178. Ibid., 235.
179. Ibid., 235–6
180. Ibid., 230.
181. Merleau-Ponty, *Le visible et l'invisible*, 22.
182. Richardson, *The Tunnel*, 236.
183. Merleau-Ponty, *Le visible et l'invisible*, 187.
184. Richardson, *The Tunnel*, 237.
185. Bronfen, *Dorothy Richardson's Art of Memory*, 12.
186. Richardson, *The Tunnel*, 167.
187. Bronfen, *Dorothy Richardson's Art of Memory*, 134.
188. Haraway, *Simians, Cyborgs, and Women*, 173.
189. Sussman, *Victorians and the Machine*, 3.
190. Ibid., 12, 3.

191. 'Reported road casualties in Great Britain: provisional estimates year ending June 2019', Department for Transport, 28 November 2019, available at <https://assets.publishing.service.gov.uk/government/uploads/system/uploads/attachment_data/file/848485/road-casualties-year-ending-june-2019.pdf> (accessed 13 October 2020).
192. Rudyard Kipling, *The Letters of Rudyard Kipling, 1900–10* (Basingstoke: Macmillian, 1996), 151.
193. The 1980s and 1990s witnessed various attempts to invent human-powered aeroplanes and helicopters. See Wilson, Papadopoulos and Whitt, *Bicycling Science*, 420–9.
194. Bodkin, *Dora Myrl*, 242.
195. Ibid., 243–4.
196. Watson and Gray, *The Penguin Book of the Bicycle*, 84–5.
197. György Lukács, *History and Class Consciousness: Studies in Marxist Dialectics* (Cambridge, MA: MIT Press, 1971), 181.
198. Leblanc, *Voici des ailes*, 26.
199. Ibid., 20.
200. Ibid., 34–5.
201. Ibid., 80.
202. G. K. Chesterton, 'The Free Man and the Ford Car' [1925], in *Delphi Complete Works of G. K. Chesterton*, vol. I (Hastings: Delphi Classics, 2013), 547.
203. Ibid., 548.
204. Ibid., 550.
205. Ibid., 551.
206. Ibid., 550.
207. Ibid., 545.
208. Steve Jobs, 'Computers are like a bicycle for our minds', YouTube, 1 June 2006, available at <https://www.youtube.com/watch?v=ob_GX50Za6c&feature=youtube_gdata_player> (accessed 5 March 2020).
209. James D. Schwartz, 'How Apple's "Macintosh" almost became the "Bicycle"', *The Urban Country*, 8 January 2012, available at <http://www.theurbancountry.com/2012/01/how-apples-macintosh-almost-became.html> (accessed 17 July 2020).
210. Williams, *Keywords*, 201.
211. Marx, *Capital*, I, 497, 496.
212. Ibid., I, 499.
213. Ibid., I, 492.
214. Bouet, *Signification du sport*, 19.
215. Martin Heidegger, 'Being and Time', in *The Question Concerning Technology, and Other Essays*, trans. William Lovitt (New York: Harper and Row, 1977), 95–107.
216. Margaret Linley, 'The Living Transport Machine: George Eliot's *Middlemarch*', in *Transport in British Fiction: Technologies of Movement, 1840–1940*, ed. Andrew F. Humphries and Adrienne E. Gavin (Basingstoke: Palgrave Macmillan, 2015), 86.

217. Marcel Mauss, *Les techniques du corps* (Chicoutimi: J.-M. Tremblay, 2002).
218. Lewis Mumford, *Art and Technics* (New York: Columbia University Press, 1952), 80.
219. Ibid., 79.
220. Sussman, *Victorians and the Machine*, 208.
221. Ibid., 216.
222. Allen, *Miss Cayley's Adventures*, 48, author's italics.
223. There was a worldwide, short-lived craze for chainless bicycles around the turn of the century. See Michael Grutzner, 'The Chainless Bicycle Craze in Germany around 1900', *Cycle History* 18 (2007), 100–7.
224. Allen, *Wheel Magic*, viii.

Chapter 4

Moving Forward: Space, Time and the Bicycle

> Life is like riding a bicycle. To keep your balance you must keep moving.
> Albert Einstein[1]

At a time when scientific discoveries such as Einstein's theory of relativity (1905) were transforming contemporary understandings of time and space, mass and energy, the new mobility of the bicycle offered a compelling vantage point on our surroundings. Einstein recognised the importance of technology in shaping our understanding of the world around us; in his short version of the special and general theory of relativity (published in 1920), he makes extensive use of the image of a moving train to illustrate his findings to a non-specialised readership.[2] Moreover, it has been argued that his work on electrical machines at the Swiss Patent Office as a young man may have led him to his game-changing insight into the fundamental nature of and relationship between space and time.[3] His theory rejected the traditional conception of time as absolute and universal, showing that it was dependent on frame of reference, speed and spatial position. Time and space cannot be considered separately, but are intertwined in the continuum of spacetime; moreover, many different spacetimes may coexist and overlap. Einstein is widely cited as having said of his famous theory, 'I thought of that while riding my bicycle.' While there appears to be no firm evidence for this claim, the legend holds that the physicist was inspired when contemplating the beam of light from his moving bicycle.[4] Whether or not the claim is apocryphal, Einstein was part of the generation who first discovered this transformative individual form of mobility along with the unique interaction with time and space it offered. Bicycles played a key role in the spatial transformations occuring at the turn of the century; as Glen Norcliffe observes, 'Personal geographies are transformed by cycling [. . .] It follows that bicycles have reconfigured space, and continually do so.'[5] The ways in which they do this, and how writers conveyed this experience in text, will be the focus of this final chapter.

I first engage with the role of cycling in the formation of an accelerated, subjective, commodified modernity. Texts allow us to explore how the bicycle interacted with the emerging technologies of photography and cinema in framing landscapes, and participated in a 'colonising' outlook towards space that would reach its apogee in the automobile era. Yet, just as cyclists manage to straddle mechanical and corporeal registers, so they integrate elements of this appropriative spatial mode into a form of mobility that remains firmly grounded in bodily animation of localities. Marc Desportes notes that a 'desire for a spatial experience that would fully engage the body' characterised the work of writers and artists at the end of the nineteenth century.[6] This yearning for an embodied, mobile experience of space reflects the reality of those who were discovering the new technology of the bicycle at this time. Cycling authors bear witness to a reconnection with their surroundings and a rejection of the compression or destruction of space and time produced by mechanised means of transport such as trains, cars and aeroplanes. Cyclists sought to engage with in-between, overlooked and forgotten spaces, challenging the contemporary focus on departure, destination, efficiency and speed. Travellers on two wheels re-established a connection with a pre-industrial space, in which the journey, the people met and the places traversed by the moving and active body once again became invested with meaning. As such, I argue that the bicycle ultimately offered an alternative to the 'automobility' paradigm, which John Urry sees as a defining element of early twentieth-century modernity.

As well as impacting on contemporary representations of space, cycling introduced a particular relationship to time and progress. While the cyclist was initially seen as an avatar of modernity and associated with futuristic visions of progress, the figure soon became associated with nostalgia. From the early years of the twentieth century, bicycles appear in texts in relation to a sense of history that itself was a paradoxical expression of modernity. I engage with diverging contemporary standpoints on the modernity and anti-modernity of the bicycle, while reflecting on the technology's place within the theories of those who have considered the specific role of various transportation technologies in shaping modernity. This study reveals that the bicycle not only helped generate the changes occurring in society at large, it also contested them. In the short narrative that opens F. T. Marinetti's *Futurist Manifesto* (1909) – a celebration of the aesthetic value of speed, violence, machinery and war – the car-driving narrator comes across a pair of cyclists who get in his way.

> suddenly there were two cyclists right in front of me, cutting me off, as if trying to prove me wrong, wobbling like two lines of reasoning, equally persuasive and yet contradictory. Their stupid argument was being discussed right in my path . . . What a bore! Damn! . . . I stopped short, and to my disgust rolled over into a ditch, with my wheels in the air.[7]

Bicycles were decidedly not part of the Futurists' pantheon, which readily included motor cars, aeroplanes and modern weaponry, yet they were a considerable obstacle for the speed-crazed car driver. They are 'persuasive' and 'contradictory', both participating in modernity and rejecting it, and their innocuous 'wobbling' is capable of sending the car driver into a ditch. Poised on the cusp of modernity, the bicycle allows us to conceptualise a unique window of time when an efficient, individual and modern means of transport accelerated daily life while ensuring that a human-scaled, embodied relationship to time and space was respected. The bicycle's rapid change in status from novelty to antiquity provided it with new counter-cultural possibilities. As it ceased to be seen as modern in the early years of the twentieth century, authors on both sides of the Channel reclaimed the bicycle as a means to connect with the slower time of the pre-industrial past, and to reject the negative influences of runaway technological progress.

Cycling and 'Automobility'

> Once some public utility went faster than 15 mph, equity declined and the scarcity of both time and space increased.
>
> Ivan Illich[8]

According to John Urry, the psychological transformations that accompanied rapid, individual mobility made a crucial contribution to shaping the modern subject. Urry argues that 'collective' or 'clock' time and the 'panoramic gaze' of the railway age was replaced by 'fragmented' or 'instantaneous' time in the era of mechanised, autonomous mobility. He claims that such an outlook came to characterise the twentieth century, replacing 'the pattern of nineteenth century "public mobility"' with 'individualised mobility'.[9] Automobility has expanded into all areas of life in the developed world, Urry argues, and continues to define our fleeting onscreen interactions in the digital age. It is a system that gives us an impression of freedom while in fact obliging us to be extremely flexible and adaptable, effectively making us dependent on a machine, estranging us from our bodies, altering our sensory perception of our environment and alienating us from others. Zack Furness adopts Urry's framework in order to 'reposition bicycling as less of an influence on the system of automobility than its initial point of origin', arguing that it 'previews some of the major problems and prospects of automobility that would later become enshrined in American car culture'.[10] Here I consider three key elements of the automobility model – the photographic gaze, the colonising impetus and mobile subjectivity – alongside early accounts of cycling in literature. I show that while the bicycle may have helped plant some of the seeds of the automobility paradigm, the mode of spatial interaction it proposed was radically different from the destructive and dehumanising paradigm of transport that would come to characterise the twentieth century.

Photography, Cinema and the Bicycle

Zack Furness draws on Walter Benjamin's concept of the 'aura' to argue that the bicycle was a technology that – like photography – made places accessible and so 'reproducible', limiting their aesthetic value and commodifying them to a certain extent.[11] In this and other ways, Furness maintains that the bicycle laid the foundations for the aesthetic and spatial mode later adopted by the automobile. Cycling and photography 'framed and fixed the landscape in mutually reinforcing ways', according to Furness, who terms the bicycle 'a landscaping machine' that allowed city dwellers to construct a distancing, tourist gaze of picturesque localities.[12] Furthermore, Furness points out how modern infrastructures of mobility such as metalled roads, touring maps, guides and road signs were first installed for the use of cyclists, all of which sought to place a uniform, readable framework on diverse landscapes and negate the need for individual interaction with specific localities. John Urry mainly focuses on the cultural and psychological impact of the railway, the car and, later, the computer, yet he briefly mentions the bicycle in his study *Mobilities* (2007), claiming that 'the humble bicycle paved the way for the car and for its subsequent domination of paths and pavements, roads and freeways'.[13] Furness extends

Urry's arguments to the bicycle, maintaining that cycling inaugurated an abstract, textual or photographic interaction with the environment that would be inherited and extended in the automobile era.

Where walkers a century before held out Claude glasses in order to appreciate a view,[14] many touring cyclists travelled with new models of camera specially designed for carrying on bicycles. Early tricycles were used for transporting heavy photographic equipment to picturesque spots, and the bicycle boom of the 1890s coincided with the appearance of cheap, portable cameras, which were heavily marketed at cyclists. W. S. Beekman augmented his volume on cycle touring with images taken by the photographer Allan Eric on his New England rides, claiming that the camera was an essential accessory for the modern cyclist. Beekman observes that 'an individual starting out with a twenty-five pound machine, a light cyclometer, a small bicycle clock, and a compact camera is indeed a most wonderful example of the world's progressiveness'.[15] Beekman's progressive cyclist seems to own a device for every function that the body and mind previously fulfilled, and so to no longer need his legs to walk, his eyes to see or his intelligence and memory to tell him the time and distance covered. Like Wells's Martians in *The War of the Worlds*, cyclists' bodies seem at risk of becoming incidental to the technologies that augment their physical capabilities and distort their interaction with space and other people.

The discourses that emerged around these contemporaneous technologies of photography, cinema and the bicycle offer many points of comparison, pointing at once to an extension and a mechanisation of the human senses alongside a transformation of our relationship to space. Literature bears testament to the cyclist's discovery of a novel visual interaction with place that has parallels with the young technologies of photography and cinema. Edward Thomas observed that 'in cycling chiefly ample views are to be seen, and the mist conceals them. You travel too quickly to notice many small things.'[16] In Maurice Leblanc's *Here are Wings*, the cyclist Pascal compares the perspective of the walker and the cyclist, noting that 'One will receive minute and detailed sensations, the other a vast overall sensation.'[17] These 'ample views' or 'vast overall sensation' suggest a broadening of the perspective akin to that promoted by a photographic or cinematographic outlook. Photography and cinematography were both technologies that foregrounded visual or panoramic views of landscapes, while paradoxically drawing attention to the extent to which visual perceptions might be misleading, especially when it comes to objects moving at speed. While early photography required the subject to be motionless, Eadweard Muybridge's stop-motion technique, developed in the 1860s, documented the movements of mobile animals or humans. Along with the chronophotography of Etienne-Jules Marey in France, these images recorded the precise movements of humans and animals in motion, and transformed contemporary attitudes to visual perception. Muybridge's photographs of horses, for instance, showed that all four hooves leave the ground during a gallop, something that the human eye is incapable of perceiving. Parallel developments in microscopy continued to expand the realm of the invisible, giving credence to the idea that technology's eye was omniscient, while unaugmented human vision could never be more than partial and misleading.

Alfred Jarry established a connection between photography and cycling in two literary depictions of cycle races. In *The Supermale*, the narrator describes the appearance of the eponymous super-cyclist in graphic detail, recounting how 'his entire comical silhouette, down to the details of the spokes of his bicycle, remained photographed in my retina'.[18] The narrator, another cyclist in the epic race, seems to have integrated an eerie photographic element into his vision, becoming capable of permanently inscribing a still image on to his retina. This cyborg-like description implies an augmentation of the human senses through contact with technology, a theme that was prominent in Jarry's novel, as we have seen. In the same year as *The Supermale* was published, 1903, Jarry penned a sketch entitled *The Passion Considered as an Uphill Bicycle Race*, in which Jesus and his fellow racers ride their bicycles up the hill of Golgotha. In this parody of Jesus's crucifixion, the narrator describes the end of the race in the following manner: 'Although wearing nothing, Jesus sweated. We are not certain that a female spectator wiped his face, but it is a fact that the reporter Veronica took a photograph with her Kodak.'[19] By transforming the biblical veil into a modern photograph, Jarry draws attention to the miraculous nature of contemporary technologies, which make possible godlike feats. Yet Jarry is also satirising society's obsession with spectator sports; rather than adopting the compassionate gesture of wiping the suffering man's face, this up-to-date Veronica keeps her distance and snaps a photograph, which will become a commodity for sale and distribution through newspapers, and a proof of her presence at a memorable event. The spectator remains aloof from fellow humans and their surroundings, attaching more importance to the visual representation of scenes and the physical commodity that will remain in their wake. In Guy Debord's society of the spectacle, 'all that once was directly lived has become mere representation';[20] an observation that seems even more relevant today – in the age of selfies and social media – than at the time it was written. From Debord's Marxist point of view, passive spectators mediate their relationship with the world purely through commodified images, forgoing active participation in their environment.

Photography and cycling could both encourage at once a fleeting and appropriative relationship with one's environment. Elizabeth Robins Pennell, whose husband Joseph illustrated the travel books they co-published, claimed that cycling was a way of composing an 'outdoor picture'.[21] Cyclists and photographers may have both performed a visual, commodified relationship with their surroundings, 'fetishising' them in Marxist terms, as an object to be admired and appropriated.[22] This modern gaze is humorously portrayed by Pennell in her travel account *Over the Alps on a Bicycle* (1898), in which she remarks:

> Everybody called for postcards. After Rousseau set the fashion, people wept over the sublimities of Nature which they could not see for their tears; now they turn their backs upon the spectacle and let their feelings loose upon illustrated postcards.[23]

While Pennell mocks the attitude of her fellow travellers, she and her husband are also participating in this modern, image-focused, appropriative approach to travel, which favours fragmented, secondary, visual representation of a scene over more direct, present engagement with one's surroundings. There was a form of visual commodification inherent in touring cyclists' way of seeing, given tangible manifestation in the photographs some of them took along the way.

The cinema has often been associated with the railway, with the train window mirroring the cinema screen.[24] Yet the smooth, gradually changing progression of scenes that the cyclist experiences offers an equally compelling parallel of cinematic experience. The two technologies were intertwined from their beginnings: Jacques Seray records *phénakisticope* displays in Paris theatres as early as 1870, in which the rear wheel of a Michaux velocipede was decorated with a series of images that moved as the wheel turned.[25] The Lumière brothers held their first cinematograph screenings in 1895, and some of their earliest films, such as *Sortie d'usine* (1895) and *Bataille des boules de neige* (1896), prominently feature bicycles. Several contemporary critics on cycling have established parallels between the modes of perception promoted by these two technologies, which both offer a mobile, shifting perspective from a slightly raised point of view. Edward Nye argues that 'the stream of images that rush by lead the cyclist to construct a sort of cinematographic montage of the things he sees'.[26] Didier Tronchet similarly observes that the bicycle is the vehicle that best reflects cinematic 'travelling'. While the pedestrian is attentive and mobile, Tronchet claims, 'to extend the cinematographic metaphor, he lacks travelling. It is this mode of mobile perception that is most relevant to the cyclist.'[27] As these critics highlight, cyclists' attentive observation, combined with their seated point of view (slightly above that of a pedestrian) and steady, smooth pace combine to give them what could be considered a cinematic vantage point on their surroundings.

If, as Leo Charney and Vanessa Schwartz argue, 'modernity can be best understood as inherently cinematic',[28] the bicycle might be seen as a crucial element in laying the foundations of a modernity that foregrounded the act of spectatorship and the experience of simultaneity. Stephen Kern notes how the cinema provided 'proof of the existence of simultaneous realities', an experience that inspired writers such as Arthur Craven and Guillaume Apollinaire to adopt multiple voices in their simultaneous poetry.[29] On a bicycle, successive images from different localities unite to provide one overall sense of many superimposed realities. The impression is well conveyed in a review of the *Cyclo-Guide Miran illustré*, which Alfred Jarry wrote for *Mercure de France* in 1896. Jarry describes his personal cycling aesthetic, contrasting it to the leisurely approach foregrounded by the guidebook he is reviewing:

> Rather than visiting sites and monuments, without compare we prefer the aesthetic emotion of speed in the sunlight, visual impressions succeeding one another rapidly enough so that we only recall the overall impression, and most of all so that we can live without thinking. However, we can only praise this book, a series of practical itineraries with an abundance of very good photographs of all the sites.[30]

The optical experience of the cyclist is reliant on 'the aesthetic emotion of speed', which creates the conditions for this tying together of many visual sensations into an 'overall impression'. From this perspective, cyclists become spectators of the scenes which their bicycles permit them to witness in rapid, smooth, exhilarating succession. As Jarry and others describe it, the cyclist made an important contribution to this very modern way of seeing and constructing landscapes.

Colonising Cyclists

John Urry argues that a further constituent element of the automobile outlook is the 'tourist gaze'. This implies a certain self-aggrandisement, as well as a sense of dominion over one's surroundings.[31] Zack Furness extends Urry's concept of the 'tourist gaze' to argue that early cyclists cultivated a domineering relationship to their environment, claiming that cycling went hand in hand with a 'colonizing impetus'.[32] He maintains that turn-of-the-century touring cyclists' new-found individual mobility allowed them to perform a certain sense of possession of the landscapes they passed through, especially when these were indigenous lands, as in the case of the USA.[33] In urban settings, too, the presence of cyclists could be aggressive and appropriative. Stephen Crane emphasises this in his lively portrait of a New York street in 1896, at the height of the bicycle boom:

> Once the Boulevard was a quiet avenue whose particular distinctions were its shade trees and its third foot-walk which extended in Parisian fashion down the middle of the street. Also it was noted for its billboards and its huge and slumberous apartment hotels. Now, however, it is the great thoroughfare for bicycles. On these gorgeous spring days they appear in thousands. All mankind is a-wheel apparently and a person on nothing but legs feels like a strange animal. A mighty army of wheels streams from the brick wilderness below Central Park and speeds over the asphalt. In the cool evening it returns with swaying and flashing of myriad lamps.
>
> The bicycle crowd has completely subjugated the street. The glittering wheels dominate it from end to end. The cafés and dining rooms of the apartment hotels are occupied mainly by people in bicycle clothes. Even the billboards have surrendered. They advertise wheels and lamps and tires and patent saddles with all the flaming vehemence of circus art [. . .] Everything is bicycle.[34]

In this portrait of a metamorphosing city, cyclists appear boisterously on the urban scene, making the 'slumberous' hotels and billboards seem suddenly out of date, whereas only a few years before they had been the most modern elements in the cityscape. A pedestrian no longer feels like a privileged ambulant observer, but rather like a 'strange animal', having only legs and no wheels. The military lexicon of 'subjugation', 'domination' and 'occupation', as well as the army-style uniform of the cyclists, all suggest that the arrival of these figures in the urban environment has been nothing less than an invasion. Moreover, the 'brick wilderness' from which they emerge and the asphalt laid beneath their wheels amount to a silencing of nature in the service of this new technology, with the 'shade trees' and 'foot-walk' of old being forgotten. Cyclists have taken over a space conceived for and by the now impotent urban walkers. Crane's description also emphasises the precocious link cycling established with consumerism, with flamboyant advertisements for bicycle paraphernalia lining the street.

In a European context, certain elements of this appropriative relationship might also be traced, with the bicycle acting as an outward sign of civilisation conquering barbarism. Indeed, the bicycle made its appearance when Britain and France were at the height of their colonial power, both seeking to extend their influence into distant lands across the globe. Glen Norcliffe observes that the bicycle, appearing shortly after David Livingstone's exploration of the interior of Africa in the mid-nineteenth century, participated in the formulation of new land-based approaches to conquest, where previously the model of colonisation had been largely maritime.[35] As Norcliffe argues with reference to Richard Lesclide's 1870 novel *Le tour du monde en vélocipède* (*Around the World on a Velocipede*), early cycle tourers fed into a growing interest in continental exploration. In a further example from fiction, Mary Kennard's cycling heroine Cynthia in *The Golf Lunatic and his Cycling Wife* is fascinated by explorers such as Cecil Rhodes and Kitchener. 'They were men in the true sense of the word; toiling, striving, sacrificing their lives without repine,' she reflects, before comparing her own more modest adventures with theirs: 'My horizon was limited, and duty prescribed that I should not attempt to overstep its boundaries. So my superfluous energy found vent in cycling and writing about cycling.'[36] Cynthia's adventures take place in England, yet the geographical liberation the bicycle procures encourages her to identify with men who led continental explorations on behalf of imperial Britain.

Grant Allen's 1899 novel *Hilda Wade* provides a striking example of the bicycle being mobilised as a symbol of Western civilisation confronting 'primitive' societies.[37] When the narrator Dr Hubert Cumberledge follows his betrothed, the genius detective, nurse and globe-trotter Hilda Wade, from England to Rhodesia, he first catches sight of her riding across the barren landscape on a bicycle. 'I could hardly believe my eyes,' the narrator exclaims. 'Civilisation indeed! A bicycle in these remotest wilds of Africa!'[38] Hilda's body language suggests that she has carried refined British manners into this 'crude, unfinished land', as in the following description: 'She stepped lightly from her pedals, as if it had been in the park.'[39] The bicycle plays a central role in a later scene where the couple use the vehicle to escape from murderous Matabele natives, who have slaughtered most of the white settlers in the surrounding area. Writing at the beginning of the Boer War, Allen's narrative mirrors contemporary preoccupations, while grossly misrepresenting the colonial origins of violence in what amounts to a deeply racist narrative from a present-day perspective.[40] Returning to the remote farm where they are staying to find their Boer hosts have been killed, Hilda manages to save the family's baby, and once Hubert returns she thinks up an escape plan involving her bicycle. She worries, however, that the attackers 'may have taken it . . . or ridden over and broken it'.[41] The bicycle has valiantly survived the massacre; the narrator focuses on its resilience when describing how he 'examined the bearings carefully; though there were hoof-marks close by, it had received no hurt'.[42] It is portrayed as a superior vehicle to Hubert's horse, which is tired and thirsty, as well as the animals with which the natives pursue them.

Watching the sky turn red as they ride for their lives, the narrator reflects: 'It seemed as though all nature had conspired in one unholy league with the Matabele.'[43] Nature is on the side of the 'primitive' Matabele, while progress and technology, personified in the bicycle, are aligned with the two British heroes. Hilda, having trouble cycling while holding the baby, jumps on to the horse with the infant, and Hubert takes her bicycle, allowing the pair to outpace their pursuers and arrive safely in the town of Salisbury. Hubert concludes that they were saved not only by the bicycle's speed, but also the strong impression it left on their 'uncivilised' aggressors:

> I feel sure that the novelty of the iron horse, with a woman riding it, played not a little on their superstitious fears; they suspected, no doubt, this was some ingenious new engine of war devised against them by the unaccountable white man; it might go off unexpectedly in their faces at any moment.[44]

The bicycle here exemplifies the 'superior' civilisation and technology by means of which British imperialists such as Cecil Rhodes justified and implemented their dominance of indigenous, 'primitive' people the world over. To adopt Furness's terms, 'a colonizing impetus' could indeed go hand in hand with the cyclist's gaze when the technology was associated with the industrial prowess of imperial Britain.

A sense of appropriation and domination of one's surroundings can also be traced in an account of Hoopdriver's dreams after his first day of cycling in Wells's *The Wheels of Chance*. In a description that echoes the biblical Apocalypse and prefigures the Martian invasion in *The War of the Worlds*, the sleeping Hoopdriver pedals 'Ezekiel's Wheels across the Weald of Surrey, jolting over the hills and smashing villages in his course [. . .] The villages went off one after another with a soft, squashing noise.'[45] Cycling appears to have noticeable destructive potential in Wells's imaginary; in his autobiography he explicitly connects his inspiration for both novels with his journeys through Sussex by bicycle, remarking 'I rode wherever Mr. Hoopdriver rode in that story. Later on I wheeled about the district marking down suitable places and people for destruction by the Martians.'[46] The power of technology for harm is emphasised in this surreal sequence, where the hero's bicycle allows him to wreak havoc on an otherwise peaceful setting, prefiguring the coming trauma of the automobile age. Yet Wells was an enthusiastic apostle of technological progress, and the destruction of sleepy villages by Hoopdriver's bicycle (and later, by the Martians) should not simply be read as a cautionary tale about the dangers of technology. Rather, it might be considered a joyous flight of fancy about bringing conservative, traditional communities up to date with modern life. Hoopdriver's dream highlights the fact that the bicycle exposed many traditional communities to the shock of modernity, without, however, putting their lives at risk in the manner of the automobile or the Martian invasion.[47]

Hoopdriver's second dream that night draws attention to the appropriation and commodification of landscapes that could accompany the cyclist's 'tourist gaze'. Schivelsbusch argues that '[f]or the twentieth century tourist, the world has become one huge department store of countryside and cities',[48] and this is precisely the image that Wells conveys when Hoopdriver dreams he is working in the drapery emporium. His customer, the Young Lady in Grey, asks for

> 'The Ripley Road'. So he got out the Ripley Road and unrolled it and showed it to her, and she said that would do very nicely [. . .] and he began measuring off eight miles by means of the yard measure on the counter, eight miles being a dress length, a rational dress length.[49]

Here landscape is seen as a commodity, available for sale and consumption by those with means or power, rather than being humanity's common inheritance. Moreover, this image effectively conveys the tangible effect of the bicycle on our relationship with distance, as it transforms eight miles from a significant distance into a segment of a whole, an easily rideable stretch. Hoopdriver's choice of the Ripley road in particular is a suggestive one, as it became the 'Mecca of all true wheelmen'[50] at the turn of the twentieth century, frequented by hordes of day-tripping cyclists from London.

We have seen that the cyclist's approach to people and landscapes could be associated with a colonising, appropriative outlook. Yet the democratising mobility it offered paradoxically encouraged cyclists to question concepts of social hierarchy and property. Grant Allen's narrator in *The Type-Writer Girl* offers an alternative means of interpreting the cyclist's appropriative outlook. In this novel the heroine Juliet boldly claims:

> I have large estates in Herefordshire and the adjoining counties, free of land tax. Some noble marquis, I am assured, lays claim to the bare loam, the ploughed fields, the turnips; but who counts mere mud? The rest is mine, to do as I will with [. . .] I own the stripling streams that break against sharp stones in the sloping stickles [. . .] The sky overhead is mine, mine the road under foot [. . .] All these I own, by virtue of my freehold in the saddle of my bicycle.[51]

Juliet expresses a sense of proprietorship over the countryside that her bicycle permits her to access, before promptly turning this very concept on its head. She in fact positions herself against the idea of individual property by claiming that the land belongs to anyone who beholds it. This outlook is clearly manifested in her decision to sell her belongings in London (all except her bicycle) and join an anarchist settlement. The ambivalence of the cyclist's perspective is well summed up in Juliet's pronouncement. Akin to the Victorian imperialist, she feels the land is hers since she has gained access to it, yet in the same breath she rejects the idea of ownership. In the same way, the bicycle accompanied the appropriative, tourist gaze while encouraging a critical outlook on the concept of property and, more broadly, social organisation.

Mobile Subjectivity

Furness employs the term 'mobile subjectivity' to describe the psychological and cultural impact of individual transport inaugurated by the bicycle, and later inherited by the car.[52] The ability to move rapidly and autonomously from one place to another at will introduced a form of agency that transformed cyclists' perception of themselves and their place in the world. The effect of this sudden geographical freedom was particularly transformative for women. The subjective and rapid approach to travel offered by the bicycle is in evidence in Mary Kennard's *A Guide Book for Lady Cyclists*, in which the author remarks of her first cycle tour:

> Our plans were just a little vague, and subject at any moment to modification, but that is the chief beauty of the cycle tour. You are independent of trains and stations, and can go where you like – stop where you like.[53]

It is significant that Kennard should consciously contrast the previous collective mode of railway travel, which rigidly defined times and places of departure and arrival, to the spontaneous, individual paradigm of mobility that the bicycle inaugurated. Cyclists arguably enjoy an even greater degree of mobile autonomy than car drivers, since they do not rely on petrol pumps and are often able to make mechanical repairs themselves. There is an addictive enjoyment in this fleeting approach; Kennard later remarks that 'touring had taken such a hold on us, that we were much happier on the move than stationary'.[54] The mobile subjectivity of the cyclist involves a certain self-aggrandisement, akin to the colonising outlook examined in the previous section. The first cyclists discovered a rapid, efficient means of locomotion, with which 'one can traverse a given territory six times as fast, or with one-sixth the amount of exertion, or cover six times as much space', when compared to walking, as W. S. Beekman enthused in his 1894 account *Cycle Gleanings*.[55] In the 1890s, cyclists were at the very pinnacle of technological advancement, promoting a form of individual mobility that no other vehicle could allow. As Beekman asked:

> Who can visit the hills and dales, mountains and valleys, forests and meadows, brooks and streams, in more rapid succession than the cyclist? We must wait for products of future evolutions before we can frame a different answer, that in the majority we all shout in unison 'NO ONE!'[56]

This intoxicating sense of being master of one's surroundings was a constituent element of the mobile subjectivity that Furness describes, and that helped lay the foundations for the individualist car culture that would come to characterise Western societies.

Mobile subjectivity relies on individual speed, as Beekman's superlative descriptions remind us. Several contemporary theorists have pointed to the cultural impact of subjective speed as an essential element in the construction of the modern subject. Stephen Kern argues that an accelerated relationship to time and space was inaugurated at the end of the nineteenth century, in part thanks to new transportation and communication technologies that allowed individuals to communicate and move over great distances. Kern quotes the French writer Paul Adam, who wrote that the bicycle created a 'cult of speed' for a generation that intended 'to conquer time and space'.[57] The thrilling bodily sensation of speed was central to the experience of cycling, a theme that frequently recurs in literary depictions of the pursuit. Indeed, the bicycle could allow for an experience of place mediated principally by speed, rather than by attentive interaction with one's surroundings. In *The Wheels of Chance*, Wells's hero Hoopdriver encounters a scorcher in an inn, who makes the following lament:

> There's no hurry, sir, none whatever. I came out for exercise, gentle exercise, and to notice the scenery and to botanise. And no sooner do I get on the accursed machine, than off I go hammer and tongs; I never look to right or left, never notice a flower, never see a view.[58]

Despite this cyclist's 'contemplative disposition' and his desire for a rich engagement of the senses, he feels that his machine obliges him to travel rapidly from departure to destination. In J. H. Rosny's *Roman d'un cycliste* (*Novel of a Cyclist*) (1899), cycling gives the hero Philippe an experience of 'intoxicating freedom', and the narrative repeatedly celebrates 'this triumph of human speed'.[59] Philippe does not express the frustrated desire of Wells's scorcher to travel more slowly and attentively, but a certain disconnection from his surroundings is in evidence. Rosny's cycling hero seems to fly above the earth in the following description:

> The man-bird glides above the abyss. Thanks to delicious speed, it seems that everything has grown larger in his body. He is multiple, he takes up more space, he is at one with fluids, he is freed from anxiety and analysis, he possesses the magic world.[60]

As Rosny describes, the bicycle's speed was experienced as prodigious and had the paradoxical effect of making the cyclist feel both at one with the world and in control of it. Velocity was experienced in a much more direct way than in the train or car, where the enclosure of passengers transformed it into something of an abstraction. The bicycle's first users discovered a means of individual mobility that allowed them to progress at a spellbinding speed in whatever direction they chose. It was a technology that made previously unthinkable feats a reality, altering cyclists' conception of their own capacities and revolutionising their relationship to their surroundings.

In the closing years of the nineteenth century the bicycle became a symbol of wondrous progress, incarnating for some authors a new vision of society. Writing about the inspiration for his romance *The Wheels of Chance* over forty years after its initial publication, Wells recalled that 'the bicycle was the swiftest thing upon the roads in those days, there were as yet no automobiles, and the cyclist had a lordliness, a sense of masterful adventure, that has gone from him altogether now'.[61] Wells draws attention here to the elements that constituted the bicycle's fundamental modernity (speed, adventure and a heightened sense of self-importance) while underlining its short-lived status as a modern form of transport, due to the appearance of the motor car. Yet in the bicycle's early days many writers adopted the technology as an avatar of modernity. In a French book of short stories written under the pseudonym Jehan de La Pédale, and entitled *Contes modernes. Pédalons!* (*Modern Stories. Let's Pedal!*) (1892), the famous novelist Richard O'Monroy wrote in the preface, '"Let's pedal!" has become the great rallying cry of modern societies.'[62] In one of the stories, the 'legend of the bicycle' is recounted, in which 'the angel Bicycle; (or progress, as you please)', when trying to recall the means to fly back to heaven, invents the bicycle.[63] The anonymous author here suggests that 'progress' and 'bicycle' are synonyms, painting the technology as a concrete expression of the future direction of society. While O'Monroy imagines that 'the iron horse will replace the war horse',[64] attributing a possible military role to the bicycle,[65] the majority of stories in the collection focus on the sexually liberating potential of cycling.[66] The bicycle's extreme modernity could even send its users hurtling into the future, giving impetus to the budding genre of science fiction. In Wells's *The Time Machine*, the Time Traveller's mysterious machine recalls a familiar object: it is equipped with a saddle and levers, and the Psychologist likens its rapid rotation to 'the spoke of a wheel spinning'.[67] Moreover, the hero resembles an exhausted cyclist when he returns from his journey 'dusty and dirty', and 'starving for a bit of meat'.[68] The dystopian future to which he travels suggests one possible direction in which human society might evolve as a result of gender-levelling devices such as the bicycle, since the sexes of the future have evolved to become hardly distinguishable from one another.[69] Wells included the bicycle in the panoply of new technologies that fed into his imaginary of progress and modernity, especially in the early period of its popularity. While not all early cycle enthusiasts shared the same vision of the world to come, the fact that the bicycle was brandished as a symbol of modernity, progress and the future says much about the transformative effect it had on contemporary mentalities.

Early car drivers undoubtedly inherited elements of an individualist, speed-focused mode of spatial interaction first experienced by cyclists, many of them having been keen cyclists in the 1890s.[70] Yet important differences existed from the outset: the cyclist's ability to 'go where you like – stop where you like', as Kennard described it, was predicated on a keen awareness of the body's limits as well as the type of terrain being crossed and the prevailing weather conditions. Cyclists are not trapped inside the 'the literal "iron cage" of modernity, motorized, moving and domestic', to quote Urry's description of car drivers, nor are they 'incarcerated' in the train carriage as depicted by Michel de Certeau.[71] The bicycle introduced the possibility of rapid individual mobility, but cyclists' reciprocal interaction with their surroundings and the limits placed on their movement by their gradual, human-powered progression meant that they retained a vital connection with their bodies, their surroundings and other people. J. W. Allen characterises the equivocal position of the speeding cyclist in the following description:

> You are deliciously divided between the temptations of pace, the luring corners, the rapid swerve round the curves, the rush past of that enchanting procession of beech trees, the delightful regret of the beauty you are leaving so fast – and, on the other hand, the urgent need you feel to break the pace, to dismount, to get up on that low bank and look, to absorb the curves and the shadows.[72]

Here Allen's syntax mirrors the rapid impressions of the cyclist in the first part of the sentence, before slowing down to reflect the possibility of slower movement or immobility. His description lucidly depicts the crucial difference between mechanised modes of transport and the new mobility offered by the bicycle. It is an ambivalent technology, since it allows 'the temptations of pace', providing the ability to move rapidly through landscapes, while provoking the 'urgent need' to stop and 'absorb' more closely. The cyclist experiences many rapid impressions, yet remains open to the surroundings and able to 'break the pace' at any moment. Unlike other technologies of the industrial age, the bicycle requires direct energetic input from the person using it. This kinetic involvement engenders a more attentive and engaged interaction with one's surroundings.

Like many late nineteenth-century inventions, the bicycle's passage 'from dazzling appearance to nearly transparent utility, from the spectacular and astonishing to the convenient and unremarkable'[73] was exceptionally quick. Paradoxically, the fact that the bicycle became unremarkable so rapidly also helps to constitute it as a modern artefact; since, as Tom Gunning observes, 'the attractions of a consumer society depend on novelty as much as utility'.[74] While I have shown that the bicycle prefigured certain elements of the automobility paradigm developed by Urry, it also offered a rich, embodied mode of spatial interaction that is inaccessible to a car driver or passenger. When cycling was a new and wondrous pursuit, it was frequently connected with utopian visions of the future that pointed roads to freedom, communication and equality as an alternative to the spatial, psychological and socio-economic incarceration of the automobile age.

Bike to the Future

> It is far from dreaming of a return to nature to point to the utter mechanical uselessness of cars in cities, their archaic character despite their flashy portrayal, and the possible modernity of the bicycle, in our cities just as much as in the Vietnam war.
>
> Gilles Deleuze and Félix Guattari[75]

Having considered the bicycle's contribution to the forward-looking automobility paradigm, I now turn my attention to the ways in which cyclists contributed to the emergence of specific modes of spatial and temporal interaction by reconnecting with a pre-industrial outlook. Cycling, briefly a prodigiously rapid way of getting from place to place, soon became a slow-paced, contemplative mode in an accelerated world of automobiles and aviation. The cyclist's gradual, deliberate progress may be likened to what Sue Zemka theorises as a 'practice in duration'. Zemka's key example of this practice is reading a modernist novel, an activity that she argues provided a connection with long time – or Bergson's *durée*[76] – in contrast to the 'moment-consciousness of modernity'.[77] Cyclists, like readers of modernist novels, experiment with a subjective, mobile, shifting experience of long time that is difficult to quantify with scientific methods. Several critics have argued that the desire to achieve a subjective, spatial engagement with the world is a defining feature of modernist literature, which casts off the regular pace and structure of realist fiction in order to present a geographical rather than a temporal account of reality.[78] Early twentieth-century society inherited aspects of a Victorian time-centred outlook, yet modernist literature incarnated a reaction to this tendency, reasserting spatial, embodied modes of engagement over temporal ones. Literary depictions of cyclists in the early twentieth century mirror the desire to foreground spatial connection, while experimenting with a longer, more subjective time. I argue that cyclists' backward-looking gaze challenged the compression of space and time which many critics have seen as a defining characteristic of the modern era, while forging early connections with the modernist movement in literature.

Progress and Primitivism

G. K. Chesterton's essay 'The Wheel' opens with a description of a stained glass window dating from 1643 in a church in Stoke Poges, Buckinghamshire, which depicts an angel sitting astride a two-wheeled machine resembling a draisine. Chesterton reflects that what distinguishes man from animals are wheels, 'things that are as old as mankind and yet are strictly peculiar to man, that are prehistoric but not pre-human'. He goes on to observe that

> A wheel is the sublime paradox; one part of it is always going forward and the other part always going back. Now this, as it happens, is highly similar to the proper condition of any human soul or any political state. Every sane soul or state looks at once backwards and forwards; and even goes backwards to come on.[79]

As Chesterton observes, it is the capacity of the wheel to move both backwards and forwards in its rotation that makes it such a productive symbol of a 'sane' individual or social organisation. Indeed, the wheel has long been a productive image for the passage of time itself, suggesting perpetual death and renewal. Even at times of rapid progress or violent revolution, Chesterton argues, people, like wheels, should look backwards in order to determine the best route to the future.

Chesterton's contemporary Wells provides a cautionary tale about the dangers of abandoning a sense of history in favour of a headlong rush towards progress in *The War in the Air* (1908). In this uncannily prescient novel set in a near future, the world's leading powers attack each other with deadly flying machines, resulting in mutual destruction and, finally, a return to a primitive, thinly peopled world. As Jeremy Withers shows, in this novel the bicycle represents a sober vision of rational technological progress, 'an ideal piece of technology that stalwartly outlasts all of the others'.[80] The bicycle adopts a middle ground between progress and a sense of history, in contrast to the dazzlingly modern flying machines that provoke total war and planetary destruction. The hero of *The War in the Air*, Bert Smallways, is enthusiastic about new technologies in the days before the war, when he works as a bicycle mechanic. As Withers observes, 'he is a character who straddles (literally and figuratively) both the newer and the older forms of technology'.[81] He first takes to cycling and then to motorcycling, modes of transport that seem startlingly modern to his appropriately named father and elder brother (the Smallways grow vegetables, run a modest grocery shop and resent the advertising boards and overhead railways that encroach on their vegetable patch). However, in the course of the narrative the bicycle emerges as a technology that goes counter to the general thrust of destructive technological progress.

At the start of the war Bert is an accidental passenger in a German Zeppelin, and as he witnesses the destruction of New York from the air the narrator reflects:

> It was the dissolution of an age; it was the collapse of the civilization that had trusted to machinery, and the instruments of its destruction were machines. But while the collapse of the previous great civilization, that of Rome, had been a matter of centuries, had been a thing of phase and phase like the ageing and dying of a man, this, like his killing by railway or motor-car, was one swift, conclusive smashing and an end.[82]

The mechanised transport metaphors that the narrator selects in order to convey the rapid obliteration of twentieth-century Western civilisation emphasise the role of industrial technologies in bringing about this very destruction. When Bert finally manages to return to earth, he and an American man use a pair of bicycles to bring the plans of the German airships, which happen to be in Bert's possession, to the country's president. Bert then crosses the Atlantic by boat, and walks for weeks through England to reach his home, meeting only walkers, cyclists and occasional motorcyclists. Nearly all traces of past civilisation have been wiped out, and the few survivors of the war have returned to the land and are leading a hand-to-mouth existence. The epilogue that closes the novel jumps forward a number of years and depicts Bert's son's amazement on beholding a bicycle for the first time. They are now a rare sight, but some bicycles persist in this post-apocalyptic, newly primitive world. Other technologies have pushed humanity to mutual destruction, yet the bicycle stands the test of time as a mode of transport that brings people together without engendering the ominous potential for mutual destruction.

In earlier writing, too, Wells integrated bicycles into his vision of a future that would be defined by a sense of (pre)history. In his cycling romance *The Wheels of Chance*, the hero and villain cyclists Hoopdriver and Bechamel are both described as 'primordial' or 'Palaeolithic creature[s]', in spite of the modern means of locomotion with which they are constantly associated.[83] As Richard Pearson observes, 'Wells's cultural-anthropological thinking in the 1890s was part of a cultural formation that says much about the transition from Victorian to modern(ist) society'.[84] Pearson goes on to argue that 'modernity for Wells is the recognition of the primitive fundamental nature of man, and the feeble artificial character of his civilization [. . .] Wells's modern man must understand his primitivism, or perish.'[85] The bicycle's sole reliance on human energy provided a means for reconnecting with the 'primitive' human body, and with simpler styles of living that suggested an alternative to complex, industrial, capitalist systems. Grant Allen – a trained biologist like Wells – was heavily influenced by Darwinism and stressed the importance of reconnecting to our primitive past in order to develop a healthy direction for future society. In Allen's novels, the bicycle emerges as a technology that seems capable of reminding us of our distant origins. When the heroine of *Miss Cayley's Adventures* tries out a new bicycle, she reflects that 'We ran together like parts of one mechanism. I was always famed for my circular ankle-action [. . .] I have prehistoric feet; my remote progenitors must certainly have been tree-hunting monkeys.'[86] Here the cyclist's movements recall a fundamental stage in human evolution. In his apocalyptic short story 'The Thames Valley Catastrophe' (1901), Allen placed the hero upon a bicycle.[87] While London is destroyed by a flood of lava resulting from a sudden split in a tectonic plate, the cyclist narrator is able to survive by taking to the hills. The great city cannot withstand the force of nature, yet as in *The War in the Air*, the bicycle emerges from the story as an adaptable technology on a human scale; a modern cultural achievement that frees its rider from reliance on the infrastructure of the industrial age.

Looking Back: The Cycling flâneur

The first cyclists performed an engagement with the past that corresponds to Marc Augé's definition of Baudelairean modernity, that is, 'the deliberate coexistence of different worlds'.[88] In his *Tableaux Parisiens* (1861), Charles Baudelaire (1821–67) depicts an archetypal nineteenth-century pedestrian, the *flâneur*, who seeks out traces of the past in the modern city. This complex and amorphous figure was famously theorised by Walter Benjamin as a cornerstone of modernity in *The Arcades Project* (1927–40). The *flâneur* became a crucial symbol in literature, closely associated with mid-century Paris, even if the figure may have been a cross-Channel or even pan-European construct.[89] Like turn-of-the-century cyclists, the *flâneur* of the 1860s negotiated and responded to a metamorphosing urban milieu. Where cyclists contended with increasingly busy, mechanised and fast-paced streets, the *flâneur* moved through cities undergoing profound upheaval. Baron Haussmann's renovation of Paris displaced 350,000 people, as winding medieval streets and labourers' slums made way for straight, metalled boulevards and bourgeois townhouses. In a matter of years, the city became unrecognisable, adapted to accommodate new modes of transportation and consumption.[90]

The *flâneur* has been seen as an ambivalent figure whose inherent modernity was coupled with slow, circuitous movement and a backward gaze that refused modern concepts of speed and efficiency. It is important to note that Pierre Michaux's velocipede, the first commercial two-wheeler equipped with pedals, enjoyed a moment in the limelight in Paris simultaneously with the *flâneur*. As Glen Norcliffe observes, 'it was [...] on these very boulevards [built by Haussmann] and in nearby gymnasia and parks that the prototypes of the world's first commercially produced bicycles were tested'.[91] Just as another ancestor of the safety bicycle, the draisine, has been seen as an important if overlooked cultural artefact in early nineteenth-century Britain,[92] the sociocultural impact of the velocipede craze of the 1860s has been largely neglected. Both the Parisian velocipede and *flâneurie* played an important role at the mid-century, shaping discourses around mobility, urban development and progress. In many respects, turn-of-the-century cyclists reconnected with the *flâneur* aesthetic as a protest against and alternative to the runaway pace of progress.

Cyclists inherited and renewed central traits of the *flâneur*, such as a marriage of close observation and movement, an equivocal position in and outside the crowd, and resistance to the dizzying pace of modernity. The cyclist aesthetic relied on a direct experience of speed, as we have seen, yet it also encouraged slow-paced interaction and the desire to seek out hidden traces of the past. Philippe, the hero of Rosny's *Roman d'un cycliste*, takes pleasure in cycling slowly, contrasting his bicycle to other recent technological discoveries and observing that 'There is also pleasure in going slowly, in this world where speed has become enormous – trains, cars, steamers – where a man's voice crosses the ocean in a flash.'[93] Here the bicycle allows the protagonist to reconnect with pre-industrial sensations, offering an antidote to the negation of time and space operated by a host of contemporary technologies. Yet in contrast to the *flâneur*, cyclists' novel machines made them a highly visible spectacle. Certainly, cyclists could achieve a certain anonymity thanks to their autonomous mobility which allowed them to reach far-off places where, even if they were remarkable, they were strangers. Yet their means of locomotion remained a curious sight, and the first cyclists could not avoid becoming a spectacle in both urban and rural settings. Nicholas Oddy argues that this conspicuousness in the days of the bicycle boom effectively negated any real possibility of emulating the *flâneur*, who was an anonymous observer among the crowd. Oddy claims that it was only by the first part of the twentieth century, when the bicycle had become an unremarkable part of everyday life, that 'the painter of modern life [could] mount a diamond frame roadster and cruise the boulevards and streets of the urban environment without being glanced at by others'.[94] The cyclist's observant, critical outlook was inherited from – or perhaps invented simultaneously with – the *flâneur*, but I agree with Oddy's conclusion that it was only when the technology's dazzling newness faded that cyclists were able to truly emulate the *flâneur* by dissolving into the crowd. What is more, the multiplication of ever-faster transport and communication technologies in the early twentieth century functioned to place cyclists in the position of marginal, outside observers of a rapidly accelerating reality.

The status of cyclists within the turn-of-the-century urban environment was ambivalent; they both actively participated in the acceleration of traffic and became observers and victims of the concurrent mechanisation of road transport, as motor cars, buses and trams began to criss-cross the city at speed. Yet in contrast to the *flâneur*, cyclists were not limited to one environment; their machine allowed them to explore both rural and urban spaces. The cyclist's organic movement between rural and urban environments corresponds to what Raymond Williams pinpoints as a crucial element in the experience of modernity in *The Country and the City*.[95] While the Baudelairean *flâneur* sought out traces of the past in the modern city, Glen Norcliffe observes that

> The cycling flâneur was able to rediscover these contrasts of new and old, not by strolling through urban quarters of different ages, but by pedalling from the modern city to the countryside and parks where tradition, bygone ways and nature were still in evidence.[96]

By allowing access to the countryside and the in-between spaces obliterated by the railways, the bicycle allowed a spontaneous encounter with traces of the past, an element that was central to the *flâneur*'s aesthetic. In *Wheel Magic*, J. W. Allen describes the cyclist's visceral engagement with the past in the following terms:

> To set out to visit, aforethought, some object of interest discovered in a guidebook or gazeetter, is quite a different matter [. . .] But to come upon the thing unawares may be to come suddenly to a point where present and past are one. The whole fabric of the medieval church rises before us as we stand by the old font or broken canopy.[97]

Allen's description here brings to mind Michel de Certeau's definition of spaces as localities in which layers of the past overlap and persist; he argues that 'inhabited places are like presences of absences'.[98] The unexpected discovery of the multi-layered history of places characterised by Allen was made possible by the bicycle, which invited spontaneous, individual discovery. Such encounters with the past became a privileged object of the modern tourist gaze, while simultaneously functioning as a protest against the excessive speed and mechanisation of modern life. Above all, the slow-paced, meandering exploration practised by cyclists suggested alternative means of engaging with localities.

The closing lines of Jerome K. Jerome's tale about a cycling tour, *Three Men on the Bummel*, provide a means of conceptualising the turn-of-the century cycling *flâneur*'s outlook. The narrator defines the titular German word in the following terms:

> A Bummel [. . .] I should describe as a journey, long or short, without an end; the only thing regulating it being the necessity of getting back within a given time to the point from which one started. Sometimes it is through busy streets, and sometimes through the fields and lanes; sometimes we can be spared for a few hours, and sometimes for a few days. But long or short, but here or there, our thoughts are ever on the

running of the sand. We nod and smile to many as we pass; with some we stop and talk awhile; and with a few we walk a little way. We have been much interested, and often a little tired. But on the whole we have had a pleasant time, and are sorry when 'tis over.⁹⁹

The verb *Bummeln*, like *flâner*, means to walk in a leisurely fashion, stroll or dawdle, and the approach to cycling favoured by Jerome's narrator owes a debt to the meandering, slow-paced rhythm of the walker. Both these modes of transport clearly mirror Jerome's digressive narrative style. The narrator's attitude towards time is equivocal. On the one hand, the duration of the journey is seen as immaterial: it may be long or short, lasting several hours or several days, and is 'without an end'. Yet on the other hand, the traveller's thoughts 'are ever on the running of the sand', and he must return to his point of departure 'within a given time'. During his journey the traveller experiences contrasting impressions from urban and rural environments, and interacts with those met along the way, unlike the enclosed train or car passenger. Bicycles were a technology that made possible a connected vision of city and countryside, facilitating subjective crisscrossings from one environment to the other. Much like the *flâneur*, cyclists used their progressive yet modest means of locomotion to navigate, understand or protest against the acceleration, anonymity and mechanisation of modern life.

Reclaiming and Reviving the Road

The bicycle provided access to rural spaces for an increasingly urban population, which gave renewed life to country roads that had been abandoned with the coming of the railway. As such, the bicycle not only opened up new spaces of encounter and exploration, it encouraged cyclists to forge further connections with the past by allowing them to ride the roads travelled by their ancestors. J. W. Allen enjoys the sense of history connected with cycling on main roads at night, when 'we know only that beneath our wheels is the great road along which men have travelled generation after generation; and our minds reach forward along it for a hundred miles'.¹⁰⁰ The increasing numbers of cyclists on rural roads brought about tangible changes for villages that had previously been staging posts, but which the railway had bypassed. F. W. Bockett remarks on the effect that passing cyclists had on rural communities, noting for instance that in the old-fashioned village of London Colney

> Cycling has given the village a new lease of life, and the old inn has put on a new coat of paint to attract the thousands of London wheelmen who will pass along this famous north road during the coming summer.[101]

As Bockett's description highlights, both the road and the places along it were revived by the bodily presence of cyclists. This was in stark contrast to the impact of the railway on such communities. In 1893, Elizabeth Robins Pennell vividly depicted the impact of the railway line crossing the Alps, observing that

> When it was out of sight there was no forgetting it; the black smoke hung over the valley, the smell of coal dust filled it, and everywhere were the signs of the change its coming had worked. Old posting inns and chalets were falling into ruins by the roadside. We did not meet a diligence, not a wagon, not a carriage, and only one tourist – a German on a bicycle, who tore past like a cyclone.[102]

As Pennell describes it, railways simultaneously pollute their surroundings and bring about the demise of smaller towns and older roads, whose very existence is negated in the train's headlong rush to reach its destination. In this sense they prefigured later transport technologies such as the car or the aeroplane, which Paul Virilio holds responsible for 'the *immaterial pollution* of distances'.[103] Virilio illustrates this concept with the image of flying over the Atlantic rather than sailing across it. The space of the Atlantic is effectively negated by refusing to engage with it as a 'reference ground' in order to achieve 'a sensory experience of geography'.[104] Though generally perceived as a liberating technology, Virilio points out how the aeroplane along with other motorised modes obliges us to disengage from the essential imbrication of our body in space. The speeding cyclist whom the Pennells meet on the road reminds us that cyclists' position is ambivalent. They straddle two modes; that of slow, observant travellers hoping to revive an authentic, embodied experience of space, and that of the scorcher glimpsed on an Alpine road, whose speed-focused approach prefigures that of the car driver.

With the appearance of the automobile around the turn of the century, roads became sites of danger and conflict, reflecting and amplifying social inequalities. Bockett, in 1901, sensed the end of an era, warning that

> Cyclists should enjoy the delights of this perfect road as frequently as they can, while there is yet time, for I fear the day will soon be here when

that rattling, snorting, and spitting Apollyon, the motor car, will make the road impossible for all but himself.[105]

Twelve years later, the roads Edward Thomas took on his journey to the Quantocks were 'travelled by an occasional (but not sufficiently occasional) motor car'.[106] The increasing presence of cars on the roads suddenly made them a dangerous space for the non-motorised majority. Indeed, the window of time in which cyclists brought attention back to the highways and were able to enjoy travelling on them safely was very brief. Cyclists' demands for better-quality roads led to ambitious road improvement schemes, thanks to lobbying by groups such as the League of American Wheelmen in the USA and the Bicycle Touring Club (later Cyclists' Touring Club, CTC) in the UK.[107] Yet with the rapid arrival of cars, motorists increasingly laid claim to the public highway, with attempts made to force bicycles off the road and on to newly built cycle paths from the 1930s.[108] The CTC's secretary, G. H. Stancer, wrote to *The Times* on 4 April 1934 to express his firm resistance to such schemes, arguing that 'the demand for separate tracks for cyclists is part of the campaign of motorists to appropriate public highways for their exclusive use'. Rather than building new cycle paths, the CTC was in favour of creating special roads for motor cars – motorways – and forbidding them access to the public highway. These still raging debates around use and ownership of the road were sparked in the early years of the twentieth century, when the bicycle and the car offered contrasting spatial and political approaches to engaging with the rediscovered public space of the road.

Cyclists' modest progress and openness to their surroundings encouraged them to engage with the road as a commons, a space belonging to all that could be rich in encounters. H. G. Wells's hero in *The History of Mr Polly* has a strange, idyllic vision while travelling on a suburban train. Looking out of the train window, he is depressed to observe that 'every road [. . .] was bordered by inflexible palings or iron fences or severely disciplined hedges', and begins dreaming of 'beautifully careless, unenclosed high roads'.[109] The enclosure of spaces he witnesses from the train window recalls the destruction of the English commons by Enclosure Acts from the 1750s onwards, while simultaneously mirroring Polly's social imprisonment in his role as a toiling draper. An image arises in his mind in response:

> He was haunted by the memory of what was either a half-forgotten picture or a dream; a carriage was drawn up by the wayside and four beautiful people, two men and two women graciously dressed, were dancing a formal ceremonious dance full of bows and curtseys, to the

music of a wandering fiddler they had encountered. They had been driving one way and he walking another – a happy encounter with this obvious result.[110]

Polly's pastoral, idealised vision of a convivial, creative use of the public highway is a reaction against bourgeois control of space in the early twentieth century. This imagined scene, as well as Polly's 'exploratious meanderings'[111] on his bicycle, which begin directly after the vision, are part of an attempt to free himself from the determinism of the capitalist society he inhabits. The bicycle helped reinstate the road as a space of encounter, while also reviving it as a rich literary terrain.

Edward Thomas also conveys a sense of the social and literary potential of the road when animated by human presence in his depiction of the other travellers he meets on his journey out of London one Good Friday:

> I had left behind me most cyclists from London, but I was now continually among walkers. There were a few genial muscular Christians with their daughters, and equally genial muscular agnostics with no children; bands of scientifically minded ramblers with knickerbockers, spectacles and cameras; a trio of young chaps singing their way to a pub; one or two solitaries going at five miles an hour with or without hats; several of a more sentimental school in pairs, generally chosen from both sexes, disputing as to the comparative merits of Mr. Bellock and Mr. Arthur Sidgwick; and a few country people walking, not for pleasure, but to see friends seven or eight miles away, whom perhaps they had not visited for years, and, after such a Good Friday as this, never will again.[112]

This colourful portrait of the walkers the cyclist encounters underlines his close visual and aural contact with them, as well as the sense of connection he feels to them. Whether participating in the muscular Christian movement,[113] debating about science or the relative merits of classical scholars, or sporting the latest fashions and inventions, these walkers give us a sense of intellectual ferment closely associated with their physical activity. For the perceptive, literary-minded cyclist, such encounters with various classes of people provide a rich source of inspiration. The combination of diversity and observation experienced when moving at a moderate speed on a bicycle allows the writer to paint vivid, shifting portraits of his fellow travellers and the spaces they move through. Rather than slicing through and dividing communities in the manner of a railway or a motorway, when animated by human presence the road becomes a meeting place teeming with energy and potential.

The sociologist of sport Michel Bouet characterises the cyclist's relationship to and animation of the road in the following description, insisting on the difference between the car driver's and the cyclist's outlook:

> in the case of the motor car, the road is chopped up and torn apart by speed. The road is only a pretext for speeding along, a sort of springboard or runway, forgotten as soon as it has been conquered. On a bicycle, however, the road rolls out organically, in a Bergsonian duration that unfurls its melody and that shares with the road its ever-shifting nature and inherent heterogeneity [. . .] The road is explored, examined and conquered in all its dynamic detail [. . .] The cyclist revives the road. He lives with the melody of the road, intimately close to it, visually and tactually.[114]

Here Bouet pinpoints the cyclist's active and bodily animation of the space of the road, which is not simply an obstacle to be overcome between departure and destination, but rather a vibrant and meaningful space in itself. The cyclist gives life to the road by exchanging with it and paying close attention to its details and particularities. This reflects Michel de Certeau's emphasis on the centrality of movement and physical presence in the very constitution of spaces. De Certeau argues that

> Space exists when we take into consideration directional vectors, levels of speed and the variable of time. Space is a crossing of mobile elements. It is in some sense animated by the totality of movements that take place within it [. . .] In other words, space is a place that is used.[115]

Bodily engagement with and use of space stands in contrast to the car's generation of an internal, subjective space and corresponding external non-places such as motorways and supermarkets, theorised by Marc Augé, which are lacking in active human presence or bodily animation.[116] In contrast to the train, plane or car traveller, cyclists revive the roads they travel on, reinvesting the time and the place of the journey with significance.

Approaching Urban Space in Ford Madox Ford's The Soul of London

In Ford Madox Ford's impressionistic portrait of an imperial metropolis, *The Soul of London: A Survey of a Modern City* (1905), the author reflects on the evolving contemporary relationship to space, focusing on temporal and spatial transformations and continuities in the urban environment. Ford follows in the Baudelairean tradition by engaging with the traces of the past in the city, claiming that

> This author's endeavour should be to make the Past, the sense of all the dead Londons that have gone into the producing of this child of all the ages, like a constant ground-bass beneath the higher notes of the Present.[117]

Ford is particularly interested in depicting new spatial configurations that have appeared as a result of transport and communication technologies, making the striking observation that 'We live in spacious times.'[118] Ford adopts an explicitly geographical approach, contemplating the city 'From a Distance' in the first chapter, and approaching it by means of transport in the second chapter, entitled 'Roads into London'. The author constantly seeks to depict London as a shifting entity, composed of many superimposed and overlapping spaces. The different means of entering the city – such as the motor car, the electric tram, the bicycle, on foot, the omnibus and the train – are each seen to create their own unique mode of spatial interaction. Ford considers that driving into the city leads to a loss of connection to successive localities, since cars 'fly too fast for any easy recognition of the gradual changes from country to town'.[119] This is a result of the car passengers' speed as well as their perspective and the physical sensation of riding in early roofless cars, since 'the motorist is too low down as a rule, the air presses against the eyes and half closes them'.[120] Ford presciently notes that this experience of mobility will inevitably lead us to an altered relationship to space, as we will begin 'thinking of distances, as it were, in terms of the motor car'.[121] He displays concern about the 'psychological effects' of this technology, while suggesting that the reassuring movement of the electric tram provides a more serene, contemplative and 'romantic' means of entering London.[122] The capacity of means of transport to create and transform the fabric of the city is apparent; Ford lists London's spreading suburbs before asserting that 'The electric tram is doing all this.'[123]

By 1905, Ford already considers the bicycle one 'of the older methods of communication',[124] and is not exactly enthusiastic about this means of entering the city, as shown in the following extract:

> I have always found entering London by this way to be tedious and dispiriting. You have to attend to yourself even more particularly than when you are in a motor-car; you have only half a horizon – the half that

is in front of you. You are nearer the dust when there is dust, or nearer the mud. Transition from country to town becomes rather wearisome; you think a good deal in miles. London manifests itself slowly [. . .]¹²⁵

Ford is hardly a keen cyclist, yet his depiction of the form of spatial engagement the bicycle offers is significant, as is his choice to include this mode of transport in his list of means of entering the city.¹²⁶ This description highlights cycling's liminal position between pedestrian and motorised means of transport. On the one hand, the physical effort required can make it 'tedious', 'dispiriting' and 'wearisome', with the cyclist, like the walker, being exposed to dust and mud. On the other hand, Ford suggests that the cyclist shares elements of the car driver's subjective, self-centred, visual relation to space, having only 'half a horizon' and being even more likely than a car driver to 'attend to yourself'. Yet crucially, the cyclist's steady progress makes possible an 'easy recognition of the gradual changes from country to town' that Ford recognised was impossible in a motor car. 'London manifests itself slowly'; the cyclist has time to notice and engage with the transforming landscape, as country turns to city. Cyclists' bodily presence in the space they traverse provides them with the means to creatively and meaningfully engage with urban and rural localities.

In chapter 3, 'Work in London', Ford returns to the bicycle to present it as a symbol of spatial and imaginative escape for overworked Londoners, observing that 'London, in fact, if it make men eminently materialist in their working hours [. . .] makes them by reaction astonishingly idealist in their interior souls'.¹²⁷ Ford depicts two subjects who are literally imprisoned by society's thirst for mechanised mobility; a railway signalman he once met who 'spends dreadfully long hours, high up in a sort of cage of wood and glass, above the innumerable lines of shimmering rails just outside the dim cave of a London terminus' and 'a man of forty, a cashier of a London 'bus company'.¹²⁸ The railway signalman finds release from his daily drudgery by making models of English cathedrals, while the cashier uses his spare time 'to cover, on his bicycle, every road of the United Kingdom. He inked over on his ordnance map each road that he travelled on.'¹²⁹ Both these examples illustrate how the infrastructure of mechanised mobility necessarily implies the effective imprisonment of workers for the comfort of paying passengers.¹³⁰ This is countered in both cases by a physical, manual activity that recreates or mimics a more organic interaction with spaces. The signalman seeks to reconnect with past spaces by creating models of historic buildings, thus enacting a creative, manual exchange with imagined localities.

The London cashier, on the other hand, compensates for his lack of spatial engagement and movement during his working hours by riding his bicycle throughout the country. Cycling offered the possibility of a human-centred, egalitarian, sociable connection with localities, in contrast to the mechanised means of transport proliferating at the time Ford was writing.

Ford's representation of the use of spaces may be read under the lens of Henri Lefebvre's theory concerning the fluctuating, multilayered nature of spaces. According to their use and interpretation, Lefebvre establishes three broad categories of space. First, everyday uses of space (such as living in a house or travelling to work) are considered as 'spatial practice, which includes production and reproduction [. . .] Both assured competence and a certain performance'[131] (terms he borrows from Noam Chomsky's linguistics, and which have been given renewed relevance in the work of Judith Butler).[132] Secondly, he outlines 'representations of space',[133] referring to definitions of space formulated by governments, businesses, city planners and other organs of power, and imposed on the users of such spaces by means of specific rules, signs and codes. Finally, the category of 'spaces of representation' refers to subversive spaces 'linked to the clandestine, underground side of social life, but also to art'.[134] Lefebvre insists that these three broad types of space are not separate categories, but rather constantly overlap and merge into each other. Indeed, he rejects the idea of inert space, underlining the fluctuating, dynamic aspect to any locality, which is never empty but always being acted upon and transformed by the various currents running through it. Ford's focus on the different spaces generated by various modes of transport into London is a vivid illustration of this. Moreover, Lefebvre's third category, 'spaces of representation', which he presents as a means by which the dominant capitalist logic ('representations of space') can be challenged, corresponds to the attempts made by Ford's enclosed railway signalman and bus company cashier to resist the imprisonment of their working lives and achieve meaningful, subversive spatial engagement.

Lefebvre's theory of the hegemonic use of space and means of disrupting it can be connected to the use of the bicycle by the Situationist movement in the 1950s. The bicycle was one tool used by the Situationists and movements inspired by them, such as the Provos in the Netherlands, in order to propose alternative means of interpreting and interacting with urban space. In a bid to actively contribute to the spatial arrangement of their city and counteract contemporary car-centred political choices, the Provos left white bicycles dotted around the city, intended for free public use.[135] As the critic Zack Furness shows, the Situationists 'abhorred the centrality of cars in urban design because [. . .] they saw it as a symbol of a much larger problem: a spatio-cultual arrangement designed to suppress human spontaneity and wilful participation in the city's construction'.[136] Guy Debord's 'Situationist Theses on Traffic' (1959) argues that revolutionary city planning should struggle against car-centred city design, attempting to '[b]reak these topological chains, by testing out terrains for the circulation of humans through real life'.[137] In the post-war period, the car-centred projects of city planners such as Le Corbusier in Paris and Robert Moses in New York led to an exponential rise in car ownership and resistance to the emerging trend of building cities around cars rather than people. The use of the bicycle by these movements of resistance in the 1960s and 1970s was prefigured by its symbolic and actual role at the turn of the century, when it became a means to perform an alternative, people-centred approach to the use of space.

Rediscovering Space on Two Wheels: Aldous Huxley's Crome Yellow

Aldous Huxley's first novel, *Crome Yellow* (1921), richly engages with the effects of transport technologies on spatial interactions and society, and is of particular interest to us because of the evocative description of a bicycle ride in the opening pages. Huxley explores the distortion or negation of space generated by motorised means of transport and the possibility for bodily re-engagement with space offered by the bicycle. Denis Stone is introduced to us as a character who longs to recover a physical connection to his surroundings. When the novel opens, Denis is travelling on a slow train to Crome, a stately home to which he has been invited. He is impatient to arrive, obsessed by his loss of 'Two hours. One hundred and twenty minutes', in which 'he might have done so much, so much – written the perfect poem, for example, or read the one illuminating book'.[138] His thoughts focus on time; not only on the length of the train journey and the number of stops, but also on his age: 'He was twenty-three, and oh! So agonizingly conscious of the fact.'[139] His enumeration of the various fictional stops the train makes on its journey from London – 'Bole, Tritton, Spavin Delawarr, Knipswich for Timpany, West Bowlby, and, finally, Camlet-on-the-Water'[140] – recalls de Certeau's characterisation of the 'map', which imposes an immobile, hegemonic definition of spatial practices.[141] De Certeau contrasts this bird's-eye view to the bodily spatial interaction of the walker. Denis's lack of physical stimulation is evident; agitated, he moves his belongings from one place to another within the train: 'A futile proceeding. But one must have something to do.'[142] He feels cooped up, and this pointless physical agitation betrays a desire to engage his body in his movement; to effect a mobile, physical 'tour', in de Certeau's terms, rather than travel on a fixed itinerary within the 'incarcerating' space of the railway carriage.[143]

The stasis of the journey contrasts sharply with Denis's busy movement once the train stops, when he 'jumped up', 'seized a bag in either hand' and 'ran up the train towards the van'.[144] On reaching the guard, he makes his first, 'breathless' utterance, 'A bicycle, a bicycle!', adopting the posture of 'a man of action'.[145] Denis's enthusiasm hardly affects the guard, however, who takes his time handing out various packages, stoically replying 'All in good time, sir.'[146] The guard belongs firmly to the Victorian world of the railways, a fact emphasised by his physical description as 'a large, stately man with a naval beard. One pictured him at home, drinking tea, surrounded by a numerous family.'[147] Denis's enterprising attitude is temporarily dampened by the guard's response, and Huxley employs a cycling metaphor in order to humorously convey his sentiment of deflation when faced with this inertia, describing how: 'Denis's man of action collapsed, punctured.'[148] The figure of the train guard embodies the railway's restrictive temporal framework; yet once Denis retrieves his bicycle, he is able to enact an embodied, creative engagement with space, an experience that impacts directly on the texture of the narrative.

Denis brings to mind the walker as theorised by de Certeau, who is able to escape 'the imaginary totalisations of the eye' through a bodily and 'blind' connection with space.[149] This vocabulary of bodily engagement with space is mirrored by several critics who have written about cycling: Marc Augé describes the sensation of cycling as 'a bodily connection with space', while Didier Tronchet praises the capacity the bicycle gives us to 'merge with our environment'.[150] It is as though cyclists' connection to their bodies allows them to extend their consciousness into a physical communion with their surroundings. Cyclists perform a sensory aesthetics built on mobile, multi-sensory engagement that actively animates the spaces through which they move. Denis's specific interaction with the landscape once in the saddle illustrates Marc Desportes's observation that 'Each major transport technology therefore models an original approach to the space one passes through, each major technology carries its own "landscape" within it.'[151]

The protagonist's first reflections on cycling relegate temporal considerations to the realm of the anecdotal, inviting the reader to focus on the spatial dimension. The narrator recounts how Denis 'always took his bicycle when he went into the country', promising himself that 'One day one would get up at six o'clock' and cycle through a succession of picturesque villages.[152] Yet despite this laudable intention, 'Somehow they never did get seen.'[153] Denis simply enjoys the idea that he might get up at six, but fails to put his plan into practice. While poking fun at the inertia of the dilettante protagonist, this observation also hints at his refusal of a linear approach to spatial exploration, since the imagined early start and the 'succession' of localities simply mirror the mode of travelling proposed by the railway. Rather than concentrating on the time taken or the number of stops until arrival, as he did on the train, Denis's journey to Crome is recounted in terms of the contours of the landscape he passes through and the sensations he experiences. Huxley's descriptions recall Ernest Hemingway's observation that 'It is by riding a bicycle that you learn the contours of a country best, since you have to sweat up the hills and coast down them.'[154] Moreover, a physical connection to the landscape is given expression in the correlation between the lie of the land and Denis's mood; for instance, as he reaches 'the top of the long hill which led up from Camlet station, he felt his spirits mounting'.[155] Inspired by the 'treeless sky-lines that changed as he moved' and the 'curves' in the landscape,[156] Denis begins to put his frustrated literary intentions into practice, composing lines of poetry in his head. The reader is once again invited to laugh at Denis, as his poetic efforts nearly cause him to fall off his bicycle when 'he made a gesture with his hand, as though to scoop the achieved expression out of the air'.[157] We are reminded that he is riding a vehicle that imposes certain restrictions on his body, yet the mental state it provokes suggests a transcendence of this fact. Denis's literary inspiration while cycling suggests a subjective remapping of space that contests the fixed map of the railways. Illustrating de Certeau's concept of 'semantic wandering' or the intimate link between physical movement and narration,[158] Denis seeks bodily metaphors for describing the 'curves of those little valleys', which he thinks are 'as fine as the lines of a human body'.[159] This instinctive connection between the forms of the human body and the landscape is encouraged by a technology that actively promotes a bodily connection with space.

It is 'the crest of a descent' which brings Denis's attention back to the 'outer world', when he first catches sight of Crome, his destination.

He admires the view of the old house, before speeding down the hill, to arrive 'five minutes later'.[160] This first mention of a temporal marker since leaving the train brings the reader back to the time-conscious world Denis inhabits; similarly, the distant view of the house suggests de Certeau's immobilised, 'totalising' view, rather than the embodied approach to space his bicycle journey has allowed him to adopt. Nonetheless, the bicycle opens up the possibility for sustained, bodily, creative engagement with space. In sharp contrast to the time-conscious, incarcerating experience of rail travel, Denis's cycle ride from the train station to Crome presents both a subjective means of engaging with space and an alternative narrative mode.

Denis's introductory bicycle ride may be contrasted to the arrival of Ivor by motor car half-way through the novel. The guests at Crome await the new guest, looking out upon the hills and valleys around the house. As they contemplate the landscape, the narrator recalls Denis's physical response to the 'curves of those little valleys' on his bicycle, describing how 'Under the level evening light the architecture of the land revealed itself [. . .] The surface of things had taken on a marvellous enrichment.'[161] In contrast, the motor car intrudes brutally into the landscape:

> On the opposite side of the valley, at the crest of the ridge, a cloud of dust flushed by the sunlight to rosy gold was moving rapidly along the sky-line [. . .] the dust descended into the valley and was lost. A horn with the voice of a sea-lion made itself heard, approaching. A minute later Ivor came leaping round the corner of the house. His hair waved in the wind of his own speed; he laughed as he saw them [. . .] 'Well, here I am. I've come with incredulous speed.'[162]

The speed of the motor car obliterates the specificities of the landscape just described by the narrator. The vehicle is 'a cloud of dust', at once shrouding it from the outside world and making the world invisible for its passenger. It creates its own closed-off space within the landscape, refusing to engage with the successive spaces which it enters. When it disappears entirely, it becomes an uncanny aural presence for the onlookers, incongruously suggesting the cry of a marine animal, before its driver suddenly appears among the company. Ivor embodies solely 'his own speed' rather than entering into a reciprocal relationship with the spaces and people around him. The driver has enclosed himself in a mechanised space, and thus shut himself off from the inherently collaborative construction of space as theorised by Lefebvre, de Certeau and others. It is the loss of bodily points of reference in cyberspace that Virilio sees as deeply problematic in terms of our current relationship with technology and space. He asks 'What spatiality are we referring to, in fact, when we lose our bearings and our foothold, and therefore all postural reference points?'[163] The car and other mechanised forms of transport laid the basis for this disembodied form of spatial (non-)engagement that has reached its apotheosis in the digital age.

The extension of the subjective spatial mode proposed by the car into society at large threatens to lead to a world where the only space that people engage with is that of their personal room, with no need for interaction with other people or spaces. Such a nightmare was imagined by E. M. Forster in his prophetic science fiction tale, 'The Machine Stops' (1909), which examines the theme of loss of space as a symptom of the machine age. This story depicts a distant future in which humans live in individual rooms 'like the cell of a bee',[164] with their every need supplied by the revered Machine. Due to pollution, the air outside their rooms has become unbreathable, and human interaction is limited to onscreen calls and lectures. The hero Kuno observes to his mother that 'we have lost the sense of space. We say "space is annihilated," but we have annihilated not space but the sense thereof. We have lost a part of ourselves.'[165] Space has been polluted, in Virilio's terms, due to the crippling absence of any bodily reference points within it. Faced with this realisation, walking becomes Kuno's means of subverting the inhuman logic of the machine. In an attempt to recover a sense of space, Kuno begins pacing up and down the platform outside his room, gradually gaining a sense of the concepts of '"Near" and "Far"'. These experiments lead him to the Vitruvian conclusion that 'Man is the measure [. . .] Man's feet are the measure for distance, his hands are the measure for ownership, his body is the measure for all that is lovable and desirable and strong.'[166] Forster's story warns against the consequences of handing our locomotive, social, digestive, sexual and other functions over to a machine. The future he imagines is extrapolated from his fears about the consequences of the increasing mechanisation of the society in which he lived.

Forster's contemporary Huxley introduced elements of the dystopian, mechanised world that he would later bring to life in *Brave New World* (1932) to his début novel. The owner of Crome, Mr Wimbush, imagines a world in which reliance on machines would make all human interaction superfluous:

> How gay and delightful life would be if one could get rid of all the human contacts! Perhaps, in the future, when machines have attained to a state

of perfection – for I confess that I am, like Godwin and Shelley, a believer in perfectibility, the perfectibility of machinery – then, perhaps, it will be possible for those who, like myself, desire it, to live in a dignified seclusion, surrounded by the delicate attentions of silent and graceful machines, and entirely secure from any human intrusion. It is a beautiful thought.[167]

Mr Scogan, who stands for faith in industry and technological progress, similarly imagines a future in which 'An impersonal generation will take the place of Nature's hideous system. In vast state incubators, rows upon rows of gravid bottles will supply the world with the population it requires.'[168] Via these characters, Huxley satirises those who have ultimate faith in machines, suggesting that the price to pay for over-reliance on technology is the loss of our basic humanity. As we saw in Chapter 3, the bicycle is unlike motorised means of transport as it accompanies human effort rather than usurping the body's strength. The empirical experience of cycling in the increasingly mechanised world of the early twentieth century corresponds to Kuno's experiments with walking outside his cell, or Denis's cycle ride to Crome. Cycling offered a means to re-establish the human body as the measure of distance and thus achieve authentic, embodied spatial engagement.

The bicycle stands for a version of progress that retains a keen awareness of the history of humanity and a connection to the human body. Revolution can only arise in the reclaimed space of the street, Virilio argues, when 'the multitude of passers-by [. . .] momentarily ceases being the technical relay of the machine and itself becomes a motor [. . .] in other words, *a generator of speed*'.[169] The bicycle had an equivocal position in relation to modernity, and one that rapidly evolved over the period under study here. In the late nineteenth century it was a strikingly modern instrument, and was therefore associated with various utopian visions of the future. Moreover, the rapid, individual form of mobility it inaugurated helped plant the seeds of the automobility paradigm theorised by Urry and Furness. Yet after the appearance of the motor car and the aeroplane, the bicycle was no longer a novel technology. Its tarnished modernity along with the embodied form of spatial engagement and connection to a longer time that it offered from the outset encouraged cyclists to adopt a perspective that looked backwards as well as forwards, condemning the destructive drive of motorised technologies and exploring more sober, mindful, revolutionary visions of progress. The bicycle – a thoroughly modern instrument that was nonetheless noted for its 'primitivism' from its very beginnings – is a striking symbol of the dual need for a connection to the past in the context of ever faster and potentially destructive movement into the future.

Notes

1. Albert Einstein, letter to his son Eduard (5 February 1930), quoted in Walter Isaacson, *Einstein: His Life and Universe* (New York: Simon and Schuster, 2007), 367.
2. Albert Einstein, *Relativity: The Special and The General Theory* (New York: Crown Publishers, 1961).
3. Peter Galison, 'Einstein's Clocks: The Question of Time', *Critical Inquiry* 26, no. 2 (2000), 355–89.
4. See Margaret Guroff, *The Mechanical Horse: How the Bicycle Reshaped American Life* (Austin, TX: University of Texas Press, 2016), ch. 6.
5. Norcliffe, *Critical Geographies of Cycling*, 23.
6. Desportes, *Paysages en mouvement*, 199.
7. F. T. Marinetti, 'The Founding and Manifesto of Futurism' [1909], in *Futurism: An Anthology*, ed. Lawrence Rainey, Christine Poggi and Laura Wittman (New Haven, CT: Yale University Press, 2009), 50. While the Futurist movement rejected the aesthetic of the bicycle, a range of early twentieth-century artists were inspired by the object, including Natalia Goncharova, Umberto Boccioni, Marcel Duchamp, Fernand Léger, Pablo Picasso and Fortunato Depero.
8. Illich, *Energy and Equity*, 11.
9. Urry, 'The "System" of Automobility', 36.
10. Furness, *One Less Car*, 16–17.
11. See Walter Benjamin, *The Work of Art in the Age of Mechanical Reproduction* [1935], trans. J. A Underwood (London: Penguin, 2008).
12. Furness, *One Less Car*, 41.
13. John Urry, *Mobilities* (Cambridge: Polity, 2007), 112.
14. Claude glasses were small convex mirrors used by picturesque artists and tourists in the late eighteenth and early nineteenth centuries. They were thought to give landscapes a more painterly aspect.
15. Beekman and Eric, *Cycle Gleanings*, 10.
16. Thomas, *In Pursuit of Spring*, 111.
17. Leblanc, *Voici des ailes*, 39.
18. Jarry, *Le Surmâle*, 72.
19. Jarry, *Ubu cycliste*, 94.
20. Guy Debord, *La société du spectacle* (Paris: Gallimard, 1996), 15.
21. Elizabeth Robins Pennell and Joseph Pennell, 'Twenty Years of Cycling', *Fortnightly Review*, August 1897, 91. Quoted in Furness, *One Less Car*, 41.

22. Marx, *Capital*, I, 163.
23. Elizabeth Robins Pennell and Joseph Pennell, *Over the Alps on a Bicycle* (London: T. F. Unwin, 1898), 81.
24. See Kirby, *Parallel Tracks*; Leo Charney and Vanessa R. Schwartz, *Cinema and the Invention of Modern Life* (Berkeley, CA: University of California Press, 1995).
25. Jacques Seray, *Tours de manivelles: le vélo au cinéma* (Vélizy: J. Seray, 2006), 13.
26. Nye, *A bicyclette: anthologie*, xxiv.
27. Tronchet, *Petit traité de vélosophie*, 56.
28. Charney and Schwartz, *Cinema and the Invention of Modern Life*, 2.
29. Kern, *The Culture of Time and Space*, 72.
30. Jarry, *Ubu cycliste*, 34.
31. John Urry, *The Tourist Gaze: Leisure and Travel in Contemporary Societies* (London: Sage, 1990).
32. Furness, *One Less Car*, 17.
33. Ibid., 44.
34. Stephen Crane, *The New York City Sketches of Stephen Crane, and Related Pieces*, ed. R. W. Stallman and E. R. Hagemann (New York: New York University Press, 1966), 149.
35. Glen Norcliffe, 'Velocipedes and their Riders in the 19th Century: Geographical Imaginaries in Richard Lesclide's *Le Tour du Monde en Vélocipède*', *Cycle History* 26 (2015), 72.
36. Kennard, *The Golf Lunatic and his Cycling Wife*, 72.
37. Allen's depiction of the bicycle in this novel may be contrasted to Chinua Achebe's narrative use of the 'white man's horse' in *Things Fall Apart* [1958] (London: Penguin, 2001), set in pre-colonial Nigeria in the 1890s. The first white man to arrive in the village of Abame is travelling on a bicycle. The villagers kill him and tie his bicycle to their sacred tree 'because it looked as if it would run away to call the man's friends' (p. 102). When later white settlers see the bicycle, they return to slaughter the whole village.
38. Grant Allen, *Hilda Wade, a Woman with Tenacity of Purpose* [1900] (New York: Jefferson, 2015), 72.
39. Ibid.
40. However, we later discover that the Matabele uprising was organised by an Englishman, Professor Sebastian, with the aim of assassinating Hilda, who suspects Sebastian of framing her late father for a murder.
41. Allen, *Hilda Wade*, 81.
42. Ibid.
43. Ibid., 82.
44. Ibid., 83.
45. Wells, *The Wheels of Chance*, 49.
46. Wells, *Experiment in Autobiography*, II, 543.

47. A further surreal cycling dream associated with planetary destruction occurs in another novel by Wells which I examine below, *The War in the Air*. Flying above the earth in a German war machine headed for New York, Bert dreams that he is 'riding a bicycle in an extremely perilous manner through the upper air amidst a pyrotechnic display of crackers an Bengal lights'. H. G. Wells, *The War in the Air* [1908] (London: Penguin, 2005), 156.
48. Schivelbusch, *The Railway Journey*, 197.
49. Wells, *The Wheels of Chance*, 50.
50. Armstrong and Inglis, *Short Spins Round London*, 70.
51. Allen, *The Type-Writer Girl*, 194–5.
52. Furness, *One Less Car*, 17.
53. Kennard, *A Guide Book for Lady Cyclists*, 70.
54. Ibid., 110.
55. Beekman and Eric, *Cycle Gleanings*, 9.
56. Ibid., 44.
57. Kern, *The Culture of Time and Space*, 72.
58. Wells, *The Wheels of Chance*, 21.
59. J. H. Rosny, *Le Roman d'un cycliste* (Paris: Plon, 1899), 38, 106.
60. Ibid., 115.
61. Wells, *Experiment in Autobiography*, II, 543.
62. La Pédale, *Contes modernes*, 11.
63. Ibid., 42.
64. Ibid., 13.
65. The bicycle was used in both world wars, adopting a military role that H. G. Wells also imagined for it in *Anticipations* (1901). See also Martin Caidin and Jay Barbree. *Bicycles in War* (New York: Hawthorn Books, 1974).
66. La Pédale, *Contes modernes*, 245.
67. Wells, *The Time Machine*, 24. As Paul Edwards notes in an edition of Jarry's 'Commentary for the practical construction of a time machine', the object described also closely resembles a bicycle. It has a 'fork', but runs on gyrostats instead of wheels. See the annotated edition: Alfred Jarry, 'Commentaire pour la construction pratique de la machine à explorer le temps', *Les Cahiers iconographiques de la société des amis d'Alfred Jarry* 95–96 (2002), 69–88.
68. Wells, *The Time Machine*, 26.
69. This recalls the gender-blurring associated with the bicycle that I analysed in Chapter 2.
70. Many early car enthusiasts had been keen cyclists; for instance, Mary Kennard and Louis Baudry de Saunier both wrote books advocating cycling in the 1890s before defending the motor car in their writing from the 1900s.
71. Urry, 'The "System" of Automobility', 28; Michel de Certeau, *L'invention du quotidien 1. Arts de faire* (Paris: Gallimard, 1990), 165–9.

72. Allen, *Wheel Magic*, 7.
73. Gunning, 'Re-Newing Old Technologies', 39.
74. Ibid., 40.
75. Deleuze and Guattari, *Capitalisme et schizophrénie*, 480. In the opening pages of this work (pp. 10–11) the authors offer an interesting reflection on the Freudian symbolism of the bicycle in Beckett's novels.
76. See Henri Bergson, *Introduction à la métaphysique* (Paris: PUF, 2011).
77. Zemka, *Time and the Moment*, 226–7.
78. See, for instance, Bronfen, *Dorothy Richardson's Art of Memory*; Thacker, *Moving through Modernity*.
79. Chesterton, 'The Wheel', 260–5.
80. Jeremy Withers, 'Bicycles and Warfare: The Effects of Excessive Mobility in H. G. Wells's *The War in the Air*', in *Culture on Two Wheels: The Bicycle in Literature and Film*, ed. Jeremy Withers and Daniel P. Shea (Lincoln, NE: University of Nebraska Press, 2016), 80.
81. Ibid., 81.
82. Wells, *The War in the Air*, 179–80.
83. Wells, *The Wheels of Chance*, 23, 83.
84. Richard Pearson, 'Primitive Modernity: H. G. Wells and the Prehistoric Man of the 1890s', *The Yearbook of English Studies* 37, no. 1 (2007), 58.
85. Ibid., 74.
86. Allen, *Miss Cayley's Adventures*, 51.
87. Grant Allen, 'The Thames Valley Catastrophe' [1901], in *Science Fiction by Gaslight*, ed. Sam Moskowitz (Cleveland, OH: World Publishing Company, 1968), 20–42.
88. Marc Augé, *Non-lieux: introduction à une anthropologie de la supermodernité* (Paris: Seuil, 1992), 116.
89. See the PhD thesis by Estelle Murail, 'Beyond the *Flâneur*: Walking, Passage and Crossing in London and Paris in the Nineteenth Century', King's College London; Université Paris 7-Diderot, 2014, for an examination of the complex figure of the *flâneur*. I refer to the *flâneur* as 'he' because the figure was generally seen as male; the question of female *flânerie* has been examined by several critics, however, including Janet Wolff, 'The Invisible *Flâneuse*. Women and the Literature of Modernity', *Theory, Culture & Society* 2 (November 1985), 37–46.
90. Schivelsbusch points out how Haussmann's boulevards took railways as their model, cutting heedlessly across the cityscape in straight lines and leading to the train stations on the periphery of the city. Schivelbusch, *The Railway Journey*, 182.
91. Norcliffe, *The Ride to Modernity*, 8.
92. See Rejack, 'Nothings of the Day'.
93. Rosny, *Le Roman d'un cycliste*, 112.
94. Nicolas Oddy, 'The *Flâneur* on Wheels?', in *Cycling and Society*, ed. Paul Rosen, Dave Horton and Peter Cox (Aldershot: Ashgate, 2007), 108.

95. Williams, *The Country and the City*, 264.
96. Glen Norcliffe, 'Out for a Spin: The *Flâneur* on Wheels', *Cycle History* 8 (1997), 96.
97. Allen, *Wheel Magic*, 10–11.
98. De Certeau, *L'invention du quotidien 1. Arts de faire*, 162.
99. Jerome, *Three Men on the Bummel*, 207.
100. Allen, *Wheel Magic*, 6.
101. Bockett, *Some Literary Landmarks*, 254.
102. Pennell, *Our Sentimental Journey*, 77.
103. Virilio, *La vitesse de libération*, 162, author's italics.
104. Paul Virilio, *Cybermonde: la politique du pire*, ed. Philippe Petit (Paris: Textuel, 1996), 42.
105. Bockett, *Some Literary Landmarks*, 200.
106. Thomas, *In Pursuit of Spring*, 81.
107. See Herlihy, *Bicycle*, 205.
108. See Carlton Reid, *Roads Were Not Built For Cars* (Washington DC: Island Press, 2015).
109. Wells, *Mr Polly*, 76.
110. Ibid., 77.
111. Ibid., 79.
112. Thomas, *In Pursuit of Spring*, 36.
113. On this influential Victorian movement which preached the spiritual value of physical exercise, see Donald E. Hall, *Muscular Christianity: Embodying the Victorian Age* (Cambridge: Cambridge University Press, 1994).
114. Bouet, *Signification du sport*, 194–5.
115. De Certeau, *L'invention du quotidien 1. Arts de faire*, 173.
116. Augé, *Non-lieux*.
117. Ford Madox Ford, *The Soul of London: A Survey of a Modern City* (London: Alston Rivers, 1905), xiii.
118. Ibid., 59.
119. Ibid., 37.
120. Ibid., 38.
121. Ibid., 39.
122. Ibid., 39–41.
123. Ibid., 37.
124. Ibid., 41.
125. Ibid.
126. A choice that is omitted by Andrew Thacker when discussing Ford's work (reflecting the general tendency in criticism to overlook the bicycle): 'Ford's intuition concerning the spatiality of modern life occurs in a chapter devoted to means of transport into London: by motor car, electric tram or railway.' Thacker, *Moving through Modernity*, 2.
127. Ford, *The Soul of London*, 85.

128. Ibid., 85, 86.
129. Ibid.
130. Henry James illustrates the incarcerating capacity of technology for those who make a living operating it in his story 'In the Cage' (1898). The young telegraphist on whom the story centres recognises that her position is 'that of a young person spending, in framed and wired confinement, the life of a guinea pig or a magpie'. Henry James, *Selected Tales* (London: Penguin, 2001), 314.
131. Henri Lefebvre, *La production de l'espace* (Paris: Anthropos, 1986), 42.
132. See Judith Butler, *Notes Toward a Performative Theory of Assembly* (Cambridge, MA: Harvard University Press, 2015); Butler, 'Performative Acts and Gender Constitution'.
133. Lefebvre, *La production de l'espace*, 43.
134. Ibid., 42–3.
135. Amsterdam was not always the cycling-friendly city it is today. The Provos and other Dutch movements in the post-war period were instrumental in resisting the car-centred planning which was being adopted by governments and city planners across Europe.
136. Furness, *One Less Car*, 53–4.
137. Guy Debord, 'Positions situationnistes sur la circulation' [1959], available at <http://carfree.fr/index.php/2011/04/28/positions-situationnistes-sur-la-circulation/> (accessed 4 May 2016).
138. Aldous Huxley, *Crome Yellow* [1921] (London: Penguin, 1967), 5.
139. Ibid.
140. Ibid.
141. De Certeau, *L'invention du quotidien 1. Arts de faire*, 179.
142. Huxley, *Crome Yellow*, 5.
143. De Certeau, *L'invention du quotidien 1. Arts de faire*, 170.
144. Huxley, *Crome Yellow*, 6.
145. Ibid.
146. Ibid.
147. Ibid.
148. Ibid.
149. De Certeau, *L'invention du quotidien 1. Arts de faire*, 141–2.
150. Augé, *Éloge de la bicyclette*, 30; Tronchet, *Petit traité de vélosophie*, 59.
151. Desportes, *Paysages en mouvement*, 8.
152. Huxley, *Crome Yellow*, 6.
153. Ibid.
154. Ernest Hemingway, *By-Line: Selected Articles and Dispatches of Four Decades*, ed. William White (New York: Scribner, 1967), 364.
155. Huxley, *Crome Yellow*, 6.
156. Ibid.
157. Ibid.
158. De Certeau, *L'invention du quotidien 1. Arts de faire*, 154.
159. Huxley, *Crome Yellow*, 6.

160. Ibid., 7.
161. Ibid., 6, 84–5.
162. Ibid., 85.
163. Virilio, *La vitesse de libération*, 159.
164. E. M. Forster, 'The Machine Stops' [1909], in *The Machine Stops: and Other Stories* (London: André Deutsch, 1997), 87.
165. Ibid., 100.
166. Ibid., 100.
167. Huxley, *Crome Yellow*, 162.
168. Ibid., 28.
169. Paul Virilio, *Vitesse et politique: essai de dromologie* (Paris: Galilée, 1977), 13, author's italics.

Conclusion

The seeds for this research were planted during a hiatus from study when I worked in Paris as a bicycle courier. My journeys through the city led me to reflect on the many connections between this specific form of mobility and the act of weaving texts. Like reading or writing, cycling is a solitary activity, yet one that generates its own geographies, sensory experiences and forms of interaction with others. My first, tentative explorations into the universe of early cycling literature revealed an unexpected treasure trove of sources, which I have been privileged to delve into over the course of this research. Alongside this literary dimension, being a cyclist in Paris made me aware of the political significance of the bicycle. When I arrived alone in this unknown city, I quickly discovered its cyclists and activists, who warmly welcomed me into their vibrant community. I discovered that cycling engenders solidarity, where motorised modes of transport more often foster conflict, individualism and anonymity. I forged deep links with fellow cyclists, and with my bicycle, which I maintained, cleaned, pulled apart and put back together again. The world of DIY bicycle workshops in which I became involved provides a microcosm of the network of cooperation among cyclists, who continue to create their own utopian communities in a world of increasing inequality.

My research is part of an emerging body of criticism seeking to address the overlooked literary and cultural significance of the bicycle. Despite long years of neglect, the current upsurge in interest in bicycles as literary and cultural objects has been exemplified by the recent publication of Jeremy Withers and Daniel P. Shea's edited collection *Culture on Two Wheels*.[1] The editors seek to inscribe this study in the wider 'mobility turn' which John Urry has theorised in the social sciences,[2] while aiming to fill the gap in research on the bicycle. I join with a small but growing group of scholars in writing the bicycle back into literary and cultural history. Cycling has too long been a blind spot in studies that focus on the interface between literature and modes of transport.³ Unlike many critics who occult or sideline cycling, I place the bicycle at the centre of my research in order to engage with it as an object and mode of transport which, like walking, the railway and the motor car, is singularly worthy of the attention of literary and cultural critics. We have seen that the bicycle accompanied many of the cultural changes that defined modernity at the turn of the twentieth century, while suggesting alternatives to the mechanised, commodified, accelerated, polluting, violent nature of life in the high industrial era. I have shown that the bicycle played this counter-cultural role from its earliest days, at first positioning itself as an alternative to the railway before coming to enshrine resistance to the motor car. While Zack Furness, Glen Norcliffe and John Urry have argued that the bicycle laid the basis for 'automobility' in the twentieth century, I contend that cyclists, far from being embryonic car drivers, envisioned and performed an alternative, human-centred vision of progress from the first.

Tom Gunning defines the decades from the 1870s to the First World War as a 'period of wonder', employing the term John Onians coined to describe the early modern period, when a host of amazing novelties flooded Western societies as a result of innovation and new trade routes.⁴ The bicycle was one of many wondrous objects – along with inventions such as the telephone, cinematograph, motor car and aeroplane – that transformed everyday life at the start of the twentieth century. I agree with Gunning that each new technology suggests an uncanny future direction of society at the moment of its first appearance. This vision is rapidly obscured as the object becomes familiar and unremarkable, yet Gunning claims that the initial meanings of technologies may return to the surface at any moment, if we simply pay attention:

> Herein lies the importance of the cultural archaeology of technology, the grasping again of the newness of old technologies [. . .] Even in the midst of familiarity, within the practices of everyday life, fissures open and the forgotten future reemerges, with uncanny effect. The question is, simply, is anyone watching or listening?⁵

This study's attentiveness to literature written at the time of the bicycle's appearance has allowed us to reconnect with the futures embedded in this new technology. The uncanny visions that the bicycle embodied over a hundred years ago continue to open cracks in the structure of twenty-first-century society. Numerous cycling movements are testimony to the continuing counter-cultural role of this technology. From Critical Mass bicycle rides that take place in cities across the globe each month in order to reclaim the roads from the car, to the cycling protests organised as part of the Black Lives Matter movement, to cooperative bike workshops, to the many and varied subcultures that have emerged among bike couriers or fixed-gear riders, the bicycle continues to provide a means for exploring and implementing alternative visions of society.[6] These movements take the bicycle far beyond its primary locomotive role in order to imagine a more just and equal society and begin to put it into practice. As Withers and Shea observe:

> we are living during a bicycling revolution. Not since the fervor that took hold for all things cycling related in the last few decades of the nineteenth century [. . .] have we seen the intense interest in cycling that we do now.[7]

Although the twentieth century was characterised by the mass adoption of the motor car, it also witnessed several cycling comebacks. Notably, the 1930s saw the rise of cycle touring (connected, in France, to the beginning of paid leave),[8] while from the 1970s new utilitarian and leisure cyclists rejuvenated the technology.[9] Clear parallels can be established between these periods and the present day. In the 1930s and 1970s, like today, people suffered from the consequences from the boom-and-bust nature of capitalism. In the 1970s, the oil crisis and growing awareness of global warming drew attention to the problems inherent in car dependency, and cyclists pointed to a more autonomous means of organising urban spaces and society in response.[10] The current financial and health crisis resulting from the Covid-19 pandemic, alongside an acute awareness of the looming menace of climate change, is forcing people to take stock of the impact of their transport and lifestyle choices. The bicycle provides one practical means to perform an alternative social organisation. It allows us to act locally and think globally, encouraging a more responsible outlook that moves towards a more just, equal, healthy and peaceful world.

As Zack Furness observes, 'we are still immersed in an ongoing process of defining and debating the meaning of bicycling through the stories we write, the images we capture, the films we watch, and the various digital media we use to interact'.[11] In the technology-saturated reality of the twenty-first century, the bicycle remains a means of constructing an alternative relationship to our bodies, machines, localities and communities. At the end of a century of car dependence, when onscreen interactions are increasingly replacing physical contact, and novelties such as the e-bike or e-scooter undermine the basic nature of human-powered transport, there is an urgent need to reconnect with the founding philosophy of the technology of the bicycle. As its continuing use in art, literature and cinema goes to show, cycling offers a compelling means of interpreting the world, uniting corporeal and mechanical registers in order to generate an aesthetic that participates in an alternative, empowering vision of the future.

Notes

1. Other recent studies include Smethurst, *The Bicycle*; and Steven E. Alford and Suzanne Ferriss, *An Alternative History of Bicycles and Motorcycles: Two-Wheeled Transportation and Material Culture* (Lanham, MD: Rowman and Littlefield, 2016).
2. See Urry, *Mobilities*.
3. See, for instance, Schivelbusch, *The Railway Journey*; Gavin and Humphries (eds), *Transport in British Fiction*.
4. John Onians, '"I Wonder . . .": A Short History of Amazement', in *Sight and Insight* (London: Phaidon, 1994), 10–33; Gunning, 'Re-Newing Old Technologies', 42.
5. Gunning, 'Re-Newing Old Technologies', 56.
6. For a discussion of cycling and various current-day subcultures, see Furness, *One Less Car*, 140–69.
7. Withers and Shea (eds), *Culture on Two Wheels*, 1.
8. See Bertho-Lavenir, *La Roue et le Stylo*, 337–61.
9. See Héran, *Le retour de la bicyclette*, 85–111.
10. Examples include the Provos in the Netherlands and the Situationists in France.
11. Zack Furness, 'Foreword', in *Culture on Two Wheels: The Bicycle in Literature and Film*, ed. Daniel P. Shea and Jeremy Withers (Lincoln, NE: University of Nebraska Press, 2016), x–xi.

Bibliography

Primary Sources

Achebe, Chinua. *Things Fall Apart*. 1958. London: Penguin, 2001.

Adam, Paul. *La morale des sports*. Paris: Librairie Mondiale, 1907.

Adamson, James. *Sketches of Our Information as to Railroads*. Edinburgh: Constable, 1826.

Allen, Grant. *Hilda Wade, A Woman with Tenacity of Purpose*. 1900. New York: Jefferson, 2015.

— *Miss Cayley's Adventures*. 1899. Kansas City, KS: Valancourt Books, 2008.

— 'The Thames Valley Catastrophe.' 1901. In *Science Fiction by Gaslight*. Ed. Sam Moskowitz. Cleveland, OH: World Publishing Company, 1968. 20–42.

— *The Type-Writer Girl*. 1897. Peterborough, Ont.: Broadview Press, 2004.

Allen, J. W. *Wheel Magic; Or, Revolutions of an Impressionist*. London: J. Lane, 1909.

Armstrong, Arthur C., and Harry Robert Gall Inglis. *Short Spins Round London*. London: Gall and Inglis, 1903.

Bastian, H. C. 'The Muscular Sense: Its Nature and Cortical Localisation'. *Brain* 10, no. 1 (1887): 1–89.

Baudry de Saunier, L. *Ma petite bicyclette: sa pratique*. Paris: Flammarion, 1925.

Beauvoir, Simone de. *Le sang des autres: roman*. 1945. Paris: Gallimard, 1990.

Beckett, Samuel. *Molloy*. 1951. Paris: Éditions de Minuit, 1989.

— *More Pricks than Kicks*. 1934. New York: Grove Press, 1970.

Beekman, W. S., and Allan Eric. *Cycle Gleanings: Or, Wheels and Wheeling for Business and Pleasure, and the Study of Nature*. Boston: Skinner, Bartlett, 1894.

Bennett, Arnold. *The Human Machine*. 1908. Auckland, NZ: Floating Press, 2009.

Bly, Nellie. 'Champion of her Sex.' *New York World*, 2 February 1896: 9–10.

Bockett, F. W. *Some Literary Landmarks for Pilgrims on Wheels*. London: J. M. Dent, 1901.

Bodkin, Matthias Mc Donnell. *Dora Myrl:The Lady Detective*. London: Chatto and Windus, 1900.

Brown, Charles William. *Cycling*. London: Iliffe and Son, 1895.

Buckman, Sydney Savory. 'Cycling: Its Effects on the Future of the Human Race.' *The Medical Magazine* 8, no. 2 (1899): 128–35.

Burginthere, G. B. 'Some Emotions and – No Morals; Or, How to Learn "to Bike".' In *The Humours of Cycling*. London: James Bowden, 1897. 25–8.

Burke, Edmund. *A Philosophical Enquiry into the Origin of Our Ideas of the Sublime and Beautiful*. 1757. Oxford: Oxford University Press, 1990.

Chesterton, G. K. 'Doubts about Darwinism.' 1920. In *Collected Works*. Vol. XXXII. San Francisco: Ignatius Press, 1989. 55–9.

— 'The Free Man and the Ford Car.' 1925. In *Delphi Complete Works of G. K. Chesterton*. Vol. I. Hastings: Delphi Classics, 2013. 545–56.

— 'The Wheel.' In *Delphi Complete Works of G. K. Chesterton*. Vol. I. Hastings: Delphi Classics, 2013. 260–5.

Coppen, W. J. *Romances of the Wheel: A Collection of Romantic Cycling Tales*. Coventry: Iliffe and Son, 1880.

Crane, Stephen. *The New York City Sketches of Stephen Crane, and Related Pieces*. Ed. R. W. Stallman and E. R. Hagemann. New York: New York University Press, 1966.

De Quincey, Thomas. *Confessions of an English Opium-Eater and Other Writings*. 1821. Oxford: Oxford University Press, 1998.

Deckert, Théodore. *Ode au véloce*. Bordeaux, 1890.

— *Le Tandem, conte cycliste*. Bordeaux: impr. de G. Gounouilhou, 1895.

Doyle, Arthur Conan. *Beyond the City*. 1891. London: George Newnes, 1921.

— 'The Priory School.' In *The Return of Sherlock Holmes*. 1905. London: Penguin, 2011. 124–65.

— 'The Solitary Cyclist.' In *The Return of Sherlock Holmes*. 1905. London: Penguin, 2011. 97–123.

Einstein, Albert. *Relativity: The Special and The General Theory*. 1920. Trans. Robert W. Lawson. New York: Crown Publishers, 1961.

Erskine, F. J. *Bicycling for Ladies*. London: Iliffe and Son, 1897.

— *Tricycling for Ladies, Or, Hints on the Choice & Management of Tricycles: With Suggestions on Dress, Riding & Touring*. London: Iliffe and Son, 1885.

Ford, Ford Madox. *The Soul of London: A Survey of a Modern City.* London: Alston Rivers, 1905.

Forster, E. M. *Howards End.* 1910. London: Penguin, 2000.

— 'The Machine Stops.' 1909. In *The Machine Stops: and Other Stories.* 1947. London: André Deutsch, 1997. 87–117.

Giffard, Pierre, and Albert Robida. *La Fin du cheval.* Paris: Armand Colin, 1899.

Girling, Thomas W. *Cycles and the Trade.* London: Iliffe and Son, 1898.

Gissing, George. 'A Daughter of the Lodge.' In *The House of Cobwebs, and Other Stories.* 1901. London: Constable, 1906. 175–91.

— *New Grub Street.* 1891. London: Penguin, 1968.

Harris, Ada L. *A Widow on Wheels.* London: Hutchinson, 1896.

Harris, T., et al. *On Wheels!!! By Twelve Spokes.* London: Cricket and Football Times, Bicycling and Athletic Journal, 1880.

Hemingway, Ernest. *By-Line: Selected Articles and Dispatches of Four Decades.* Ed. William White. New York: Scribner, 1967.

'How Some Wheelwomen Earn Money.' *The Hub*, 12 September 1896: 5.

Huxley, Aldous. *Crome Yellow.* 1921. Harmondsworth: Penguin, 1967.

Jackson, Edna C. 'A Fin de Cycle Incident.' In *The Humours of Cycling.* James Bowden: London, 1897. 56–65.

James, Henry. 'In the Cage.' 1898. In *Selected Tales.* London: Penguin, 2001. 314–84.

Jarry, Alfred. 'Commentaire pour la construction pratique de la machine à explorer le temps.' Ed. Paul Edwards. *Les Cahiers iconographiques de la société des amis d'Alfred Jarry* 95–96 (2002): 69–88.

— *Le Surmâle: roman moderne.* 1902. Paris: Mille et une nuits, 1996.

— *Ubu cycliste: écrits vélocipédiques.* Ed. Nicolas Martin. Toulouse: Le Pas d'Oiseau, 2007.

Jerome, Jerome K. *Three Men in a Boat.* 1889. London: Penguin, 1990.

— *Three Men on the Bummel.* 1900. London: Penguin, 1994.

Kennard, Mary E. *The Golf Lunatic and his Cycling Wife.* London: Hutchinson, 1902.

— *A Guide Book for Lady Cyclists.* London: F. V. White, 1896.

Kipling, Rudyard. *The Letters of Rudyard Kipling, 1900–10.* Basingstoke: Macmillan, 1996.

La Pédale, Jehan de. *Contes modernes. Pédalons!* Paris: Véloce-Sport, 1892.

Lawrence, D. H. *Sons and Lovers.* 1913. London: Penguin, 1983.

Leblanc, Maurice. *Voici des ailes.* 1898. Vierzon: le Pas de côté, 2012.

Leechman, George Douglas, *Safety Cycling.* London: Iliffe and Son, 1895.

Lesclide, Richard. *Le Tour du monde en vélocipède.* Paris: Bureaux de la Publication, 1870.

'Lord Bowen.' *The Spectator*, 14 April 1894: 9–10.

Lucas-Championnière, Just. *La Bicyclette*. Paris: L. Chailley, 1894.

Marinetti, F. T. 'The Founding and Manifesto of Futurism.' 1909. In *Futurism: An Anthology*. Ed. Lawrence Rainey, Christine Poggi and Laura Wittman. New Haven: Yale University Press, 2009. 49–53.

Masterman, C. F. G. *The Condition of England*. London: Methuen, 1909.

Meade, L. T. *The Cleverest Woman in England*. London: J. Nisbet, 1898.

Mecredy, R. J. *The Art and Pastime of Cycling*. Dublin: Mecredy and Kyle, 1890.

Muir, Robert James. *Plato's Dream of Wheels; Socrates, Protagoras, and the Hegeleatic Stranger; with an Appendix by Certain Cyclic Poets*. London: T. F. Unwin, 1902.

Niles Leeds, Virginia. 'A Coast and a Capture: A Bicycling Story.' In *The Humours of Cycling*. London: James Bowden, 1897. 85–93.

O'Brien, Flann. *The Third Policeman*. 1967. London: Paladin, 1988.

O'Followell, Ludovic. *Bicyclette et organes génitaux*. Paris: Baillière, 1900.

Ogden Robbins, Lawrence. 'My Match with Eileen. A Cycling Adventure in Ireland.' In *The Humours of Cycling*. London: James Bowden, 1897. 32–41.

Pemberton, A. C., et al. *The Complete Cyclist*. London: Innes, 1897.

Pennell, Elizabeth Robins. 'From Coventry to Chester on Wheels.' *The Century Magazine*, 1 September 1884: 645–55.

Pennell, Elizabeth Robins, and Joseph Pennell. *A Canterbury Pilgrimage*. London: Seeley & Co., 1885.

— *Our Sentimental Journey through France and Italy*. London: T. F. Unwin, 1893.

— *Over the Alps on a Bicycle*. London: T. F. Unwin, 1898.

— 'Twenty Years of Cycling'. *Fortnightly Review*, August 1897.

Proust, Marcel. *À la recherche du temps perdu II. À l'ombre de jeunes filles en fleurs*. [1919] *Le côté de Guermantes*. [1920–21] *Esquisses*. Paris: Gallimard, 1988.

— *À la recherche du temps perdu III. Sodome et Gomorrhe*. [1921–22] *La Prisonnière*. [1923] *Esquisses*. Paris: Gallimard, 1988.

— *À la recherche du temps perdu IV. Albertine disparue*. [1925] *Le temps retrouvé*. [1927] *Esquisses*. Paris: Gallimard, 1989.

— *Jean Santeuil*. Paris: Gallimard, 1952.

Raverat, Gwen. *Period Piece: A Cambridge Childhood*. London: Faber and Faber, 1952.

Redmond, Edmond. *Lyra Cyclus; Or, The Bards and the Bicycle*. Rochester, NY: Bacon, 1897.

Régamey, Frédéric. *Vélocipédie et automobilisme*. Tours: A. Mame et fils, 1898.

Richardson, Dorothy M. *The Tunnel.* 1919. London: Virago, 2002.

Romains, Jules. *Les Copains.* Paris: Gallimard, 1922.

Rosny, J.-H. *Le Roman d'un cycliste.* Paris: Plon, 1899.

Rumney, A. W. *A Cyclist's Note Book.* Edinburgh: W. and A. K. Johnston, 1901.

Ruskin, John. 'Letter on Cycling.' *Tit-Bits,* 31 March 1889: 399.

— *The Works of John Ruskin.* Ed. Edward Tyas Cook and Alexander D. O. Wedderburn. Cambridge: Cambridge University Press, 2009.

Shadwell, A. 'The Hidden Dangers of Cycling.' *The National Review,* 1 February 1897. 795–6.

Sterne, Laurence. *A Sentimental Journey through France and Italy.* 1768. London: Oxford University Press, 1968.

Sturmey, Henry. *The 'Indispensable' Bicyclists' Handbook, A Complete Cyclopædia on the Subject.* Coventry: Iliffe and Son, 1880.

Stutfield, Hugh. 'Tommyrotics.' *Blackwood's Magazine* 157 (June 1895): 833–45.

Thelwall, John. *The Peripatetic.* 1793. Detroit, MI: Wayne State University Press, 2001.

Thomas, Edward. *In Pursuit of Spring.* 1914. Albany, CA: Berkeley Hill Classics, 2013.

Tosetti, Amadeo. 'Pedali sul Mar Nero.' 1884. In *The Dictionary of Imaginary Places.* 1980. Ed. Alberto Manguel and Gianni Guadalupi. New York: Harcourt Brace, 2000. 395–415.

Twain, Mark. *A Connecticut Yankee in King Arthur's Court.* 1889. New York: Bantam Classics, 1983.

— 'Taming the Bicycle.' 1884. In *Collected Tales, Sketches, Speeches & Essays, 1852–1890.* New York: Literary Classics of the United States, 1992. 892–6.

Virginia, 'Array yourself becomingly.' *The Cycling World Illustrated. A Journal de Luxe,* 29 April 1896: 19.

— 'Arrayed like one of these.' *The Cycling World Illustrated. A Journal de Luxe,* 18 March 1896: 20.

Ward, Maria E. *Bicycling for Ladies.* New York: Brentano, 1896.

Wells, H. G. *Ann Veronica.* 1913. London: J. M. Dent, 1962.

— *Anticipations of the Reaction of Mechanical and Scientific Progress Upon Human Life and Thought.* 1901. Auckland, NZ: Floating Press, 2008.

— *The Correspondence of H. G. Wells.* Ed. David C. Smith. London: Pickering and Chatto, 1998.

— *Experiment in Autobiography.* 1934. London: Jonathan Cape, 1969.

— *The History of Mr Polly.* 1910. London: Pan, 1963.

— *Hoopdriver's Holiday*. 1904. Ed. Michael Timko. Lafayette, IN: Purdue University, 1964.
— *Kipps: The Story of a Simple Soul*. 1905. London: Collins, 1961.
— *A Modern Utopia*. 1905. Lincoln, NE: University of Nebraska Press, 1967.
— 'A Perfect Gentleman on Wheels.' In *The Humours of Cycling*. London: James Bowden, 1897. 5–14.
— *The Time Machine*. 1895. London: Book Club Associates, 1980.
— *Tono Bungay*. 1909. Oxford: Oxford University Press, 1997.
— *The War in the Air*. 1908. London: Penguin, 2005.
— *The War of the Worlds*. 1898. London: Penguin, 2012.
— *The Wheels of Chance, A Bicycling Idyll*. New York: Macmillan, 1896.
— *The Wheels of Chance, A Bicycling Idyll; The Time Machine*. 1896. London: J. M. Dent, 1935.
Wilson, A. J. *The Pleasures, Objects, and Advantages of Cycling*. London: Iliffe and Son, 1887.
Wishaw, Fred. 'Pogeley's Ride Down Town.' In *The Humours of Cycling*. London: James Bowden, 1897. 19–24.
Woolf, Virginia. 'Romance and the Heart. Review of *The Grand Tour*, by Romer Wilson, and *Revolving Lights*, by Dorothy Richardson.' *The Nation and the Athenaeum*, 19 May 1923. 228–9.
— *A Room of One's Own*. 1929. London: Penguin, 1992.
Zola, Émile. *Œuvres complètes. Paris fin de siècle, 1897*. Ed. Henri Mitterand, Jacques Noiray and Jean-Louis Cabanès. Vol. XVII. Paris: Nouveau Monde, 2008.

Secondary Sources

Adler, Nanci J. 'The Bicycle in Western Literature: Transformations on Two Wheels.' Master's thesis, Rollins College, 2012.
Aguiar, Marian, Charlotte Mathieson and Lynne Pearce, eds. *Mobilities, Literature, Culture*. New York: Palgrave Macmillan, 2019.
Alderson, Frederick. *Bicycling: A History*. New York: Praeger, 1972.
Alford, Steven, and Suzanne Ferriss. *An Alternative History of Bicycles and Motorcycles: Two-Wheeled Transportation and Material Culture*. Lanham, MD: Rowman and Littlefield, 2016.
Altick, Richard D. *The English Common Reader: A Social History of the Mass Reading Public, 1800–1900*. Chicago: University of Chicago Press, 1957.
Anderson, Benedict R. *Imagined Communities: Reflections on the Origin and Spread of Nationalism*. 1982. London: Verso, 1991.

Appadurai, Arjun, ed. *The Social Life of Things: Commodities in Cultural Perspective*. Cambridge: Cambridge University Press, 1986.

Ardis, Ann L. *New Women, New Novels: Feminism and Early Modernism*. New Brunswick, NJ: Rutgers University Press, 1990.

Armstrong, Tim. *Modernism, Technology, and the Body: A Cultural Study*. Cambridge: Cambridge University Press, 1998.

Aronson, Sidney H. 'The Sociology of the Bicycle.' *Social Forces* 30, no. 3 (1952): 305–12.

Augé, Marc. *Éloge de la bicyclette*. Paris: Payot & Rivages, 2008.

— *Non-lieux: introduction à une anthropologie de la supermodernité*. Paris: Seuil, 1992.

Bakhtin, Mikhail M. *Rabelais and His World*. 1965. Trans. Hélène Iswolsky. Bloomington, IN: Indiana University Press, 1984.

Barathieu, Agnès. *Les mobiles de Marcel Proust: une sémantique du déplacement*. Villeneuve d'Ascq: Presses universitaires du Septentrion, 2002.

Barthes, Roland. 'Le Tour de France comme épopée.' In *Mythologies*. Paris: Seuil, 1957. 125–36.

Beaumont, Matthew, and Michael J. Freeman. *The Railway and Modernity: Time, Space, and the Machine Ensemble*. Oxford: Peter Lang, 2007.

Belmont, Justin Daniel. *The Art of Bicycling: A Treasury of Poems*. Halcottsville, NY: Breakaway Books, 2005.

Benjamin, Walter. *The Arcades Project*. 1927–40. Ed. Rolf Tiedemann. Trans. Howard Eiland and Kevin McLaughlin. Cambridge, MA: Belknap Press of Harvard University Press, 1999.

— *Charles Baudelaire: A Lyric Poet in the Era of High Capitalism*. Trans. Harry Zohn. London: NLB, 1973.

— 'On Some Motifs in Baudelaire.' 1940. In *Illuminations*. Ed. Hannah Arendt. Trans. Harry Zohn. London: Fontana, 1992. 155–200.

— *The Work of Art in the Age of Mechanical Reproduction*. 1935. Trans. J. A. Underwood. London: Penguin, 2008.

Bennett, Jane. *Vibrant Matter: A Political Ecology of Things*. Durham, NC: Duke University Press, 2010.

Bergson, Henri. *Durée et simultanéité. À propos de la théorie d'Einstein*. Paris: Librairie Félix Alcan, 1922.

— *L'évolution créatrice*. 1907. Paris: PUF, 1948.

— *Introduction à la métaphysique*. 1903. Paris: PUF, 2011.

— *Le rire: essai sur la signification du comique*. 1900. Paris: PUF, 1981.

Bertho-Lavenir, Catherine. *La Roue et le Stylo: comment nous sommes devenus touristes*. Paris: Editions Odile Jacob, 1999.

Besse, Nadine, and André Vant. 'A New View of Late 19th Century Cycle Publicity Posters.' *Cycle History* 5 (1994): 117–23.

Bijker, Wiebe E. *Of Bicycles, Bakelites, and Bulbs: Toward a Theory of Sociotechnical Change*. Cambridge, MA: MIT Press, 1995.

Bijker, Wiebe E., Thomas Parke Hughes and T. J. Pinch, eds. *The Social Construction of Technological Systems: New Directions in the Sociology and History of Technology*. Cambridge, MA: MIT Press, 1987.

Bouet, Michel. *Signification du sport*. Paris: Editions universitaires, 1968.

Brogan, Una. 'Albertine the Cyclist: A Queer Feminist Bicycle Ride through Proust's *In Search of Lost Time*.' In *Culture on Two Wheels: The Bicycle in Literature and Film*. Ed. Jeremy Withers and Daniel P. Shea. Lincoln, NE: University of Nebraska Press, 2016. 116–35.

— 'Cycling and Narrative Structure: H. G. Wells's *The Wheels of Chance* and Maurice Leblanc's *Voici des ailes*.' In *Mobilities, Literature, Culture*. Ed. Marian Aguiar, Charlotte Mathieson and Lynne Pearce. New York: Palgrave Macmillan, 2019. 237–57.

— 'Liberation on Two Wheels: Social Change and the Bicycle in H. G. Wells's *Kipps* and *The History of Mr Polly*.' *The Wellsian* 41 (2018): 5–27.

Bronfen, Elisabeth. *Dorothy Richardson's Art of Memory: Space, Identity, Text*. Trans. Victoria Appelbe. Manchester: Manchester University Press, 1999.

Brown, Bill, ed. *Things*. Chicago: University of Chicago Press, 2004.

Buchanan, Dave. 'Cycling and the Picturesque: Illustrated Cycle-Travel Writing of the 1880s.' *Cycle History* 19 (2008): 67–72.

— 'Pilgrims on Wheels: The Pennells, F. W. Bockett, and Literary Cycle-Travels.' In *Culture on Two Wheels: The Bicycle in Literature and Film*. Ed. Jeremy Withers and Daniel P. Shea. Lincoln, NE: University of Nebraska Press, 2016. 19–40.

Butler, Judith. *Notes Toward a Performative Theory of Assembly*. Cambridge, MA: Harvard University Press, 2015.

— 'Performative Acts and Gender Constitution: An Essay in Phenomenonology and Feminist Theory.' *Theatre Journal* 40, no. 4 (1988): 519–31.

Caidin, Martin, and Jay Barbree. *Bicycles in War*. New York: Hawthorn Books, 1974.

Carey, John. *The Intellectuals and the Masses: Pride and Prejudice among the Literary Intelligentsia, 1880–1939*. New York: St Martin's Press, 1992.

Charney, Leo, and Vanessa R. Schwartz. *Cinema and the Invention of Modern Life*. Berkeley, CA: University of California Press, 1995.

Choi, Yoonjoung. 'The Bi-Cycling Mr Hoopdriver: Counter-Sporting Victorian Reviving the Carnivalesque.' *Critical Survey* 24, no. 1 (2012): 102–15.

Clais, Anne-Marie. 'Portrait de femmes en cyclistes ou l'invention du féminin pluriel.' *Les cahiers de médiologie* 5, no. 1 (1998): 69–79.

Clayton, Nick. 'SCOT: Does It Answer?' *Technology and Culture* 43, no. 2 (2002): 351–60.

Cohen, William A. *Embodied: Victorian Literature and the Senses.* Minneapolis, MN: University of Minnesota Press, 2009.

Corbin, Alain, ed. *L'avènement des loisirs: 1850–1960.* Paris: Aubier, 1995.

Coverley, Merlin. *The Art of Wandering: The Writer as Walker.* Harpenden: Oldcastle Books, 2012.

Crary, Jonathan. *Techniques of the Observer: On Vision and Modernity in the Nineteenth Century.* Cambridge, MA: MIT Press, 1990.

— 'Unbinding Vision: Manet and the Attentive Observer in the Late Nineteenth Century.' In *Cinema and the Invention of Modern Life.* Ed. Leo Charney and Vanessa R. Schwartz. Berkeley, CA: University of California Press, 1991. 46–68.

Cropper, Corry. 'Like a Furnace: Alfred Jarry's *The Supermale*, Doping and the Limits of Positivism.' In *Culture on Two Wheels: The Bicycle in Literature and Film.* Ed. Jeremy Withers and Daniel P. Shea. Lincoln, NE: University of Nebraska Press, 2016. 94–115.

Cunningham, Gail. *The New Woman and the Victorian Novel.* London: Macmillan, 1978.

— 'Seizing the Reins: Women, Girls and Horses.' In *Image and Power: Women in Fiction in the Twentieth Century.* Ed. Sarah Sceats and Gail Cunningham. London: Longman, 1996. 65–77.

Daly, Nicholas. *Literature, Technology, and Modernity, 1860–2000.* Cambridge: Cambridge University Press, 2004.

Danius, Sara. *The Senses of Modernism: Technology, Perception, and Aesthetics.* Ithaca, NY: Cornell University Press, 2002.

Day, Jon. *Cyclogeography: Journeys of a London Bicycle Courier.* London: Notting Hill Editions, 2015.

De Certeau, Michel. *L'invention du quotidien 1. Arts de faire.* 1980. Paris: Gallimard, 1990.

Debord, Guy. 'Positions situationnistes sur la circulation.' 1959. Accessed 4 May 2016. <http://carfree.fr/index.php/2011/04/28/positions-situationnistes-sur-la-circulation/>.

— *La société du spectacle.* 1967. Paris: Gallimard, 1996.

Delerm, Philippe. *La première gorgée de bière et autres plaisirs minuscules: récits.* Paris: Gallimard, 1997.

Deleuze, Gilles, and Félix Guattari. *Capitalisme et schizophrénie: l'anti-Oedipe.* Paris: Les Éditions de minuit, 1980.

Derrida, Jacques. *Spectres de Marx: l'état de la dette, le travail du deuil et la nouvelle Internationale.* Paris: Galilée, 1993.

Desportes, Marc. *Paysages en mouvement : transports et perception de l'espace, XVIIIe–XXe siècle.* Paris: Gallimard, 2005.

Diesbach, Ghislain de. *Proust*. Paris: Perrin, 1991.
Dodge, Pryor, and David V. Herlihy. *The Bicycle*. Paris: Flammarion, 1996.
Draper, Michael. *H. G. Wells*. London: Macmillan, 1987.
Dubbelboer, Marieke. 'Un univers mécanique: la machine chez Alfred Jarry.' *French Studies* 58, no. 4 (2004): 471–83.
Edensor, Tim. 'Rhythm and Arrhythmia.' In *The Routledge Handbook of Mobilities*. Abingdon: Routledge, 2014. 163–71.
Erhard, Hans. 'Cycling or Roller Skating: The Resistible Rise of Personal Mobility.' *Cycle History* 5 (1994): 129–32.
Featherstone, Mike. 'The *Flâneur*, the City and Virtual Public Life.' *Urban Studies* 35, no. 5–6 (1998): 909–25.
Foucault, Michel. *Histoire de la sexualité*. Paris: Gallimard, 1976.
— *Les mots et les choses; une archéologie des sciences humaines*. Paris: Gallimard, 1966.
Furness, Zack. 'Foreword.' In *Culture on Two Wheels: The Bicycle in Literature and Film*. Ed. Daniel P. Shea and Jeremy Withers. Lincoln, NE: University of Nebraska Press, 2016. ix–xiv.
— *One Less Car: Bicycling and the Politics of Automobility*. Philadelphia, PA: Temple University Press, 2010.
Fyfe, Aileen. *Steam-Powered Knowledge: William Chambers and the Business of Publishing, 1820–1860*. Chicago: University of Chicago Press, 2012.
Gaillard, Françoise. 'A l'ombre des jeunes filles en vélo ou l'invention de la jeunesse.' *Les cahiers de médiologie* 5, no. 1 (1998): 81–5.
Galison, Peter. 'Einstein's Clocks: The Question of Time'. *Critical Inquiry* 26, no. 2 (2000): 355–89.
Garvey, Ellen Gruber. *The Adman in the Parlor: Magazines and the Gendering of Consumer Culture, 1880s to 1910s*. New York: Oxford University Press, 1996.
Gavin, Adrienne E., and Andrew F. Humphries, eds. *Transport in British Fiction: Technologies of Movement, 1840–1940*. Basingstoke: Palgrave Macmillan, 2015.
Giraud, Hélène. *Le goût du vélo*. Paris: Mercure de France, 2011.
Goody, Alex. *Technology, Literature and Culture*. Cambridge: Polity, 2011.
Griffin, Brian. *Cycling in Victorian Ireland*. Dublin: Nonsuch Publishing, 2006.
— 'The Romance of the Wheel: Cycling, Fiction and Late Nineteenth-Century Ireland.' *Sport in History Sport in History* 29, no. 2 (2009): 277–95.
Grimshaw, Anne. *The Horse, a Bibliography of British Books, 1851–1976*. London: Library Association, 1982.
Grossman, Jonathan H. *Charles Dickens's Networks: Public Transport and the Novel*. Oxford: Oxford University Press, 2012.

Grutzner, Michael. 'The Chainless Bicycle Craze in Germany around 1900.' *Cycle History* 18 (2007): 100–7.

Guevara, J. Josh. 'The Mechanisms. Light and Miraculous: The Convivial Bicycle in Literature and Film.' PhD diss., University of California Santa Cruz, 2012.

Gunning, Tom. 'Re-Newing Old Technologies: Astonishment, Second Nature, and the Uncanny in Technology from the Previous Turn of the Century.' In *Rethinking Media Change: The Aesthetics of Transition*. Ed. David Thorburn and Henry Jenkins. Cambridge, MA: MIT Press, 2003. 39–61.

— 'Tracing the Individual Body: Photography, Detectives, and Early Cinema.' In *Cinema and the Invention of Modern Life*. Ed. Leo Charney and Vanessa R. Schwartz. Berkeley, CA: University of California Press, 1995. 15–45.

Guroff, Margaret. *The Mechanical Horse: How the Bicycle Reshaped American Life*. Austin, TX: University of Texas Press, 2016.

Hadlock, Philip G. 'Men, Machines, and the Modernity of Knowledge in Alfred Jarry's "Le Surmâle".' *SubStance* 35, no. 3 (2006): 131–48.

Halberstam, Judith. *Female Masculinity*. Durham, NC: Duke University Press, 1998.

Hall, Donald E. *Muscular Christianity: Embodying the Victorian Age*. Cambridge: Cambridge University Press, 1994.

Haraway, Donna. *Simians, Cyborgs, and Women: The Reinvention of Nature*. New York: Routledge, 1991.

Heidegger, Martin. *The Question Concerning Technology, and Other Essays*. 1954. Trans. William Lovitt. New York: Harper and Row, 1977.

Héran, Frédéric. *Le retour de la bicyclette: une histoire des déplacements urbains en Europe, de 1817 à 2050*. Paris: la Découverte, 2014.

Herlihy, David V. *Bicycle: The History*. New Haven, CT: Yale University Press, 2004.

— 'Who Invented the Bicycle – Lallement in 1863 or Michaux in 1861?' *Cycle History* 4 (1993): 11–26.

Hodder, Ian. *Entangled: An Archaeology of the Relationships Between Humans and Things*. Malden, MA: Wiley-Blackwell, 2012.

Illich, Ivan. *Energy and Equity*. New York: Harper and Row, 1974.

— *Tools for Conviviality*. New York: Harper and Row, 1973.

Isaacson, Walter. *Einstein: His Life and Universe*. New York: Simon and Schuster, 2007.

James, Simon J. 'Fin-de-Cycle: Romance and the Real in *The Wheels of Chance*.' In *H. G. Wells: Interdisciplinary Essays*. Ed. Steven McLean. Newcastle upon Tyne: Cambridge Scholars Publishing, 2008. 34–48.

— *Maps of Utopia: H. G. Wells, Modernity and the End of Culture*. Oxford: Oxford University Press, 2012.

Jarvis, Robin. *Romantic Writing and Pedestrian Travel*. Basingstoke: Macmillan, 1997.

Jungnickel, Kat. *Bikes and Bloomers: Victorian Women Inventors and their Extraordinary Cycle Wear*. London: Goldsmiths Press, 2018.

Kern, Stephen. *The Culture of Time and Space 1880–1918*. Cambridge, MA: Harvard University Press, 1983.

Kirby, Lynne. *Parallel Tracks: The Railroad and Silent Cinema*. Durham, NC: Duke University Press, 1997.

Kirkham, Pat, ed. *The Gendered Object*. Manchester: Manchester University Press, 1996.

Kittler, Friedrich A. *Discourse Networks 1800/1900*. Trans. Michael Metteer. Stanford, CA: Stanford University Press, 1990.

— *Gramophone, Film, Typewriter*. Trans. Geoffrey Winthrop-Young and Michael Wutz. Stanford, CA: Stanford University Press, 1999.

Knapp, Bettina L. 'Jarry's "The Supermale": The Sex Machine, the Food Machine, and the Bicycle Race: Is It a Question of Adaptation?' *Nineteenth-Century French Studies* 18, no. 3/4 (1990): 492–507.

Kobayashi, Keizō. 'The Inventor of the Lallement Pattern: Michaux, Olivier, or Lallement Himself?' *Cycle History* 1 (1990): 100–9.

— *Pour une bibliographie du cyclisme: répertoire des livres en langue française édités entre 1818 et 1983: la bicyclette sous tous ses aspects*. Paris: Fédération française de cyclotourisme, 1984.

Latour, Bruno. *Aramis ou L'amour des techniques*. Paris: La Découverte, 1992.

— *Nous n'avons jamais été modernes: essai d'anthropologie symétrique*. Paris: La Découverte, 1997.

— *Reassembling the Social: An Introduction to Actor-Network Theory*. Oxford: Oxford University Press, 2005.

Ledger, Sally. *The New Woman: Fiction and Feminism at the Fin de Siècle*. Manchester: Manchester University Press, 1997.

Leed, Eric J. *The Mind of a Traveler: From Gilgamesh to Global Tourism*. New York: Basic Books, 1991.

Lefebvre, Henri. *La production de l'espace*. Paris: Anthropos, 1986.

Lenskyj, Helen. *Out on the Field: Gender, Sport, and Sexualities*. Toronto: Women's Press, 2003.

Lewis, Jeremy. 'Introduction.' In Jerome K. Jerome, *Three Men in a Boat*. Oxford: Oxford University Press, 2000. vii–xxx.

Linley, Margaret. 'The Living Transport Machine: George Eliot's *Middlemarch*.' In *Transport in British Fiction: Technologies of Movement, 1840–1940*. Ed. Andrew F. Humphries and Adrienne E. Gavin. Basingstoke: Palgrave Macmillan, 2015. 85–100.

Lloyd, Rosemary. 'Reinventing Pegasus: Bicycles and the Fin-de-Siècle Imagination.' *Dix-Neuf* 4, no. 1 (2013): 52–60.

Lucas, John. 'Discovering England: The View from the Train.' *Literature & History* 6, no. 2 (1997): 37–55.

Lukács, György. *History and Class Consciousness: Studies in Marxist Dialectics*. 1923. Cambridge, MA: MIT Press, 1971.

— *The Theory of the Novel: A Historico-Philosophical Essay on the Forms of Great Epic Literature*. 1920. Trans. Anna Bostock. London: Merlin Press, 1988.

MacKenzie, Jeanne. *Cycling*. Oxford: Oxford University Press, 1981.

Mackintosh, Phillip Gordon. 'A Bourgeois Geography of Domestic Bicycling: Using Public Space Responsibly in Toronto and Niagara-on-the-Lake, 1890–1900.' *Journal of Historical Sociology* 20, no. 1–2 (2007): 126–57.

Mackintosh, Phillip Gordon, and Glen Norcliffe. '*Flâneurie* on Bicycles: Acquiescence to Women in Public in the 1890s.' *CAG Canadian Geographer / Le Géographe Canadien* 50, no. 1 (2006): 17–37.

MacLeod, Christine. *Heroes of Invention: Technology, Liberalism and British Identity, 1750–1914*. Cambridge: Cambridge University Press, 2007.

Macnaghten, Phil, and John Urry, eds. *Contested Natures*. London: Sage, 1998.

Macy, Sue. *A Sport-Loving Society: Victorian and Edwardian Middle-Class England at Play*. London: Routledge, 2006.

— *Wheels of Change: How Women Rode the Bicycle to Freedom*. Washington DC: National Geographic Society, 2011.

Marks, Patricia. *Bicycles, Bangs, and Bloomers: The New Woman in the Popular Press*. Lexington, KY: University Press of Kentucky, 1990.

Marx, Karl. *Capital: A Critique of Political Economy*. 1867. Trans. Ben Fowkes. Vol. 1. London: Penguin/New Left Review, 1990.

Marx, Leo. *The Machine in the Garden: Technology and the Pastoral Ideal in America*. New York: Oxford University Press, 1964.

Mason, Jennifer. 'Animal Bodies: Corporeality, Class, and Subject Formation in *The Wide, Wide World*.' *Nineteenth-Century Literature* 54, no. 4 (2000): 503–33.

Mauss, Marcel. 1934. *Les techniques du corps*. Chicoutimi: J.-M. Tremblay, 2002.

McGonagle, Seamus. *The Bicycle in Life, Love, War, and Literature*. South Brunswick: Pelham Books, 1969.

McGurn, James. *On Your Bicycle: An Illustrated History of Cycling*. New York: Facts on File, 1987.

Meiner, Carsten Henrik. *Le carrosse littéraire et l'invention du hasard*. Paris: PUF, 2008.

Melada, Ivan. 'Review of *Socialist Propaganda in the Twentieth Century British Novel*, by David Smith.' *Studies in the Novel* 12, no. 1 (1980): 95–7.

Menke, Richard. *Telegraphic Realism: Victorian Fiction and Other Information Systems*. Stanford, CA: Stanford University Press, 2008.

Merleau-Ponty, Maurice. *Le visible et l'invisible*. Ed. Claude Lefort. Paris: Gallimard, 1964.

Mills, Russell. 'Thinking about Thinking about Cycles'. *Cycle History* 5 (1995): 11–18.

Mumby, Frank Arthur. *Publishing and Bookselling*. London: Cape, 1974.

Mumford, Lewis. *Art and Technics*. New York: Columbia University Press, 1952.

Murail, Estelle. 'Beyond the *Flâneur*: Walking, Passage and Crossing in London and Paris in the Nineteenth Century.' PhD thesis, King's College London; Université Paris 7-Diderot, 2014.

Nelson, Carolyn Christensen, ed. *A New Woman Reader: Fiction, Articles, and Drama of the 1890s*. Orchard Park, NY: Broadview Press, 2001.

Norcliffe, Glen. *Critical Geographies of Cycling: History, Political Economy and Culture*. Burlington, VT: Ashgate, 2015.

— 'G-COT.' *Science, Technology, & Human Values* 34, no. 4 (2009): 449–75.

— 'Out for a Spin: The *Flâneur* on Wheels.' *Cycle History* 8 (1997): 93–100.

— *The Ride to Modernity: The Bicycle in Canada, 1869–1900*. Toronto: University of Toronto Press, 2001.

— 'The Rise of the Coventry Bicycle Industry and the Geographical Construction of Technology.' *Cycle History* 15 (2004): 41–58.

— 'Velocipedes and their Riders in the 19th Century: Geographical Imaginaries in Richard Lesclide's *Le Tour du Monde en Vélocipède*.' *Cycle History* 26 (2015): 71–5.

Nye, Edward. *A bicyclette: anthologie*. Paris: Sortilèges, 2000.

Oddy, Nicholas. 'Bicycles.' In *The Gendered Object*. Ed. Pat Kirkham. Manchester: Manchester University Press, 2006. 60–9.

— 'Cycling in the Drawing Room.' *Cycle History* 11 (2000): 169–76.

— 'The *Flâneur* on Wheels?' In *Cycling and Society*. Ed. Paul Rosen, Dave Horton and Peter Cox. Aldershot: Ashgate, 2007. 97–11.

Onians, John. '"I Wonder . . .": A Short History of Amazement.' In *Sight and Insight*. London: Phaidon, 1994. 10–33.

Pearson, Richard. 'Primitive Modernity: H. G. Wells and the Prehistoric Man of the 1890s.' *The Yearbook of English Studies* 37, no. 1 (2007): 58–74.

Pick, Daniel. *Faces of Degeneration: A European Disorder, c.1848–c.1918*. Cambridge: Cambridge University Press, 1989.

Prynn, David. 'The Clarion Clubs, Rambling and the Holiday Associations in Britain since the 1890s.' *Journal of Contemporary History* 11, no. 2/3 (1976): 65–77.

Pye, Denis. *Fellowship Is Life: The National Clarion Cycling Club, 1895–1995*. Bolton: Clarion, 1995.

Raab, Alon. 'Wheels of Fire: Writers on Bicycles.' *World Literature Today* 86, no. 5 (2012): 22–31.

Rabinbach, Anson. *The Human Motor: Energy, Fatigue, and the Origins of Modernity*. Berkeley, CA: University of California Press, 1990.

Rachline, François. 'Le vélo du baron.' *L'Économie Politique* 38, no. 2 (2008): 101–6.

Reid, Carlton. *Roads Were Not Built For Cars*. Washington DC: Island Press, 2015.

Rejack, Brian. 'Nothings of the Day: The Velocipede, the Dandy, and the Cockney.' *Romanticism* 19, no. 3 (2013): 291–309.

Reynolds, Siân. 'Albertine's Bicycle, or: Women and French Identity during the Belle Epoque.' *Literature & History* 10, no. 1 (2001): 28–41.

Richardson, Angelique, and Chris Willis, eds. *The New Woman in Fiction and in Fact: Fin de Siècle Feminisms*. Basingstoke: Palgrave, 2001.

Ritchie, Andrew. *King of the Road: An Illustrated History of Cycling*. London: Wildwood House, 1975.

— *Quest for Speed: A History of Early Bicycle Racing 1868–1903*. Santa Clarita, CA: A. Ritchie, 2011.

Robinson, Jeffrey Cane. *The Walk: Notes on a Romantic Image*. Norman, OK: University of Oklahoma Press, 1989.

Rosa, Hartmut. *High-Speed Society: Social Acceleration, Power, and Modernity*. Trans. William E. Scheuerman. University Park, PA: Pennsylvania State University Press, 2009.

Rosen, Paul, Peter Cox and David Horton, eds. *Cycling and Society*. Aldershot: Ashgate, 2007.

Roston, Murray. *The Comic Mode in English Literature from the Middle Ages to Today*. London: Continuum, 2011.

Rush, Anita. 'The Bicycle Boom of the Gay Nineties: A Reassessment.' *Material Culture Review / Revue de La Culture Matérielle* 18 (June 1983): 1–12.

Sceats, Sarah, and Gail Cunningham, eds. *Image and Power: Women in Fiction in the Twentieth Century*. London: Longman, 1996.

Schivelbusch, Wolfgang. *The Railway Journey: The Industrialization of Time and Space in the 19th Century*. 1979. Trans. Anslem Hollo. Berkeley, CA: University of California Press, 1986.

Sedgwick, Eve Kosofsky. *Between Men: English Literature and Male Homosocial Desire*. New York: Columbia University Press, 1985.

Seltzer, Mark. *Bodies and Machines*. New York: Routledge, 1992.

Seray, Jacques. *Tours de manivelles: le vélo au cinéma*. Vélizy: J. Seray, 2006.

Shrimpton, Andrew. 'The Cultural Significance of Cycling c. 1870–1900.' Master's diss., University of York, 1991.

Siegert, Bernhard. *Relays: Literature as an Epoch of the Postal System.* Stanford, CA: Stanford University Press, 1999.

Simmel, Georg. 'The Metropolis and Mental Life.' 1903. Trans. Kurt H. Wolff. In *The Sociology of Georg Simmel.* London: Free Press, 1950. 409–24.

Simpson, Claire S. 'Capitalising on Curiosity: Women's Professional Cycle Racing in the Late-Nineteenth Century.' In *Cycling and Society.* Ed. Dave Horton, Paul Rosen and Peter Cox. Aldershot: Ashgate, 2007. 47–65.

Smethurst, Paul. *The Bicycle: Towards a Global History.* Basingstoke: Palgrave Macmillan, 2015.

Smith, Cyril Stanley. *A History of Metallography: The Development of Ideas on the Structure of Metals before 1890.* Cambridge, MA: MIT Press, 1988.

Smith, Robert A. *A Social History of the Bicycle: Its Early Life and Times in America.* New York: American Heritage Press, 1972.

So, Hiroshi. '*The Wheels of Chance* and the Discourse of Improvement of Health.' *The Wellsian: The Journal of the H. G. Wells Society* 29, no. 1 (2006): 37–47.

Solnit, Rebecca. *Wanderlust: A History of Walking.* New York: Viking, 2000.

Spinney, Justin. 'Cycling the City: Non-Place and the Sensory Construction of Meaning in a Mobile Practice.' In *Cycling and Society.* Ed. Dave Horton, Paul Rosen and Peter Cox. Aldershot: Ashgate, 2007. 25–45.

Starrs, James E., and Kevin Schaeffer. *The Literary Cyclist.* New York: Breakaway Books, 1997.

Sussman, Herbert L. *Victorians and the Machine: The Literary Response to Technology.* Cambridge, MA: Harvard University Press, 1968.

Thacker, Andrew. *Moving through Modernity: Space and Geography in Modernism.* Manchester: Manchester University Press, 2003.

Thiesset, Pierre, and Quentin Thomasset, eds. *Les bienfaits de la vélocipédie: anthologie.* Vierzon: le Pas de côté, 2013.

Thompson, Christopher. 'Controlling the Working Class Sports Hero In Order to Control the Masses? The Social Philosophy of Sport of Henri Desgrange.' *Stadion* 27 (2001): 139–51.

— 'Corps, sexe et bicyclette.' *Les Cahiers de médiologie* 5, no. 1 (1998): 59–67.

— 'Regeneration, Dégénérescence, and the Medical Debate about Bicycling in Fin-de-Siècle France.' In *Sport et santé dans l'histoire/ Sport and Health in History.* Ed. Thierry Terret. Sankt Augustin: Academia Verlag, 1999. 339–46.

— *The Tour de France: A Cultural History.* Berkeley, CA: University of California Press, 2006.

Thompson, Christopher, and Fiona Ratkoff. 'Un troisième sexe? Les bourgeoises et la bicyclette dans la France fin de siècle.' *Le mouvement social* 192 (2000): 9–39.

Thornton, Sara. *Advertising, Subjectivity, and the Nineteenth-Century Novel: Dickens, Balzac, and the Language of the Walls.* Basingstoke: Palgrave Macmillan, 2009.

Thorold, Peter. *The Motoring Age: The Automobile and Britain 1896–1939.* London: Profile Books, 2003.

Thurschwell, Pamela. *Literature, Technology, and Magical Thinking, 1880–1920.* Cambridge: Cambridge University Press, 2001.

Tronchet, Didier. *Petit traité de vélosophie: réinventer la ville à vélo.* Paris: Plon, 2014.

Urry, John. *Mobilities.* Cambridge: Polity, 2007.

— 'The "System" of Automobility.' *Theory, Culture & Society* 21, no. 4–5 (2004): 25–39.

— *The Tourist Gaze: Leisure and Travel in Contemporary Societies.* London: Sage, 1990.

Vallet, Odon. 'Vélo, bicyclette: histoire des mots.' *Les cahiers de médiologie* 5, no. 1 (1998): 15–18.

Virilio, Paul. *Cybermonde: la politique du pire.* Ed. Philippe Petit. Paris: Textuel, 1996.

— *The Original Accident.* Trans. Julie Rose. Cambridge: Polity, 2007.

— *La vitesse de libération: essai.* Paris: Galilée, 1995.

— *Vitesse et politique: essai de dromologie.* Paris: Galilée, 1977.

Virilio, Paul, and Philippe Petit. *Politics of the Very Worst: An Interview by Philippe Petit.* Trans. Sylvère Lotringer. New York: Semiotext(e), 1999.

Walker, Linda. 'Party Political Women: A Comparative Study of Liberal Women and the Primrose League, 1890–1914.' In *Equal or Different: Women's Politics, 1800–1914.* Ed. Jane Rendall. Oxford: Blackwell, 1987. 165–91.

Wallace, Anne D. *Walking, Literature, and English Culture: The Origins and Uses of Peripatetic in the Nineteenth Century.* Oxford: Clarendon Press, 1994.

Wanggren, Lena. 'The Freedom Machine: The New Woman and the Bicycle.' In *Transport in British Fiction: Technologies of Movement, 1840–1940.* Ed. Adrienne E. Gavin and Andrew Humphries. London: Palgrave, 2015. 123–35.

Watson, Nicola J. *The Literary Tourist: Readers and Places in Romantic & Victorian Britain.* Basingstoke: Palgrave Macmillan, 2007.

Watson, Roderick, and Martin Gray. *The Penguin Book of the Bicycle.* London: Penguin, 1978.

Weber, Eugen. *France, Fin de Siècle.* Cambridge, MA: Belknap Press of Harvard University Press, 1986.

Wenzel, Peter, and Sven Strasen, eds. *Discourses of Mobility, Mobility of Discourse: The Conceptualization of Trains, Cars and Planes in 19th- and 20th-Century Poetry.* Trier: WVT, 2010.

Williams, Edward. *The Pocket Bibliography of Cycling Books.* Wolverhampton: Edward Williams, 1993.

Williams, Raymond. *The Country and the City.* Oxford: Oxford University Press, 1973.

— *Keywords: A Vocabulary of Culture and Society.* London: Fontana, 1988.

Williamson, Geoffrey. *Wheels within Wheels: The Story of the Starleys of Coventry.* London: Bles, 1966.

Willis, Chris. 'Heaven Defend Me from Political or Highly-Educated Women! Packaging the New Woman for Mass Consumption.' In *The New Woman in Fiction and in Fact: Fin de Siècle Feminisms.* Ed. Angelique Richardson and Chris Willis. Basingstoke: Palgrave, 2001. 53–65.

Wilson, David Gordon, Jim Papadopoulos and Frank Rowland Whitt. *Bicycling Science.* 3rd edn. Cambridge, MA: MIT Press, 2004.

Withers, Jeremy. 'Bicycles and Warfare: The Effects of Excessive Mobility in H. G. Wells's *The War in the Air.*' In *Culture on Two Wheels: The Bicycle in Literature and Film.* Ed. Jeremy Withers and Daniel P. Shea. Lincoln, NE: University of Nebraska Press, 2016. 78–93.

— 'Bicycles, Tricycles, and Tripods: Late Victorian Cycling and Wells's *The War of the Worlds.*' *The Wellsian* 36 (2013): 39–51.

Withers, Jeremy, and Daniel P. Shea, eds. *Culture on Two Wheels: The Bicycle in Literature and Film.* Lincoln, NE: University of Nebraska Press, 2016.

Wohl, Robert. *A Passion for Wings: Aviation and the Western Imagination, 1908–1918.* New Haven, CT: Yale University Press, 1994.

Wolff, Janet. 'The Invisible *Flâneuse.* Women and the Literature of Modernity.' *Theory, Culture & Society* 2 (November 1985): 37–46.

Woodruff, William. *The Rise of the British Rubber Industry During the Nineteenth Century.* Liverpool: Liverpool University Press, 1958.

Zemka, Sue. *Time and the Moment in Victorian Literature and Society.* Cambridge: Cambridge University Press, 2011.

Zupančič, Alenka. *The Odd One In: On Comedy.* Cambridge, MA: MIT Press, 2008.

Websites and Blogs

'Bicycle Chosen as Best Invention.' *BBC News*, 5 May 2005. Accessed 18 September 2015. <http://news.bbc.co.uk/2/hi/technology/4513929.stm>

Gates, Jasper. 'Vélivre: Reading and Riding.' *The Dusty Musette*, 25 November 2011. Accessed 15 January 2015. <http://dustymusette.blogspot.fr/2011/11/velivre-reading-and-riding.html.>

Hanlon, Sheila. 'Women's cycling.' Accessed 4 October 2020. <http://www.sheilahanlon.com/>

Hawkins, Kaitlin, and Eliza Robertson. 'Books on Two Wheels: The Cycling Reading List.' *World Literature Today*. Accessed 18 March 2015. <http://www.worldliteraturetoday.org/books-two-wheels-cycling-reading-list#.VQl7HmZJ_m0>

Hoefer, Carsten. 'Bicycle Touring: A Short Illustrated History of the Bicycle.' *Crazyguyonabike*. Accessed 9 October 2014. <http://www.crazyguyonabike.com/doc/?doc_id=1889>.

Jobs, Steve. 'Computers are like a bicycle for our minds.' YouTube, 1 June 2006. Accessed 5 March 2015. <https://www.youtube.com/watch?v=ob_GX50Za6c&feature=youtube_gdata_player>.

Manners, Will. *The Victorian Cyclist*. Accessed 12 July 2016. <https://thevictoriancyclist.wordpress.com>.

Mattix, Micah. 'Literary Cycles.' *Wall Street Journal*, 26 June 2013. Accessed 16 October 2014. <http://online.wsj.com/news/articles/SB10001424127887323683504578567760447206752>.

Orgebin, Philippe, Hervé Le Cahain and Jean-Yves Mounier. *Biblio-Cycles*. Accessed 18 March 2020. <http://biblio-cyclesdephilippeorgebin.hautetfort.com>.

Peirpert, Jim. 'Literary Musings.' *Jim's Bike Blog*, 29 August 2012. Accessed 23 February 2020. <https://jimsbikeblog.wordpress.com/category/literary-musings/>

'Reported road casualties in Great Britain: provisional estimates year ending June 2019.' Department for Transport, 28 November 2019. Accessed 13 October 2020. <https://assets.publishing.service.gov.uk/government/uploads/system/uploads/attachment_data/file/848485/road-casualties-year-ending-june-2019.pdf>.

'Road Safety History 1861–1903.' Road Safety UK. Accessed 8 July 2016. <http://www.roadsafetyuk.co.uk/history1.htm.>

Schwartz, James D. 'How Apple's "Macintosh" almost became the "Bicycle".' *The Urban Country*, 8 January 2012. Accessed 17 July 2020. <http://www.theurbancountry.com/2012/01/how-apples-macintosh-almost-became.html>.

Williams, Zoe. 'Join the Wheel World.' *The Guardian*, 5 May 2012. Accessed 4 January 2016. <http://www.theguardian.com/travel/2012/may/05/urban-cycling-zoe-williams>

Index

Achebe, Chinua, *Things Fall Apart*, 243n
aeroplanes, 9, 27, 187–8, 202n, 229
Allen, Grant
  Hilda Wade, 40–1, 213–14
  Miss Cayley's Adventures, 102, 103–5, 106, 113, 135n, 194, 224
  'The Thames Valley Catastrophe', 224
  The Type-Writer Girl, 102, 104, 135n, 216
  The Woman Who Did, 100
Allen, J. W., *Wheel Magic*, 47, 48, 56, 93–4, 147–8, 162, 164–5, 173, 195, 220, 227, 228
Armstrong, Tim, 148–9
Augé, Marc, 30, 83, 98, 225, 232, 237

Bakhtin, Mikhail, 38, 80
Barathieu, Agnès, 119–20, 122, 127, 138n
Baudelaire, Charles, 225, 233
Beekman, W. S., and Eric Allan, *Cycle Gleanings*, 166, 171, 208, 217
Benjamin, Walter, 43, 65n, 163, 225
Bergson, Henri, 44–52, 221

Bijker, Wiebe, et al., 5, 72, 153
Bockett, F. W., *Some Literary Landmarks for Pilgrims on Wheels*, 19, 22–7, 55–6, 58, 72, 152, 153, 171–2, 228–30
Bodkin, Matthias Mc Donnell, *Dora Myrl, The Lady Detective*, 41, 100, 106, 187–8
Bouet, Michel, 167, 170, 192, 232
Bronfen, Elisabeth, 180, 185–6
Burke, Edmund, 174

Carey, John, 58, 70, 92–3
cars, 9, 10, 13, 25–6, 71–2, 87–8, 91, 93, 98, 133n, 147–8, 150, 161, 167, 175–6, 182, 187, 189, 190, 206, 207, 216–17, 220–1, 223, 229–30, 232–4, 236, 239–40, 241, 244n, 250–2
Chesterton, G. K.
  'The Free Man and the Ford Car', 190
  'The Wheel', 146, 222
cinema, 207–11, 252
coaches, 8, 9, 23, 32, 35, 36, 56, 78, 83, 167–8, 230–1
Cohen, William, 181, 184
Coppen, W. J., *Romances of the Wheel*, 162–3
Crane, Stephen, 212–13

Crary, Jonathan, 166
cycle paths, 76, 230
cycle racing, 7, 79, 104–5, 112–13, 120–1, 156
cycle touring, 21–7, 30, 47, 93–4, 117, 166, 172–3, 208, 210, 212, 217, 230, 251
Cyclists' Touring Club (CTC), 230
cycle travel writing, 21–7

Daly, Nicholas, 164–5
Darwin, Charles, 2–3, 77, 119, 146–7, 153, 196n, 224
Da Vinci, Leonardo, 2, 189–90
Day, Jon, 54
Debord, Guy, 209–10
De Certeau, Michel, 220, 227, 232, 236–9
Deleuze, Gilles, and Félix Guattari, 221, 245n
De Quincey, Thomas, 20, 56, 168–9
Derrida, Jacques, 31
Desportes, Marc, 10, 205, 237
Doyle, Arthur Conan, 42
  Beyond the City, 106, 114–16
  'The Priory School', 42–3
  'The Solitary Cyclist', 42–3
Drais, Baron Karl von, 2
Dunlop, John, 2

Edensor, Tim, 31
Einstein, Albert, 49, 204
electric bicycles, 4, 168, 193, 252

feminism, 99, 106, 115–17, 118–30, 121, 134n
flâneur, 35, 225–8
Ford, Ford Madox, *The Soul of London*, 232–6

Forster, E. M.
  Howards End, 36
  'The Machine Stops', 240
Foucault, Michel, 124
Furness, Zack, 10, 108–9, 150, 207, 212, 214, 216–17, 251
futurism, 206

Garvey, Ellen Gruber, 31, 59, 107–8, 112
gender, 80–1, 101, 111, 113, 115, 118–30, 181, 183, 219
Gissing, George, 74–5
  'A Daughter of the Lodge', 116–17
  New Grub Street, 54, 57–8
Griffin, Brian, 38–9, 41
Gunning, Tom, 5, 43, 221, 250

Halberstam, Judith, 125
Haraway, Donna Jeanne, 123, 186
Harris, Ada L., *A Widow on Wheels*, 100, 106
Heidegger, Martin, 192
Hemingway, Ernest, 238
Herlihy, David V., 71, 130n
history of the bicycle, 1–5
  célérifère, 2
  chainless bicycle, 194, 203n
  draisine, 2, 5, 21, 61n, 71, 134n, 222, 225
  ordinary bicycle, 2, 4, 39, 45–6, 53, 162
  safety bicycle, 2, 4, 5, 6, 53, 59, 79, 162
  velocipede, 2, 3, 5, 6, 13n, 113, 150, 155, 210, 225
horses, 8, 9, 33, 36, 39, 43, 66n, 71, 73, 129, 143–4, 153, 167–8, 179, 214, 219, 243n
Huxley, Aldous, *Crome Yellow*, 236–42

Illich, Ivan, 69, 168–9

James, Henry, 76, 247n
Jarry, Alfred, 211, 244n
  'The Passion Considered as an Uphill Bicycle Race', 209
  The Supermale, 155–61, 198n, 209
Jerome, Jerome K., *Three Men on the Bummel*, 45, 49–50, 60, 66n, 74, 152, 162, 194, 227–8
Jerome, Jerome K., H. G. Wells et al., *The Humours of Cycling*, 41, 48, 81
Jobs, Steve, 191
Jungnickel, Kat, 136n

Kennard, Mary E., 29, 244n
  A Guide Book for Lady Cyclists, 29–30, 59, 73, 102, 110–12, 142, 151, 217, 220
  The Golf Lunatic and His Cycling Wife, 101–2, 105–6, 117, 151–2, 213
Kern, Stephen, 9–10, 211, 218
Kipling, Rudyard, 186, 187, 193
Kittler, Friedrich A., 8, 107

Lallement, Pierre, 13–14
La Pédale, Jehan de, *Modern Stories. Let's Pedal!*, 209
Latour, Bruno, 6, 140–1
Leblanc, Maurice, *Here are Wings*, 27–38, 57, 125, 167, 174–7, 189–90, 208
Lefebvre, Henri, 235
Lukács, György, 35, 189

Marinetti, F. T., 206
Marx, Karl, 143, 169, 189, 191
Mauss, Marcel, 192
Meade, L. T., *The Cleverest Woman in England*, 106
mechanics, 106, 150–5, 179, 194, 197n

Mecredy, R. J., *The Art and Pastime of Cycling*, 2–4, 143, 162
Meiner, Carsten Henrik, 9, 32, 35
Merleau-Ponty, Maurice, 176–7, 182–5
Michaux, Pierre, 2, 21, 210, 225
modernism, 89–90, 177, 221–2
Muir, Robert James, *Plato's Dream of Wheels*, 48, 143–4
Mumford, Lewis, 192–3
Muybridge, Eadweard, 209

New Woman, 19, 40, 69, 81, 99–107
Norcliffe, Glen, 10, 88, 99, 204–5, 213, 225, 227, 250

O'Brien, Flann, *The Third Policeman*, 66n, 154
Oddy, Nicholas, 51–2, 111, 226

Pennell, Joseph and Elizabeth Robins, 22, 61n, 62n, 210
  Our Sentimental Journey through France and Italy, 21–5
  Over the Alps on a Bicycle, 210, 229
photography, 205, 207–11
primitivism, 222–4
Proust, Marcel, *In Search of Lost Time*, 118–30
Provos, 235–6, 247n, 252n

Rabinbach, Anson, 155, 158
Rachline, François, 142–3
railways, 5–6, 8–9, 23, 33, 34, 40, 41, 53, 56, 64n, 71, 75, 83, 140, 162, 164–7, 173, 175–6, 182, 190, 206, 210, 217, 227, 228–9, 231, 234–5, 237–8, 245n, 250

rational dress, 101, 105, 110–11, 119, 124–5, 215
Redmond, Edmond, *Lyra Cyclus*, 54, 55
Régamey, Frédéric, *Vélocipédie et automobilisme*, 162–3
Richardson, Dorothy, *The Tunnel*, 56, 110, 177–186
Ritchie, Andrew, 16n, 150, 155–6
Romains, Jules, *Les copains*, 52
Rosa, Hartmut, 164
Rosny, J. H., *Roman d'un cycliste*, 218, 226
Rumney, A. W., *A Cyclist's Note Book*, 158, 172, 174
Ruskin, John, 23, 167

Schivelbusch, Wolfgang, 8, 144–5, 166, 245n
Shea, Daniel, 10–11, 249, 251
Shelley, Mary, *Frankenstein*, 187
Simmel, Georg, 84–5
Situationists, 235–6
social class, 5, 25, 40, 58, 70–98, 80–1, 111, 113, 115–17, 120–1, 151, 172, 181
socialism, 70–3, 76, 87, 91, 98, 134n
songs, 54, 67n
Starley, James, 2
Starley, J. K., 2, 4
Sterne, Laurence, 22–4
Sussman, Herbert L. 39–40, 76–7, 186, 193–4

telephones, 181
Thomas, Edward, *In Pursuit of Spring*, 22–7, 170–1
Thompson, Christopher, 79, 99, 119, 120
Thurschwell, Pamela, 130, 181, 183
Tour de France, 79, 156, 158

trams, 53, 57, 89, 121, 233
Twain, Mark
  A Connecticut Yankee in King Arthur's Court, 39
  'Taming the Bicycle', 142–3

Urry, John, 49, 150, 206–8, 212, 220

Virilio, Paul, 149–50, 161–2, 229, 240, 241

walking, 9, 19–27, 35, 55–6, 72, 86, 88–9, 93, 97–8, 144–5, 167, 169, 170, 176, 183–4, 192, 208, 212–13, 228, 231, 236–7, 240
Wells, H. G., 12, 15n, 49, 59–60, 74–8, 186, 219–20, 224
  Ann Veronica, 101
  Anticipations, 75–6, 244n
  Experiment in Autobiography, 74–5, 215, 219
  Hoopdriver's Holiday, 116
  Kipps, 15n, 75, 82–92
  Modern Utopia, A, 76
  'Perfect Gentleman on Wheels, A', 40, 81–2
  The History of Mr Polly, 15n, 39, 50–1, 92–8, 230–1
  The Time Machine, 77, 117, 219
  The War in the Air, 15n, 222–4, 244n
  The War of the Worlds, 145–8, 208
  The Wheels of Chance, 15n, 27–38, 40, 47, 57, 76, 78–82, 101, 104, 114, 115–16, 147, 154, 173, 215–16, 218, 219, 224
Williams, Raymond, 42, 140, 191, 227

Withers, Jeremy, 10–11, 145, 148, 223, 249, 251
Woolf, Virginia, 164
  A Room of One's Own, 105

Zemka, Sue, 34, 164, 221
Zola, Émile, 57
  Paris, 103
Zupančič, Alenka, 49